DANGER ZONE
THE STORY OF
THE QUEENSTOWN COMMAND

ADMIRAL SIR LEWIS BAYLY, K.C.B., K.C.M.G., C.V.O.
On board the United States Destroyer *Cushing* at Queenstown.

DANGER ZONE

THE STORY OF
THE QUEENSTOWN COMMAND

By
E. KEBLE CHATTERTON
Author of
" The Sea-Raiders," etc., etc.

WITH FOREWORD BY
WILLIAM S. SIMS
Rear Admiral, U. S. Navy

With 40 *plates*
and
3 *maps*

The Naval & Military Press Ltd

Published by

The Naval & Military Press Ltd
Unit 5 Riverside, Brambleside
Bellbrook Industrial Estate
Uckfield, East Sussex
TN22 1QQ England

Tel: +44 (0)1825 749494

www.naval-military-press.com
www.nmarchive.com

In reprinting in facsimile from the original, any imperfections are inevitably reproduced and the quality may fall short of modern type and cartographic standards.

Copyright, 1934,
By E. Keble Chatterton

All rights reserved

TO COMMEMORATE
THE 'PULLTOGETHER' SPIRIT
OF TWO NAVIES

"The part that Queenstown played during the Great War is not generally known, by reason of the very necessary veil of secrecy that was drawn over its work. Some day the full story will be told, and it will prove to be thrilling and amazing, for some of the most daring exploits were performed by the craft based on this port."
"THE TIMES," June 17, 1919.

"When history is finally written, the Queenstown Command will stand out as the finest example of the right spirit of co-operation between our two great countries."
Mr. FRANKLIN D. ROOSEVELT,
when Governor of New York.

"ADMIRAL BAYLY and ADMIRAL PRINGLE; the British Navy and the United States Navy—in the story of the Queenstown days there is no separating them nor distinguishing between them, for the very essence of the 'pull together' is the fusion of the two elements in one. And now, when friendship between the two peoples, especially between their Navies, is of capital importance to the world, it is good to dwell on the thought of amity that grew like a flower out of the grossness of war, and is blooming still after sixteen dangerous years of peace."

"THE TIMES," May 31, 1934.

FOREWORD

The Hon. Franklin D. Roosevelt, when Governor of New York, did not overstate the case in declaring that "the Queenstown Command will stand out as the finest example of the right spirit of coöperation between our two great countries."

Mr. Chatterton's participation in this campaign has fitted him to describe it with complete professional understanding; his account also does full justice to a campaign marked by daring, the dogged performance of difficult tasks, and by dramatic incidents — a campaign upon whose successful outcome depended the safety of the Allies' main lines of oversea supply for food, munitions and troops.

When an army springs a surprise weapon or method on the enemy, the secret is out, and the press can make the most of the story. When fleets clash, the details of the action are soon world news. But submarine warfare is chiefly a series of engagements between individual submarines and anti-submarine forces. If a weapon or method employed by the latter results in sinking or capturing the sub, it can be used again. The fate of those who do not return remains a mystery, and that undermines the enemy's morale. Hence the importance of keeping from the enemy all knowledge of anti-submarine operations; and this can be done only by keeping such knowledge from our own people.

The mystery that thus surrounds the whole business gives free scope to the imagination of the writers of press "stories" based upon the opinions of home "experts" and the yarns of the third mates of tramp steamers. The result is practically complete misinformation. This of course does not prevent the press from criticising supposed methods and advising the "Principal Dignitaries" what should be done about it. Thus all the gallant actions of the anti-submarine forces are performed not only in profound silence, but also under the sting of ignorant criticism, which of course crystallizes into mistaken public opinion.

It is therefore important that in due time the actual facts be related; that the public be informed of the devotion, energy and effectiveness with which the forces of both nations carried out their arduous and dangerous duties in keeping open the essential lines of supply in the face of an elusive enemy. This is a yarn which will interest any person who admires daring and devotion, but which should, under the circumstances, be of very particular interest to all Americans.

To my mind, the real significance of this story, both as history and as a human document, is the demonstration of a wartime coöperation so cordial and complete that it is an outstanding example of an entirely frictionless association between allies in war. It is indeed an outstanding example of the inestimable benefit to a common cause of a real brotherhood of the sea.

The submarine warfare in European waters has been described in many books, but the story of the Queenstown Command is something else again. No one who had the good fortune to be a guest at Admiralty House in Queenstown during the war, as it was often my privilege to be, is likely to forget the spirit of whole-hearted coöperation that permeated the entire command. An American officer who served overseas has well described the atmosphere of the Queenstown Command as follows: "In 1917 and 1918 in Irish waters, our light naval forces were so closely commingled, in all vital respects, with those of Great Britain, that only expert observation could tell them apart. Those forces were of two nations, but they were one unit performing arduous service of high importance. Their commander was a British admiral, who year after year managed the administration and the operations of those numerous ships with scarcely an hour's respite. He did not work too much with papers. He commanded most actively and dealt with a large number of subordinates face to face. Therefore large numbers of us came to know him personally and we carried out of the war a feeling toward that commander of respect and affection which will last throughout our lives."

The spirit that pervaded Admiralty House has been perpetuated in the unique Queenstown Association — comprising all those who served under Admiral Bayly on the Irish station — which keeps alive the mutual esteem, and I can truly say the affection, of those who carried on so successfully under such difficult and dangerous conditions. This organization gives a dinner from time to time; the occasion of the most recent one,

FOREWORD

which took place in New York on June 8, 1934, was to honor Admiral Bayly. He had come to this country with his niece, Miss Voysey, the much beloved hostess of Admiralty House, to present a tablet in memory of Admiral Pringle, who was his American Chief of Staff at Queenstown — a unique tribute from an officer of one navy to an officer of another.

I believe that American readers will find this book not only entertaining and inspiring, but a demonstration of the fundamental good will between our two great nations.

WILLIAM S. SIMS
Rear Admiral, U. S. Navy

Marion, Mass.
September, 1934

PREFACE

This is the full and thrilling story of those naval operations carried out in an area which a German Admiral once described as "the decisive U-boat theatres"; for these waters were "the highways of the world's traffic."

Whilst the general reader is familiar with what happened in many other War theatres, he has till now been unable to appreciate all that was done under the Queenstown Command. With its mystery ships, sloop flotillas, its armed trawlers, drifters, M.L.'s; and—during the second phase—its American destroyers, submarine-chasers, British and American submarines as well as rescue tugs, all serving under Admiral Sir Lewis Bayly, this immense miscellaneous fleet was responsible for the safety of shipping passing through the submarine zone to keep the United Kingdom from starvation.

If this volume is overdue, and has taken many years to compile, it is now at length possible to present all the facts in their appropriate value and see the events as one connected whole. To have published it earlier would have meant the presentation of an incomplete picture; to have delayed much longer would have meant the loss of much invaluable personal evidence. It was my privilege to have been serving in command of patrol vessels on this station during two of the most important War years; to have had personal knowledge of many historic occasions; to have heard (immediately after the events) the narratives from the very officers who played the leading parts in great dramas. In short, the following chapters are based on first-hand information supplemented by some thousands of documents placed at my disposal.

These have included numerous private and War Diaries, considerable private correspondence carried on during the strenuous months by highly-placed naval officers, impressions set down at the time; and much else. Without the most generous assistance and enthusiasm of these friends—as well on the Active and the Retired Lists—it would have been impossible to carry through this task. Apart from historical reasons, one of the motives animating this book has been the desire to perpetuate the co-operation of Anglo-American naval

DANGER ZONE

forces that were based on Queenstown. "War may exacerbate enmities," said the London *Times* newspaper, referring to Admiral Bayly's last visit to America; "it can also foster friendships. And at Queenstown in 1917 and 1918 friendships were born and brought to maturity which may well outlast in memory the lives of those whom they linked together."

Where such thorough and spontaneous assistance has been rendered in regard to data and illustrations, it is not easy to make full acknowledgment. I desire most especially to offer the following my best thanks for all their courtesy and invaluable aid: Admiral Sir Lewis Bayly, K.C.B., K.C.M.G., C.V.O.; Admiral W. S. Sims, U.S.N.; Rear-Admiral S. W. Bryant, U.S.N.; Rear-Admiral B. B. Wygant, U.S.N.; Rear-Admiral W. N. Vernou, U.S.N.; Rear-Admiral A. W. Johnson, U.S.N.; Rear-Admiral R. F. Zogbaum, U.S.N.; Rear-Admiral J. K. Taussig, U.S.N.; Commander F. W. Hanan, D.S.O., R.N.; Captain D. C. Hanrahan, U.S.N.; Captain Halsey Powell, U.S.N.; Captain G. F. W. Wilson, D.S.O., R.N.; Captain S. H. Simpson, D.S.O., R.N.; Commander Roger Williams, U.S.N.; Commander G. B. Vroom, U.S.N.; Commander C. R. Cowap, R.D., R.N.R.; Lieut.-Commander A. T. Emerson, U.S.N.; Mr. Junius S. Morgan; Mr. C. Blake Pitt; Mr. H. W. Dwight Rudd; and Miss Voysey, C.B.E.

If any should find his name has been omitted, either here or in the text, I beg that he will not impute to me ingratitude.

E. KEBLE CHATTERTON.

CONTENTS

CHAP.		PAGE
I.	WESTERN APPROACHES	13
II.	THE WAR COMES WEST	20
III.	THE *LUSITANIA* CRISIS	31
IV.	THE BIG PROBLEM	44
V.	CHANGE IN COMMAND	58
VI.	NEW MEASURES	68
VII.	PATROLS *VERSUS* SUBMARINES	79
VIII.	TRAP-SHIPS	90
IX.	QUEENSTOWN SLOOPS	101
X.	NARROW ESCAPES	112
XI.	THE U-BOAT CAMPAIGN	120
XII.	SINN FEIN AND GERMANY	138
XIII.	THE EASTER REBELLION AND THE SEA	148
XIV.	NAVAL DETECTION	169
XV.	TRAGEDY OF THE SEA	184
XVI.	A NEW PHASE BEGINS	197
XVII.	TORPEDOES AND MINES	209
XVIII.	THE CRITICAL MONTH	221
XIX.	HAIL, COLUMBIA!	236
XX.	THE RIGHT SPIRIT	245
XXI.	A MAN'S LIFE	258
XXII.	DEATH AND DELIVERANCE	279
XXIII.	PLUCK AND ENTERPRISE	291
XXIV.	DESTROYERS AND *U* 58	298
XXV.	DOWN TO THE DEPTHS	318
XXVI.	A BAND OF BROTHERS	327
XXVII.	*OLYMPIC* AND *U* 103	336
XXVIII.	UP THE IRISH SEA	348
XXIX.	RESCUE SHIPS	360
XXX.	VICTORY	377
	APPENDIX A	384
	APPENDIX B	385
	INDEX	387

LIST OF ILLUSTRATIONS

	FACING PAGE
ADMIRAL SIR LEWIS BAYLY, K.C.B., K.C.M.G., C.V.O.	*Frontispiece*
QUEENSTOWN FROM THE HARBOUR	18
S.S. *LUSITANIA*	36
GRAVES OF THE *LUSITANIA* VICTIMS	36
ADMIRAL SIR LEWIS BAYLY	66
A BEREHAVEN PATROL VESSEL	72
A QUEENSTOWN SLOOP	72
SURVIVORS	74
THE GREEN BARGE	74
QUEENSTOWN HARBOUR	84
THE "SLOOP" GARDEN	84
THE COMMANDER-IN-CHIEF, COAST OF IRELAND	158
CAPTAIN OF THE GERMAN SUBMARINE *UB* 48	232
MAY 4, 1917	244
MAKING HISTORY	244
GETTING READY FOR SEA	246
DEPTH CHARGES	246
ACROSS THE ATLANTIC	248
CONVOY INWARD BOUND	248
ON CONVOY DUTY	250
U.S. NAVAL MEN'S CLUB, QUEENSTOWN	254
Q-SHIP *ZYLPHA*	264
Q-SHIP *ZYLPHA*	264
FIGHTING FATE	266
Q-SHIP *ZYLPHA*	266
Q-SHIP *ZYLPHA*	268
Q-SHIP *ZYLPHA*	268
BARELY AFLOAT	282
MOTHER AND DAUGHTERS	282
HER LAST AGONY	284
CAPTAIN (NOW VICE-ADMIRAL) GORDON CAMPBELL, V.C., D.S.O., R.N.	284
U.S.S. *CASSIN*	298
U.S.S. *SHAW*	298
U.S.S. *FANNING*	300
FOUR-FUNNELLED AMERICAN DESTROYER	300

	FACING PAGE
U 58	302
Depth-charge Wins!	304
"Kamerad! Kamerad!"	306
Salving a Submarine	308
German Submarine Prisoner	308
Peril by Sea	310
The Great Storm	312
The Great Storm	312
Sinking of the United States Steamer *Covington*	314
American Transport	314
The American Mystery Ship *Santee*	316
Depth Charge	318
What a Torpedo Does	318
"They Could Roll!"	328
Patrol Drifter	332
On Patrol	332
"Heave Away!"	346
Torpedoed Oil-Tanker	346
H.M.S. *Kilfree*	352
A Rare Sight	352
Inspecting U.S.S. *Melville*	362
Aboard an American Destroyer	362
First Sea Lord and Chief of Naval Staff	364
The Commander-in-Chief	376
Silver Rose Bowl Presented to Admiral Bayly	378
Where British and American Naval Officers Met	378
U.S.S. *Pulltogether*	380
After the War	382

DANGER ZONE
THE STORY OF
THE QUEENSTOWN COMMAND

CHAPTER I

WESTERN APPROACHES

THE unprecedented improvement which, during the last hundred years, has completely revolutionised sea-transportation is responsible for a curious modification of geographical values: communities are reckoned as distant from each other less by a definite number of miles than by a measure of facilities for travel. And the safer, the more easy, the more pleasant you make the passage from one country to a second, so much more quickly and more substantially will be erected a kind of bridge, which not merely encourages the exchange of trade as well as of ideas, but also joins those two peoples firmly and closely, even though the ocean be many hundreds of miles at its narrowest.

There was a time, even after the old packet ships and the early transatlantic steamers, when no passenger thought of crossing from England to America except for some urgent cause, but then such an undertaking had been considered with heavy solemnity in the first place. Ships were small and very much at the mercy of wind or wave, cabins were cheerless, comforts were lacking. In short, the unreliable and uncertain period at sea, with all its horrors and inconveniences, but especially its suggestion of death, maintained in the public mind such a distaste for voyaging that Americans and Britons were still mutual strangers. But quickly followed the luxury liners of immense tonnage, perfect safety, and considerable speed. With what result? Distance was ignored, a few days afloat amid an environment of pleasure were an attraction to leave the shore; and to many overwrought men of affairs this sea-change was the first opportunity in months for rest from routine.

Thus has London become in these latter years far nearer to New York, or Boston, than the map would seem to indicate. The average British citizen in his daily life is to-day more concerned with what is happening in the United States than with what may be going on in Ireland; and this notwithstanding that England is, geographically, quite adjacent to Dublin or Queenstown. For every visitor who crosses from

England to Ireland there are some hundreds who take a trip over the Atlantic; indeed, the leading British journals—except in a time of political crisis—contain on their daily sheets few references to events on the other side of St. George's Channel, merely because their readers have little or no interest regarding the Emerald Island. Conversely, every item sent over by a newspaper's New York correspondent is printed and read as of primary importance.

During the present century this increase of travel, of commerce; this closer contact in such matters as finance, art, literature, drama, and so on; have steadily been drawing Britain and the United States towards one common standard in thought, as well as conduct. And this has been occurring throughout the very period when Ireland has been withdrawing herself within herself; as far away from English life and ideas as she can, by all her persuasion, determine. So, even just before the Great War, an Englishman finding himself perchance in the streets of Cork was conscious of a strange, foreign, alien background such as he never experienced when walking along Broadway or down Fifth Avenue.

By the year 1914 Queenstown and Cork Harbour had become to the average Englishman just places on the map that, in the normal round of social life, rarely had need to be mentioned or thought of. So long as Liverpool continued to be the principal British port for transatlantic passengers, Cork Harbour week by week used to see the New York liners anchor within its green shores long enough to discharge pilot and pick up mails. Only during the worst winter storms did weather prevent these steamers from calling, and in consequence compel their Liverpool pilots to be carried on to New York and back. But with the change over from Liverpool to Southampton, the introduction of mammoth liners which now called at Cherbourg and ignored Queenstown, the connection between Irish and English life became slighter than ever. A handful of sportsmen at certain seasons went over to hunt or fish, only to return home with strange tales of the people.

Now, even so late as the year mentioned there were still three noble harbours of the world where occasionally you could be sure of finding some tall sailing ship, barque-rigged, coming in, going out, or waiting for orders. Sydney, Falmouth, Queenstown [1] have been privileged to behold such glorious sights year after year. Certainly, when the War started, these relics of a glorious epoch were becoming fewer, whilst none was being built to replace any which passed out. Nevertheless, during even the first three years of hostilities an occasional barque would be seen approaching the south-west Irish coast, and those of us happening to be on patrol off the Fastnet felt a thrill of fear lest all that white canvas might immediately advertise her presence to some invisible U-boat. Always it was with a feeling of relief that we saw her pass on from our assigned area to the next. Uninsurable, generally ill-manned, these survivors from a bygone age made some plucky voyages through dangerous zones without the slightest armament, and with little or no escort.

After weeks at sea, not infrequently these sailing ships had the ill luck to arrive off Mizen Head or Cape Clear in thick weather—terribly anxious hours for any master mariner having no machinery for clawing off a lee shore, but a situation rendered worse by the danger zones of submarine and mine. Within two years I recollect three such vessels at different dates coming in from the Atlantic, each getting embayed, not one of them knowing where she was, yet miraculously in the end all three were extricated from that which seemed final peril. But of these incidents we can say more in subsequent chapters.

It was during the finest weather, when winds were light and the barnacled barque could scarce keep way, when visibility was unlimited, and her t'gallant masts could be seen for miles and hours ahead, that such a vessel was the easiest victim for any German submarine waiting in the neighbourhood of Galley Head or the Old Head of Kinsale. Thus, long before the War reached its crisis, there had been swept from the sea practically every British and French ocean-going sailing ship. Never again would Queenstown shelter in its wide expanse those salt-stained bulwarks and picturesque spars of a great canvas fleet.

To many people, even long after that memorable August

[1] It matters not whether we call the harbour after Queenstown or Cork. Certain maps and charts prefer the former, others choose the latter.

1914, it was something of a shock when they were reminded that Queenstown still possessed one considerable link, in that it continued to be a base of the Royal Navy: not in the same prime category as Portsmouth or Devonport, yet at least it was a second-class depot such as existed across St. George's Channel at Pembroke. Within its magnificent natural harbour, Queenstown liked to boast that there was room enough for the whole British Fleet when once the mile-wide channel of approach had been negotiated. The latter is just a couple of miles in length, twisting right and left between the fort-crowned cliffs before suddenly bursting into a glorious maritime lake some five miles broad, east and west, against a background of Devonshire-like country. Thousands of seafarers throughout the ages have given thanks that during prevailing south-west and southerly winds the entrance from Roche's Point is practicable for sailing ships during really heavy weather, although the bends make it awkward for the very largest of modern steamers. Even the great Drake was once grateful for finding here a safe retreat from the Spaniards, and the place of his anchorage is known to this day as Drake's Pool.

As you come in from the boisterous Atlantic, and heavy seas which smite the Irish coast most days of the year, beginning in mid-September and rarely modifying till May, there is a most pleasing softness characterising the atmosphere. So mild and agreeable is this salubrious climate that it tends rather to soothe than invigorate. Before hostilities broke out with Germany, here was maintained a nice pleasant station unaccustomed to violent excitements, a kind of Service backwater right away from the world's turmoil, and most convenient if you happened to enjoy outdoor sports; yet it was not usually sought for by the most ambitious officers. No capital ships were based here, and the dockyard was normally employed maintaining in a condition of sea-readiness that old-fashioned Training Squadron which consisted of eight old cruisers. Not one of them was less than twenty-two years old in 1914, and the biggest was of only 7,700 tons. Actually these " Edgar " class were employed during the initial weeks of the War under Admiral de Chair off the north coast of Scotland enforcing the blockade; but they proved themselves so incapable of enduring bad weather—more than half of them narrowly escaped disaster—that by early December seven of them had been paid off, whilst the eighth had been sunk in action.

Queenstown itself is a collection of houses rising from the slope of a hill on the south side of Great Island, with the Roman Catholic cathedral as its most conspicuous building near the top, close to which stood Admiralty House. The hill is steep, and you descend to a somewhat dull main thoroughfare of second-rate shops, inferior hotels, a long shipping quay, and the Royal Cork Yacht Clubhouse. Approaching from seaward, you will have passed by this time three other islands—Spike, Rocky, and Haulbowline. The first is the largest, and was at one period a convict establishment; the second was excavated to form a powder magazine; and the third, lying opposite to the Yacht Club, contained not merely large ordnance stores, but also an excellent naval dockyard with a twelve-acre basin, naval storehouses, facilities for dry-docking, a hospital, workshops, foundry, and other conveniences.

In peace time the number of dockyard employees at Haulbowline was always small, and, after the first week of war, when the last old training cruiser had been hurried off to join Admiral de Chair in the north, there remained little enough work to be done. During the next few months various other cruisers came in to fuel, or for small repairs; but they soon went out again into the Atlantic. It was Haulbowline, likewise, which had a brief busy spell when two divisions of the British Expeditionary Force came to be embarked and despatched; yet once again life at Queenstown settled down pretty much as before. The ferry-steamers and picket-boats kept running between town quay and dockyard, sport had come to an end; but the North Sea, Heligoland Bight, and all the war regions, seemed to be infinitely remote.

With the Grand Fleet stationed at the northern extremity of Scotland, it was unthinkable that the enemy's High Sea Fleet, or any single ship, would ever break through to the wide ocean. True, there existed a possibility that some raid in force might be made in the English Channel against the British Army transports, though it was scarcely probable these enemies would come west of Land's End, unless on their way to harass the trade routes in the North or South Atlantic. As to submarines, no one entertained the slightest apprehension that these could venture out beyond the North Sea confines, inasmuch as under-water craft of any nation had never made a passage so long as the distance from Germany to the south of Ireland and back.

On the whole, then, any intelligent person would have been justified in prophesying that the War would hardly reach the Queenstown area. Here up the hill at Admiralty House, whose balconies looked forth over dockyard, anchorage, islands, and down to the harbour's very entrance, was Vice-Admiral Sir Charles H. Coke, K.C.V.O. His official appointment was "Senior Officer on the Coast of Ireland," and already at the commencement of hostilities he had been here for more than three years. Until a short time previously his flag had been flying in the old training cruiser *Endymion*, but after the naval review at Spithead in July she had gone to Devonport before steaming up to Scotland. Queenstown harbour was now comparatively empty, and its four ancient torpedo-boats were not suitable for much higher service than to roll and patrol immediately at the entrance off Roche's Point. Their fighting value was of the slightest, yet in keeping with the unimportant character which at least this part of the British Isles was expected to play in the big drama.

Outside, however, was stationed the 11th Cruiser Squadron, under Rear-Admiral Phipps Hornby, comprising those none-too-modern vessels *Venus*, *Minerva*, *Doris*, *Isis*, and *Juno*. Within the first three days they were on their beat, sixty miles west of the Fastnet; there placed so as to cover liners, cargo carriers, and tramp steamers approaching the British Isles from the Atlantic. Until it seemed fairly certain that German naval forces would not make forthwith an attack on the terminals of these trade routes, along which so much of Britain's essential food supplies must be brought, the 11th Cruiser Squadron was a very prudent and necessary defence; and Queenstown an equally handy base for fuel and repairs. The cruiser *Drake* was also sent to this area, and only five hours before war actually broke out she had come beyond the Fastnet, picked up the Cunard liner *Carmania* and was escorting her home.

QUEENSTOWN FROM THE HARBOUR

The Admiral's flagstaff will be seen to the right of the cathedral.

As illustrating the great shortage of cruisers in the British Navy, it is to be noted that barely had this squadron been on its area for a week than its services were demanded for a purpose other than commerce protection. The enemy had sprung no surprise down the English Channel, but he still might emerge and fall upon the British Armies in transit. Therefore, while an Army division was being sent by sea from Ireland to France, the cruisers had to be moved to the north-east and south-east of the Emerald Isle so as to form a temporary, but closer, barrier against any possible Atlantic onslaught. For, during those first days, when the air seemed full of rumours and nothing definite or clear-cut could be surmised, there had arisen a reasonable conjecture that raiders were already coming up the Atlantic. The imagined crisis passed, and the centre of anti-raider operations was presently shifted.

CHAPTER II

THE WAR COMES WEST

It was not till hostilities had been going on for most of three months that the first shock smote Ireland, yet the incident was kept so secret that the whole truth and nothing but the truth was hidden from the public till after the War.

On the night of October 22 the ex-North German Lloyd liner *Berlin*, which had succeeded in stealing up the Norwegian coast, thence passing between the Faroes and Iceland, southwards now in the direction of the Donegal coast, laid a terrible minefield off Tory Island, which four days later caused the S.S. *Manchester Commerce* to founder. She was outward bound from Manchester to Quebec when she struck one of these deadly black " eggs," so that her master, together with thirteen of her crew, were lost. Next day H.M.S. *Audacious*, one of the Fleet's crack battleships, was mined a mile farther south and sent to the bottom in spite of the most praiseworthy efforts to save her. It so happened that the White Star liner *Olympic* was in the neighbourhood, being on her way from Liverpool to America. In response to distress signals she arrived on the sad scene, and took the *Audacious* in tow for a while; but the result was foreseen.

Now, apart from the serious effect on the Grand Fleet movements and its Commander-in-Chief, this minefield, so mysteriously laid, was the initial happening to create the same urgent necessity for auxiliary craft already required off the English and Scottish coasts. At that date none but the Germans knew whether the Tory Island trap had been laid by surface ship. Genuine man-of-war? Disguised neutral? Submarines? Who could surmise? The first thing was to sweep up these dangers to shipping, and the second to send out all the available patrol vessels, that they might keep vigilant guard.

In those early days, when every ship of the Royal Navy was still too few, the problem of improvising a subsidiary fleet of steam yachts, trawlers, drifters, paddle-steamers (only a few weeks before busy running trips for summer visitors), had already developed. In response to Admiral Jellicoe's request, four minesweeping trawlers were hurried north from Milford Haven in Wales, others were sent from the North Sea, paddle-steamers arrived from the Clyde, and, in spite of the foul weather or the heavy ocean swell off northern Ireland, these crews from fishing and commercial vessels had by Christmas located the minefield's limits. To sweep them all was a slow, dangerous, boring job; but by the following April (1915) most of these mines had either been cleared up or had drifted away to the west shores of Scotland. Nevertheless, a Norwegian grain-ship foundered in the Tory Island area during that same month, and even in the year 1917 the region was not quite clear.

But, while it was impossible to station patrols everywhere in Irish waters, this Tory Island danger might be repeated at other points where normally there was much traffic, and something thorough must be done in selected regions to thwart future incursions. Now to-day, some twenty years afterwards, we are able to view events from two opposite angles; but in that first critical autumn, imagination and cautious reasoning had to make up for uncertainty. To the British Naval authorities it looked as if the selection of Tory Island was plainly to entrap the Atlantic liners which at this date—for safety's sake—were again running from Liverpool rather than Southampton; and the next minelaying effort would probably be directed to the Mersey entrance. Therefore both approaches to the Irish Sea must be guarded, north and south.

At this period of anxious suspense it was for some time believed that a submarine had laid the trap. That being so, future U-boat visitors must be shut out from the Irish Sea, and so from the Liverpool approaches. Actually, the *Berlin* had intended depositing her cargo of death in the Firth of Clyde, but her original aim was frustrated by navigational difficulties created by no lights burning on Rathlin Island, Mull of Cantyre, or up the Clyde. She got clean away after doing her job, never dared to try to reach Germany again, but had just coal enough to steam into a Norwegian fjord, and on November 17 bring up abreast of Trondheim, where she was interned. Now, to deny enemy submarines a passage down the Irish Sea, it was decided to barrage the North Channel, which is that neck of water where the north-east of Ireland comes closest to the south-west of Scotland. The idea was to employ large numbers of steam-drifters, which only a few weeks previously had been engaged in the herring fishery, but henceforth were to tow a special type of nets backwards and forwards in the hope of making it impossible for any underwater craft to avoid entanglement.

So a base was established at Larne, hundreds of drifters were sent to the coast of Ireland, and they began operating in an area thirty miles long by twenty-two miles wide. At each end of this thirty-mile stretch cruised armed patrols, so that if the U-boat dived to pass under the area it would be in an exhausted condition by the time it must rise near the patrol vessels. Half a dozen of England's finest steam yachts had also been taken over and armed with guns. For a while these beautiful craft (such as the *Valiant*, *Sapphire*, and *Medusa*) were employed as a flying squadron to hunt in the Irish Sea, Kingstown was opened as an auxiliary naval base, armed trawlers were hurriedly fitted out for patrolling, whilst at the southern end, where St. George's Channel separates Ireland from Wales, another net barrage was attempted.

For the latter it was decided to make Milford the base, under the care of Rear-Admiral C. H. Dare, and from this Welsh haven there was presently maintained a most ambitious scheme. By the time sufficient numbers of drifters had been collected, there was stretched across St. George's Channel a vast mobile barrage, whilst to the north the important route Kingstown to Holyhead was being watched by a chain of steam trawlers and other improvised war vessels.

Thus within the first few months of hostilities had been set going the four new bases of Larne, Kingstown, Milford, and Liverpool, where ex-fishing fleets and yachts could be coaled, their boilers cleaned, repairs made, crews rested, supplies taken aboard, and the organisation directed. On paper, at least, it seemed as if all those hundreds of active patrols, and all those miles upon miles of nets, would make the Irish Sea into a peaceful lake for the perfect safety of merchant ships passing on their lawful occasions. Liverpool and the Mersey would not be menaced, the Irish passenger-mail service to Holyhead would not be endangered, and the enemy must go farther afield.

But with a distance of sixty miles across from Wales to Ireland this Milford mobile barrage was in practice not capable of perfection. To maintain such a permanent and unbroken line over even a large section during summer gales and winter storms, with fishing skippers getting their ships out of position, or nets becoming tangled up by the tide, and all kinds of unexpected complications occurring—this, in the strict sense, was a quite impracticable project. Gallant and splendid, patient and long-suffering as were officers and men, it would have been impracticable to make this barrier entirely submarine-proof. At their best the net fleets were likely to be inconveniences to any enterprising enemy rather than insuperable obstacles; but as to that the future would decide. For the present, then, only along the north and eastern Irish coasts were considerable measures adopted, whilst even now Queenstown was hardly affected. First thing in the morning, perhaps, a pair of trawlers would come out and do a routine sweep with their tethered wires off the harbour entrance, but then they would go back to their anchorage. " No mines found. Nothing to report."

And so the daily routine went on during the first winter.

But next developed, with interesting and logical sequence, a phase that startled the world's greatest submarine experts, whether in Germany or elsewhere. It was to expand from a phase into a campaign so vast and far-reaching that the United States felt the same jolt, no matter how many miles of sea intervened, nor how uninterested officially at that date were her statesmen. We can, indeed, with all the facts before us in our post-war epoch, perceive the hand of fate slowly but inevitably manifesting itself in the North Sea, then stretching farther and farther west towards Ireland, closer yet closer, till its fingers touch the remoter shores, and at last beckon right across the Atlantic to the American nation.

For at the outbreak of war the seagoing and offensive capabilities of submarines were unknown, and by no means fully tried. But forthwith one or two daring pioneers in the German U-boat service began to achieve some remarkable successes. At the end of August 1914 Lieut.-Commander Hersing in *U 21* left Germany for a North Sea cruise, and on September 2, about one and a half hours before midnight, he had the audacity to go right up to the Forth Bridge. There were no defensive nets on the Firth at that time, but the battle-cruiser *Invincible* happened to be in harbour, and would have been definitely torpedoed but for the fact that Hersing's periscope was sighted. This caused the batteries to open fire and the *Invincible* to send picket-boats out to hunt. With only a little more determination Hersing could have bagged his victim, and have had a fair chance of escaping; but what with the strong tides gurgling under the Forth Bridge, the awkwardness of navigating in strange waters after dark when submerged, and the sudden fire opened against him; no one could blame him for abandoning his project and retreating.

Nor had he long to wait for success to meet him. Off May Island he came up with H.M.S. *Pathfinder*, Captain F. Martin-Leake, flotilla-leader of the Forth Destroyer Patrol. Ten miles south-east of the island, about 4.30 in the afternoon of September 5, Hersing's torpedo hit the *Pathfinder*, which disappeared in less than five minutes, with the loss of most men, though the wounded Captain Martin-Leake himself was picked up. This charming and very courteous English gentleman, member of a family renowned for gallantry, not merely lived to command another ship, but also to have his revenge; for, when commanding officer of the armoured cruiser *Achilles*, he and the *Dundee* some months later engaged the German raider *Rena* so effectively as to sink her. Not long after that, in turn, we find him at Queenstown as Flag Captain, winning and deserving a great respect among the Anglo-American naval forces. He lived till after the War, became an Admiral, and, by a curious twist of fate, his death was caused through an accident along a country road.

The essential feature of Hersing's achievement lay in the fact that this was the first U-boat victory in the War, and he reached home safely, to be greeted as a hero. His example was immediately an inspiration, no less than an incentive, to other submarine captains. These new under-water craft possessed remarkable potentialities. So September 20 saw Lieut.-Commander Weddigen leaving Heligoland in *U* 9 to intercept British transports off the Belgian coast. Whilst on his way thither early on the morning of the 22nd, in the Maas lightship vicinity (west from the Hook of Holland), he sighted the three British cruisers *Aboukir*, *Cressy*, and *Hogue*. At 7.30 a.m. they were all afloat; at 8.35 a.m. all three had been torpedoed by him. They foundered with heavy loss of life, and Weddigen, having used up all his torpedoes, went back home without having been able to interfere with the transports.

The sensational announcement in the English evening papers that three " *Cressys* " had been wiped off the Navy List as if by the wave of a man's arm, has never been forgotten: it remained one of the most dramatic surprises throughout four amazing years. Weddigen was to find himself the second hero in his country's submarine service, and yet again did example have an almost immediate influence on brother officers: for the first time in history the Dover Straits were next violated by a U-boat and a brilliant coup was barely frustrated.

The date was September 27, which I have personal cause to remember, since I happened to be bringing an auxiliary patrol vessel up the English Channel from Portsmouth, bound through the Straits northward. I had passed into Dover Harbour by the western entrance, anchored among destroyers and some old-type cruisers, then rowed off to call on the Admiral. It was while waiting aboard his flagship, and just outside his open door, that a conversation he was having with another officer suddenly quickened my pulse.

". . . Enemy submarine in the Straits. . . . Beginning to come farther west now. In future we must expect them to penetrate down Channel."

It was a thrilling moment; for not since the days of Napoleon had a hostile craft cruised in those waters. I recollect feeling singularly lucky to have listened in at such an historic occasion, yet consumed with mingled anger and amazement. What seemed so excellent was the Admiral's complete lack of emotion: his voice exhibited no more feeling than if he were reading from a railway time-table.

Actually it was *U* 18 (Lieut.-Commander Hennig) who that day had attacked the light cruiser *Attentive*, which would have been quite a satisfactory result for the German, given a little more luck. The cruiser chanced to be—like the *Pathfinder*—a flotilla leader. The loss of such another within the same week as the *Cressy* disaster would have stunned the British public too seriously, but fortunately the *Attentive* escaped the torpedo.

What followed?

Whilst two more torpedoings occurred in the North Sea, the Dover Straits were quiet for a whole month, till the French S.S. *Amiral Ganteaume*, with Belgian refugees, was torpedoed off Cape Gris Nez on October 26, followed five days later by the sinking of H.M.S. *Hermes* at the hands of a submarine eight miles W.N.W. of Calais. Barely a fortnight followed, and another warship was sunk in the Straits: this time it was H.M.S. *Niger*, which was sent to the bottom off Deal by *U* 12 on November 11. Less than one more fortnight passed and the British S.S. *Malachite* was off Cape de la Heve near Havre, when *U* 21 shelled her, causing her to take fire and founder. Three days later in the same locality the same submarine by gunfire sank the British S.S. *Primo*.

The situation by the end of the first November was this: The unsuspected U-boats had proved themselves a terrible menace to cruisers and merchant steamers, in the Dover Straits no less than the North Sea. But Hersing with *U* 21 had broken further records, (*a*) by enterprising so far west as the neighbourhood of Havre, (*b*) by using a deck gun as a means of attack, thus saving the limited number of torpedoes which a submarine can carry and enabling the cruise to be lengthened as regards time. There ensued another month when submarines were curiously inactive, but on the last night of the year came the climax, when *U* 24 (which had but recently joined the German Flanders flotilla based on Bruges) arrived so far down the English Channel as to reach West Bay, between Portland Bill and the Start.

Now it so happened that during December 31 a British battle squadron was exercising in West Bay. Several weeks had elapsed since an enemy submarine had been reported in the English Channel, but never had one been heard of so far down as Portland. Unknown to anyone else, however, Lieut.-Commander Schneider in *U* 24 had been trying throughout that afternoon to get into a position suitable for attack. Night had long since fallen, heavy weather was impending, the sea had already begun to rise, and the time was nearly half-past two in the morning. The conditions for successful submarine attack under protection of invisibility were thus perfect, and the sad result followed that the *Formidable*, last battleship in the line, was torpedoed and eventually sank.

Nothing succeeds like success, and whilst the British naval authorities now concentrated their efforts on making the Dover Straits impassable for submarines, using to that end a barrage of nets and drifters, there must inevitably be a period ere theory was put into practice. To manufacture so many miles of wire netting, to collect so many steam drifters from North Sea ports and send them to begin a routine rolling athwart the strong Dover tides, demanded weeks. But meanwhile Hersing aspired to break both his own and Schneider's records. On January 23, after the usual lull which already the reader will have noticed, U 21 set out from Germany, came through the Dover Straits by night, thence proceeded the whole length of the English Channel, turned north, and passed the Welsh coast into the Irish Sea, being the first enemy submarine ever to have done so.

Off Bardsey Island (northern end of Cardigan Bay) she was sighted by an armed drifter, but carried on past Holyhead and Liverpool, next up the Lancashire coast till she had reached Walney Island. This is a narrow eight-mile stretch of land fronting Barrow-in-Furness, where existed not merely an airship shed, but some of the most important shipbuilding works and munition factories in Great Britain. It was shortly before two o'clock in the afternoon of January 29 that Walney Fort sighted a submarine to seaward, travelling south on the surface. The German was having a thorough good look round and taking her time, yet the ridiculous situation was that the soldiers on shore had no definite knowledge as to her nationality. Barrow was a place where numbers of British submarines had been built, or came to be repaired. Was this one of the latter?

Forty minutes passed before her hostility could be determined, but Hersing now opened fire on the airship shed; the Walney guns replied, but no damage was done by either side. U 21 quickly submerged, carried on south, and began operations off the Mersey. Here next day she captured and sank by bombs (again demonstrating Hersing's economical methods) the three British steamers *Ben Cruachan*, *Linda Blanche*, and *Kilcoan*. She then resumed her return voyage homeward, though when coming down the Irish Sea and some thirty miles north-west of Fishguard she herself was sighted and attacked by the *Vanduara*, one of the armed yachts previously mentioned already patrolling this area.

Now, the immediate sequels to this intrepid voyage were notable. Admittedly, to British imaginations Hersing had conveyed unpleasant fears as to the future. The great port of Liverpool, with its daily procession of shipping to and from all regions of the world, was most seriously threatened. Without any warning the approaches had been brought within the danger area, and the Irish Sea could no longer be reckoned safe. Having regard to the absolute necessity for using Liverpool as the gateway, through which entered the country's food and other essential supplies, the future prospect appeared serious beyond all exaggeration. And nothing could be done except to go on multiplying nets, drifters, trawlers, or any available patrol vessels.

In Germany, however, the safe return of $U\,21$ synchronised with a declaration (on February 4) that the waters round Great Britain and Ireland were now in the War Zone, that from February 18 the German submarine blockade would begin, and every merchant ship met with in that zone would be destroyed. This, as we now know, was the enemy's reply to the British blockade established off the North Scottish coast. The enemy was careful not to declare a blockade in so many words, because he possessed at that time only twenty-three submarines, though forty-two large ones and 127 small ones were on order. He was driven to inaugurate this campaign not merely because already the certainty of starvation by the British blockade was now only a matter of a few short years, but for the reason that the retreat from the Marne, and the High Sea Fleet's inactivity, had created the need for some bold onslaught.

Thus it was, then, that at the end of six months' warfare Germany's naval activities had gradually spread from the North Sea. Obviously her submarines would not be content with this advance. Now that $U\,21$ had got home to Wilhelmshaven and reported that the Dover nets at present stretched for less than ten miles across the Straits, leaving another eleven miles unbarraged; and that by timing one's arrival at this line so that the first of a west-going tide coincided with one of the dark hours it was quite practicable to overcome the only obstacle in the English Channel; nothing could prevent other submarines from doing all that Hersing had accomplished. British shipping could be attacked either in the immediate approaches to Liverpool or much farther to the south-west, where Atlantic vessels were wont to make their first landfall or navigational departure.

We know, on the authority of our late enemy Captain A. Gayer, that if a U-boat outward bound arrived ahead of her tide, and intended to negotiate the Dover Straits by day, she would lie on the seabed to the north of the Ruytingen Bank, and then proceed submerged when the favourable stream began. If she essayed the Straits passage by night, she remained on the surface, kept a smart look-out for any gaps in the net-line, occasionally became temporarily entangled, but on the whole found little difficulty. That which surprised these U-boat officers was that the British Admiralty had been so slow in denying the Straits. Of course it is easy to be wise after making a mistake, but the truth may at once be admitted: this net idea was not a reliable barrier. Indeed, not till the last year of hostilities and efficient minefields were laid, was the Dover defile any more difficult to a U-boat than a wooden gate to an active pedestrian.

On the other hand, Germany confessedly made a great error in beginning this new campaign so early as February; for only two boats were ready. That is to say, U 30 had in fact started out on her western cruise slightly before February 18, and U 8 was able to sail on the appointed day; but the next pair, U 20 and U 27, did not leave the Ems for the Irish Sea till February 25. And if you ask why out of twenty-three only four were available, the answer is quite plain. Submarines are temperamental, tricky craft. After every little voyage each U-boat needed a careful overhaul, and this meant a number of days in dock. Thus what with that period, plus the days spent on the way out to her allotted patrol, plus more days wasted during her return journey, the actual time for sinking ships in British waters did not amount to much. And this is the explanation of those short, sharp bursts we have noted in the English Channel, followed by several weeks of uneventfulness.

Now, at the much later stage, when Germany's shipyards had finally been able to deliver most of the 169 new craft, the same difficulty still presented itself, though not so acutely. Whilst more boats were in commission, more work was required of them, and their operational areas had extended much farther away from home : consequently the voyaging was longer, whilst the days off Ireland, or wherever the location might be, had not been proportionately increased.

We shall do well to emphasise the interesting fact that between August 1914 and February 1915 the submarine for Germany had so ably, yet so surprisingly quickly, made herself a most valuable war weapon that no supply could keep up with the sudden demand. It was but ten years previously that the Germania Yard received its first order for three ten-knot submarines—to be used in the Russian Navy. Not till three years before the War had our enemy evolved his own efficient U-boats with reliable heavy-oil engines, but with the precise intent of employing them not as harbour defences: they were to be used oversea for attack in British waters. At length, when engine troubles had been conquered, it was feared that no crews could endure being at sea more than three days. But, after numerous medical experiments and the introduction of oxygen, trial cruises in the North Sea had proved that a week out from port was not intolerable. Only, as we have witnessed, after the commencement of war was it demonstrated by Hersing that men could live and be tossed about in these steel shells during a whole fortnight and be none the worse; which was just the remaining bit of information that had to be determined ere a blockade by U-boats could become a practicable proposition.

CHAPTER III

THE *LUSITANIA* CRISIS

RESULTS of Hersing's adventurous enterprise, and of the enemy's new policy, were not long in being made manifest; on February 20, when ten miles east of Point Lynas, Anglesey (in the Liverpool district), *U* 30, without any warning, torpedoed the British S.S. *Cambank*, 3112 tons, and sent her to the bottom with the loss of four lives. On the same day the S.S. *Downshire* was sunk off the Isle of Man. *U* 8, however, whilst on her way home fouled one of the Dover drifter's nets, was chased and shelled by destroyers, to whom the German crew surrendered before the submarine sank.

Whilst *U* 20 (Lieut.-Commander Schwieger) and *U* 27 (Lieut.-Commander Wegener) both started out from the Ems on February 25, the former travelled by the Dover Straits and English Channel to the Irish Sea; the Isle of Man; visiting also the Bristol Channel. The other boat inaugurated for submarines a new route which was to be invaluable later on as an alternative to the Dover passage; for Wegener went up the North Sea, round the coast of Scotland, thence south into the Irish Sea as far as the Isle of Man also. This was no ordinary achievement. To have navigated, in the depth of winter, motor-driven vessels through so many anxious miles; to have endured the heavy weather, the cold, and damp discomfort; but also to have returned home safely, exhibited a professional ability that betokened a grave future peril to Allied shipping. Nor was that all.

These two, between them, became responsible for the following sinkings of British steamers: the *Bengrove* (3840 tons) on March 7 off Ilfracombe; two days later the *Princess Victoria* (1108 tons) off Liverpool Bar; three days later the *Andalusian* (2349 tons), to the north-west of the Scillies; and on the following day the *Hartdale* (3839 tons) off the Irish coast of County Down. In addition to the above, three steamers were attacked, but escaped; one in the Bristol Channel got away because of superior speed, as did another off Liverpool Bar, but the third when in that vicinity survived only on account of the torpedo having missed. But perhaps the most sensational and significant item at this period occurred on March 14, twelve miles south-west of Inishturk Island, when a submarine set on fire the British S.S. *Atalanta*. Actually the steamer was salved and towed into port, but the unsettling surprise lay in the fact that the enemy had now come right out into the Atlantic off the west of Ireland.

That was yet another record of endurance and originality, since there now remained no coast of the British Isles, nor any of the sea approaches, too distant from Germany for submarine attack. Our enemy had also the sound sense to make her pioneer captains into experts of some particular area. Hersing was so super-brilliant that his services were needed elsewhere; but Schwieger and Wegener, following their first trips, became specialists for the Irish waters, and henceforth their duty was to " take care of " those important trade-routes which concentrated off the Fastnet, followed the south Irish coast, and led up to Liverpool Bar. I would ask the reader please to keep in mind the names of Schwieger and Wegener, for reasons that will soon be apparent, whilst adding that Wegener, during the early hours of March 11, brought off another genuine triumph. By this time he was just outside the Coast of Ireland area, at the southern end of the Firth of Clyde near Corsewall Point, when at 5 a.m. he sank by torpedo H.M.S. *Bayano*, one of Admiral de Chair's Blockade Squadron. The loss of this vessel on a night so dark that the enemy lying on the surface, stopped and waiting, could not be discerned, also emphasised our weakness in defence.

The position indicated that Wegener had made light of that mobile net barrage across the North Channel. Already not less than eighty drifters were based on Larne, and all shipping was compelled to pass to the south of Rathlin Island. Nevertheless, he had got through once when coming south, and again succeeded when returning home northabout. But if we seek a reply to the question, How was escape possible? the explanation is ready. The net drifters could not work in the worst weather, and this region is exposed to the ruthless Atlantic. What with the strong tides, dangerous overfalls, heavy seas, rain and mist, with no safe anchorage adjacent, but gaunt wild cliffs and barely two months in the year of tolerable conditions, these little vessels could not be an infallible protection.

Moreover, any seaman will agree that on a black night, with the usual Atlantic swell beating against the rocks, the commanding officer of a nine-knot drifter is not likely to keep quite close up to a lee shore. On the other hand, using fair tide and the cover of darkness, the experienced U-boat captain will watch for his chance, make for the gap, and get clear of net obstructions. Indeed, looking back on the past, one may deplore the reliance which for many a vital month was placed on anti-submarine nets. As mobile defences and traps they were of more trouble than utility wherever tides and waves could interfere. It was solely when firmly fixed —as, for instance, across a harbour entrance—that they possessed positive value. Furthermore, even so early as March, U-boats were being fitted at the foredeck with a permanent saw whose teeth would tear netting to pieces. This fixture continued in use up till the end of the War, and I have noticed it on a number of surrendered U-boats.

By the end of March (1915) the position was this: To the enemy belonged a bold initiative, that needed only time for its broadening effect, against shipping found off the British Isles. To counteract this no offensive was undertaken with a view to destroying German submarine bases, but efforts were expended on perfecting the nets, increasing their extent, and multiplying the number of drifters across the Dover Straits, as well as in the North Channel and St. George's Channel. It is true that *U* 32 (whose captain was Lieut.-Commander Freiherr von Spiegel, later destined to become an important visitor in Irish waters),[1] early in April, whilst bound west down the Dover Straits, and submerged, did have a trying experience. She collided with one of the nets, so was compelled to dive down and sit waiting on the bottom till kindly night followed. Then, coming to the surface, it was found that the net was foul of the conning-tower and festooning the sides. After some trouble she got free of all encumbrance, but at the end of her cruise in western waters preferred to return home via Scotland and the North Sea rather than tackle the Straits.

[1] See Chapter XVIII.

This incident, rare as it was, had an interesting effect, which lasted for the next two months, and Admiral Jellicoe remarked on the larger number of U-boats which during April were passing round Scotland. Now, it was by reason of von Spiegel's narrow escape that Germany's biggest submarines were forbidden to use the Dover route and ordered to voyage north-about whether going or coming; only the small UB and UC types of the Flanders flotilla being unaffected by this regulation. Thus it was that Hersing in *U* 21, whose orders were now to leave for the Mediterranean, saw before him a task more difficult than submarines of any nationality had so far faced. He was bound for the Adriatic, which, even by the English Channel, would mean a voyage more lengthy than an under-water craft had ever hitherto contemplated, but now that he must go right round the north of Scotland and outside Ireland, the undertaking was serious indeed. That he left the Ems on Sunday, April 25, and had just enough oil fuel to reach Cattaro on May 13, is remembered as another of Hersing's able achievements. The havoc which he wrought presently at the Dardanelles is beyond our story.

But whilst his departure from the Irish scene would have been appreciated—had we been made aware of it—this skilful officer passed on his tradition to successors, who were to create precedents and to alter the course of international history. Let us immediately see how one of the greatest of crimes was enacted in the most casual manner.

I have just mentioned Lieut.-Commander Schwieger and *U* 20. It was on the morning of the last day of April that he set forth in his submarine from Borkum Roads again bound for Ireland. A few weeks previously, Lieut.-Commander Freiherr von Förstner in *U* 28 had been to the Bristol Channel, where on March 27, to the west of Lundy Island, he had torpedoed and sunk the two British steamers *South Point* (3837 tons) and *Aguila* (2114 tons); whilst next day, besides chasing the *Dunedin* (4796 tons), which escaped by superior speed, he torpedoed the *Falaba* (4806 tons).

It is necessary to stress the *Falaba* incident because of what followed less than six weeks later. It was a Sunday, and she was on her way south down the St. George's Channel carrying many passengers, when Förstner stopped her and ordered her master to abandon ship. Before this demand could be obeyed—even whilst the boats were being swung out —*U* 28, with incredible brutality, loosed off a torpedo, so that 104 lives were lost, including that of the master. This was the first passenger ship to be sunk by a U-boat since the submarine blockade commenced, but German callousness roused so great an indignation as to sweep across the world like a mighty wave.

A month's lull ensued in this western area until the British S.S. *Fulgent* and the Russian S.S. *Svorono* were destroyed by a submarine off those bleak islands, the Blaskets, which form such an impressive group on the Kerry coast. Now this activity on the Atlantic side of Ireland, following the previously mentioned *Atalanta* affair, showed that the enemy was fairly encircling Ireland in his search for merchant vessels. Two lives had been lost in the *Fulgent*, and the date was April 30, which coincided with Schwieger's departure from Borkum, thus proving that another U-boat had already begun operating in Irish waters before his arrival.

It is not possible to say exactly on which day Schwieger arrived in *U* 20 off the south Irish cliffs, though we know definitely that he was there by May 7, and that a second submarine was operating likewise. The following activities are but introductory scenes leading up to the amazing crisis of a spring afternoon. On May 4 the British S.S. *Cayo Romano* was off the Fastnet when a torpedo was fired at her, but fortunately the missile missed. Next day, just after half-past five in the evening, the sailing schooner *Earl of Lathom* was coming along, some eight miles south-west from that prominent cape the Old Head of Kinsale, when a submarine sank her by gunfire. Four hours later the enemy was seen a little nearer to the east—that is to say, to the south of Queenstown Harbour entrance, but well placed so as to be on the track of ocean-going steamers.

On the forenoon of the 6th, this same U-boat, or her opposite number, had come so near to the harbour entrance as to be only 400 yards from Daunt's Rock buoy, where she was seen at 9.45 a.m. It would therefore be reasonable to suppose that she was hovering about for a special purpose:

sooner or later an important steamer might be expected to pass along these shores in or out of Queenstown. It is difficult to separate the movements of this submarine from those of another, for, whilst a U-boat early that evening was seen farther west off Castletownsend, there is no sort of doubt that a submarine at 7 a.m. and 1 p.m. was sighted off south-east Ireland, near the Coningbeg lightship. For two steamers, each of just under 6000 tons, were torpedoed and sunk in the latter neighbourhood.

Knowing (as we do from the above) that Hersing left Germany on April 25, and Schwieger on April 30; knowing also that the cruising speed of these two units on the surface was ten knots, but liable to be modified when butting into heavy weather; we can get a good idea concerning their progress. For, by a curious coincidence, the S.S. *Teriesias* happened to be making a voyage off the Portuguese coast, and to be thirty-six miles N.W. by N. of those well-known rocks the Burlings, when she met Hersing's $U\,21$ steering south, flying no colours, and awash. That was on May 6, the German being twelve days out. A rough reckoning persuades me to believe that Schwieger in $U\,20$, voyaging by the same route past the Orkneys and Hebrides, would not reach the south-west Irish coast before May 6, and it seems probable that his immediate predecessor, who arrived there at least two days earlier, was gradually working east towards Coningbeg, off which would be a position most favourable when attacking a liner bound up the Irish Sea for Liverpool.

That night a wireless message was sent out by the Admiral at Queenstown to the homeward-bound Cunarder *Lusitania* advising her to avoid headlands, pass harbours at full speed and keep in mid-channel, adding that submarines were off the Fastnet. This signal the *Lusitania* acknowledged having received. At this stage the historic sea drama becomes quicker and more tense. In April she had left England with passengers and mails for New York, and the accompanying photograph is of special interest: it was taken by another Cunard officer as she steamed west on what was to be her final voyage outward bound. With tragic inevitability and destined doom she left New York on May 1, whilst $U\,20$ was still in

S.S. *LUSITANIA*
Photograph taken in April 1915 on her last voyage to America.

GRAVES OF THE *LUSITANIA* VICTIMS
At Queenstown.

the North Sea. Fate was arranging during the intervening week that they should meet at a lonely rendezvous not far from Queenstown.

In spite of the War, it was essential that connection between the United States and Great Britain should be not wholly broken. Business people of both nations still had need to cross the Atlantic; private individuals, financial houses, diplomats and others required that the trans-oceanic postal service be maintained so far as possible. Therefore, notwithstanding the threat contained in Germany's Submarine Declaration, already carried into execution against the liner *Falaba*, the Cunard Steamship Company decided that they could run that crack ship the *Lusitania* once a month, though not at her maximum speed. By this date many of the best crews had joined the Army or Royal Navy, and the demand for munition workers or other Government employees was daily becoming acute; but the *Lusitania* could economise in labour and fuel provided six of her boilers were closed down.

This was decreed, yet even now she was capable of a speed of twenty-one knots, so that when she entered the danger zone and zigzagged she should have more than a fair chance of eluding any of the contemporary U-boats, whose maximum speed when submerged was only nine knots and could be maintained for not more than one hour. The *Lusitania* was unarmed, carried no troops when she came out of New York, and the voyage was uneventful till she approached the Fastnet area on May 7. Being about to enter the danger zone, Captain Turner, her master, ordered lifeboats to be swung out, bulkhead doors and portholes to be closed, and doubled his look-outs. He was bound for Liverpool, and a 30,000-ton ship had, of course, to work her tide into the Mersey. At the present speed *Lusitania* would be ahead of her tide, which would not serve for crossing Liverpool Bar till 4 a.m. on May 8. At 8 a.m. on May 7 Captain Turner accordingly eased down to eighteen knots. This to me seems a most natural and reasonable proceeding, and far wiser than waiting about off the Mersey, where submarines had already found victims. Whether in peace or war, the handling of such a great ship is a full-size man's job, and his anxieties increase proportionately as he gets nearer his landfall.

Having spent most of my war service patrolling in the Fastnet neighbourhood through all the seasons and every kind of weather, I would emphasise the frequency of fog and thick atmosphere, which makes it most difficult, and even impossible, for an Atlantic ship to sight the coast. That is why so many able navigators and fine ships come to grief off south-west Ireland. It is my experience that the month of May is particularly bad for fogs anywhere near the Mizen Head, Brow Head, or the Fastnet. Indeed, one of the most vivid of my recollections was being sent, in May 1916, from Berehaven to grope round the Mizen and Brow for a vessel that had at the end of her Atlantic voyage lost herself and got seriously ashore in the Fastnet region during the same fog that we were so heartily blaming.

Well, just a year previously, Captain Turner encountered a similar fog in the same locality. He had barely eased to eighteen knots when it became thick, so that, as he expected to pick up the Irish coast very shortly, he wisely reduced speed to fifteen knots. Luckily, just about noon the weather cleared, as it sometimes does when the May sun at its zenith disperses the mist. So now the rocks and cliffs of Ireland suddenly revealed themselves, and he was able to identify Brow Head, fix his position, lay a course S. 87 E. parallel with the south coast, and increase speed to the previous eighteen knots, which was henceforth maintained. Almost simultaneously with sighting Brow Head he received a wireless signal from Queenstown, which was a general warning to all ships that submarines were active in the southern part of the Irish Channel and had last been heard of near the Coningbeg lightship. *Lusitania* acknowledged this message, but an hour later Queenstown flashed out a final one to the effect that a submarine was active five miles south of Cape Clear, and was last seen proceeding west. Now, this message Captain Turner did not acknowledge, but if he received it he was doubtless too occupied with the double anxiety of unseen enemy and a possibly returning fog.

At 12.40 p.m. he had altered course to N. 67 E. so as to come nearer the land and get a more certain grip on his position: in other words, he wanted to pick up the prominent Old Head of Kinsale, which he now identified also. Exactly an hour later he swung back on to his S. 87 E. course, and at 1.50 p.m. began to take what is technically known as a four-point bearing.[1] It was now clear weather, and Captain Turner, with the wisdom and prudence of a most experienced navigator, was letting slip no opportunity for accurately ascertaining his ship's position. Having regard to the fact that he must presently alter course past the Coningbeg and Tuskar to find himself in the more restricted waters of the Irish Sea, surely he acted as any other shipmaster would have done in such circumstances?

Twenty minutes passed, the passengers were below enjoying the comfort of lunching whilst the sea was smooth: to-morrow they would breakfast in the still more peaceful Mersey? But, all of a sudden, the great climax burst when the ship's Second Officer sighted a torpedo rushing towards the starboard side from a distance estimated at 200 to 500 yards. The accompanying photograph of *Lusitania's* side will be studied in conjunction with the statement that this torpedo struck her between the third and fourth funnels. By the sudden inrush of water the liner's engines were disabled almost immediately, but the wireless operator was able to send out an S.O.S. signal at once, giving her position as ten miles south of the Old Head of Kinsale.

It was about 2.15 p.m. when this startling news reached Queenstown, and Admiral Coke wasted no time in despatching every available craft to her assistance. But what actually were these vessels? For their numbers and characters form a curious commentary on the naval importance of Queenstown area at that date.

Now, Queenstown, with its sub-base Berehaven (some eighty miles to the westward at the south-west end of Bantry Bay), had been charged with the duty of patrolling this south and south-western Irish coast, and for that, as well as other purposes, there were roughly two dozen steam trawlers, tugs, steam yachts, a drifter, torpedo-boats, plus two or three very

---

[1] This practice is based on the well-known instance where, two angles of a triangle being equal to one another, then the sides opposite to these are also equal. Thus, after noting when a headland bears four points on the ship's bow, the bearing is again taken when the headland is eight points, the distance run in the meanwhile being the distance at which the ship now passes the headland.

small motor yachts. In addition, might be mentioned an examination vessel which lay off Queenstown entrance and inspected all ships wishing to enter.

At any given moment some of these units must be of no practical value, since they might be in port coaling, refitting, or resting their crews. At the time when *Lusitania* was struck, the three trawlers *Sarba*, *Heron*, and *Bluebell* were patrolling to the eastward between Kinsale and Ballycotton; the three trawlers *Freesia*, *Verbena*, and *Restango* to the westward between Kinsale and Mizen Head; whilst the four trawlers *Indian Empire*, *Clifton*, *Maximus*, and *Reliance* were doing the easternmost patrol of all—from Ballycotton to Carnsore Point. Thus the south Irish coastline of some 150 miles was being watched by ten steam trawlers, whose best speed did not surpass, but was considerably inferior to, that of a U-boat's maximum of fifteen knots on the surface. It was rarely that one of these trawlers could steam at more than ten knots, but nine knots could be reckoned as about the average.

The latter corresponded with the submerged maximum speed of a German submarine, so that even if the trawler had a gun (usually a twelve-pounder) and a few lance bombs, she was too slow for chasing the enemy, whose twenty-pounder gun or guns could (and did) outrange the trawler. Thus this patrol force, guarding the inshore trade routes along which passed some of the most valuable Atlantic steamships, could only be regarded as quite inadequate against the newly inaugurated submarine blockade.

On this historic and fateful occasion the weak forces based on Berehaven were patrolling the district around the lonely Fastnet rock. Thus the trawler *Luneda* was south of the Mizen Head, the little motor yacht *Seagull* had sighted *U* 20 off Cape Clear and rushed into Baltimore to report; whilst another small motor craft, *Aptera*, was in the Kinsale vicinity. The yacht *Scadaun* happened to be in Berehaven, but just about the time of *Lusitania's* tragedy was starting off to investigate the report sent by *Seagull*.

It will be quite obvious to the reader that these two German submarines merely by submerging now and then, preserving vigilance through the periscope and coming to the surface fairly frequently when no patrols were about, could, over an area of 150 square miles, do an immense amount of damage, provided that the targets passed by day, did not zigzag irregularly, and kept fairly to the accustomed traffic lanes. Given reasonable luck, a clear atmosphere to see approaching such a tall hull as the *Lusitania*, conspicuous with her characteristic four funnels and lofty masts, almost any U-boat standing off and on for a few miles from the Old Head of Kinsale could have a 75 per cent. chance of sinking the Cunarder. It is true that on May 7 the sea here was calm, and therefore Schwieger was handicapped somewhat in respect of concealment; since the roughness of waves forms an excellent cover to hide a periscope. But, unfortunately, no patrol was near enough to cause the slightest inconvenience, so the German could just wait, watch, take his bearing of the oncoming victim, go ahead, stop, alter helm a little—and finally fire the torpedo.

Contrary to what was believed at the time, it is now fairly certain that only one torpedo was used. Schwieger himself in his diary denied that a second was fired. Although, as commanding officer, he was responsible for his U-boat and personnel, it is fair to say that quite possibly he never meant to sink *Lusitania*. It was stated in Germany by some, who served in these boats, that the navigating warrant officer who fired the torpedo from *U* 20 did so without waiting his captain's orders, and eventually received punishment. And if the reader asks: Then what was Schwieger doing to have trimmed his boat well down below surface, and to be using the periscope as if intent on attack? I would answer as follows.

Two years later, in these very waters, a British Admiral came steaming along with his flag flying aboard his flagship. It was a period of the War when some of the British submarines had been sent to patrol off the Irish coast against U-boats. The former, anxious to lose no opportunity for periscope practice, were always quietly but efficiently making themselves more and more expert. One day, a certain British captain sighted the flagship approaching, submerged to periscope depth, waited and watched, and finally got the Admiral's vessel so nicely framed in the lens that only the word had to be given and a torpedo would have caused the sea to be strewn with wreckage.

We shall never quite know whether accidental pressure on

a super-sensitive trigger may have been influenced by excitement of the moment. Against this theory must certainly be stressed those very definite rumours persistent in New York that *Lusitania* was to be sunk; and it may be something more than chance which brought *U* 20 from Germany to the Old Head of Kinsale just at the right time.

Fire and smoke were seen, the great hull and massive funnels heeled to starboard, she was already down by the head, and at 2.30 p.m. she had disappeared, with a loss of 1198 men, women, and children. Now, besides those patrol units already mentioned, and out on their respective beats, Admiral Coke in Queenstown from his balcony could look down on to the following up harbour: The tugs *Stormcock* and *Warrior*; the four torpedo-boats; three trawlers coaling; and the drifter *Golden Effort*, which had recently come round from Scotland in connection with the boom defence that was being laid across Queenstown Harbour. Round the corner was the armed yacht *Greta*, though she was in a state of refitting, and unable to move.

But the only two vessels immediately available were the *Stormcock* and *Warrior*, who got away out of the harbour quickly. The rest moved off with all the speed practicable. Both the trawlers *Brock* (Lieut.-Commander T. B. H. Whytehead, R.N.R.) and *Bradford* suddenly stopped coaling, raised steam, and went. The *Flying Fox*, *Golden Effort*, and the three torpedo-boats 050, 052, 055 sped to sea, whilst Queenstown flashed a message to the *Indian Empire*, which was fitted with wireless. She chanced to be off Mine Head at that hour, so she had about fifty miles to steam before reaching the scene of disaster. The *Freesia* also had wireless, and she could be summoned; but she was right away west by the Fastnet. Still, every vessel with engines that could move gradually concentrated on the sad area, and even the examination steamer *Julia* for once left her job to look after itself.

That evening began the mournful return of tugs and trawlers to bring in the living with the dead; men and women picked up with such little clothing that they were glad to accept the blankets and most of the clothes belonging to these auxiliary vessels. The trawler *Bluebell* brought in Captain Turner alive (though he had been in the water for nearly three hours), one other officer, and some passengers. At 8.30 p.m. arrived *Stormcock* alongside the Cunard Wharf, but followed by the *Indian Empire* (Lieut. W. H. Wood, R.N.R.) with no less than 170 souls—the largest number of survivors brought in by any vessel. On board now were only three of Lieut. Wood's crew, the rest being away in boats scouring the sea for more people still in their struggle against death. About 7 p.m. the Third Intermediate Officer of *Lusitania* was also picked up by a trawler.

But of all those who lunched in *Lusitania* that day, by far the greater number never partook of another meal: their bodies either found sepulchre in those very waters where at a subsequent date the enemy laid mines for the same purpose of entrapping steamships, or were tenderly laid to rest in the Queenstown soil.

CHAPTER IV

THE BIG PROBLEM

WE need not stop to sympathise with Captain Turner at the sudden loss of his fine ship and the ruination of a successful career. After the official investigation, presided over by Lord Mersey, this eminent Judge was careful to state that blame ought not to be imputed to the captain for ignoring the wireless messages sent by Queenstown, since they were rather in the nature of advice than orders: they were never intended to deprive him of his skilled decision. This point, I consider, deserves emphasis. He was free to handle his vessel and use any defensive tactics that he deemed best. Had he been a naval officer and received those Queenstown signals, he must, on the contrary, have obeyed them implicitly.

There are plenty of his own profession who to this day criticise Captain Turner for his action in approaching so near to the coast, though many mariners will argue otherwise. Although he lived for nearly twenty years longer, he might long since have been dead; for never again was he entrusted with such responsibility as a *Lusitania*, and all his long experience of the Atlantic in every kind of vessel ceased to have value.

But the international results of *Lusitania's* loss were so real that the thud of Schwieger's torpedo could be felt throughout every civilised country. In America was aroused such anger at the ruthless slaughter of her citizens that for a while it looked as if she would now enter the War on the Allies' side. Political notes were exchanged across the Atlantic, the U-boat commanders were forbidden to sink large passenger ships, and for a few weeks this order was obeyed. It was, indeed, thought that both the *Lusitania* and the *Falaba* affairs would thereafter be mere isolated horrors never to be repeated; though we shall presently find that events worked out differently.

Truth is not always so obvious that it can be grasped without trouble, and Schwieger's torpedo stirred up all sorts of complications. Whilst no less an authority than the late Grand-Admiral Tirpitz left it on record that submarine warfare had "no effect in securing the ultimate victory of the German people," yet it still had "material enough to create incidents and quarrels with the Americans"; and already Mr. Gerard, the United States Ambassador, had been instructed to remind Germany that, during any blockade, neutrals also had rights; yet the whole situation during this first spring was still very delicate. But why?

Frankly, Britain, by her blockade—though she also was careful not to call it by that name—had become unpopular internationally, and the position regarding Anglo-American trade connections was fraught with peril. Germany's attitude was that her submarine effort was merely an essential measure of self-defence and a reply to the British blockade, which threatened to starve her into submission; and here the enemy foresaw with perfect accuracy the inevitable. On the other hand, the British blockade was stopping foodstuffs and cotton coming from America destined for Germany, and this angered part of the American public against Britain. Furthermore, the American nation embraced so many families of German and Irish descent that an immense influence in Wall Street and the Senate could be exerted against any practical sympathy with Britain, however much private individuals and the press might feel about the *Lusitania*.

Even just before this fateful May it had needed all the clever diplomacy, the patience, and self-control of Sir Edward Grey, Mr. W. H. Page (the American Ambassador in London), President Wilson and Sir Cecil Spring-Rice (the British Ambassador in Washington) to maintain an atmosphere of calm and a spirit of reasonable discussion. With just one tactless mistake on either side, a terrible crisis might quite easily have followed, and the world owes more to these men of good-will for their cautious restraint during the first quarter of 1915 than has ever been fully appreciated.

But when the *Lusitania* climax came on the top of the contraband troubles, and some American traders were still crying out that the British Blockading Squadron had robbed them of their normal markets in Hamburg, whilst other United States citizens were perfectly happy piling up fortunes in supplying munitions and food to Britain and France, it was difficult for President Wilson to know how he should act for the good of his country. Whilst one party urged him to enter the War against the British blockade, and another body of opinion was for instantly coming in against Germany's submarine blockade, yet a third section insisted on traditional aloofness from European troubles. Was ever a nation's leader faced with a more awkward dilemma than was President Wilson that May? Should he plunge the United States into this European War?

It was on May 12 that the United States despatched the first Note of protest to Germany, who replied on May 31; and a second Note was sent from Washington in June. But meanwhile the enemy continued to roam about off the Irish coast and sink wherever he had an opportunity. He was playing the game of attack-and-disappear, and our patrols, though alert and eager, scarcely had a chance of sighting and fighting. But what could be done? It seems to-day regrettable that British naval strategy did not include determined raids on German U-boat bases, thus destroying the menace at its source. Since, however, such raids were not undertaken, and we allowed the enemy in increasing numbers to cruise off our shores, there remained no choice except to multiply the patrol trawlers and net-drifters.

Thus, whilst one lot of drifters was now based at Fleetwood ready to meet any further attacks on Walney Island, the great Milford fleet of ex-fishing vessels was patrolling the southern Irish Sea from Bardsey Island in the north to Newquay on the Cornish coast in the south, and across to Ireland. Admiral Dare's units were so numerous that one could not fail to be impressed by these hundreds of small ships with their rough, hearty fishermen crews. Nets were laid off such spots as the Smalls (Welsh coast), Lundy Island in the Bristol Channel, Hartland Point, or in Barnstaple Bay, where it was believed that U-boats sought shelter during strong easterly winds. A squadron of six able steam yachts, each unit armed with at least two twelve-pounders, was during May likewise assigned to Milford. These cruised about as far west as the Fastnet, up and down the traffic route, but always ready for concentration on a given position if a submarine warning was sent forth by wireless.

As a further precaution the upper part of the Irish Sea was being patrolled with even more meticulous care. Every night from 6 p.m. to 10.30 p.m., before the departure of the night steamer from Dublin to Holyhead, one lot of trawlers cruised about as scouts whenever troops were crossing to England. Other patrols were steaming up and down the east Irish coast and along the north Welsh coast past Anglesey to Liverpool Bar; nets being also shot off the South Stack (Anglesey), the Calf of Man, and the Mull of Galloway. These traps would be left for a couple or even five days with mines ready to explode if a U-boat came along; but very rarely indeed were they of the slightest service, for the buoys gave considerable trouble, and the mines had a habit of misbehaving.

By the end of May, too, there were over 150 of these net drifters at Larne, to barrage the North Channel. Day and night a vast fleet of these little steamers kept under way, continuously towing their nets to form a double line across towards the opposite shores of Scotland. The cost of this one area alone was considerable; for in addition to the items of coal and stores, and wear and tear of nets, must be reckoned the monthly pay of 1500 men. Four days after the loss of the *Lusitania* eight Scottish drifters were commissioned to be based on Queenstown. They could be sent to lay their nets off any required headland or some suspicious bay, and during the ensuing months were thus employed as convenient.

Admiral Coke realised full well that his Queenstown armed trawlers were too slow for chasing a submarine which was obstinate enough to remain on the surface; and, indeed, the picture of a fifteen-knot U-boat impudently walking away from a ten-knot trawler beyond gun-range was extremely galling. In vain the Admiral asked for a dozen destroyers, whose speed would have been invaluable; but the Grand Fleet and Commodore Tyrwhitt at Harwich needed all the best, whilst many of the older destroyers could not be spared from other parts of the North Sea or the Dover Straits. So Queenstown, notwithstanding its recently proved weakness in patrols, still continued to be a kind of poor relative, the Navy's Cinderella, not considered worthy of too much attention by her proud sisters.

If at this date President Wilson could only have helped with a couple of flotillas! But the return of the *Mayflower* was not yet due.

So the task had to be borne in the best manner then possible. Only four days after the *Lusitania* foundered either Schwieger or his fellow U-boat was still at work off Queenstown harbour entrance, for the trawler *Brock* (now under Lieut. Cannell, R.N.R.), which had so quickly rushed towards the sinking Cunarder, received a surprise. The time was 10.30 p.m., and the position only four miles south-west of Daunt's Rock lightship—once so familiar an object to transatlantic travellers. Suddenly the *Brock* saw the conning-tower and wash of a submarine; but on that same day a U-boat had likewise been off Ballycotton, and in Tramore Bay, Waterford, farther east. Even after yet another three days these two submarines were still at work, since on May 14 one came into Tramore Bay and Ballycotton Bay, whilst the other showed herself towards the Fastnet area of Baltimore. In other words, the enemy was lying off each end at the south Irish coast, and was therefore excellently placed for capturing vessels making either their landfall or departure. Like a ripe pear, any unsuspecting ship must presently fall into German hands.

In an earlier chapter we spoke of those handsome ocean-going sailing ships which used to get their first sight and smell of land down here after weary weeks at sea. During most days of the year the wind blows from the south-west, thus enabling a vessel under canvas to have a fair breeze to Queenstown, Liverpool, or the Bristol Channel. But in June, or the latter part of May, when the barometer is high and the weather anti-cyclonic, a spell of light easterly winds may settle, and that was the condition which obtained during the third week of May 1915.

For about seven days that fine old sailing vessel *Glenholm* (1968 tons), one of the few that still belonged to British owners, had been boxing about in the vicinity of Mizen Head and the Fastnet lighthouse, but could make no actual progress against the east wind. Then at last, on May 21, she had reached out seaward nicely clear of the land, so that she was sixteen miles W.S.W. of the Fastnet. Of course she was the ready " ripe pear," and was quickly collected. Schwieger—or one of his friends—could not help observing that mass of white canvas isolated from all patrols, so he put a torpedo into her, and down she went. Another chapter of sailing-ship history closed!

It is true that the Berehaven Auxiliary Patrol vessels had already increased to the number of seven: the steam yacht *Aster*, the trawlers *Ina Williams, Lucida, Luneda, Reindeer, Drake*, and *Bempton*. But even if all these could be on their beat simultaneously, and not one coaling in port, what was such a handful when spread over that south-west corner with such long fjords as Bantry Bay and Dunmanus Bay, Roaringwater Bay, and innumerable lonely coves away from habitation, where a U-boat could come to anchor for a quiet night's rest? And one has to remember that Ireland, besides breeding pigs, is the most fertile country in the world for startling rumour. The cock-and-bull stories invented by some simple non-seafaring peasant living on the cliff-top, narrated to his neighbour, who enlarged upon the dramatic aspects and then spread them through the crowd on next market-day, would finally come to the ears of the Irish Constabulary, and so to the Admiral at Queenstown. He, in turn, and duty bound, would send one of his steam yachts, or trawlers, or drifters, to investigate this strange story. In most cases the narrative was pure myth, having no more initial foundation than an imaginative sense of the sensational. Two well-known instances of this class may be mentioned.

One favourite yarn was that a U-boat used to come into Dunmanus Bay, and that in a secluded cove, mostly sheltered by a rock, there was a rough quay, alongside which a U-boat arrived periodically to fill up with petrol, this fuel being brought down to the quay by a farmer of strong Sinn Fein sympathies. It was even suggested that after *Lusitania* succumbed, two U-boats motored into this bay. Now, three months later—if I may anticipate—when Admiral Coke had been succeeded by Sir Lewis Bayly and many changes took place—an armed drifter was sent by Admiral Bayly to investigate that rumour, and I worked my ship alongside this quay. Certainly it was secluded enough and, at a later date, I learned that once, during naval manœuvres years previously, an enterprising torpedo-boat had achieved some success by hiding herself there.

But, apart from the cart-ruts and an old black shed, there was no potential evidence, and after every particle of the story had been examined this was the residuum of truth: The quay and shed were on occasions used when some small coaster brought goods that were temporarily housed ashore, whence they were carted up the mountain-side to the farms. Dunmanus certainly was a Sinn Fein peninsula even in 1915, and witnesses were convinced that just after the *Lusitania* two submarines came into Dunmanus Bay. But there is no sort of veracity in connection with the petrol. In the first place, was it likely that a U-boat captain would run things so fine as to be glad of a few odd tins from an Irish farmer? And, secondly, these overseas U-boats did not use petrol. Their Diesel engines consumed heavy oil. As to the " marvellous " yarn of the U-boat officer who was said to have landed somewhere on the west coast of Ireland, to have visited a local cinema, and afterwards to have displayed the printed programme before the eyes of some torpedoed crew—this also may be dismissed as mere fiction. In those days of war rumours and unexpected happenings, the mind of the public was in a mood to accept amazing, and even ridiculous, assertions. But the pity of it all consisted in the waste of time, ships, and men who were diverted from their lawful occasions.

That the attack on *Lusitania* was no mere separate instance, or that the two submarines had voyaged solely for that one purpose and no other, is disproved by the prolonged visits now being made. On the day after *Glenholm's* finale a submarine was again sighted near the Fastnet, and on the evening of May 25 came indisputable testimony that U-boats were even going out nearly fifty miles from Ireland into the Atlantic, thus making quite certain of evading the coastal patrols. For the American S.S. *Nebraskan* was now to be a victim. She was of 2824 tons, registered in New York, and owned by the Hawaiian Steamship Company. On May 24 she had left Liverpool in ballast, come round the south of Ireland, and just before 8.30 p.m. was forty-eight miles west of the Fastnet —well clear of what was then regarded as the danger zone.

Suddenly an unseen submarine fired a torpedo which caused a violent shock and terrific explosion, bursting the hatch and deck at No. 1 hold, hurling the cargo-derrick thirty feet into the air, and immediately filling that hold with water. The look-out sighted no missile, but the Chief Engineer happened to be gazing on to the sea and saw what might have been a torpedo's wake—just before the explosion.

What to do? The *Nebraskan* in the lonely Atlantic, night coming on, and the perilous U-boat area fifty miles astern. If she tried carrying on towards New York, she would founder. If she put about towards land, she might get another torpedo any moment.

A difficult situation for the steamer's master! Literally between the German and the deep blue sea!

Miraculously, the *Nebraskan* kept afloat; her engines were intact, and she was able to bleat an S.O.S. on her wireless; but it had been expected that she would sink, and the crew had already taken to the boats. Now, once again, the patrols were luckily able to rush forth at the right opportunity. The armed yacht *Scadaun* (Lieut. Wybrants Olphert, R.N.R.) at that hour was patrolling off the south coast and near Castlehaven. Her wireless operator intercepted *Nebraskan's* call, so Lieut. Olphert started at full speed towards the position which *Nebraskan* gave, wirelessing that he was on his way. From Berehaven also was despatched the armed yacht *Aster*.

Through the night these two small vessels steamed and rolled athwart the Atlantic swell, and before 2 a.m. they picked up the *Nebraskan* some twenty-six miles west of the Fastnet, steaming slowly eastward. Cheered by the shore station's reply that a couple of naval vessels were coming to her assistance, the American steamer had recalled her boats and turned back. With *Aster* stationed astern and *Scadaun* ahead, the procession started, after *Nebraskan* had been instructed to obscure all lights. Suspenseful hours ensued, and the enemy might now have completed his attack. At first a course was set for Berehaven, which was the nearest port, though *Nebraskan* asked that he might be escorted all the way to Liverpool. Olphert wirelessed to Admiral Coke at Queenstown, and permission was given.

But it turned out to be a risky trip. The trio came safely past Queenstown without having another encounter, and rounded the Tuskar at a good wide berth of eleven miles, though the sight of this stricken steamer would have surely tempted any U-boat to do its worst. In place of this ephemeral foe, there was waiting man's eternal enemy. For when shelter of the south coast had been lost and the Irish Channel was entered, a nasty north-east wind with a heavy sea had to be encountered. By this time the *Nebraskan* was well down at the head, and in no condition for braving waves; if she foundered now, it would be hard luck, yet not surprising. Instead of the normal fair south-wester, the north-easter meant a head wind all the way to Mersey Bar.

But Lieut. Olphert was an excellent seaman, who had formerly been an officer in a New Zealand liner. In order to get any possible shelter, he convoyed his charge over towards the Welsh shore, crept up under Anglesey, and at the end of an anxious, trying time the *Nebraskan*[1] one evening at nine o'clock arrived safely at Liverpool, whence she had started.

So the anti-submarine game went on, with the Queenstown patrols doing their inadequate best right around the south and west coasts from Carnsore Point to Sybil Point, north of Dingle Bay. In clear weather by day you would meet several of these trawlers slowly steaming in company abreast of each other, two miles apart, keeping out on a traffic line some ten or fifteen miles from land. Then at nightfall they would close the cliffs, move along the coast, and pay surprise visits to bays where the enemy might be lurking. It was customary for a U-boat, after coming round Scotland, to make the coast of Ireland at the north side of County Mayo, and it was off this north-west corner on May 24 that the trawler *Norbreck*, by her vigilance, was able to save another of those sailing ships. Under the very quarter of this barque was nestling a U-boat, and in a short time there would have been a barque no more. The *Norbreck* steamed towards the enemy at full speed, fired shots, and the enemy replied. The latter then made off and the sailing ship escaped.

Two days later one more British steamer, the *Morwenna* (1414 tons), was sunk by torpedo well south of the Fastnet; four days later still, the White Star liner *Megantic* (14,878 tons) off the south of Ireland was chased by a submarine, but got away through superior speed; whilst the 11,000-ton S.S. *Demerara* on the last of this month saved herself by using a gun with which she was defensively armed. On this same

---

[1] The *Nebraskan* was not the first American steamer to be torpedoed, for on May 1 the American S.S. *Gulflight* was thus injured off the Scillies, but taken into port later.

THE BIG PROBLEM

day in the St. George's and Bristol Channels three other steamships had narrow escapes.

It is now common knowledge that the positions of German submarines, coming up or down the North Sea, were as a rule ascertained by means of our directional wireless stations on the east coast. Daily a U-boat would flash home a signal to report her existence, but she failed to appreciate that in so doing she equally announced her presence and exact position to the British Navy. Thus, after a little while, it became possible not only to follow her daily progress and know roughly when to expect her off western Ireland, but also to identify her call signs. At the end of a certain period, and time for her refit, she would be expected back on her operational area. Sure enough, with typical German method, she would begin her own special technique, and it was always easy to know if a new-comer strange to Irish waters had been sent.

Sometimes things would happen a little differently and cause wonder; a brief bout of attack slightly off the usual localities—and then silence. Now, when this sort of strategy occurred, it simply meant that the enemy was on passage. Since the Dover nets compelled him to go round Ireland, he might as well sink whatever came within range. But there were also those, such as *U 35*, whose track could be followed almost circling the British Isles. On June 4, having just arrived from the north, she sank the *George and Mary* sailing vessel off the Mayo coast, carried on south and into the Irish Sea, thence down towards the Scillies. But at this time *U 34* was also operating round Ireland, the pair of them doing considerable harm, though both were seriously endangered, and by the same trawler.

Her name was the *Ina Williams*, commanded by Sub-Lieut. Nettleingham, R.N.R., a very keen and hard-working officer who had spent many years in sail and steam. Based on Berehaven, he was patrolling on June 1 in the Fastnet zone—a dozen miles south-west of Mizen Head—when at 8 a.m. a large submarine was sighted three miles distant on the port bow. Nettleingham hauled towards the latter with all possible speed, ordered the gunner to take steady aim and fire. Range 5000 yards. The aim was accurate, but there had been too much deflection, as the shot fell just for'ard of the conning-tower. Quickly the gun was reloaded, but alas! owing to the electric firing gear developing a defect, a misfire happened. The gunner withdrew his cartridge, reloaded, and again fired. This time the submarine was in the act of diving, and avoided the fate which threatened. Although the *Ina Williams* steamed about in the vicinity for another five hours, nothing further was seen, and the enemy had departed wisely for some quieter berth.

On June 5, in practically the same spot, *Ina Williams* had another fight against a U-boat, with a similar result. The scene had thus shifted gradually to the south-west, yet soon the enemy was working his way east in the final direction of Milford.

Now, the first of *Ina Williams'* submarines was almost certainly *U* 34; for this was the German who on the same day, to the south-east of Cape Clear, captured and sank the fishing steam trawler *Victoria*, involving the loss of her skipper and six hands; and at 5.30 on the morning of June 2, in the same district, came across the Cardiff fishing steam trawler *Hirose*. This recently built vessel was outward bound for her fishing grounds, and was proceeding at nine knots (her full speed), the boatswain and third hand being on watch.

At that hour, even on a bright June morning, human nature is not at its brightest, so the two fishermen received quite a jolt when the long, low hull of *U* 34 rose up and a 4·1-inch gun came into action. The boatswain sang out below to Skipper Francis Ward: "Come up! There's shells flying all around!"

Up tumbled the skipper, looked about, and saw *U* 34 some distance astern. He called all hands, stopped engines, and the shelling ceased. He then put *Hirose's* engines again full speed ahead, but the shelling once more started. This time Ward not merely rang down to stop, but ordered the ship's boat to be lowered, whereupon the firing ended and the submarine came up alongside on the surface.

"Leave your ship! I will give you five minutes!" commanded a German officer, looking over the conning-tower.

The *Hirose*, being totally unarmed and not a warrior, had but to obey. The crew jumped into their boat, rowed to the submarine, and were told to come aboard. Inside, to their great surprise, were four other fishermen, being survivors of the trawler *Victoria*. The German captain next sent three of *U* 34's men with bombs to destroy the *Hirose*, but not before bringing off Ward's chart-room clock and binoculars. Finally, an hour having gone by, the enemy placed the ten men from *Hirose* and the four men of *Victoria* into the former's boat and left them to fare as they might, exposed to the Atlantic. Before long a strong W.S.W. wind piped up with an ugly sea. There they were, fourteen men overcrowding a boat without a sail, and likely to die of starvation, thirst, or to be drowned by crashing waves.

The fishermen dug out the boat's canvas cover, called it a sail, hoisted an oar as mast, and ran all that day and through the night before an atrocious sea. Luckily, after twenty-four hours their small speck of a craft was observed by the S.S. *Ballater* of Liverpool. That such a tiny object in a welter of wave and foam should have been spotted at 6.30 a.m. is a tribute to the steamer's efficient look-out. Yet, owing to the heavy weather, there was considerable difficulty in getting the fishermen on board. Even then they were in quite a bad way through exhaustion and their food having been soaked, but at four that afternoon they were safely landed at Milford. A short voyage already to have been out and home again!

During the next fortnight came an alarming list of sinkings, which included still more of those glorious old sailing ships. In the notorious Fastnet slaughter zone was destroyed the British barque *Sunlight* (1433 tons); between Queenstown and Lundy Island both the *Express* and *Susannah* schooners (on the same day), the Russian barque *Thomasina*, the Norwegian barque *Bellgrade*, and the British four-masted barque *Crown of India*—the last mentioned being an exceptionally noble creature of 2034 tons—followed by that bigger and more historic British barque *Dumfriesshire*, of 2622 tons. And besides the above were steamers of most sorts and sizes. The outlook was really most serious; yet, by a curious mental perversion, created by excessive optimism, the British nation refused to read the true signs. It was all "Business as usual"; "The War will soon end."

Actually the Submarine War had scarcely begun. If,

with so few U-boats, the enemy could do pretty much what he liked from Ireland to Wales and the Scillies, what was going to happen when a hundred or two of these craft were scattered more freely about the Western Approaches?

In those busy days, so full of surprises and sorrows, there was not time enough for broad, constructive reasoning and appraisement of situation; yet how strange it seems to-day that, whilst the Grand Fleet and High Sea Fleet were both in harbour, the sea warfare off the British Isles was for the most part being waged by submarines and fishermen. To-day the incongruity of employing untutored, simple-hearted yet brave seamen, knowing everything about trawls and nets but nothing about gunnery or naval tactics, with only a handful of Merchant Service officers to lead such units; whilst against this improvised force came the most highly specialised type of modern craft, with regular Service men trained to the last degree—this mismatching of forces and disproportionate display stands out significant of the confused strategy then prevalent. The fishermen were eager but untrained, their discipline not yet tightened up, their gunnery indifferent, though capable of being made good. Wireless communication aboard these ships was still bad, a fresh mind was sorely needed possessing organising genius and tremendous driving power, so that wireless and gunnery, discipline and initiative might combine with blunt gallantry as one perfect whole.

The hour was fast approaching when such a naval director must be sought out by the British Admiralty, and entrusted with the great U-boat problem now beginning to dominate the Western Approaches. The time was ripe, the British nation had rarely experienced such a shock as *Lusitania* provided, and now reform was in the air. Neither in France, nor at the Dardanelles, neither off the Belgian coast, nor in Irish waters, was the outlook any too bright. But a clean sweep occurred at the end of May 1915, when a new Government was elected. On May 22 the veteran Lord Fisher resigned his appointment as First Sea Lord at the Admiralty, and this was followed by the resignation of Mr. Winston Churchill, the First Lord. Two days later Mr. Balfour succeeded Mr. Churchill, and on May 27 Admiral Sir Henry Jackson was appointed to succeed Lord Fisher.

THE BIG PROBLEM 57

It was from this change over that a notable transformation was to be made in the Irish naval command, and the most far-reaching effects were to be set in motion. It needed a few strenuous weeks for Mr. Balfour and Sir Henry Jackson to settle into their respective duties, but suddenly, one summer day, the big decision came.

CHAPTER V

CHANGE IN COMMAND

For something drastic had to be done, and the excellent seaman-like material must be used in the best possible manner. That these fisher folk were enduring, plucky, ardent for any dangerous job, cannot be more interestingly illustrated than by the following two examples.

We have just mentioned the three-masted Norwegian barque *Bellgrade*, which $U\ 35$ on June 12 had shelled so heartlessly. That same morning she was sighted by the Milford patrol vessels, whose crew boarded her and found her to be abandoned, with sails furled aloft, the hull low in the water, and stern submerged to a depth of four feet. So they tried to salve her, and took her in tow with a 100-fathom rope of three-inch wire. Three net-drifters, *Cromorna*, *Ivy Green*, and *Marys* (all from Scotland's fisheries), began the task, the first two tugging ahead, and the last keeping a look-out astern for the enemy.

Making for the Welsh coast some seventy miles away against an easterly wind and agitated sea was a slow, wearisome job, yet they kept going at four knots, until at 5 a.m. on June 14 wind and waves defeated them and the three-inch wire parted. Sticking to the undertaking, they were endeavouring again to take her in tow when the *Bellgrade* gave a horrible list in the sea trough and completely capsized, turning keel up. Luckily those fisher hands who had been put aboard the barque managed to scramble off like squirrels, and were all rescued, though one man was injured by an iron cathead which struck him as the vessel turned over.

No longer was it possible to do anything with her, and the drifters were running short of coal; so the latter steamed off to Milford Haven, leaving an armed trawler to warn passing ships of this obstruction. Lying in the middle of the Irish Channel, she might have caused disaster to some Liverpool liner in the darkness, so for the next week there had ever to be one of the Milford patrols standing by, until the day came when she was finally towed into St. Bride's Bay, where this neutral victim of the enemy was anchored. Apart from the value of hull, spars, sails, and fittings, the *Bellgrade* had a cargo worth £50,000, so the fishermen-warriors had been able to render good service.

Now, whilst the *Bellgrade* was still wallowing about and the three drifters had gone in, there departed from Liverpool the British S.S. *Turnwell* (4264 tons) in ballast. Dropping down the Mersey late in the afternoon, she came south, rounded the Tuskar, and was well on her way for New York. But on June 16, when thirty-five miles W.S.W. of the Tuskar, her Second Officer sighted a submarine's periscope only 200 yards away on the port quarter. It was now 1.40 p.m., and he summoned Captain A. E. Humby to the bridge. By this time the submarine was running awash, and plainly visible, with her crew on deck. She fired a shell, which missed *Turnwell*, though a second burst close alongside, amidships. The German now signalled for the steamer to be abandoned, whereupon all hands—thirty-three in number—left the ship in three boats.

The *Turnwell* was next boarded by four German seamen armed with bombs, so that shortly afterwards an explosion occurred and the steamer took a heavy list. Thus ended Act I. But note the curious development. At this moment steamed on to the scene S.S. *Trafford*. She was but a small coaster of 215 tons and on her way to Cork. The submarine, like the fable of the dog with a piece of meat, now left her first prize and made off for the second. The *Trafford's* master was named Hughes, and he was not lacking in grit, for at once he made for the U-boat, went hard aport, and was just about to ram when the German, at a distance of 130 yards, took refuge by submerging. Not till it was one and a half miles away did the submarine return to surface, but at that safe range opened fire with her 4·1-inch gun. Altogether it loosed off seventeen rounds, six of them hitting the unfortunate little *Trafford*, one striking the foot of the foremast, whilst another struck the boiler. Finis!

Stopped, stunned, and sinking, the coaster was abandoned, disappearing below at about 2.30 p.m. This easy victory, however, allowed the submarine to resume her attention to the *Turnwell*. The enemy for a while tried the previously reported dodge of hiding under her intended victim's quarter, ready to spring a surprise on the next steamer. But it so happened that this time the German was to receive the unexpected; for on came several of the Milford patrols with their fishermen, headed by the *Good Luck*. This was too much, so the enemy dived into obscurity and departed westward in the hope of other fortune. The patrols searched and hunted, and then picked up both steamers' crews.

Now, fate that afternoon had taught the submarine's commander a simple but severe lesson against greed. An hour previous the *Turnwell* was his, but next she was taken from him in exchange for the *Trafford*: 215 tons for 4264 tons. A bad bargain! For the *Turnwell*, notwithstanding her damage by the bombs and shells, did not founder as expected. Presently Captain Humby with his officers and men returned aboard, and found one hold full of water with another leaking badly. The engines were in good order, the pumps worked all right, so, escorted by two of the patrols, the steamer was turned round and proceeded at ten knots in the direction of Milford, where happily she arrived early the next morning.

Shift the scene now some miles farther west, and advance the date to June 27. Another Liverpool steamer, the *Kenmare* (1330 tons), was on her way past the south Irish coast bound for New York. Again the time was a few minutes after 1 p.m. She was four miles from the Waterford shore, and abreast of Ardmore Head, when a U-boat showed up on the surface a couple of miles away and coming towards the *Kenmare's* port side at full speed. Trapped? Well, there seemed but two alternatives: either to be sunk in deep water, or to run the ship ashore.

The captain reasoned quickly, and decided that he would try to shake the enemy off by superior speed if practicable; and Queenstown harbour was less than thirty miles distant. But if the *Kenmare* could not escape, he would beach her in Ardmore Bay. So he put his helm hard aport, the engines were whacked up to utmost speed, the firemen responding so splendidly that she was doing about fifteen knots. The submarine was thus brought astern and had a less easy target, but gave chase and began firing with her 4·1-inch. And forthwith a curious thing happened.

Somewhere in the vicinity was the Queenstown armed

trawler *Rodney* doing her patrol. Now, her Skipper Watmore—another of those rough, hearty fishermen in naval uniform—was suddenly startled by the sound of shots: one, two, four, seven—eight of them! Looking round, he could not see whence they were coming, but his ears gave him some idea of direction, and thither he steamed at full speed, so that presently the submarine became visible. He immediately opened fire, and the second shot dropped so very close that the enemy hurried off without stopping to fight.

The German, of course, with his superiority of speed and range (to say nothing of his torpedoes), was much more than a match for the slow trawler with her three-pounder. But Watmore and his hearties were as gallant as the old admiral after whom the trawler was named. Down below men were shovelling coal into the furnace, and soon the ship was travelling faster than she had any right; but Watmore was one of those Grimsby fellows, brought up in the hard conditions of the North Sea and Dogger Bank, accustomed to be called on for any emergency—be it fog up the Humber and an eight-knot tide, or hurrying home with a fine catch of fish through a merciless winter's gale.

To chase a U-boat in June weather off the green coast of Ireland had all the attraction of a Grimsby football game. " Away we went after him for all we were worth," related Watmore. " We kept up the chase for one hour, and firing all the time; but he at length got out of our range, as he was going about fifteen knots. We still kept steaming after him, and he was leaving a lot of oil in his wake. In a cloud of smoke he disappeared altogether." The enemy had made his offing, and could now submerge to his nine knots. But that is by no means all the story.

The *Rodney* certainly did not sink the enemy, but definitely saved the *Kenmare*, as well as enabling three other vessels to get away. *Rodney* also believed that one of his first shots actually hit the submarine, and this seems quite possible; for the enemy then altered course and passed close to an open boat. Now, that same submarine, shortly before meeting with the *Kenmare*, had sunk the small 243-ton steamer *Lucena* by gunfire, so that the latter's crew were rowing about. It was *Lucena's* captain who was able to notice that the German crew were running around on deck in great excitement and that the fleeing U-boat had a hole in her hull, out of which oil was spurting; therefore Skipper Watmore's twenty-two shells had not all been wasted.

But this little incident exhibited another typical bit of fisherman pluck. By mere coincidence the steam trawler *Cevic* was also on the scene. She was not armed, had nothing to do with the Navy, and chanced to be one of those Fleetwood vessels which go out to fish in the Atlantic near the Porcupine Bank. However, gun or no gun, the Fleetwood skipper belonged to the same Sea Brotherhood as the Grimsby captain. The German evidently took the *Cevic* for a patrol, for one trawler looked the same as any other and retained even her fishing number on the bows. When suddenly the U-boat bobbed up three-quarters of a mile away and began firing at *Cevic*, the latter had no hesitation in steering straight at full speed for the enemy in hope of ramming her by steel bows against steel hull. And in order to attract the attention of all other patrols in the district, the Fleetwood skipper tugged at his steam whistle and fastened it down to keep it blowing.

This trawler, when fired at, was undamaged, as also may be said of *Rodney*. The *Kenmare*, however, was rescued only just in time, since already fourteen shells had come her way, cutting the rigging and bursting on deck, so that captain and crew were half suffocated. It was only after sinking the *Lucena*, exactly an hour earlier, that this grey submarine had motored off towards the *Kenmare*. The *Rodney* picked up the crew of the *Lucena* and cruised about for another hour near the spot where oil was last seen on the surface; but such wounds were capable of being plugged, so the enemy was not destroyed, and remained in the neighbourhood, showing himself (if no trawlers were about) just long enough to sink a merchant ship and then again submerge.

In this way the 77-ton schooner *Edith* of Barrow was sunk that day at noon just before the *Lucena*, whilst two days later the 5000-ton S.S. *Scottish Monarch* was likewise sent to the bottom off the same coast, though some forty miles to the southward; for the enemy realised that the fisherman-patrols near the land were pretty prompt foes. The British Admiralty also were of this opinion, and awarded the sum of £20 to the *Rodney*, together with a similar sum to the *Cevic*, and the same fine spirit of these temporary fighting men was being exhibited in other parts of the Irish area, as, for example, on June 13, when the armed trawlers *Vera* and *Roxano*, based on Larne, engaged a submarine.

But the enemy's blockade was, in truth, more successful than were the British measures to overcome the menace at this time. In order to harass the U-boats' operations in the triangle formed by Milford–Scillies–Queenstown, through which must pass most of the Atlantic-borne supplies not merely for the British Army, but also for its civilians, an endeavour was now being made so to arrange the patrols that they might be concentrated around the locality where a submarine had last been sighted. Still, it is one thing to sit in a comfortable office with a flat chart in front, to measure off distances and draw intersecting lines based on the latest wireless reports, optimistically believing that the hunters will presently announce that the fox has been surrounded. It is, however, quite a different story when the fox goes to earth; or—to speak without simile—when the enemy has for a brief period taken flight beneath the waves and cleared off in an unknown direction, leaving the yachts and trawlers bewildered, whilst a few hours later a signal comes into the land office proving that the same submarine some thirty miles farther west has begun shelling or torpedoing another batch of shipping.

The enemy was going from strength to strength. Not more than about half a dozen of these under-water craft were at sea simultaneously on any selected day—omitting that smaller class of UC boats operating in the North Sea and Dover neighbourhood. The 210-feet U-boats, with fuel endurance for more than 5000 miles—enough to cross the Atlantic twice—were directing their united attention against the Western Approaches, with a determination to starve Britain in the same way that Germany was to be starved by the British blockade. In fact, a most desperate international race had begun, to decide which party should be the first to arrive with the gift of death. All those occasional incidents off the north-east English coast, the north and west coasts of Scotland, when sinkings of some small coasters occurred, were but minor events that happened casually during a U-boat's six-day voyage to the south of Ireland. Her main objective, her positive reason for leaving Germany, was to make that Queenstown triangle too dangerous, thereby closing down Liverpool, together with those Bristol Channel ports of Cardiff and Avonmouth, besides making the western gate of the English Channel impossible of entry.

It was rather like stationing some ferocious individuals heavily armed outside a family's front door to assassinate the butcher's boy, the baker's man, and every person carrying means of sustaining the human body.

How long could we stand this sort of thing? How could the family's food still get within the door? That was the problem which had to be considered by the new First Lord of the Admiralty. No longer was the English Channel in itself dangerous, but rather its Atlantic porch; and unless the guard here were strengthened, the most obvious but serious results would soon be causing a crisis. Starvation, ruin, riots, at home; the War lost on the Continent and at sea! Yes: it was time that something was done about it. This June had been a terrible month. At that time I happened to be serving at Milford, and the almost daily sight of torpedoed or gunned mariners being brought into the Haven on the crowded deck of some drifter or trawler patrol was a sickening reminder that all was not well. The critical Queenstown situation demanded new methods and a reorganisation of these Western Approaches; which is to say that it required an Admiral of exceptional creative ability, initiative, driving force; of dauntless courage, independent judgment; experienced in flotillas, and possessing a genius for control.

Queenstown was such a long way from Whitehall in more senses than one; for if the physical distance were not great, the journey was most tedious, the human background to Cork Harbour generally unsympathetic and anti-British. But, apart from that, the enemy and our western patrols between them were in effect waging a separate or subsidiary naval war. In actuality (though not yet in name) the " Senior Officer on the Coast of Ireland " was " Commander-in-Chief

Western Approaches," with his dockyard at Haulbowline, and various sub-bases round the area, but with problems in many respects quite different from those in Scotland or the Dover Straits.

The Admiralty looked forth, and decided to offer this heavy responsibility to Vice-Admiral Sir Lewis Bayly, K.C.B., K.C.M.G., C.V.O., whose career might have been specially predestined to deal with future naval history having Queenstown as its centre. Seven years before the War he had been appointed the first Commodore of Flotillas, and it is general knowledge to-day that Commodore Bayly, by sheer force of character, trained and organised the British destroyer service in such a manner that his influence there has never been lost. He has been rightly called by that official historian, Sir Julian Corbett, " the father of destroyer tactics and organisation "; who, after being the second flag officer of the Royal Naval War College for over two years, commanded the First Battle-Cruiser Squadron, with his flag in the *Lion*, subsequently commanding the First Battle Squadron in the Grand Fleet.

For years this oncoming war with Germany had to Admiral Bayly been something real, to be pondered over, weighed, prepared for seriously. He himself had studied naval history of the past in the same manner as the late Admiral Mahan, extracting from previous events those solid strategical principles which are unalterable, though ships may discard sail for steam. And I happen to know that throughout 1914–1918 he was ever comparing present problems with their historical prototypes, foreseeing what must inevitably follow as a result of certain events. For, just as every fiction-writer or playwright well knows that in all the world there are but thirty-six dramatic situations; and the art of conjuring is still more limited; so in the art of war the same situations continue to arise through the ages. A blockade, for example, is a blockade; whether being wrought by German submarines off Ireland or by British armed merchant cruisers off Scotland. The two differed in many details and complications: yet in principle and ultimate result they proceeded on parallel lines.

Nevertheless, Admiral Bayly was no mere antiquarian, but

so modern as to have been the first flag officer who ever employed a smoke screen for a tactical purpose during naval battle exercises; and with startling success. This is worthy of being remembered, since so much has been said recently as to its employment by the enemy at Jutland and the invaluable means it afforded the High Sea Fleet Admiral of extricating himself from a tight corner. This same manner of using smoke was likewise the cloak by which some of our slow cargo-carrying steamers managed to avoid being torpedoed by U-boats.

In July 1915, Sir Lewis Bayly happened again to be at Greenwich, serving as President of the Royal Naval College, when Mr. Balfour, the First Lord, sent for him, and invited him to accept the Queenstown command, which by this date had entirely altered its restful character of a year before. In this interview at the Admiralty it was pointed out how important Queenstown had become, because of the protection now increasingly necessary to ships arriving from the United States with munitions of war, guns, machinery, and so on.

The Admiral's reply was characteristic. He took pencil and chart, then, with Queenstown as a centre, drew a circle which included the Scillies, Milford Haven, Irish Sea, North Channel, and all the waters round Ireland inclusive of the base at Berehaven.

"If I can have command in that circle," he stipulated; "and if you will give me a fast cruiser, I will go to Queenstown."

Here was the "father of destroyer tactics and organisation," the independent naval thinker, the Admiral of resolute courage and immense driving power, accepting a most difficult and complicated duty, with a mere handful of fishing vessels as flotillas, and a vast plan to be worked out. Destroyers just then were as much desired and appropriated for the North Sea as gold is by the bankers. Cruisers were so very much needed for guarding the trade routes, and as scouts for the Grand Fleet, that the supply had long since given out—armed liners had replaced them and were being employed in many localities.

Still, the Admiralty agreed. Not merely to all that the pencilled circle enclosed; but also to the fast cruiser. Big

ADMIRAL SIR LEWIS BAYLY

When in command of the Royal Naval College, Greenwich. (The lines formed part of the Admiral's large-scale war map on the lawn, indicating the military situation in 1915.)

decisions are sometimes made in the fewest minutes, and it was decided that Sir Lewis should have H.M.S. *Adventure*, a fast scout, one of the prettiest ships in the Navy, and destined to become as much part of Queenstown as Admiralty House.[1] It was now July 12. Eight days later the Admiral hauled down his flag at Greenwich and went aboard the *Adventure* at Gravesend, and on July 22 landed at Queenstown, went up the hill and succeeded Vice-Admiral Sir Charles Coke.

A new chapter of naval history was now to begin.

[1] H.M.S. *Adventure*, 2940 tons, twenty-five knots, completed in 1905. Commanded by Captain (now Vice-Admiral Sir George) Hyde.

CHAPTER VI

NEW MEASURES

THE sea has ever been the finest school for character. From time immemorial it has stamped its sons not merely with that clear-cut, open-air visage, the keen blue eyes, and the frank manner; but also with a distinctive personality that is too well known to need emphasis. Read, for illustration, any book of memoirs by some distinguished General and compare them with *My Life at Sea*, written by an Admiral. The result of totally different Service influences is most interesting to note. Speaking comprehensively, the soldier's style is jerky, staccato, as opposed to a wave-like, rhythmic flow of the naval officer. The former writes with obvious effort, but the latter has always had the more vivid imagination and a natural narrative ability.

So, also, as a consequence of three centuries of sea traditions, those who have submitted their careers to the routine, the training and influence of the Royal Navy, come to view life's problems from the same angle. For example, in any gallery of naval prints, showing the portraits of England's famous Admirals during the eighteenth century, will be found a striking generic similarity. And, indeed, during our own epoch, both in fiction and drama, there is a recognised type which is supposed by the public to represent every modern British Admiral.

Now, Sir Lewis Bayly has always been too independent and original in his methods to fit any stereotype or category. The most loyal of friends, a staunch disciplinarian, a most faithful servant to his Sovereign, with the sympathy of a woman and the courage of a lion, the new inhabitant of Admiralty House, Queenstown, was also one whom no person or circumstance could by any effort whatsoever divert by so much as a fraction of an inch from the objective before him. The ablest men in any walk of life are those who have taught themselves how to recognise instantly the essential from the dispensable, the main from the subsidiary. In the handling of squadrons, individual ships, men, and even crises, Admiral Bayly's methods were direct, by the shortest route; his orders unequivocal, with an economy in words and clarity of thought that never failed to impress.

Almost his first act at Queenstown was to issue a signal that all social calls were to be regarded as having been made and returned. The new Admiral was filled with the single concern of the War that was going on just outside the harbour; all other things were of little or no import. Thus Admiralty House became during the initial weeks transformed into a Navy Office, and even the drawing-room was now partitioned off so that two-thirds of it might be used for Service business and only one-third for its original purpose. It was, likewise, much more necessary that the Admiral should be able to see at a glance on the chart the position of his ships, and to plot the position of an approaching vessel carrying valuable cargo, than that the billiard-table should be available. If an important steamer from the United States, and bringing to Avonmouth or Liverpool munitions for the Allies, were about to enter the danger zone west of the Fastnet, it was necessary to ascertain which was the patrol craft nearest her and to be sent as escort. So Haulbowline Dockyard was instructed to build a wooden cover over the full-sized table, and thereon the chart was laid, ships' positions being marked by little flags.

The Admiral decided from the first that this was not the time for social entertainment and that invitations would be extended only to Commanding Officers, with the primary object of keeping in close touch, understanding their problems, and maintaining warlike efficiency. Then to be tackled was that ever-present problem that Ireland, though geographically part of the British Isles, was in political feeling outside them. During his interview at the Admiralty in Whitehall that July day, Sir Lewis Bayly was informed that considerable leakage of naval information had been going on for some time, and, seeing how many thousands of southern Irishmen were against England emerging victorious from the War, it was going to be very difficult to stop this emanation.

But the following were the measures promptly inaugurated.

First, as to the secrecy of signals. At the bottom of the garden at Admiralty House, Queenstown, was a signal station, readily seen from the ships in the harbour below. Supposing, for instance, the Admiral wished to order a ship instantly to raise steam and rescue a *Lusitania* or chase a submarine, the custom had been to send that signal first from the House to the bottom of the garden by messenger; then it would be semaphored or morsed *en clair* to the vessel concerned. Thus any German spy or Sinn Feiner sufficiently practised in signalling could pick up no little naval intelligence by daily watchfulness. To overcome this, a cable was now connected from the Admiral's house, down the hill, across the harbour to Haulbowline, where a signal station was established. This cut out all prominence, and it would be much less easy for an unauthorised person to intercept signals. But all signals concerning either the movements of ships or other matters of importance were henceforth signalled in code, and had to be decoded by the ship's commanding officer.

Thus the signal station in Admiralty House grounds was closed down altogether. An order was also issued that no person was to be allowed on board any man-of-war or armed vessel unless in uniform, or on naval or dockyard duty. This, of course, meant that no civilian friend of either officers or men could visit the ships even at a time when there was little enough contrast to the boring life afloat; but the regulation was a very necessary one in a country where it was hard to tell friend from foe. And the Vice-Admiral Commanding at Queenstown had to be a diplomatist no less than a naval officer, since there was likewise the religious difficulty to be faced.

Queenstown was for the most part a Roman Catholic community, and the cathedral stood adjacent to Admiralty House, near to which resided the Roman Catholic Bishop of Cloyne, the Most Reverend Robert Browne—the Church and the Navy, side by side, dominating the hill, and the two most powerful forces in the place! There was just a conceivable possibility that these two might pull in opposite ways, and that serious friction might last throughout the War. Indeed, almost the first experience of the new Admiral was a visit from one of the clergy concerning the attendance of sailors at Sunday Mass.

So Admiral Bayly himself went along to call on the Bishop, and to discuss matters in a manner customary among neighbours. " I pointed out to him that he was really the most important personage in Queenstown, and that things would be better in every way if we worked together. The Bishop entirely agreed, and from that moment began a friendship between us that has lasted until now. We always exchange Christmas greetings every year."

Here was a splendid example of two distinguished men, without the slightest variation of their consciences or the least disloyalty to duty, exhibiting goodwill and mutual respect. No delicate situation ever arose between them which could not be smoothed out; and the following brief story will show that the ensuing benefits were not exclusively on the Navy's side. "About the end of 1916," says the Admiral, "the Bishop told me that the forty-two bells of the cathedral were at Liverpool waiting safe transit to Queenstown. Could I help him? I said: 'Yes. Send them over in the next steamer, and we will obey the Scriptural injunction to watch and pray. I will watch. And you pray?' The scheme succeeded, and the bells arrived safely."

Now, having once organised communications and the House, the next thing was to collect ships for the job. Under the Admiral's command were those several hundred trawlers, drifters, and motor-boats based on Queenstown, Kingstown, Larne, Killybegs, Berehaven, Milford, and the Scillies, a few armed yachts, and the old-time torpedo-boats previously mentioned; but, since other vessels of greater speed were also required, and no destroyers could be spared, the Admiralty had promised him a number of sloops as soon as they could be got ready. At the beginning of the War not one single British harbour had been safe against torpedo attack, and it was only just about the date when Sir Lewis Bayly reached Queenstown that this had been made secure by a boom defence consisting of wire nets, with a " gate " in the middle; a couple of trawlers here being moored, whose windlasses could slack out and lower the netting to allow entry of vessels. It was now possible to afford absolute safety within the harbour, however busy the U-boats might be outside; and the Queenstown space was so great that security applied even to colliers or any other kinds of necessary ships.

But these sloops?

The word suggested anything, for during the last three or four centuries it had been applied to all kinds of craft—from small, fore-and-aft rigged vessels to gunboats. It has always been a convenient term to be used for units that are neither capital ships nor cruisers. Soon after the outbreak of war it became manifest that after all the suitable merchant ships had been taken up for mine-sweeping, it would be necessary for the Admiralty to build others. They were to be of simple design, single-screw, and—in order to hasten their construction—to adopt mercantile practice with regard to both hull and engines. This decision enabled the work to be spread over various firms accustomed to build liners and cargo-carriers. As a triumph of creation these sloops fairly broke the record: the decision to build was made only in December 1914, yet by May 22 of the following year the first two had not merely been launched, engined, armed, and fitted out, but had done their trials, been fully commissioned, and steamed off to join the Grand Fleet.

The next dozen were to be placed under Admiral Bayly, and by the end of July the first of them began to reach Queenstown. The accompanying photograph will show the appearance of this new type, which was to play a most conspicuous part in Irish waters till the end of hostilities. No class of vessel, having regard to size and cost, ever did such excellent work or saved so many million pounds' worth of shipping from destruction. Originally designed for mine-sweeping, they were chiefly used for anti-submarine work and convoying, yet on special occasions after the enemy had spasms of laying his black " eggs " it was easy enough to fit requisite gear and send the sloops out to mine-sweep by pairs.

Actually they were small cruisers, armed at first with a couple of twelve-pounders, and very economical in coal. Twin-funnelled, with cruiser sterns, they were often taken by U-boats for cross-Channel steamers of the sort running from Dover to Calais. The length was 267 ft., beam 33 ft., draught 11 ft., displacement 1250 tons, and the speed varied. Some steamed as high as sixteen knots; others were not so good by a couple of knots. They were lively in a seaway, and I often used to note their tendency to pitch; but it was just their liveliness which made them such excellent seaboats. Summer and winter, in heavy Atlantic gales, thick fogs, during more than three strenuous years the Queenstown sloops were to do their fine service. How many merchant captains and

A BEREHAVEN PATROL VESSEL.
H.M. Drifter *Daisy VI*.

A QUEENSTOWN SLOOP
Putting to sea.

crews were picked up by them out of the lonely Atlantic and saved from chilly deaths, or how much the shipping lines owe to these small cruisers could be reckoned only in large figures. Commanded by senior Lieutenants or Lieut.-Commanders, usually from the Grand Fleet or on the Retired List, who had never commanded anything bigger than a picket-boat previously, the sloops provided first-class opportunities for any ambitious young officer who was bored with spending the first war months as a watch-keeper swinging round a buoy at Scapa Flow.

But these sloops were no pleasure yachts, and they had the faculty for wearing out any officer whose nerves were not one hundred per cent. strong. Winters off the Irish coast are not merciful, and some fellows either broke down after the first few months or applied for other jobs. For the most part these keen captains stuck it out till the Armistice; and until the first American Naval Forces began to arrive, in May 1917, the sloops (which never numbered more than thirteen) worked and worked to the limit of human endurance. Nor did their labours go unrewarded, since there was scarcely one commanding officer for whom the Admiral was not instrumental in obtaining either the D.S.O. or promotion to Commander.

"I wondered," thought Admiral Bayly on their arrival at Queenstown, "how they would get on in the heavy gales off the coast; and was very proud after the first to find that they all came out of it with very little damage to themselves, thus showing that they had been handled with skill and seamanship —a proof of the Navy's excellent training."

It was well and most necessary that the sloops should now, one by one, be sent to this area; else how could the underwater enemy be kept on the move, or shipless mariners rescued? Even from the very first Queenstown sloops were justified in nicknaming themselves the "Irish Lifeboat Service." For the enemy was still maliciously busy: a sailing vessel and a steamer some thirty or forty miles west of the Fastnet, and a couple of steamers in the Irish Channel neighbourhood, having already been sunk in the first part of July, whilst barely a week after the Admiral's arrival in the *Adventure* another fine steamer had been torpedoed nine miles south of the Fastnet, causing the loss of seven lives.

This was the 5223-ton S.S. *Iberian*, on July 30, the enemy being Commander Baron von Förstner [1] in *U* 28. Fortunately, H.M.S. *Sunflower*, one of the new sloops, got to the scene and rescued the survivors. Lieut.-Commander J. C. Cole-Hamilton, R.N., who had retired before the War, but was now in command of the *Sunflower*, describes in a private letter those first impressions as they steamed back to Queenstown, " with three dead in the ward-room, a badly-wounded man in each officer's cabin, every scrap of our food eaten by the quite filthy crew of cattlemen, and the *Sunflower* in an awful mess." But on arrival in the port, to meet the *Sunflower* came the practical, keen-eyed Admiral himself, already afloat in his green barge, that was to become so familiar during these years to many British and American naval officers.

" Tell your ship's company," the well-known voice congratulated, " they've done very well." It was the first of a hundred tactful encouragements made at just the right moment. But not less characteristic was the order which immediately followed. " Get away to sea again as quickly as you can ! " [2]

Efficiency ! Hurry on with the big job ! Go out after the enemy ! That was the spirit which was now very much alive at Queenstown. Any officer who came there knew that he was about to be worked to the limit; but he also soon learned that the Admiral was working himself not less furiously. He was here, there, and somewhere else in a flash of time. Up the hill in his office, across the water in Haulbowline Dockyard, off round the harbour in his barge. Nothing missed his attention; nothing was too much trouble. Take the following as a thumbnail sketch.

Scene: Queenstown Harbour aboard the same sloop *Sunflower*.

Time: Summer's morning, but the fog is so thick that

---

[1] This German officer at a later date related in the *Deutsche Allgemeine Zeitung* that about twenty-five seconds after the *Iberian* sank there was a violent explosion, and a few seconds subsequently a gigantic sea-monster, 60 ft. long, in shape like a crocodile, with four legs terminating in fins, was hurled writhing and struggling into the air. Five other witnesses in the conning-tower also saw it.

[2] Compare this with the almost identical words with which the first of the American destroyer captains was greeted two years later. (See Chapter XX.)

SURVIVORS
From a vessel sunk by a German submarine.

THE GREEN BARGE
Of Admiral Bayly at Queenstown.

visibility is less than five yards. Her captain is walking irritably up and down his bridge, hoping the fog will lift and enable him to up-anchor. He wants to be out at sea, but first the boom-defence gate has to be negotiated, and if he is not lucky he will be into it, with his propeller fouled by wire-netting.

Suddenly, out of the fog, comes the churning of a smaller propeller alongside, and a hail from a voice that must be the Admiral's.

" Good morning ! "

" Good morning, sir ! "

" Going to sea ? "

" Yes, sir ! Pilot says he can't find the gate till it clears a bit."

" Oh ! Is *that* what you're waiting for ? Come on ! I'll show you the way."

So the ubiquitous barge went ahead and located the boom, the sloop hove in anchor and crept close after her, " with our stem' almost rubbing against the barge's stern." Another few minutes and the fog-bound *Sunflower* was beyond the gate heading out for her Atlantic patrol. Not even a thick fog must now keep a ship in harbour.

But long before this—years before—the name of Queenstown's new Admiral was known throughout the Service as the enemy of all slackness, a fair and just judge, but no friend to an officer who did not think of his ship and his duty before all other things. Sure as fate any such delinquent would reveal his failing and as quickly " be returned to store."

Now, that was in peace time. What must it be like under war conditions at Queenstown ?

The following impression has been given me by one of the ablest of the sloop captains, who, after doing months of great work in the *Jessamine*, took command of a mystery Q-ship, and won a D.S.O. Captain Salisbury H. Simpson, R.N., writes :

" While serving in the cruiser *Argyll* during a refit at Devonport in October 1915, I was appointed to command one of the new sloops building at Newcastle-on-Tyne named *Jessamine*. When I heard that she was going to Queenstown, and that I should serve under Admiral Sir Lewis Bayly, I suffered from a cold shiver. Although I had never met Admiral Bayly, I had heard sufficient from those who had served under him; who never mentioned his name except with awe and reverence. So, knowing my own limitations, I wondered how long I should last under his command.

"After a filthy trip from Newcastle to Queenstown via the Pentland Firth (during which the ward-room alone had five leaks through the deck), we arrived at Queenstown. Before going on shore to call on the Vice-Admiral, I was reminded by my engineer officer that a week in harbour was needed to get the hurriedly-built *Jessamine's* machinery in proper sea-going order and to put right a number of small defects such as invariably manifest themselves during the first days of any new ship at sea. Having toiled up the steep hill to Admiralty House, I found Sir Lewis Bayly in his garden hard at work, assisted by his niece, Miss Voysey. Having reported myself, the Admiral then asked when I would be ready for sea, so I replied that, having regard to the mess in which the builders had left the *Jessamine*, a week in harbour was desirable."

Now, every schoolboy knows that there is no more unconditioned pleasure than to watch a new boy on the first day of term answering a test question in exactly the wrong manner. A few weeks later that newcomer will look forward with the same delight to hearing another arrival making the same mistake. In a later chapter [1] we shall find an American officer emerging from the Queenstown catechism with full marks, and saying the right sentence at the right moment. But not every British or American at the first interview realised that his enthusiasm and preparedness for war were immediately to be put under proof and the result announced by the officer's own lips. It required a little warning if a new commanding officer were to answer, straight off the tongue, "Ready, sir? My ship is ready for sea now in all respects save fuel, sir, and she'll have completed coaling to-night."

But hardly one newcomer in a dozen would ever think of this super-excellent response. So Lieut.-Commander Simpson's plea for his engine department was received with as much warmth as can be found in crystal icicles.

"You will proceed to sea at eight o'clock to-morrow

[1] See Chapter XX.

morning," the Admiral dismissed him quickly. " Good day to you."

And the *Jessamine's* captain descended the hill to his ship.

But that sort of test was never repeated: the " new boy " had learned his lesson, and the other fellows in this great Queenstown school (that was to bring out the best in every officer's character and lead him ultimately to distinction) had either gone through this preliminary trial already, or would very shortly have its experience. The unexpected question was just part of the vast new scheme which had to be set going, and this initiation into the Queenstown Patrol could not fail to leave a serious impression. Here was a time of grave events; the war at sea had just begun, Queenstown was on the flank of the nation's food routes, and those marine lanes were unsafe to travel. Much was expected of these new sloops and their young captains to make the steamship tracks through Irish waters such that liners or cargo-carriers, grainships or cattle-boats, could come along towards Liverpool and the Bristol Channel yet not be destroyed during the last part of their voyage.

" This was my first experience of Sir Lewis Bayly, and it made a lasting impression," records the same officer. " In that short visit I summed up my future Admiral, and it was the beginning of a happy two-and-a-half years' service under his flag, when I learned not only to respect and admire him, but also to love him. As an example of his consideration for his captains, it was by no means uncommon, when a sloop was securing to her buoy after a patrol of five days at sea, for the commanding officer to receive a signal from the Admiral worded thus: ' If you have nothing better to do, will you dine and stay the night at Admiralty House ? ' On one occasion, having just accepted this kind invitation, I was going ashore in the *Jessamine's* motor-boat when the latter broke down between ship and landing-steps, the night also being very dark and the tide strong.

" The result was that after racing up the hill I arrived breathless and half an hour late for dinner. Having apologised and explained the unfortunate cause of my delay, I noticed that the Admiral said nothing, and I imagined he was extremely annoyed. But actually his mind was working to get efficiency restored to the motor-boat. Lifting up the telephone he began speaking with the dockyard chief engineer, instructed him to have the *Jessamine's* motor-boat taken in hand at once, get its engine overhauled, and everything to be finished by 7 a.m. to-morrow. Result? The job was done by the appointed time, and that motor never gave any further trouble."

CHAPTER VII

PATROLS *VERSUS* SUBMARINES

Such was the new discipline, the new activity, the ardent spirit that enthused all whose duty consisted in carrying out orders at sea. For the Admiral all this control and direction; the strategy of patrols; the responsibility for the safety of valuable heavy-laden steamers passing through his area; the supervision of Haulbowline Dockyard; the rapidly growing numbers of trawlers and drifters; the immense amount of official correspondence and paper work; the hourly incoming and outgoing telegrams and wireless signals, made more dramatic by the enemy's latest phase of ruthlessness, or the sinking of another crack liner—this was a task so heavy, so thankless at times, that in those early days it might by some have seemed unbearable.

And it was largely a one-man job. As his secretary there had arrived with the Admiral a most experienced officer, Fleet Paymaster (now Paymaster Rear-Admiral) H. R. Russell, who had been some time secretary to Admiral Sir Berkeley Milne, Commander-in-Chief of the Mediterranean Fleet. Fleet Paymaster Russell brought, besides his long familiarity with this special work, a genius for organisation and a technical knowledge of naval details not always possessed by those in charge of a Flag Officer's business department. But even here existed human limits of endurance, and day after day, week after week he would be still toiling at these documents till 2 a.m., then begin again before 9 a.m.

But we have just seen Admiral Bayly in the garden with his niece, and there are to-day many naval officers, active or retired, American or British, who will consider this environment of green lawn and coloured flowers to be the right background for introducing the lady who did so much to help on the naval endeavour. What Admiralty House and its hospitality were to mean for nerve-tired sailors, and how much Miss Voysey as hostess did in that capacity, providing unforgettable benefits through most of four historic years, are still remembered and talked about on both sides of the Atlantic. In those days, after being cooped up in a comparatively small ship, and only a handful of brother officers with whom to exchange ideas, it was no inconsiderable privilege to come out of the turbulent Atlantic and arrive with one's suit-case up the hill. To enjoy again a white table-cloth, the warmth of a fireside, the comfort of a bedroom away from one's restless ship; to be allowed to present, informally over a cigarette or pipe, the problems of one's own particular patrol for the Admiral's advice, information, or assistance; and then on the morrow to go down aboard again—this was to resume the daily round and common task with recreated energy and freshly kindled enthusiasm. "There were many very interesting evenings round the fire," Admiral Bayly remembers, "while the youngsters described their experiences in their new occupations. No. 9 room was always kept empty, so as to be ready for such a visitor." Thus, not only was the younger officer able to understand exactly what was in his Admiral's mind when the ship was back on patrol and some wireless order came through; but the Big Chief himself was able to know his fleet more intimately, the personnel, their capabilities, their problems and the scope for improvement.

Thus was efficiency gained, useless correspondence entirely cut out, and valuable time saved.

But, in default of the necessary staff, it was Miss Voysey who quietly and unobtrusively assisted her uncle even in matters that might ordinarily have been part of a Flag Lieutenant's duty. To many people, no doubt, it seemed strange that so distinguished an Admiral had entered on his command here without a Flag Lieutenant, and without a Flag Commander, yet this was hardly the time to increase personal staff when everywhere, on land and sea, men were so badly needed. So she and the Admiral used to move the flags about the chart each day, whereby the position of any patrol vessel could be instantly perceived, and each alteration kept up to date.

The Admiral also assigned to each sloop area a letter of the alphabet, but, to prevent this becoming known to unauthorised persons, such a letter was changed at unequal intervals. With a view to making it easier for all concerned to remember the different areas, so that when a captain was ordered from one to another he could not misunderstand where he was to go, these area-initials (reading from east to west) composed a word. Since no two areas must duplicate the same letter, it sometimes became difficult to find a word with eight or nine different letters corresponding to the number of areas. The word "mediator," for example, was suitable, whereas "remember" was most unsuitable; and in such details as this there was opportunity for the imaginative ability of a woman already closely in touch with every section of Queenstown routine.

We have seen both the strength and the weakness of the slow trawlers; but the sloops had nearly twice the former's speed, double the armament, six times the men, perfect wireless communication, and twelve times the tonnage. This meant a considerable improvement, since a wider and deeper patrol section could be covered and a more rapid concentration made in response to a Morse signal. It became possible to station sloops along the entire south Irish coast, from the Tuskar to the Fastnet, each vessel taking care of a section fifty miles north and south, thirty miles east and west. Thus the full extent of a submarine's likely hunting ground, including all the traffic routes, now became so well covered that even if by chance a sloop were at the furthest extremity when an S.O.S. call buzzed through, she should be able to reach the torpedoed steamer in three hours; but the probability was that a sloop in the next area would have arrived on the scene even earlier still.

To keep these little cruisers at sea for five days with only a couple of days in harbour, yet maintain personnel, engines, hulls, and fittings in a high state of fighting efficiency, was no small achievement of organisation. During those two days the ship had to go alongside collier and laboriously fill bunkers with so many tons; food and other stores had to be fetched aboard, and any defect made good, whether arising from fair wear and tear, unfair seas, or any other cause. To this end the dockyard, its officials and men, its facilities and store-houses, were kept ever in readiness to deal with any emergency, and really help a captain by answering his needs instead of tying him up in a muddle of red tape. Labourers might have to toil on night-shifts, a dry-dock be filled and emptied, men working overtime. But what of it? The sloops were fighting for the nation's bread and meat, for the Army's bully beef and bullets.

Another thoughtful consideration of the Admiral was to allow each sloop at once to draw fires when she had come into port and secured to her buoy, collier, or alongside the dockyard wall. This enabled the engineering staff to get on with their jobs immediately, and if the ship had to be moved, this was done by means of tugs. It was the auxiliary machinery in these sloops which used to give no little trouble, but a great blessing was conferred on a worried engineer officer when he knew that there would be time to let it get cold and be dealt with promptly.

This side of an Admiral's work is by no means the least important, yet, even in spite of the best construction which public money can buy, and the greatest attention expended on upkeep, it is very true that mechanical creations can be most unreliable and temperamental. Even the modern motorist is convinced of that by bitter experience. But especially does the failing pertain to that complex class, the destroyer. At one period three of these most modern units were sent from the North Sea to Queenstown, and great was the Admiral's joy as he welcomed such invaluable vessels . . . until one by one each destroyer captain climbed the hill to report. The acid test was awaiting him.

" And when will you be ready for sea ? "

" Well, sir, my boilers require cleaning," said one.

" My destroyer needs to be dry-docked," apologised a second.

And the third had some other complaint. That settled the destroyers' Queenstown fate, and they were (in Navy parlance) speedily " returned to store," which means that they were sent back to the North Sea. Their Commodore on that bleak coast felt a little hurt that three of his very " top-line " force should be dismissed so lightly, and the following two wireless messages were exchanged :

" Commodore to Vice-Admiral Commanding : Sorry my destroyers were not much use to you."

Reply from Queenstown :

" Vice-Admiral Commanding to Commodore : Why say ' *much* ' ? "

One of the less easy problems at Queenstown was concerned with recreation. It is quite obvious that to keep officers and men fit and happy, they must be given whatever opportunity might be possible for getting a walk ashore. Even the keenest mariner soon reaches a stage when he hates the sight of his mess-mates, and loathes the very inside of his ship; yet a run on land for a few hours, a complete change of environment, the sight of a pretty girl, perhaps a meal in a restaurant, an entertainment in some theatre, will create a complete mental transformation. He returns aboard satiated with the beach, fed up with town life, and to-morrow is quite glad when the ship puts to sea.

In Queenstown, however, the local attractions were practically nil. Neither music-halls nor cinemas, nor any other amusement existed nearer than Cork. This meant a train journey both ways, with always a possibility of being insulted or maltreated for wearing the King's uniform. Even at Queenstown itself, whose inhabitants drew so much of their income from the Navy, most of the people were either lacking in sympathy or deliberately antagonistic, so that every now and again there would be an ugly " scrap," followed by one more public-house being put out of bounds by the Admiral as punishment for the ill-treatment of his sailors.

For commanding officers the beautiful little walled-in enclosure near the bottom of Admiralty House garden was reserved exclusively. It was quiet, restful, shut in by trees and hedges, with fruit ripening on an old stone wall, and just peeping over the trees could be seen the tall mast from which fluttered the Admiral's flag. It was a gracious gesture that here, at least, was a plot they could call their own and from which it was quite impossible to see any part of their ship. Here, too, was a well-kept tennis lawn with a flower-border limning the gravel paths.

Before long, naturally enough, this enclosure became known as the Sloop Garden. Now, the names of these ships had all been called after flowers. The *Sunflower* and *Jessamine* we have already mentioned, but soon were to come the *Zinnia* and *Begonia*, *Laburnum*, *Lavender*, followed by the *Daffodil*, *Primrose*, *Tamarisk*, *Snowdrop*, *Camellia*, *Viola*, *Delphinium*. Each sloop captain regarded it as a matter of honour to plant, sooner or later, as suitable leave and season permitted, that floral stem which signified his own ship, and presently there flourished an herbaceous border bright with maritime meaning. Thus to enjoy exercise amid a setting so charming formed the best antidote for tired nerves and eyes that had kept long vigil for submarines.

As to the Admiral, his presence being continuously necessitated by the ceaseless flow of signals even at meal-times, by the frequent orders that must be sparked out to the patrols, and the important decisions which hourly had to be made, only on Saturday afternoons could he find time for a long walk. Then the Admiralty sent him a motor-car: at least, that was what it purported to be, though actually it was a "cast-off" from the Royal Naval Air Service. It seemed to the Admiral that what was not good enough for the R.N.A.S. could by no manner of reasoning be up to Navy standard; wherefore he returned the questionable vehicle, and their Lordships sent him a perfectly good one instead. About this time Lord Barrymore gave the run of his estate at Fota for Sir Lewis Bayly's convenience, who could now use it in much the same manner as commanding officers were occupying the Sloop Garden. This was pretty well all the hospitality which the Vice-Admiral Commanding accepted throughout these strenuous years; and, having announced that he would enter no private house so long as the War should last, his precious time could be spent solely on the things which mattered.

And indeed things mattered very considerably this August. Never since the War started, a year before, had the sinkings of merchant vessels reached the appalling figure of this month, and never was it again touched until October 1916. August 1915 will ever be known as one of the most critical periods, when 135,153 tons of shipping were sent to destruction. Now, it is an interesting and notable fact that, notwithstanding the large number of submarine officers and boats which the enemy sent forth from time to time, most of the damage was done by a select few who were specially skilled and successful, whilst the average drew many a blank. Particularly able were those captains who were already U-boat experts in the early days of hostilities.

The reader will recollect $U\,27$ (Wegener) and $U\,24$

QUEENSTOWN HARBOUR
Royal Cork Yacht Club in the foreground. Admiralty House is to the right of cathedral.

THE "SLOOP" GARDEN
With the Admiral's flagstaff in the background.

(Schneider) as being mentioned in our second and third chapters. The former had ever since March been one of the pioneers in the Irish Sea, whilst the latter had won notoriety by sinking the *Formidable*. Both officers were representative of the sharpest steel with which Germany was now waging her blockade warfare. It was on August 4 that Lieut.-Commander Wegener set out from home bound for the Irish coast in $U\,27$, and about the same time Lieut.-Commander Max Valentiner in $U\,38$ likewise started for the southern part of the Irish Sea. That Valentiner was another of the enemy's "star turns" will immediately be appreciated, for in five days he sank twenty-two cargo vessels, five trawlers, and three sailing ships in the vicinity of St. George's Channel, Ushant, and the English Channel's western mouth. His attacks were made chiefly by gunfire and during hazy weather. Thirty sinkings in five days!

During this same month $U\,34$, $U\,35$, followed by $U\,33$ and $U\,39$, left Germany for the Mediterranean, but their orders allowed them to sink shipping so far as the English Channel, which accounts for the loss of three steamers. Thus it was that never previously had so many U-boats been simultaneously operating in Ireland's neighbourhood. But omitting from our inquiry these four transients, let us watch Schneider and Wegener leaving in their wake smoke and wreckage wherever they went.

$U\,24$'s voyage began on August 5. After motoring up the North Sea, right round Scotland, the west and south of Ireland, Schneider brought her up the Irish Sea, and at daybreak of August 16 was off the Cumberland coast; that dreary region of muddy harbours, coal dust, and dismal cliffs. Factories and collieries have robbed this locality of any beauty, yet in a time of war such spheres of production were more to be desired than any æsthetic attraction. Being now abreast of Lowca, which is half-way between Workington and Whitehaven, the enemy was ready for his morning hate.

Lowca is merely a village, whose chief justification for being on the map is that it contains some small works where naphtha, benzol, and coke are produced. Sunrise this fine, calm, hazy morn was at 4.53, but shortly after four o'clock

U 24, carrying one gun for'ard and another aft, was seen from Harrington Harbour moving along the coast about a mile from the coke-ovens. Three minutes before the sun leapt up Schneider opened fire on the works, but the shooting was such that the first dozen shots effected little damage. The next three or four dozen, however, were all direct hits on the works, a total of fifty-five shells being fired within twenty-five minutes. Apart from bursting a fifty-gallon drum of benzol, setting it on fire, and damage done in the works to the extent of £800, no serious results had been brought about, and not a single casualty. Nor did this visit have any effect on the War, since work was held up during only four days.

But it is worth remarking that our enemy knew exactly what he was about, and this should carry a warning for the future. The Germans in their official communication twelve days later made no vague claim to have bombarded the coast, but correctly stated they had "shelled the benzol works and the benzol storage tanks as well as the coke-ovens." How did they know so much? Why had such an out-of-the-way village as Lowca ever come into their ken?

The answer is that only two years previously a hundred of Lowca's coke-ovens had been erected by a certain German firm, whilst the crude-naphtha and refining plants had been constructed by a second German company. The latter had brought over their own labourers, of whom some were such enthusiastic photographers that they took snapshots of the works from various positions, including views from the sea. Thus was it possible to give Schneider not merely detailed plans down to the minutest details, but some useful pictures. This bombardment instantly suggests comparison with Hersing's attack on Walney by U 21 at the end of January, but it should be mentioned that if Schneider made a more deliberate display there was no reason to the contrary; for coast defences in that district were non-existent.

It is a testimony to the increased efficiency of North Channel net-drifters that Schneider did not return home by that strait, but must needs come all the way round Ireland west about. Proceeding down the Irish Sea again, U 24 was attacked by a patrol trawler off the Tuskar and, after passing through St. George's Channel, was south off the Old Head of Kinsale by August 19. It so happened that very heavy weather had been experienced that week, which had made it impossible for the Milford drifters to maintain a good line of nets for the thirty-five miles stretch from the Tuskar to the Smalls, but it is quite certain that all these three submarines—$U\,24$, $U\,27$, and $U\,38$—in this very neighbourhood were having an exciting time whenever the patrols could see them.

Thus, two days before the Lowca bombardment Skipper Pascoe Philip Glanville in his trawler *Amadavit*, armed with only a six-pounder, shelled and chased one U-boat, got so close as to smother the enemy's conning-tower with the spray from a bursting shell, and was able to rescue the S.S. *Maxton*—just in time—from being sunk. On that same day the armed yacht *Sabrina* chased a submarine, which was probably $U\,38$; but on the 17th (*i.e.* the day following the Lowca affair) the armed trawler *Ann Ford Melville*, likewise in the Tuskar area, fired at a submerging U-boat, whilst nearly three hours later the armed trawler *Spider*, farther south, roughly midway between the Old Head of Kinsale and Lundy Island, in spite of the mist chased and kept firing at a U-boat till the latter had to find safety below surface. By so doing was the S.S. *City of Liverpool* (an Army transport on her way from Calais to Manchester) saved.

It is very evident that Schneider, Wegener, and Valentiner were now making a concentration well to the south of Ireland in a region which is contained in the area Fastnet–Ushant–Land's End–Milford–Tuskar; that is to say, they were operating across the entire Western Approaches, which include the ship routes towards the English Channel ports no less than those of Liverpool and the Bristol Channel. An ambitious undertaking, yet merely an extension of that principle which had entrapped the *Lusitania*. The strategy was sound, simple, and bound to succeed, inasmuch as these were the essential highroads if steamers were still to enter British ports from the Atlantic.

I have taken the trouble to plot down on a chart the positions where, from August 17 and during the next few days, patrol vessels sighted U-boats, or the latter molested steamers, and the above conclusions are instantly manifested. It would have been impossible for three submarines to have maintained this barrier for long, yet while it lasted it was a most formidable expression of the enemy's blockade. And by August 19 the centre of effort had been moved to a locality which was from about fifty to seventy miles S. by W. of the Old Head of Kinsale, or some distance farther south than the last scene of *Lusitania*.

That both Wegener and Schneider were present is beyond dispute. On the 19th *U* 24 was some forty-eight miles from the Kinsale Head, and molested the stricken S.S. *Dunsley* (4930 tons), which had been captured by gunfire and was already doomed. Before giving her the knock-out blow, however, there came in sight a big liner three times her size. Just now Schneider had developed a certain nervousness of liners, for, in St. George's Channel, on the way down, his attack on the Ellerman liner *City of Exeter* had been received with shells from the steamer's defensive armament. Schneider therefore now dived.

Certainly, if you have ever looked through a periscope at a great Atlantic liner zigzagging towards you, the sight of this menacing mass and the sharp forefoot is unforgettable. That she was a passenger ship must have been patent from all her tophamper. That he could not have forgotten the *Lusitania* sensation, and world-anger, must equally have been certain. Nevertheless, by some sudden decision, perhaps in an impulse of blind anger, Schneider repeated the offence of Schwieger. He fired a torpedo at close range, and the result was that the well-known White Star S.S. *Arabic* (15,801 tons), went down with the loss of forty-four people, to keep the Cunarder company. Fortunately, most of 400 persons were saved, but among those lost were several American citizens, so the man who sank the *Formidable* was now likely to embroil his country in a pretty diplomatic dilemma. But that very afternoon, only twenty-five miles away, Wegener was doing his stuff also.

For at three o'clock the S.S. *Nicosian* (6369 tons) was captured by *U* 27, and was shelled at a range of a thousand yards. Fortunately, the Q-ship *Baralong* (Lieut.-Commander Godfrey Herbert, R.N.) was cruising in the neighbourhood, picked up the wireless " S.O.S.," altered course, soon sighted the submarine as well as the steamer's boats, and so completely fooled Wegener that before the German could make off, thirty-four shells were fired from the *Baralong*, and most of them scored hits. Within less than two minutes U 27 and Wegener disappeared, never again to be seen by human eye. There were no survivors. In spite of being down by the head, the steamer managed to keep afloat, and was towed in the direction of Bristol Channel, finally reaching port. But on this same day, and adjacent to this locality, both the sailing vessel *St. Olaf* and the S.S. *New York City* (2970 tons) were also sent to the bottom by U-boat gunfire. Four days later a couple of bigger steamers, the *Trafalgar* (4572 tons) and *Silvia* (5268 tons), were destroyed a little nearer the Fastnet.

Thus the first twelve months of war had made the south Irish waters of the Atlantic a veritable graveyard for shipping of all sorts—from the world's biggest steamers down to sailing craft and submarines. But these activities of mid-August were to provide some notable sequels.

CHAPTER VIII

TRAP-SHIPS

No one more than Admiral Bayly himself appreciated the terrible seriousness of this shipping situation off the coast. With a fleet consisting at this date of eight sloops, three steam yachts, twenty-four trawlers, and four motor-boats (having yachtsmen personnel patrolling the inshore bays and creeks), how inadequate was his force against the ubiquitous and rarely visible enemy! Queenstown possessed not even one decoy ship, for the *Baralong* had come all the way from Falmouth to gain her victory.

It was quite impossible to make the Western Approaches safe for shipping unless the patrols were considerably strengthened. Almost every one of the Queenstown trawlers was defensively engaged on escort duty, but what was required now were about twenty-four sloops, twelve destroyers, and six decoy steamers of the *Baralong* type. To the Admiral only three methods were practicable for combatting the U-boats: protection, evasion, prevention. Of these the first was being carried out so far as the paucity of armed vessels permitted. Evasion was possible only where sea-room would be unlimited, as in the Atlantic: it was almost impossible when making the land, or off lightships and promontories which must be rounded, or in such straits as St. George's Channel. But the only satisfactory method was that of stopping the enemy's exits, blocking up his ports of departure. Sooner or later, he foresaw that this would have to be attempted; and, looking back on the past, it seems a pity that the gallant efforts to bung up Zeebrugge as well as Ostende were not made till the last few months of War.

Twenty years ago the value of naval history—the application of lessons from the past to solve problems of modern warfare—was very far from being appreciated by the Service as it is to-day. There were, indeed, some Flag Officers who could already interpret previous developments in present-day terms; but, just as one of the greatest Generals in France early in the War during a critical day recognised the threat of such a situation as military history had taught him must never be allowed to mature, and therefore instinct must give way to logic; so Admiral Bayly, with his mind alive with naval history, at the end of his first month in Queenstown could discern the same inevitable conclusions about to spring from similar circumstances.

That is to say, the blocking-up would not be easy, and might even fail at first—as the operation had at Santiago and Port Arthur—but it might have to be attempted a second time [1] and might still not succeed. The submarine had its historical precursor in the privateer of sailing-ship days, when we endeavoured, both in the West Indies and along the north coast of France, to destroy the wasps by attacking the wasps' nest. What in principle was effected by us then could, and should, be attempted to-day.

Unfortunately, this attitude failed to commend itself in certain quarters, and the strictly *defensive* methods continued. As to increasing the Queenstown patrols by so many destroyers and sloops, that could not be done, because the Grand Fleet still needed the latter to sweep North Sea tracks clear of mines and the former to act as an anti-submarine screen. But a couple of decoy-ships, colliers or tramp steamers suitably armed, should presently be sent to serve under Sir Lewis Bayly. It is worth adding that at this date the Admiralty thought very little of decoy-ships. Off and on this sort of vessel had been out on cruises ever since November 1914, several steamer-types had been tried, and the *Baralong* had tramped about over 12,000 miles before Wegener brought her luck.

Of course, this decoy idea—" Mystery ship " as the class came to be known informally, " Q-ship " as it was called officially, " Trap-ship " as it was eventually designated by German officers—again came from history. The notion was employed not merely so far back as the seventeenth and eighteenth centuries; on land at least it derived directly from the classical wooden horse of Troy. But the sudden success of the *Baralong*, synchronising with the sensational loss of the *Arabic*, clearly suggested that other *Baralongs* might be more useful than armed yachts.

Now when the big White Star liner's funnels finally dis-

[1] As indeed happened at Ostende in the spring of 1918.

appeared into the sea, there had been caused such a commotion that waves of indignation were felt so far away as the United States. Here was another *Lusitania* crime, differing in degree, but not in kind. Must America still stand aside and suffer these insults? Or could she bring such diplomatic pressure to bear on Germany as to prevent this sort of thing happening a third time?

The excitement spread east, and caused a sharp difference of opinion at German General Headquarters. On the one side distinguished officers, such as Admiral Tirpitz and the Chief of the German Admiralty Staff, energetically insisted that the U-boat war against sea-borne commerce must on no account be abandoned: this sword was far too mighty a weapon to be sheathed. Opposed to the party were men like Bethmann-Hollweg, the Imperial Chancellor, and the Chief of the Naval Cabinet, who were in favour of placating America and assuring Washington that U-boat captains had received precise orders *not* to sink passenger steamers without warning, or without seeing that passengers were safe.

The dispute continued till August 27, when the Emperor decided in favour of the Bethmann-Hollweg party, and on September 1 the German Government informed the American Government that the latter's demands for the limitation of submarine activity were now accepted. In the meanwhile, Count Bernstorff—without having previously been so authorised—declared that the submarine captain who sank *Arabic* would be punished for having exceeded orders. It was on August 30 that Germany issued instructions to her U-boat officers forbidding them in future to sink small passenger steamers without warning. Of course it required about three weeks before this drastic and unwelcome decision could be communicated to the most distant boats still at sea. To-day we know, through Captain Gayer,[1] who was co-head of the German Admiralty's Submarine Department, that such an order was received as something impracticable. How could a submarine's commanding officer discriminate between a small passenger steamer and a cargo-carrier?

So after the sinking of the S.S. *Urbino* on September 24, the U-boat campaign in the waters of the British Isles came

[1] *Die Deutschen U-Boote.*

to a stop until the following March;[1] and attacks[2] were transferred to the Mediterranean, where there could be no expectation of creating further difficulties with Washington. Thus, whilst not yet in the War, President Wilson and the American nation were already a much more potent influence on the German blockade than is usually understood.

Now, we have just made mention of *U* 39 and *U* 33, the former being commanded by Lieut.-Commander W. Forstmann, and the latter by Lieut.-Commander Gansser. When these set out from Germany for the Mediterranean via Scotland and Ireland, they were despatched just before the new order had been issued to submarine captains. It was on August 27 that Forstmann began his voyage, so that (reckoning the usual six-day passage) he should be off the Fastnet on September 2, but a good deal to the westward, before laying a course well to windward of the Bay of Biscay.

With typical Teutonic punctuality, *U* 39 on September 2 at 7 p.m. was ninety-five miles west of the Fastnet lighthouse, when she had the good fortune to cross the track of that fine four-masted British barque *William T. Lewis* (2166 tons), registered at Greenock. Her master, Captain E. Manning, suddenly sighted the submarine, which hoisted the two-flag signal: " Show your nationality." After the Red Ensign had been hoisted, Forstmann then fired a shot across the barque's bows and hoisted: " B.A.," meaning " Can your damage be repaired at sea?" But in the excitement the German signalman had evidently pulled the wrong end of his halyard, and the flags flapped upside down. What he really intended was " A.B.," meaning " Abandon your ship at once." And this is how Captain Manning interpreted it.

The submarine approached, the barque's crew took to their boats, for shells came crashing into the rigging before there was any chance to answer the signal. Next the German hailed Manning, and ordered him to deliver up the ship's papers. Whilst they were being examined, Manning said to Forstmann, " You aren't going to leave me adrift all night,

---

[1] With the exception of a week's spasm from December 20 to 28, 1915, when U-boats on passage to the Dardanelles brought sudden havoc off Ireland. (See Chapter X.)
[2] The smaller class of submarine minelayers in the North Sea still carried on.

are you?" The weather was squally, the lonely Atlantic presently becoming dark and heavy-waved, and the nearest land was too distant for any pleasure in open-boat sailing.

The German officer saw no reason for sympathy.

"You have a good boat, a compass, sails, and a chart? What more do you want?"

So, having pumped some additional shells into the poor old sailing vessel, and being convinced that one more survivor of the Golden Age would quickly become another of Davy Jones' museum-pieces, the U-boat departed, and night settled down. She carried on to the southward, was not seen till she had passed through Gibraltar Straits, and on September 8 was heading to the south-east, preparatory to sinking next day one British and two French steamers. As to Manning and his crew, they drifted about till, most providentially, a Danish vessel observed them; and, having regard to the size of a ship's boat compared with Atlantic seas, the chances of being observed by even the most vigilant look-out were pretty slender. After a while the Danish vessel met one of the patrol craft nearer land, so transferred the distressed mariners, who were now brought into Berehaven.

But to these unfortunates came another surprise.

The barque was laden with timber valued at a total of £10,500, the loss of ship and freight after coming across the ocean being a bitter blow. Judge of Captain Manning's emotion, therefore, when he learned that his ship, in spite of all the German shells, had not sunk! It was the timber which kept her afloat, so that the London S.S. *Balakani* on September 4 had discovered the derelict, taken her in tow, and brought her into the nearest convenient harbour, which was Berehaven. I remember what an impressive picture this little drama made. The *Balakani* was an oil-tanker, and I can still remember her off Berehaven on a September day butting into a head sea, escorted by armed trawlers which had come out to guard her. But still more wonderful to my eyes was the *William T. Lewis*, and I noted in my diary the terrible shell-holes at her bows, on the quarter, the stern, and even right through the foremast. Much more damage had been caused by splinters, and even her bollards had been shot away, yet the clever salvage expert who was sent down to Berehaven made such a capital job of the repairs—notwithstanding the lack of facilities in this outlandish fjord—that one day the *William T. Lewis* was again taken to sea. She arrived safely at Plymouth, where the timber was discharged, and if the news ever reached Forstmann he must have been not less astonished than Manning had been on resuming command.

As for the *Balakani*, this Samaritan presently fell among thieves: that is to say, she had proceeded on her way towards Hull, and on September 9 was off the Thames Estuary, when by sheer misfortune she struck mines laid by one of the UC-boats. She foundered with the loss of nine lives, so that her voyage was more disastrous than the barque's. Subsequently the Admiralty Court made a very handsome award to the crew of the *Balakani*, amounting to one-half of the £10,500 value. Thus the steamer's owners were to have £3500, the master £400, the crew £1,330, plus an extra £20 to the mate who did special service by boat.

Lieut.-Commander Gansser in *U* 33 departed from Borkum only a day after Forstmann, but was off the Fastnet two days later than the attack on *William T. Lewis*. Indeed, it is remarkable that *U* 33 did not come across the *Balakani* in the act of towing the maimed barque. Nevertheless, Gansser can never complain of his luck. For, on September 4, shortly after midnight (having three days earlier sunk the S.S. *Whitfield* when ninety-five miles north of Cape Wrath), he torpedoed the S.S. *Cymbeline* some twenty-nine miles west of the Fastnet, causing the loss of six lives. He then continued his voyage on the surface at about ten knots till 11.45 a.m., when, in a position 137 miles S.W. by W. of the Fastnet, he sank the S.S. *Mimosa* by gunfire. Five hours passed, and he came up with the Norwegian vessel *Storesand*, which he despatched also. Total: three ships in one day. He then steered a southerly course until September 6 at 3 p.m., by which time he had got past the Bay of Biscay and was ninety-eight miles west of Cape Finisterre. The S.S. *John Hardie* came along, was shelled, and sent to the bottom, after which *U* 33 carried on, passed through Gibraltar Straits, though at noon on September 9 she was fired on half a dozen times by H.M. Torpedo Boat No. 95, so dived and got away unhurt.

But at this time there was also a third submarine, which operated between south-west Ireland right across the Bay of Biscay in a south-east direction to the Gironde mouth. She may have been *U* 38 (Valentiner), but her course can be followed with conviction from 4.30 a.m. on September 4, when she was ninety miles west of the Fastnet, and another barque was sent down to the Great Maritime Museum, though this time the victim was not British, but the Norwegian *Glimt*. On that same day, and in the same locality, she made the finest haul since the *Arabic's* loss; for the 10,920-ton liner *Hesperian* was torpedoed without warning; thirty-two people perished, but happily several hundred survivors were rescued by Commander Cole-Hamilton in the sloop *Sunflower*. Before that day was over the S.S. *Dictator* and the S.S. *Douro* were also at the bottom, and so the horrible destruction continued till September 8, by which time the S.S. *Mora* in the Bay of Biscay closed the list till a fortnight later; since this enemy was now on her way home by the same route, and *U* 41 must come out to take her place. Now, this interval between the departure of one submarine and the arrival of another explains the fortnight's sudden lull between September 8 and 23.

Thus we come to the dramatic incident, which caused great uneasiness in Germany and a new encouragement among those who happened to be serving off Ireland.

The commanding officer of *U* 41 was Lieut.-Commander Hansen, and she was a comparatively new boat, having been commissioned at Kiel as recently as the previous February. On April 15 she had left Wilhelmshaven for her first trip; then had followed two more. But on September 12 she again started from Wilhelmshaven bound for the Western Approaches. These dates are interesting, as proving that in five months only three voyages could be made, and that, having wasted twelve days on each trip (coming and going), no less than thirty-six days of the voyages were to be deducted from time available on the Irish station. Therefore, to justify his existence, Hansen or any other submarine captain must be a quick worker when once the right spot had been reached. Food, fuel, fresh water, men's nerves, minor defects, would all hold out for a certain period, yet not indefinitely.

It follows that a smart officer would study his chart to note where the trade routes were certain to be fairly thick with traffic. However much the British Government might modify the steamer lanes, there was only one way into the Atlantic mouth of the English Channel, whilst the Irish Channel was still more subject to physical conditions. So, having once arrived at what might be termed an inevitable, chance-proof, spot well clear of land as well as of patrols, the U-boat had merely to wait the shortest while and bag three or four of the bigger ships in a couple of days before wireless alarms again diverted vessels.

By keeping on a line from Fastnet to Ushant, thus proceeding in a roughly south-east direction, cruising over the surface at an economical ten knots, but always ready to dive, and ever keeping a smart look-out for a funnel's smoke on the horizon, was almost sure to bring success, except in thick weather. For this line not merely crosses the local paths round Cape Clear, the Scillies, and Ushant, but is the barrier between the outside world and the main British ports.

On September 23, then, $U\,41$ was well down this line—that is to say, some seventy-nine miles S.E. of the Fastnet, when she sighted the S.S. *Anglo-Colombian* (4792 tons) and sank her. On the same day, but seven miles farther down the line, she sank the S.S. *Chancellor* (4586 tons) and the S.S. *Hesione* (3663 tons). By nine o'clock on the following forenoon $U\,41$ had got more than half her distance across in the direction of Ushant, and was actually sixty-seven miles S.W. by W. of the Bishop Rock, Scillies, when she was rewarded by a fourth victim. This was a much bigger vessel, the S.S. *Urbino* (6651 tons) of the Wilson Line, and into her Hansen poured so many shells that soon she was lying over, on fire, with a heavy list. But the adversary had not quite completed his job when he saw another steamer approaching. Here was to be the fifth victim in two days' operation.

$U\,41$ accordingly quitted the *Urbino*, submerged, had a good look round through the periscope, became convinced all was well, returned to the surface and signalled the new arrival. It was a fine, clear September morning, the *Urbino's* crew had taken to their boats and waited afar off to count the minutes before Hansen reopened fire. Stranger and submarine were approaching on converging courses, but now the former was ordered to " Stop instantly," followed by a signal to bring her papers on board. So the steamer stopped, lowered a boat, and the submarine had her for'ard gun manned under the charge of Oberleutnant Crompton. Just for a moment let us leave them in this suspenseful situation: the two craft separated by only 700 yards, Crompton about to give the order for his gunner to fire, and the steamer hurriedly trying to get a boat into the water.

We may now explain that the steamer was none other than that "mystery" or decoy-ship *Baralong*, though she had since the last engagement changed her name to *Wyandra*. She had also got a new skipper, Lieut.-Commander Herbert being succeeded by Lieut.-Commander A. Wilmot-Smith, R.N. This had been done because of the furore which arose in Germany over the loss of $U\,27$, the Kaiser himself being extremely indignant. On the evening of September 23 the *Baralong* again happened to be in Falmouth when news was received that the *Anglo-Colombian* had been sunk in the given position at 9.45 a.m. that day. Admiral Bayly instructed *Baralong* to go out, in order to try and intercept a submarine which seemed to be working towards Ushant or the Bay of Biscay.

After rounding the Lizard, *Baralong* steered in a W.S.W. direction, and night passed as she came nearer to the Fastnet–Ushant line. At 9.45 a.m. on the following day the decoy-ship's officer-of-the-watch reported a steamer right ahead " stopped, and blowing off steam," the distance being about eight miles. It was quite obvious what must be wrong and that a U-boat could be not far away. The *Baralong* accordingly kept steadily on towards what turned out to be the *Urbino*, and Wilmot-Smith got ready for immediate action. After getting a little closer, sure enough a submarine's conning-tower was made out, and next came Hansen's decision to dive.

It may be added that since a month before this decoy had so altered her external appearance as to be unrecognisable: whatever details had reached Germany indirectly from those who had belonged to the *Nicosian* now signified nothing. And, indeed, it was part of a captain's skill that he could in a very few hours, even at sea, completely transform his " trap " ship by means of paint, false derricks, new funnel-markings, and many other ingenuities. In short, Hansen was fooled from the very first, and Wilmot-Smith endeavoured to impose his will on the German, altering course to the southward so as to compel his rival—if he really intended an attack—to appear on the surface and use his oil-engines.

The ruse succeeded; $U\,41$ surfaced, came full speed so as to head the steamer off; and next was hoisted bunting to " Stop instantly." The submarine then went closer, and the decoy proceeded under easy steam. Having got the enemy about two points on the starboard bow, Wilmot-Smith kept her on that bearing until the separating distance was only 700 yards, whereupon the " mystery " ship put her helm hard a-starboard, so that her head went off to port, thereby allowing guns on the starboard quarter and stern to bear. By now the range was a mere 500 yards, and the order was given to " Open fire ! " So excellent was the shooting that the second round hit $U\,41$ at the conning-tower base, and then several other shells struck also. The enemy replied with one round from one of her two guns, but this hopeless effort failed to find a target. Panic-stricken men were seen deserting their guns and making for the conning-tower hatch, but at this moment another shell struck that tower, blowing Hansen and half a dozen men (who were inside) to pieces. Five more direct hits struck the hull, she gave a heavy list to port, and with a big inclination at the stern disappeared.

But any attempt to escape by invisibility was short-lived. She was found to be leaking so badly that the main bilge-pump became ineffective, and a terrible fate threatened all. Down and down the boat went, and in spite of releasing safety weights, she sank to the phenomenal depth of 258 feet. Diving tanks were now blown out by the compressed air, and only then did her bows as well as her conning-tower appear above water. To those still alive within it seemed an age: actually she had been down only half a minute. Large quantities of steam and smoke burst forth, below she went for the last time, followed by an explosion of air and welling-up of oil which covered the surface. For she had gone down in water so deep that the pressure crushed hull and bulkheads as a child smashes a paper bag.

The German crew had numbered thirty-two, including four commissioned officers. The only survivors were Oberleut. Crompton and Navigating Warrant Officer Gudan, who were rescued by the *Baralong*. The former remembered nothing after hearing the order to dive immediately, for he had been badly wounded whilst entering the conning-tower. But unfortunately the *Urbino* had sunk also, assistance having arrived just too late, though no lives were lost aboard the Wilson liner; her entire personnel of forty-two officers and men being picked up. Fate played some curious pranks during the War, and when the *Baralong* got under way without even so much as a scratch on her side, she had passengers both British and German. Soon after midnight she again passed the Lizard and arrived in Falmouth.

On that return trip Captain Allanson Hick was able to fill in the gaps of the story, to mention that his *Urbino* had been homeward bound from New York to Hull, and to relate how badly the dead Germans had behaved; for nineteen of them were on the submarine's deck and jeered at the master mariner in his open boat whilst his fine ship wallowed in her last agony. And presently, by a curious mentality, the German newspapers which had approved the sinking of the *Falaba*, *Lusitania*, and *Arabic*, passenger steamers, now rose in their wrath and considered the sinking of $U\,41$ a murderous act.

In England the victory over a dangerous enemy was hailed with delight wherever the half-secret was made known. Lieut.-Commander Wilmot-Smith was awarded a D.S.O., Engineer Lieut. J. M. Dowie, R.N.R., was given a D.S.C., whilst two of the crew received each a D.S.M. But the direct result of these two successful actions by the same disguised ship, having the appearance of the most inoffensive tramp-steamer, was to take over and fit out more decoys for service under Sir Lewis Bayly. Obvious reasons demanded that the *Baralong* should not continue in her old area, so she was ordered off south to the Mediterranean, where the U-boats were already engaged in a new campaign.

CHAPTER IX

QUEENSTOWN SLOOPS

"As soon as I am to the west of Cape Clear," remarked a coasting mariner some years ago, "I always bid farewell to civilisation; for beyond that headland both people and scenery belong to another age."

Certainly in those bleak cliffs and primitive inhabitants of south-west Ireland there is something which to the average town-dweller of Britain or America seems altogether different. The outlook on life, the value which is set on romantic idealism, the singular lack of practical enterprise (as we know it), the fidelity to ancient traditions, the indifference to a competitive spirit, have made this part of the world to appear not less than two centuries behind most other countries. I recollect one of the Cape Clear Island fishermen stoutly defending his cause when accused of pillaging an Atlantic steamer which had the misfortune to end her days on the rocks. Apart from the bales of cotton which formed her cargo, were the copper and brass pipes in her engine-room, and all making up a considerable sum if reckoned in money. But British laws, or naval threats, meant nothing to these remote inhabitants. Their way of regarding the wreck was analogous to the manner in which a merchant welcomes good trade, or a farmer sees the sun ripening his crops.

"God has indeed sent that wreck for the benefit of us all on Cape Clear Island," insisted the accused. "And if we should leave the cotton or the copper to itself, we'd niver deserve any luck agin!"

A little farther north lies Bere Island, so placed by Nature as to create that haven which both in peace and the last War has been invaluable to naval ships of all sorts. It was one of the British military garrison on Bere Island who through sheer boredom described Berehaven as a place that is covered with mist for five days of the week, and with rain for the other two. However unjust such a statement might be during such months as June or August, the description, if applied to autumn, winter, and spring, is scarcely exaggerated. Long years ago the first dwellers on Bere Island arrived in their simple vessels from northern Africa, and neither off the Fastnet nor the Mizen were sea-waves then any less tyrannical than to-day. But, in spite of all the traditional tales and fairy legends, or the more firmly founded stories of Druids and Celts, this locality at the southern end of Bantry Bay is yet both full of sea-history and empty of those attractions which appeal to modern warriors.

So quickly do gales set in off this coast, that they frequently precede any warning given by the barometer. So inhospitable is the littoral that raids and invasions have more usually failed than succeeded. In the seventeenth and eighteenth centuries both the Spanish and French fleets, respectively, were scattered by sudden storms off the coast; and the heights of Hungry Hill, dominating the more sheltered waters of Berehaven, have looked down on almost every kind of craft that history has provided—from dug-outs to destroyers of British or American build, from the Elizabethan exploration ship *Desire* (of that great pioneer Davis) down to the twentieth-century submarines.

It was two and a half years before the Great War that for the first time I beheld, early one chilly morning of December, the mist-covered top of Hungry Hill, and from the bridge of the world's crack battle-cruiser. As the guest of Rear-Admiral Bayly in H.M.S. *Lion*, I was given the singular privilege of coming to sea in that famous ship which not many months later was to be present in the North Sea actions as Admiral Beatty's flagship. Two items especially impressed themselves on my mind. The first was when Admiral Bayly asked me ashore to climb Hungry Hill, and it was one of the many lessons which I had still to learn in perseverance. I forget how long it took us to reach the top and come back, though I did hear that it beat the Navy's existing record for time. Such was the pace set, and such the conquering energy of my distinguished host, that I felt an intense shame because the speed for me very shortly must be no longer tolerable. Twenty years his junior, I was just about to suggest a temporary halt, when there came suddenly and most welcomely the order:

"Heave-to, Scribe!"

My leg-muscles were stiff for many a long day after that adventure, but the joy of that short sentence still survives.

Glancing up at the Hill from the *Lion's* deck that same day,

I do remember saying: " Well, it's the last time either those slopes or Berehaven will ever pass within my gaze. For the battle-cruisers have arrived only for a special purpose, and no such invitation will again come my way."

But how vain a thing is man's prophecy! The months flew by, a World War began, events big and little followed in strange sequence. In August of 1915 I happened to be serving afloat at Milford, when H.M.S. *Adventure*, flying the flag of Sir Lewis Bayly, came in and anchored for a brief official visit. Before I could get alongside to pay my respects, the energetic Admiral was already pacing his quarter-deck. His eyes missed nothing—not even the salute of a temporary naval officer.

" Hallo! What are *you* doing here ? "

" Not much good, sir. Very bored, sir."

" Would you like to serve under me in Ireland ? "

(Already the *Adventure's* anchor was up, and her propellers had begun to churn the water.) " I should like nothing in the world so much " (shouting at the top of my voice, in fear that the noise of wind and propellers might rob me of this unexpected chance). " It is most kind . . ."

" Then I will ask the Admiralty for you by wireless."

The appointment was approved, and two nights after the torpedoing of *Arabic* I crossed from Fishguard to Queenstown. Up the hill into Admiralty House for orders. Everything strictly " Service." Everything working with quiet, but immense, determination. A queue of officers waiting to enter the Admiral's chart-lined room. At last my turn, and the clearest orders given with the greatest economy of words.

" You are to command the drifter *Daisy VI*, now lying at Haulbowline Dockyard. Complete fitting out. Report when ready for sea. You will be based on Berehaven for special service."

Down the hill . . . across the harbour . . . six busy days fitting out; practising gunnery and use of a nasty dangerous explosive sweep; taking in rapid-laying nets for any area suspected of containing a submarine . . . coaling ship . . . drawing stores . . . and then, one bright morning, with a light N.E. wind, steaming down the coast towards Berehaven! Hungry Hill again, mist-topped as before, deep shadows in the glens, waterfalls, yellow and black rocks, gorse, turquoise sea, a blue-and-white August sky.

But soon followed the autumn gales, with the mists turning into thick rain, and the cliffs of Dunmanus Bay resisting the monstrous seas that came bursting out of the Atlantic. It was the first of a series which surprised drifters and sloops, ocean-going sailing ships, and hefty steel trawlers alike. The fun began on the evening of October 27, and by 6 p.m. the barometer had gradually dropped the amazing extent of eleven-tenths, when the Norwegian barque *Pehr Ugland* of Arendal, in the thick driving rain and S.W. gale, suddenly found herself heading straight for Mizen Head, with the steep rocks close to leeward: the first landfall after coming up the South Atlantic.

This fine vessel—one more of a dying race—had been built in the year 1891, and was of 1293 tons. Owned by Messrs. J. L. Ugland, she had left Antofagasta, Chile, on July 6 for Queenstown " for orders," with a cargo comprising " 21,961 bags of nitrate of soda, and sixty-five Spanish quintals." Her master, Captain Aanonsen, was a magnificent sailorman, with pluck and a cool head: otherwise immediate disaster would have happened. It was unfortunate that he should have got a few miles to the north of his reckoning, whereas he ought to have been well south of Cape Clear. In peace time he might have fared better, for Mizen Head lighthouse would have been showing its guidance; but too many navigational aids for U-boats could not be allowed.

Captain Aanonsen was horrified to see the cliff very close, tried to stay his ship, but she refused to come about, so wore round. The lighthouse men fired rockets, the barque's crew thought the end had come and donned lifebelts. It was a period of terrible suspense, but the ship just avoided Mizen Head, and then nearly got on to Three Castles Head. Throughout that wild night the gale continued merciless; there were no lights, the captain had only a small-scale chart, so he jilled about off the entrance to Dunmanus Bay between Three Castles and Sheep's Heads till dawn, when he ran up Dunmanus Bay, finally coming to anchor off Two Point Island.

This happened to be within my special area, so I went

alongside and boarded the barque, examined her papers, and in Captain Aanonsen's cabin listened to the story of an almost miraculous escape from death. The whole crew were still a bit shaken with the night's adventures, but there was one fellow among them who had reason to wonder why he had spent these last four months coming from South America only to be robbed of his ultimate aim. His name appeared last on the list as Ernst von Acker, and he had signed on as a Belgian, being rated as an A.B. His hopes of reaching home were now delayed for several years, since he turned out to be a German who had been born in Westphalia in 1875 and must be locked up in the local depot of the Royal Irish Constabulary preliminary to being interned. The barque, however, experienced better luck. Instructions came from her owners that she was to make for Bordeaux, and on November 5 she departed with a most favourable breeze, the wind that day having suddenly become north-east. So she had been remarkably lucky in having got in and out of Dunmanus Bay by her own efforts and without injury.

But three days after her departure these Irish gales began a new intensity which gradually worked up to a grand climax. War or no war, Nature was not to be cheated of her self-expression. Whereas in England a drop of three-tenths is warning enough that some hard blow approaches, we now saw the glass take a dive of six-tenths. That south-wester finished its anger for a while, but on November 11 there was every indication of further trouble. The wind had backed to south-east, the atmosphere was thick with mist, the barometer fell nine-tenths in twenty-four hours, and during the night another four-tenths were added to the score. One wondered if Ireland was about to be blown off the map altogether! Suddenly the wind flew round to south-west, and by morning the glass was still falling, so that already it registered 28·6.

A very heavy swell came running in, and at 1.20 p.m. the wind had veered to north-east with amazing vigour. At a later date the Captain of the *William T. Lewis*,[1] who had in his long sailing career been twenty-five times round Cape Horn, assured me that this north-easter reached hurricane force. I am sure he was not guilty of exaggeration, for one of the

[1] See Chapter VIII.

squalls snapped off the end of the gaff aboard my *Daisy VI* and blew the mizzen sail out of its bolt-rope. But we were steaming along in comparative shelter under the tall cliffs. The coasting S.S. *Loch Leven* came running for shelter into a cove and brought up to her anchor with many fathoms of chain, but dangerously near some jagged rocks which waited to leeward. A few hours later the mountains were covered with snow.

Not since the year 1861 had such a storm visited Ireland; in one small estate a thousand trees were knocked down, and for three days both roads were blocked, neither telegraphic nor postal communication being possible during that period between Bantry and Berehaven, so that the *Daisy VI* temporarily acted as mail-ship immediately the gale eased up.

But it was this cyclonic storm which gave the Queenstown sloops their first real testing, and provided some most interesting data as to the capabilities of this new man-of-war type. The *Iris* fared not too well, being thrown on her beam ends, and two men washed overboard, though one was saved. Eventually this sloop came through safely, but only after a most trying experience, during which the whole of her ward-room furniture was smashed to small pieces. Captain G. F. W. Wilson, R.N., who was then commanding the *Zinnia* and had put to sea that forenoon from Queenstown, has kindly lent me his private log-book, from which the following extracts are taken :—

> During afternoon wind veered through N.N.W. to N.N.E., rapidly increasing to a gale.
>
> 4.0 p.m. Hove-to N.N.E. 7 knots. Wind increased to hurricane force, and very rough confused sea, so that ship became unmanageable. Unable to set main trysail,[1] so spread canvas screen on main rigging, and at last brought up to N.N.W.
>
> 9.0 p.m. Wind N.N.E., force 10–11. Very rough sea, driving hail and rain. Glass leaping up, ship having just passed centre of depression.
>
> 11.0 p.m. At last got about and steered E. by N., sighting Kinsale at 11.30. The foremost gun carried away securing chains, demolished training stops and kept crashing against foremast, shaking ship throughout. Engines racing dangerously. Speed through water about 3 knots.

[1] In order to steady them, a certain amount of sail could be set aboard these sloops, and this was found a great help during heavy Atlantic weather.

Next morning she steamed into Queenstown for repairs, with wireless aerial carried away, one of her starboard boats stove-in, main trysail and much canvas gear tattered.

Not less unpleasant was the *Jessamine's* experience. Captain Salisbury H. Simpson, R.N., tells me his sloop was a hundred miles south-west of the Fastnet that memorable day. At first it was just dull and cloudy, with a smooth sea, "but an ominous warning of an approaching storm, for the barometer was below 29°. While at lunch, I received a message from the officer of the watch to say that the sea was getting up. Within ten minutes we had to have fiddles on the table, as the sea had become like the South Downs for rolling expanse. From the upper bridge—a height of about forty feet—it was impossible to see over the next wave ahead; but the marvellous seaworthiness of the 'Flower' class sloops as 'hill-climbers' now demonstrated itself. Each wave looked as if it would break on board and swamp the ship, but each time she rode like a duck over its towering height, with the foc'sle just flush with the wave-crest. Owing to the shallow draught of the single propeller, the latter would race in the air as the ship slid down a wave's side, and the hull would shake like a jelly till once more the crest had been passed. We found that by keeping a speed of about six to seven knots, and the sea about four points on the bow, these little ships could ride out any gale in safety."

Nevertheless, the *Jessamine*, like her sisters, did not escape from this November gale completely immune. In the middle of the storm the telemotor steering-gear gave out, and before the alternative method of steering could be connected up, the helm crept hard-over, with the result that the sloop got broadside on to these enormous rollers. Moreover, it was night! Before the *Jessamine* could be brought back on to her course, she was rolling forty degrees; whilst so much water had poured down below, through the few openings giving access to the living-quarters, that even the heavy Service arm-chairs in the ward-room were floating about against the ship's side.

All these three years the sloops kept the sea with a pluck and pertinacity that had never been surpassed in naval history by small vessels. Even those gallant units of Admiral de Chair, which at this time were maintaining the British blockade between Iceland and Scotland, were of much bigger tonnage, and less unkindly to their personnel. The little "Flower" units of Queenstown must needs be not less efficient in the dark nights of winter than in the sunny days of June; for the enemy's strategy was not crystal clear, and the reason for his occasional mysterious lulls, or the date of his new operations, could not be guessed. The sloops must remain out on their respective areas so long as ever their hulls would float and their engines move round. Whenever Atlantic weather became too atrocious, speed would be reduced to about four knots, trysail would be set aft, and with barely steerage way the miniature "cruiser" would lie close to the wind making one point leeway. But to forsake the sphere of duty and run for shelter would have been unthinkable.

This sloop-patrol through every sort of Atlantic weather may well be compared with the British blockading squadrons which remained at sea off Brest during the Napoleonic wars; and I should like to set down here some pertinent remarks which Admiral Bayly has given me. "In many ways," he writes, "the sloops had a harder time. Thus, the ships off Brest were under sail, which steadied them in heavy weather much more effectively than was possible in these small steamships. The Brest blockaders had their decks comparatively dry, they were not driven along under a press of canvas, for they had to remain within a few miles of their station; and, being sailing ships, they never proceeded head to wind. But when a gale arrived from west or south-west, they ran before the wind to shelter in Cawsand Bay, or Torbay, the French Fleet simultaneously being unable to come out.

"On the other hand, our sailing men-of-war suffered from bad food, and often bad drinking water. Large numbers of the crews were pressed men who were on board against their will; whose sleeping-quarters were damp and cramped. Men were punished with severity, that being the contemporary idea of keeping discipline. Whilst the sloops had better quarters, with better food for the men, and generally were dry below the upper deck, they did not shelter in bad weather, but frequently had to steam head to wind when maintaining their station; with the accompanying severe discomfort of continuous vibration, and the upper deck practically under water."

During those harassing weeks when liners were being sunk right and left, it was difficult, or even impossible, for sloops to continue patrolling; wireless instructions would send them off at full speed to rescue torpedoed passengers and crews. The escorting of some valuable steamer through the danger zone so far as Liverpool or the English Channel mouth could be exceedingly inconvenient unless that ship had a speed of at least fourteen knots. For example, one homeward-bound vessel with a rich cargo could do no better than eight knots. She was convoyed from the Fastnet to the Mersey during a long, tiresome interval that caused the sloop to be away from her patrol for several days. On another occasion the cable S.S. *Telconia* was about three weeks either off the Fastnet repairing an Atlantic telegraph line, or in harbour waiting for the weather to moderate. Lest she should fall a victim to one of the U-boats, a sloop must stand by her, this again upsetting routine.

There were incidents, too, which could be very trying both to the Admiral and his commanding officers—as, for instance, when some expected merchant ship failed to arrive at the rendezvous with any punctuality, or indeed at all. One very dark night a sloop was at sea with instructions to meet and escort a certain vessel, whose name (let us assume) was the S.S. *Nonesuch*. Arrived at the given latitude and longitude, the sloop waited, and in due time along came a vessel of sorts. Was this the *Nonesuch*?

The sloop called her up by Morse across the leaden sea, but in vain. No answer was forthcoming; each time the dots and dashes were flashed by the former it seemed as if the merchant vessel increased her speed, whilst ignoring signals utterly. Finally the sloop kept up only by going faster and faster, till she reached the limit—seventeen knots. The race went on until the sloop picked up the following wireless message at close distance:

"Am being chased by 17-knot submarine. S.S. *Nonesuch*. Lat. . . . Long. . . ."

Presently that would reach Admiralty House, sloops would be sent out of their areas to assist, and once more the patrol arrangements suffer modification. But this particular "Flower" escort was now able to convince the *Nonesuch*, whose S.O.S. was promptly cancelled and explained before any further inconvenience had resulted. Nor was this by any means the last instance of one friend mistaking another for a foe.

But, peace or war, every winter finds some steamer so battered about well out in the Atlantic that she may never reach even Queenstown unless aid is despatched quickly and an accurate rendezvous has been wirelessed. Sometimes it is the case of a single-screw vessel with a broken tail-shaft, or her rudder carried away. On other occasions it has been the loss of her funnel, or the serious shifting of cargo.

Now that it happened to be war-time, such rescues belonged to the Navy, and news came through that the 4142-ton S.S. *Pomeranian* was disabled beyond the Fastnet with a broken rudder and smashed sternpost. On Monday morning away went the two sloops *Zinnia* and *Daffodil* out of Queenstown, accompanied by the tug *Warrior*. A heavy sea was still running, but they were able to maintain a nine-knots speed, and at the end of twenty-four hours had reached the presumed area. Opening out to a distance of two miles apart, the trio began their search, without success. Other events, however, began to happen.

At 10.30 a.m. the *Daffodil's* steering-gear became defective, but the tug broke down altogether. For the next three hours *Zinnia* stood by the latter in a heavy sea, until finally the *Warrior* reported she was leaking seriously. The situation, therefore, had become both awkward and annoying. Instead of the tug being one of the assistants, she must perforce be herself aided. The *Zinnia* sent across an 11½-inch grass warp by veering it astern, and to this was connected a 3½-inch wire. As the two ships rolled to the heavy ocean swell, this evolution was not easy, and when the sloop began towing the tug through the steep green valleys it became immediately evident that a long, arduous task had been undertaken.

The position was in Lat. 51.40 N., Long. 12.25 W., and presently the *Daffodil* wirelessed she had found the *Pomeranian* some distance farther north. The two sloops, each with her respective charge, continued to make slow progress throughout Tuesday towards the Irish coast until 5.15 a.m. on Wednesday, when the *Zinnia's* grass warp parted. By this time the sea had moderated slightly, and the wind had gone round to west;

yet again there was considerable difficulty in renewing connection. The warp was sent to the *Warrior* by means of the sloop's whaler, but it was still Atlantic night, and the tug unfortunately allowed the rope to snap whilst being hauled in.

For the two vessels in close proximity obviously the risk of colliding was not small; and had they rolled against each other but once, immense damage could scarcely have been avoided. At daylight the *Zinnia's* captain essayed a pretty bit of seamanship, and laid his bows sufficiently near to throw a heaving-line aboard the other. By this time the *Warrior's* crew, either from fatigue or sea-sickness, were incapable of acting promptly, so that another trying delay ensued before a couple of wires had been made fast and progress resumed.

It was now 8 a.m., and anxiety continued, but by skilful caution these wires were not given opportunity for breaking; for three half-hundredweight sinkers were slid down by shackles along the wires, thereby obtaining the necessary spring. Finally, at noon of Wednesday the useless tug was brought safely into Berehaven and anchored. Thus freed of one burden, the *Zinnia* hurried back into the Atlantic, only to find that besides the fresh wind and sea it had become foggy. At half-past nine that night she located three ships. The first was *Daffodil*, acting as escort, the other two being the *Pomeranian* and a vessel named the *Montfort*. The arrangement was a little unusual, though technically excellent: whilst the *Pomeranian* could not steer herself because of the broken rudder, she had plenty of power. So she took the *Montfort* in tow, who was able to act the part of a rudder, and steer the *Pomeranian's* stern as requisite.

Niceties were quite impossible, the two steamers yawed so badly that an accurate course was out of the question; but, luckily, the weather cleared, wind and sea moderated, permitting a speed of seven knots to be maintained. Keeping station on either side of their convoy, the two sloops ultimately arrived, late on Thursday afternoon, outside Queenstown Harbour, where the *Pomeranian* was handed over to local tugs. Thus both *Zinnia* and *Daffodil* had been taken off their normal beat during four days, and must now go in to coal ere proceeding to patrol their respective areas.

CHAPTER X

NARROW ESCAPES

THE last week of the year 1915 was to be for the Queenstown Command just one long thrill after another. Three months without any visit by U-boats had, none the less, been kept lively by a long succession of gales; but now we were to have both worse storms and more submarines.

It happened on this wise. Two of the enemy were outward bound from Germany to the Mediterranean, and whilst passing on their way halted just long enough to carry out a notable enterprise, the scene being the south-east and south Irish coasts. Ever since the *Urbino* sinking on September 24 [1] U-boats had kept out of those waters where *U* 41 suffered destruction; but on Christmas Day at 1.35 p.m. (the very annual hour when a seaman's mind is least warlike) the British S.S. *Van Stirum* was suddenly pounced upon. She was an Admiralty transport of 3284 tons, and was steaming through the Irish Channel, being about nine miles W. by S. of the Smalls.

For some while the steamer made every endeavour to escape, but two U-boats were co-operating against her, German shells began to register hits, and at 2.20 p.m. the *Van Stirum* sent out a wireless call:

"Done for. Pick us up five miles south of the Smalls."

A quarter of an hour later one more shell carried away her wireless aerial, she had to be abandoned, and a torpedo passing under one of the partially-lowered boats struck the steamer abreast of her engine-room. This did not sink her, but it killed the boatswain, who happened to be an American citizen from Michigan, blowing him to pieces. At 4.15 p.m. one of the two submarines came along and resumed the shelling, yet even now the *Van Stirum* declined to founder. The first vessel to arrive on the scene of this drama was the Belgian trawler *Nadine*. Like others of her nationality, who had found British help after the fall of Ostende, she was fishing out of Milford. Hearing the firing of guns, her skipper knew something was wrong, so hauled up his trawl and steamed in

[1] See Chapter VIII.

the direction of the sound. Here he discovered the survivors in boats, picked them up and landed them by midnight at Milford. Four patrol vessels of that port presently located the still floating *Van Stirum*, took her in tow, wrestled with her for two whole days and nights, brought her within four miles of the South Arklow lightship, when at last the steamer collapsed to founder in thirty fathoms of water.

Meanwhile the submarines had moved farther south to catch other victims, on December 26 sinking the two steamers *Ministre Beernart* and *Cottingham* sixteen miles S.W. of Lundy Island. Nothing happened on the following day, but by the morning of December 28 one of the U-boats had reached within five miles of the very spot where *Lusitania* sank on May 7; for at 6.30 a.m. the inward-bound British oil-tanker *El Zorro* (5989 tons) happened to be ten miles south of the Old Head of Kinsale, when up rose an enemy to the surface and demanded the steamer's surrender. Captain Mitchell, instead of obeying, went full speed in an effort to escape, and simultaneously wirelessed for help—this call reaching Queenstown almost instantly.

But the submarine's surface speed was such that she kept up with the steamer and pounded her with shells which caused serious hull damage, killing the Chief Engineer. Next followed a torpedo, whose explosion quickly indicated a hit. Captain Mitchell now gave orders for the crew of thirty-two to abandon ship, and they took to the boats. Shells still poured on to the *El Zorro*, so the survivors remained under the lee side for protection, and ultimately a second torpedo was fired, causing large volumes of smoke to rise in the air. Nevertheless, the oil-tanker persistently continued to float.

Now, in response to her bleating, there had been sent out from Queenstown the armed yacht *Greta* and two of those old torpedo-boats previously mentioned. A couple of tugs were likewise despatched, but because of the heavy sea could not make headway; for, if ever foul weather existed, it was now more than begun. In an earlier chapter reference was made to H.M.S. *Adventure*, which first brought Sir Lewis Bayly to Queenstown. Since that date the Admiral ever kept her in readiness to get under way at half an hour's notice by day, and two hours' by night. He used her occasionally to visit the patrols at sea, as also the other ports under his orders, such as Milford, Berehaven, and the Scillies. Equally she was there in case a German raider approached the station, and it will always be a matter for regret that every one of these disguised vessels gave Ireland the widest berth: otherwise a most glorious engagement would have followed.

If news came in over the ether that some vessel had got in distress, Admiral Bayly might suddenly announce: "I am going to sea in half an hour to try and save her." With him went his faithful Coxswain Wade (who had served under him in the *Lion*) and his Steward Murray: both, at a minute's notice, dropped their other duties at Admiralty House and hurried down to the harbour. So to-day at 8 a.m., only ninety minutes after *El Zorro's* signal, the *Adventure*, flying the Admiral's flag, slipped her buoy and departed. She hurried to the south of the Old Head of Kinsale, and began hunting the enemy thence towards the Fastnet.

Spick and span in her grey paint, lean of hull and fine-bowed, with smoke pouring from her four slim funnels, gun-crews at action stations, the *Adventure* was a most impressive sight to anyone, but singularly beautiful to every ship-lover. Even after twenty years the picture of her arouses deep emotion. But this Tuesday, December 28, must be remembered as one of the greatest occasions in her career. At 12.45 p.m., whilst still searching for the foe, *Adventure's* wireless picked up an S.O.S. from the Leyland liner *Huronian*, a fine new steamer of 8766 tons, who was eight miles S. by E. of the Fastnet, and had just been torpedoed.

Off raced the grey flagship at twenty-two knots, and a quarter of an hour later came up with her. It was a most timely arrival, for the *Huronian* was on her way from across the Atlantic with a valuable cargo of grain and cotton: a few minutes later the second torpedo would have settled her fate. The *Adventure* caused the U-boat to disappear and scurry away below the surface without stopping to complete the attack. For some while the flagship steamed quickly in the neighbourhood, but then came forth the two sloops *Begonia* and *Camellia*, together with the armed trawler *Bempton*, who escorted the liner safely into Berehaven, severely wounded though not mortally. The *Adventure* spent the next hours patrolling north and south in the gale that was gradually rising, but if she had been able to rob the enemy of his prey it was only by a small margin that the submarine succeeded in escaping.

Perhaps the reader will forgive a personal impression of that afternoon to confirm the kind of weather which awaited *Adventure*. H.M. drifter *Daisy VI*, in accordance with routine, happened to be at Queenstown for periodical boiler-cleaning, which enabled us to have a few days' Christmas leave. Crossing via the Holyhead–Kingstown night boat had been wild enough, but more fun was to follow. Reaching Queenstown by train at 1.10 p.m.—the very moment that *Huronian* was being plucked out of disaster—I heard the first tidings of this sudden U-boat activity. We were to push off and reach Berehaven without waste of time. This allowed no opportunity to check the dockyard's work of refitting, but by 2.20 p.m. we had raised steam enough, got a few days' provisions aboard, and were off down the harbour. The Irish Sea the preceding night had been kinder to the mail-steamer than to the Milford patrol drifters, forty of them being slightly damaged in what was officially described as " a severe gale," whilst thirty more were injured badly. Presently the wind reached hurricane force, causing the loss of H.M. drifters *Ferndale* and *Ladysmith*; the former whilst trying to enter Milford Haven, the latter being driven on to Skokham Island. In each case all hands were drowned.

As we emerged past Roche's Point into the heavy Atlantic swell and headed westward, it quickly became apparent that this was all in violent contrast to the pleasant London Christmas —its festivities and " business-as-usual " atmosphere. First of all came the sickening sight of the *El Zorro* struggling gamely to keep afloat, trying to limp into harbour with the assistance of the yacht *Greta*, half a dozen trawlers and tugs. She had over eight thousand tons of oil, which the nation badly needed, and her crew had already returned on board; but, as we passed, we could see that only a miracle would prevent her from foundering. A few hours later she had to be anchored near Daunt's Rock lightship, and the trawler *Freesia*, notwithstanding the terrible sea, succeeded in taking off all the crew except one man, who lost his life whilst trying to jump to the trawler's deck. In the darkness it was impossible to save him.

For the fine seamanship displayed, the *Freesia's* skipper afterwards received special commendation from the Admiralty, but unfortunately the gale was such that *El Zorro* that night dragged her anchor, drove ashore at Man-of-War Cove, broke in two, lost all her oil, and for months afterwards remained a ghastly chaos of rusted jagged steel plates. I never passed that marine skeleton without a shudder.

Now, as we headed towards the Old Head of Kinsale, the next unpleasant surprise was to find that the *Daisy's* hitherto reliable compass had gone mad: whereas we were steering west, this overhead compass indicated south-west! There had been no time to test it before leaving, but the dockyard people in recanvassing the bridge-house top had taken up the compass correcting-bars and replaced them in the *opposite* way, thus making the deviation hopeless. The long winter night came on, and so did the reinforced gale, with rain so thick that visibility was almost nil. We were off Galley Head lighthouse about 8 p.m., having a rock-girt coast under our lee; the glass had fallen six-tenths since quitting Queenstown, the seas were monstrous, and, bravely as the ship behaved, it would have been sheer folly to ask her to round Cape Clear on a night such as that.

With reefed (winter) mizzen set, steaming at less than nine knots, she made better weather of it than many a vessel ten times her size; but how would she fare off the Fastnet? And should I be justified in driving her past an unlit coast, in thick atmosphere, with no accurate means of navigation? To run for one of the creeks such as Castlehaven or Glandore, or to attempt Baltimore under these conditions would have been criminal. I therefore decided to stand off and on all night from Galley Head, so as to glimpse its light occasionally through the mist, steaming so slowly (five knots) as almost to be hove-to. Course? I had made it a practice during the War always to carry on me one of those half-crown pocket compasses, in case fate ever made us take to the boats. So to-night we steered by that.

The other two matters which caused some anxiety were: (*a*) the presence of submarines in this vicinity, and (*b*) the possibility of sudden collision, for we were steaming athwart the trade route of vessels proceeding between New York and Liverpool. On the one hand, seaman-like prudence seemed to demand that we should show navigation lights, whilst war sense insisted we should not advertise our presence. I therefore compromised by displaying not my masthead, but only side lights. Moreover, I reversed the latter, *i.e.* letting them be seen from astern, in such a manner that they would interfere with a torpedo's aim, yet might be seen from the high bridge of a liner.

To cut this story short, it remains only to add that, apart from the suspense, the occasional heavy sea which walloped on deck, the annoyance of rats (which had joined us whilst lying in Queenstown), the night ended without further incident, though it was not till ten the next morning that we dared grope our way towards the coast. Eventually Berehaven was reached just after one gale ended and another was beginning. In the fjord lying to her anchor was the *Huronian*, with her fore-part shattered by the torpedo, and later I was to be a guest aboard her. Captain A. H. Highton, her master, had been fifty-one years at sea. He told me the whole thrilling story of how the *Adventure* had saved him from certain destruction, and I asked him what he thought of the weather during our night off Galley Head.

He told me he had logged it as "a fresh gale." Subsequently it was interesting also to learn that Commander G. F. Hyde of the *Adventure* described it as a "heavy E.S.E. gale, high short sea, rain." For the flagship, on her way back to Queenstown during the early hours of December 29, had to reduce speed till she was doing only eight knots. On New Year's Day followed yet another storm of amazing force, so that no patrol vessels (sloops or otherwise) were able to move out of Berehaven, and liberty men could not get back to their ships. Even in Queenstown Harbour communication between shore and Haulbowline was suspended until after 3 p.m; yet out at sea merchant shipping went through a trying experience, the S.S. *Pascal*, for example, losing all her boats and having her steering gear carried away.

But the most remarkable occurrence was that which affected the four-masted Norwegian barquentine *Renfield*. This was a vessel of 1112 tons and 209 feet long: one of those fine steel sailing ships for which Russell & Co. of Port Glasgow made themselves famous as builders in the 'nineties; the *Renfield* having been launched in 1895. I had imagined that the *Pehr Ugland's* escape from getting ashore on Mizen Head established a record; but the *Renfield* beat it easily. She was bound from Capetown to Glasgow with a cargo of maize, and was off south-west Ireland when she got blown to leeward of her course. Her captain told me the whole impressive story, when I went alongside her soon after her arrival. He was Norwegian by birth, but brought up in Australia as a British subject. A first-class sailor-man, he possessed an extra-master's certificate, had spent most of his life in sail, but this New Year's Day of 1916 surpassed all his previous thrills.

One of the nastiest corners of this coast is off the Bull, Cow, and Calf Rocks, which lie at the end of that peninsula which separates Kenmare River from Bantry Bay. It is an inhospitable place even in June, with always an ugly sea; but in the winter there is nothing but atrocious and terrifying waves coming all the way from America to hurl themselves against these rocks. Unfortunately, when in this vicinity the *Renfield* was overcome by the hurricane, so that most of her canvas and two of her boats were carried away. One sea lopped over, and swept over the side half of one lifeboat together with the compass. The captain found two time-honoured bits of seamanship most effective: towing a ninety-fathom warp over the stern, and pouring oil down the " heads " forward. All the same, his ship only just avoided getting on to the Bull. Compelled to up-helm, he had (like the *Pehr Ugland's* master) only a small-scale chart of Ireland, but he ran up Bantry Bay *under bare poles*, not knowing which of these fjords he had entered. Bantry Bay is fortunately wide till you come to the top, and about thirty miles long, with plenty of water. Otherwise this blind navigation would have spelt disaster.

Suddenly the end came in sight where a road runs down to the sea, so he let go anchor barely in time: it dragged some distance, and when the *Renfield* swung head to wind her stern was close to the shore—in fact, barely afloat. She was in a tight corner, and could never get out unaided. Therefore, on the Sunday afternoon, when the gale began to ease, a trawler with *Daisy VI* was sent to tow the barquentine to a safe anchorage, which was all done by nightfall. The crew consisted of several nationalities, including Belgians and Swedes, and it took them two hours to weigh anchor. Round and round they walked with their capstan bars, singing the old sea-shanties for perhaps the last time they will be heard in those waters, leaving with us an indelible impression. But if ever a good ship was lucky, her name is *Renfield*, for whilst she had lost £500 of canvas, her hull and cargo were valued at £36,000; and next day another S.W. gale started up.

Nor was this the last occasion when patrol vessels of the Queenstown Command extricated a sailing ship. But that story must come later.

CHAPTER XI

THE U-BOAT CAMPAIGN

HUMAN imagination delights in drama, since the very essence of life is action and contest from birth till death; but let there be added the element of mystery, and all interest becomes dominated, enslaved, tyrannised, till the finale. For we cannot long exist in a state of suspense, and must pass through uncertainty to find that which is a satisfying solution—no matter whether the pursuit is in the sphere of fiction or of plain fact.

But the finest setting for drama and mystery is against a background of sea and sky, always changing, yet the same untamed environment. In all naval warfare, as opposed to military operations on land, there proceeds the dual struggle between man and man, as well as man against waves and wind. Thus, all sea hostilities have for us an attractiveness of peculiar intensity. Throughout the years 1914–1918, and day after day, were occurring incidents and surprises which seemed so incredible, so exceptional, that a novelist would have been laughed at for using them as parts of his theme.

Take, for example, the following extract from a commanding officer's log, written with no other motive than to state bare truth :—

> Sighted an upturned boat. Proceeded alongside boat and righted it. All gear inside, including sails; also a rug and coat. In pocket of latter a Japanese passport, photo, and seaman's discharge ticket. Name Isaike Lam. Boat and coat full of bullet holes, and life-belts saturated with oil. Remained in vicinity for three hours, but no sign of anything.

No body, dead or living! No clues to the bullet-holes! No ship in sight! Nevertheless, with just this plain statement to work upon, what a glorious mystery of the sea could be elaborated!

Or watch the hand of fate on that splendid French sailing ship *Bougainville* as she passed through suspense to finality :—

> Tuesday. 4 p.m. Sighted French barque *Bougainville* in Lat. 50.45 N., Long. 10.20 W.

Saturday. 4.30 p.m. Sighted barque *Bougainville* again. Noon position was Lat. 50.54 N., Long. 7.5 W.

(On the following Tuesday, *Bougainville* was sunk by submarine 60 miles south of Coningbeg Lightship.)

She had thus hovered for a week between safety and danger; for on March 4 (1916) Germany resumed off Ireland that U-boat campaign which had ceased on September 24, always excepting the brief spasm of Christmas week by the two submarines en route for the Mediterranean.

How the French ship's loss was avenged immediately, by a combination of mystery and powerful drama, we shall presently appreciate; but that this surprise was practicable must be traced back to the inspiration begotten by the *Baralong*. The decoy ship having so undoubtedly proved her worth against the elusive enemy, two tramp steamers had been taken over from the Merchant Service in September 1915 and fitted out as disguised men-of-war. These were, respectively, the *Lodorer* (3207 tons) and the *Zylpha* (2917 tons), each having concealed guns not exceeding twelve-pounders. The former was commissioned at Devonport, the latter at Portsmouth, during October, and were sent to serve under Admiral Bayly. Shortly afterwards the squadron of steam yachts which had been patrolling off the Irish coast, being based on Milford, was despatched to the Mediterranean; which was just as well. For no type of improvised warship proved herself so disappointing as these pleasure craft, and no class was to be so successful as the disguised tramps. About this time also a slight modification was made in the Queenstown area, whereby the Scilly Isles reverted to the Devonport command.

Much has been written in recent years concerning the Q-ships,[1] so that it is necessary here only to tell the principal activities briefly, and to add fresh matter obtained at first hand. A new generation has grown up since those days, and there are many officers on the active list to-day who never beheld a mystery ship: so let the following description of the *Zylpha*, given to me by her one-time First Lieutenant (now

[1] See *Q-Boat Adventures*, by Lieut.-Commander Harold Auten, V.C., R.N.R.; and *My Mystery Ships*, by Vice-Admiral Gordon Campbell, V.C., D.S.O.; for personal narratives. *Q-Ships and Their Story*, by E. Keble Chatterton, is a general history.

Commander Cowap, R.N.R., of the Cunard Line), suffice for perpetuating a picture.

"The *Zylpha* was an old-fashioned tramp steamer more than twenty years old, with a speed of about seven knots. Flush-decked from forward to abaft the engine-room, with a well deck and poop aft,[1] she carried an armament of three twelve-pounders (18 cwt.), two being concealed in deck-houses forward on either bow, and one aft on the poop. Around this latter was erected a wooden box to represent a small deck-house. On going into action, this box collapsed with one pull of a lever. The forward deck-houses were fitted with flaps, which could be dropped very quickly. Actually it was a matter of seconds to bring the guns into action when required. She also carried at a later date two depth-charges on the poop, which could be released by means of a mechanism worked from the bridge.

"Numbers 1, 3 and 4 holds were packed with timber to give buoyancy in case the ship was torpedoed. Number 2 hold was filled with coal for the boilers, in addition to the regular bunker space. The ship thus had a very large steaming radius, and it was seldom necessary to coal her. The forward shelter deck was converted into crew's quarters, hospital, dispensary, Paymaster's office, and store-rooms. Through the various bulkheads openings were cut, so that it was possible to move under cover from right forward in the ship to the after part of the engine-room, as also to the bridge. Communication to the forward guns was established by means of man-holes through the upper deck into the deck-houses. The two forward gun-crews' messes were immediately under their respective guns, the men being always kept near their guns. The after-gun's crew lived in the after-part of the poop. Since this gun could not be reached except by going along the after-deck in full view of any interested spectator, the crew remained there day and night.

"There they had to sit monotonously with very little light and nothing to do except clean their gun, from dawn until dark. To vary their routine, reliefs were sent in the morning before daylight, and at night after dark; but this gun's crew always slept by their gun. The captain lived in the chart room under

[1] See illustrations in Chapter XXI.

the bridge, and the officers in the poop, which was fitted up in very much the same manner as in a sailing ship. Under the chart-room were the hand-steering gear and a room (originally used as apprentices' quarters) converted into the captain's office. It also became the action station of the small-arms party under the Paymaster with two Lewis guns, a Maxim, rifles, and Mills bombs. All guns in the ship could be manned in a minimum of time, the only people compelled to show themselves on the upper deck being (at most) a couple of officers in their poop cabins.

"The routine on board below decks was very much the same as in a man-of-war, except that neither officers nor men wore naval uniform. But discipline had to be exceptionally strict. The crew had to realise that after the ship was 'abandoned' during an action, she was supposed to have been deserted wholly: any sign or sound of occupancy would give the show away. The slogan therefore was: 'Go to your stations, and stay at your stations, without noise and without showing yourselves—at any cost.' We were a heterogeneous crowd. The captain was R.N., all the officers R.N.R., most of the ratings were active service, but some were R.N.R. On the whole, they were magnificent; all were volunteers, many of them being 'hard cases' who had joined *Zylpha* with the intention of getting away from big-ship routine. If they found Q-ship life infinitely more irksome and less comfortable, they appreciated the necessity for all the precautions and responded splendidly.

"The chief discomfort for the crew was the absolute necessity of keeping below decks during daylight hours. A tramp, such as the *Zylpha*, ordinarily would carry a crew of about twenty all told, of whom the greatest number ever visible on deck at sea would be four. Because of our guns we had to carry about fifty men, and whilst anyone was allowed on deck after dark, they were forbidden to smoke. Action stations, abandon ship, and other drills were carried out frequently: sometimes after dark we dropped disguise and exercised guns on a given bearing."

To the *Zylpha* Lieut.-Commander J. K. McLeod, R.N., was appointed as "master"; to the *Lodorer* came Lieutenant Gordon Campbell, R.N., from one of the Devonport destroyers. And it was this officer whose originality and brave enterprise were largely responsible for the Q-ship technique that soon became standardised. Roughly, the latter consisted in luring the submarine on to launch her attack. Then the Q-ship expected to be torpedoed in the opening round of the fight, but her skilful skipper would try so to manœuvre that his vessel received the wound in one of the holds where damage might be less serious. He relied on the packed timber to keep him afloat some hours.

Having been torpedoed, he would next send away the abandon-ship party, numbering about twenty—the normal size of such a tramp's crew. These warriors departed in the steamer's lifeboats, having been carefully drilled to act the part and tell the right tale, if questioned by the U-boat, as to name of ship, port of registry, where bound, where from. An officer pretended to be the master, and carried with him what purported to be the ship's papers, since these were always asked for by the enemy. The "panic party" were instructed to pull away in their boats from the ship, so that all guns of the decoy might bear freely on the target when the right moment should arrive.

At this stage began that terrible time of suspense, of fateful uncertainty. To all outward appearance the mystery vessel was deserted: actually the guns' crews and captain were waiting for the next round to develop. Usually the submarine would now cruise round the tramp steamer, examining the latter from below surface with periscope up; and this period to the British naval officer seemed an eternity. Having at last satisfied herself that after all here was but a genuine, dirty old collier, the submarine would then rise into visibility and approach the lifeboats in order to collect evidence of identity, demand the ship's papers, and (sometimes) take the alleged master as prisoner.

The supreme test of an able Q-ship commander was to know how long delay should be tolerated and when the psychological moment for opening fire had come. Impetuosity and procrastination were equally bad: a hit must be obtained very quickly and with absolute certainty, since the enemy was nervously shy, keyed-up, suspicious. The first flash of a trap-ship's gun would cause instant flight and concealment by submerging. Throughout this trying interval the British commanding officer was lying on his stomach peering through a crack in the bridge canvas dodger, seeing everything, forming his own conclusions of the immediate future, reckoning range, keeping his men alert by a running commentary down the voice-pipes, steadying their excitement, warning them to stand-by. . . . Then, all of a sudden, would come the staccato order. The enemy was now nicely within range and bearing at a convenient angle.

Open fire! Up White Ensign! Down guises! Bang went the guns, and shells struck the U-boat's conning-tower. In a few short minutes the enemy would be sinking for the last occasion, and the tramp's panic party would be rowing rapidly to pick up German survivors. Perhaps at dawn the Q-ship would come steaming innocently up Queenstown Harbour to be repaired by the dockyard, whilst her well-trained troupe of actors went home for ten days' leave, there to receive both decorations and congratulations.

That was the scheme of events if every detail went well without a hitch and the enemy acted his part normally. Sometimes things happened awkwardly, and the U-boat kept right out of the British twelve-pounders' range. By remaining on the surface a long way off, and making deliberate firing from her superior 4·1-inch gun or guns, the German could drop death on the torpedoed vessel, compelling the concealed warriors either to show themselves or perish. In such circumstances the best course was to call up the sloops by wireless and be towed, sinking perhaps, as far as Berehaven; for that U-boat would presently send a radio, warning the nearest submarine of a decoy's presence, giving details as to appearance. Until the tramp had been reconstructed, repainted, externally altered, she could be no further use in baiting the enemy.

Now, the renewed submarine campaign came to Ireland on March 4, 1916, when the S.S. *Teutonian* (4824 tons) was torpedoed thirty-six miles S.W. of the Fastnet, followed by the sailing vessel *Willie's* loss through U-boat gunfire sixty miles N.W. of that rock on the 16th. At 8.30 p.m. on this date, and in about the same position, the S.S. *Berwindvale* (5242 tons) happened to be passing, with 280,000 bushels of wheat, from Galveston, bound for Avonmouth, when the submarine torpedoed her twice and shelled her as well. Fortunately, the sloop *Primrose* arrived before it was too late, rescued the grain ship from certain destruction, and brought her into Berehaven, where for many a day the action of salt water on wheat created an odorous reminder.

These March days had become suddenly intense, and it is now very plain that the enemy was making a fierce concentration off Ireland. On Monday, the 20th, a large submarine was sighted off the mouth of the River Shannon, and next day the S.S. *Aranmore* was torpedoed farther north, some distance from the Mayo coast. Evidently more than one U-boat shared this western side, for next morning at 6.40 Lieut.-Commander Gordon Campbell in the Q-ship *Farnborough*[1] was steaming off the S.W. coast into the Atlantic when $U\,68$ was sighted awash about five miles away. Twenty minutes later came a torpedo, which missed. Next the enemy broke surface and began shelling, so the *Farnborough* stopped, blew off steam, and "abandoned ship," whilst Commander Campbell and his gun-crews waited on board. The enemy closed to 800 yards and again fired, whereupon the Q-ship dropped all disguise, replied with all three twelve pounders, hit the German several times, and saw $U\,68$ disappear. The *Farnborough* then steamed at her full speed of about nine knots over the position, dropped an explosive depth-charge, which caused the submarine to rise almost perpendicularly, displaying a large gash in her bows. At point-blank range five more rounds were now fired into the conning-tower, so that once again the U-boat disappeared. In order to make doubly sure, two more depth-charges were loosed off, after which there rose over the sea much oil and bits of wood. Thus, with remarkable despatch, the decoy-collier not merely saved herself, but defeated $U\,68$ with the loss of thirty-eight Germans, no survivors emerging.

This victory—the firstfruits of Admiral Bayly's extended decoy strategy—had immense moral effect on the Queenstown

---

[1] This was the previously mentioned *Lodorer*. On passage from Devonport to Queenstown she had changed her name, because report had got about that she was something very different from what she pretended to be. Throughout that vile winter she had cruised with her "ill-kempt" crew and "slovenly" appearance, having no luck.

patrols. Besides winning promotion and a D.S.O. for her captain, other decorations for her officers and men, together with £1000 and prize bounty, the *Farnborough* roused such enthusiasm in the sloops' personnel that many officers and ratings were eager to be allotted one of these trap-ships. Coming at the end of an exceptionally severe winter that had tried men's morale considerably, no event at sea could have brought such inspiring courage.

Nevertheless, the situation could not be regarded as healthy. Shipping was being slaughtered like defenceless sheep. Only the day after (March 23), the S.S. *Eveline* (2605 tons), when off the south Irish coast, only escaped total loss because another U-boat's torpedo just missed. Friday the 24th was one of those busy occasions when the Admiral deemed it necessary to leave his Secretary, Paymaster Commander Russell, in temporary charge of headquarters while the Senior Officer himself went afloat in the *Adventure*. More than a hundred miles west of the Fastnet the S.S. *Phrygia* was attacked by a submarine, but escaped; though at the opposite end of Ireland, some thirty miles N.E. of Malin Head, the S.S. *Englishman* received a torpedo which caused the loss of a 5257-ton ship and ten lives.

Throughout that wet triangle Fastnet–Scillies–Tuskar the sloops were having a strenuous time whilst the enemy played his hit-and-submerge tactics with repeated good fortune. It was a game of hide-and-seek, with valuable vessels and more precious lives for stakes. In the days when naval warfare had been waged by ships under sail, at least one could see the foe and his strength for some distance: surprise had scarcely been practicable, and a sea engagement was rather a protracted affair. But all had been changed by modern invention; and elusiveness (no less than rapid action on the part of U-boat as well as patrol) now complicated the struggle beyond all expectation.

Take, for illustration, Lady Day. A submarine had been reported within three miles of the Fastnet, and all the forenoon H.M.S. *Zinnia* cruised about this vicinity hopeful, expectant, yet seeing nothing. Along came a merchant steamer, which the sloop began to escort through an area notorious for trouble. The steamer turned out to be American, who had actually seen the U-boat passing a few miles to the south, but bound eastward. Sure enough, at 2.30 p.m. this enemy was reported farther east off the Cork coast, and half an hour later the *Zinnia* was patrolling that spot. Here she remained till 5 p.m., when a west-bound steamer approached, who had to be escorted through the Fastnet zone.

Meanwhile what happened?

At 5 p.m. this 25th of March the Russian barquentine *Ottomar*, which had left British Guiana on February 6 bound for Liverpool, was sailing a course to give Ireland the widest possible berth, being now forty-five miles S.S.E. of the Fastnet, when *U* 44 unfortunately appeared out of a lonely sea. The ship, under canvas, was heading to the north-east, the submarine coming up on the barquentine's port quarter. The sea had been choppy all day, with a strong W.N.W. wind, and any marine artist would have found a glorious subject in that thrilling race between these two contrasted types: the *Ottomar*, under a press of sail, another of that grand old marine aristocracy soon to vanish for ever, fleeing for her life from a greenish-grey whale-like monstrosity more than 213 feet long and able to motor at over fourteen knots through the waves. As we shall learn presently, even to practised eyes she looked (bows-on) like a tramp-steamer.

Gradually *U* 44 won the race, and when half a mile off opened fire, shooting away *Ottomar's* peak halyards, mainsheet, outer-jib, though, curiously, neither hull nor crew received injury. It was again bad luck that after traversing the ocean, and her destination comparatively near, the barquentine should be waylaid. But nothing is more helpless than a sailing vessel in war-time, so her master must surrender. He luffed up into the wind, the enemy ceased fire and ordered ship to be abandoned. Launching their boat on to the rough waters, the sailormen got in and rowed towards *U* 44, whose captain asked in German for the ship's name, where from, whither bound, and nature of her cargo. On being told that the cargo was timber, the master received a surprise: timber not being contraband, the German informed him the *Ottomar* might proceed, so back on board the crew could go.

By this time the boat had got well to leeward, making it impossible for the rowers to regain their vessel. The submarine tried taking the boat in tow, but the latter shipped much water and turned turtle. Finding themselves in the sea, the sailors swam to the submarine, and all were hauled out except the boatswain, who had managed to right the boat, and he was picked up an hour later. Whilst no lives were lost, this was to be the last they ever saw of their ship; for they were sent below immediately, and then the enemy changed his intention. Opening fire again, he shelled the barquentine till she sank.

A strange change of environment indeed for those who had so recently been looking forward to being paid off and enjoying shore pleasures! For three nights and days they cruised in the belly of this steel whale, and from such evidence as marks on the inside of books as well as the Germans' caps it was pretty evident that this was *U* 44; though, when asked, the captors feigned her to be *U* 287! (No such number had yet been reached in the German submarine service.) Now, the barquentine's master kept his eyes open all the time, though he was not allowed to see much or to have any idea of the courses steered. One night, however, he did observe a red light flashing, and this he timed: the flashes were at intervals of thirty seconds. The U-boat commander told him they were off the Scillies.

Most probably this was an intentional lie, lest the prisoner should know too much. My own opinion is that they were nowhere in that vicinity, but off south-east Ireland, where also this enemy sank the S.S. *Manchester Engineer*. For whilst Round Island (Scillies) exhibits a red light, and its neighbour the Wolf Rock has a group flashing red and white light every thirty seconds, the Barrels Lightship (south-east Ireland) has a red light which gives two flashes every thirty seconds also. It was about 7 a.m. on March 27 that this U-boat torpedoed and sank the S.S. *Manchester Engineer*, and the barquentine's master not merely heard the torpedo leave the tube, but also felt the concussion when it struck the steamer. From other sources we know that the *Manchester Engineer* [1] went down off the south-east Irish coast, some twenty miles W. by S. of Coningbeg Lightship.

Naturally, all these foreign guests were a serious embarrass-

[1] She was taken in tow by the sloop *Lavender* for a time, but her bows already were awash, and salvage became impossible.

ment, both as regards space and food. Although there was sausage, ham, sauerkraut, and drinking water, this had to last thirty men plus six officers till they reached Germany; so the U-boat captain was about to dismiss his visitors into the *Manchester Engineer's* boats when an armed trawler appeared. *U* 44 then submerged quickly and came west, for at 5.10 p.m. on the next day (28th) she was sighted by H.M.S. *Zinnia* seven miles from Galley Head. The German captain told the barquentine's master that at this time a British patrol vessel fired on him. How true this statement is may be seen from the sloop captain's log:—

> 5.15 p.m. . . . Course W. 12 knots. Sighted hostile sub. on surface bearing S. 10 W. about 5 miles. Sub. was painted a greenish grey and had no periscope or cowls visible. She appeared very much like a tramp steamer approaching bows on at a long distance; but was actually steering about W. Two shots were fired at her with range of 4000 and 6000 yards, but both fell short. Sub. after remaining up for abt. 4 mins. dived and disappeared altogether. *Daffodil* arrived later and assisted in search until dark, but no more was seen.

Two hours later, and not far from here, *U* 44 sighted the Irish fishing smack *Pet*, so came to the surface, put the Russian crew aboard her, and thus they were landed at Baltimore. This incident naturally caused no small interest along the coast.

The German commanding officer had told the barquentine's master that three other U-boats were operating round Ireland, and that *U* 44 [1] expected to be out another fortnight or three weeks. Both these statements seem true, for on the same day (28th) was torpedoed the S.S. *Eagle Point*, about twenty miles south of the Fastnet area; and one of these three was responsible for what happened on March 29 a hundred miles farther to the south-east.

The enemy had good reason to hate the sight of a sloop, since this ubiquitous class of vessel had long since begun to impose her will and to cheat U-boats of their prey; so we all expected that no opportunity would be lost for revenge. On this Wednesday at 1.48 p.m. H.M.S. *Begonia* was patrolling

---

[1] *U* 44 on August 5, 1917, torpedoed the Q-ship *Chagford* when about 120 miles N.W. of Tory Island, sinking her; but was also herself damaged. On August 12, whilst going home, she was sunk by H.M.S. *Oracle* off the north of Scotland.

when a torpedo struck her on the port side abreast the foremost boiler-room, and ten minutes later a periscope showed up 500 yards away on the port quarter. These sloops had been so designed that if they should hit a mine forward, they would not immediately sink; and the magazine had wisely been placed aft. Therefore *Begonia*, though in a bad way, still floated, and opened fire at the submarine, which dived, only to reappear 200 yards off. The latter now fired a second torpedo, which passed under the sloop: a most narrow escape.

It is probable that a shell from *Begonia's* foremost gun did some damage, for it exploded on the enemy's periscope. Most likely the German had to withdraw to effect repairs, since nearly four hours elapsed ere she was again observed. This time she kept over five miles away, stationary, and then disappeared in a south-east direction without completing her attack. None the less, *Begonia* was in a sad state, with a huge hole in her side, and a twenty degree list, one man killed, one missing, and one dangerously wounded. In addition, her main steam-pipe had been carried away, her wireless put out of action, thus robbing her of motion or speech. How much longer she might have rolled about before finally foundering of her wounds, or being given the death-blow by a second submarine, is matter for conjecture. Luckily that ancient Brotherhood of the Sea had not altogether departed.

About 8 p.m. the American S.S. *Siberia* fell in with her, came near and passed *Begonia's* messages (asking for help) by wireless. The *Siberia*, like a good friend, also stood by until assistance could arrive. The nearest sloop happened to be the *Snowdrop*, which immediately proceeded to the given position and came up at 10 p.m., *Siberia* then continuing on her course. The *Zinnia* was escorting the S.S. *City of Glasgow* past Galley Head when she heard this startling news, so went off full speed to the south-east through the night. Before 3 a.m. *Snowdrop* had made a fine evolution and secured *Begonia's* wire hawsers in spite of the darkness and a certain amount of sea then running. With her was *Zinnia*, and towing began towards Queenstown. The Admiral had also sent the tug *Warrior*, together with an armed trawler. The cavalcade advanced slowly, but patience was rewarded finally when at 8.30 that night *Begonia* was brought safely into harbour and docked. There she remained until the following August, for during these weeks she was not merely repaired, but transformed into a Q-ship with a counter to replace her cruiser stern, derricks added, and so on. Thus ingeniously disguised to resemble a cargo vessel, she did good work under Lieut.-Commander Basil S. Noake, R.N., till she was sunk by the enemy in October 1917 as Q 10.

The conversion of this and other " Flower " sloops from warships to resemble medium-sized merchantmen was one of the cleverest and most ingenious achievements of Haulbowline Dockyard. The *Tulip*, *Tamarisk*, *Aubrietia*, and *Heather* were all so changed that they fooled most, though not quite every one, of the U-boats. This art of mystification as regards externals became highly specialised, and its success evolved from two minds striving together on a difficult job. To Admiral Bayly and Mr. J. F. Walker, the Dockyard Constructor at Haulbowline, must always belong the Navy's gratitude for the ingenious effects worked out with patience and originality.

Some time after the *Farnborough* and *Zylpha* reached Queenstown, the Admiralty sent a couple more, but the choice had been made with too little imagination. These vessels were of such superior tonnage that to let them pretend they were coasting along Ireland would have fooled no one: their size and build intended them for ocean voyaging, so Admiral Bayly sent them for an anti-submarine cruise in the Mediterranean. Unfortunately, the Senior Officer out there kept them in harbour during three weeks because so many U-boats were roaming about. On another occasion Queenstown was assigned for decoy patrol a vessel that should pretend to be a cross-Atlantic steamer and be seen making her way along the normal liner lane. Actually she turned out to be a steamship with rubbing-strakes prominently showing just above the water-line—the kind of coaster which spends most of her time in and out of harbour, alongside quays. Had this " mystery " ship been instructed to operate well away from land in the Atlantic, suspicion must have been aroused immediately; for U-boats were now each carrying an experienced mercantile officer whose knowledge of detail would mean much.

Finally, the Admiralty was persuaded to let Queenstown

choose and purchase its own mystery ships. A Q-ship officer would be sent over to Cardiff, or to search any likely port, select a steamer of about 4000 tons having the necessary fittings on upper deck for concealment of guns; and with him went a naval constructor to make sure her frames were able to endure weight as well as strain. She would then be brought round to Haulbowline Dockyard, where Mr. Walker had her photographed broadside on, after which he would note the best places for guns, take down the deck-houses and remove hatchways or ventilators or whatever was to be used as gun-position and look-out. The guns would then be mounted, deck-houses put back, the ship once more photographed broadside on; the second portrait being compared with the first. Why? In order to make certain that no pilots or enemy experts might suspect any item of her appearance.

Queenstown thus developed a tradition, its reputation for fitting out Q-ships was neither surpassed nor rivalled; yet Haulbowline was not Devonport or Portsmouth. Ireland was largely unsympathetic, anti-British, and even an enemy country. No doubt (as the Admiral realised only too well) some of these disguises were reported to Germany by certain workmen employed at Haulbowline: indeed, such was the strange situation of affairs that when the Rebellion of Easter 1916 occurred, some of the local employees turned out to be wholly inimical. Q-ship warfare at sea was a wild gamble with death, the odds being slightly against even the cleverest captain. Secrecy of movement, of disguise details, of sailing date, was as difficult as essential when so many spies were about.

But the actual ship alterations were entrusted only to picked, trustworthy men, and even with that precaution there still remained something else to be done. On the quiet perhaps a spy in the dockyard had photographed her when ready for sea. Presently that pictorial intelligence would reach Germany. All right! It was part of Admiral Bayly's scheme that after a Q-ship left harbour she was in some significant manner altered by lowering one of her masts, repainting funnel markings, altering derricks. This would be done at sea the first night, but before coming back to Queenstown she would again be changed to her original condition. Sometimes these vessels would pretend to be foreign neutrals, *e.g.* Dutch or

Norwegian. In those days it was customary for neutrals to have their national colours painted on the hull. Both British Q-ships and German raiders occasionally copied this practice —quite legitimately, provided that before coming into action the White Ensign of the respective country was hoisted. The Queenstown mystery ships used to have a couple of boards, each about four feet square, and hinged together, hanging outside. On these was painted a neutral flag, but before opening fire the upper board was released so that it dropped over the lower board, obliterating the neutral colours.

Few chapters of the War at sea will be in subsequent years so well remembered, and no series of single-ship actions has left behind such glamour, as those of the mystery squadron. Nevertheless, no type of vessel—not even the submarine—was so merciless to personnel. It was very rare that any commanding officer could endure the strain beyond nine or twelve months. Night and day it was one protracted suspense, yet the ship might cruise for months without firing a shot, and every day her people were fighting their own despondency. " Gordon Campbell was at Admiralty House one evening, and said he had been nine months in his *Farnborough*," relates Sir Lewis Bayly; " he had never seen an enemy submarine, and would end the War without firing a gun. At that date he was a Lieut.-Commander, yet within a year he had sunk U-boats, been promoted to Commander and Captain, won a V.C. and D.S.O."

But sudden and comprehensive changes were characteristic of all activities off that coast, so that surprising developments became woven into routine, till the ordinary affairs, by a curious reversal, appeared to be exceptional. Scarcely had we learned of the *Farnborough's* success after so many dull weeks than she was again in action. This time the scene was also off southwest Ireland in Lat. 51.57 N., Long. 11.2 W.; that is to say, some twenty-five miles west of Dingle Bay. At 6.30 p.m. of April 15 Commander Campbell was steaming north in the hope of intercepting a U-boat which had been reported off the Orkneys two days previously and might be expected off the west Irish coast. It was a calm, misty day, and two miles away to starboard was another steamer. Suddenly between the two ships a U-boat broke surface, which hoisted T A F

("Bring your papers on board"), whereupon *Farnborough* stopped, blew off steam, but then quietly kept going ahead towards the enemy, which was more than 200 feet long, and armed with two guns.

In order to gain time, the Q-ship pretended she could not understand the enemy's signal, but also closed the range appreciably, then lowered a boat with the ship's papers, and the stage was set for another neat engagement; but at 6.40 p.m. the German fired her foremost gun, and the shell passed over the ship. Unfortunately, one of *Farnborough's* crew (not being able to see what was happening) thought this was the Q-ship opening fire, so he also fired. This spoiled Campbell's day, forced him to instant action at 1000 yards and certainly the submarine was damaged; but the enemy dived and managed to get away. This proved to be doubly regrettable, since the warning and details presently to reach Germany concerning British trap-ships would make the operations against U-boats much more difficult and more risky. The other steamer was the Dutch *Soerakarta*, bound from the East Indies to Rotterdam via Falmouth and Kirkwall. One of our Berehaven armed trawlers, *Ina Williams*, was only two miles away, heard the firing, came along at full speed ready to open attack, but by this time the incident had passed into history and an enemy crew was thinking unkindly of all tramp steamers.

Of course, this facility in deceiving the Germans had been a success in itself, and it proved that the disguised ship was still likely to be the most effective solution of an increasing problem. Only those of us who went aboard Q-ships, or passed them at sea, ever realised how perfect was the visual simulation. And if friends were deceived, how much more readily would a foe be fooled! In proof whereof let me anticipate a few months, and tell the following story in Admiral Bayly's own words concerning the Q-ship *Dunraven*, in which Commander Campbell eventually won further distinction. Admiral Sims had already reached Queenstown from America and was being shown over the latest decoy.

"One day I took Admiral Sims on board the *Dunraven*, the most perfectly fitted mystery ship. On reaching the deck, he caught hold of the rigging, but it came away in his hand. He leaned against a ventilator, and it gently subsided. He then asked me whether anything in the ship was fixed and reliable, but was told that while he could safely lean against the mast or the funnel, little else would stand his weight."

By the spring of 1916 the Queenstown Q-ships consisted of *Farnborough*, *Zylpha*, *Vala*, and *Penshurst*, which cruised not merely off the south and south-west Irish coasts, but between Milford Haven and the Scillies, off the western mouth of the English Channel, and the whole length of the Irish Sea, thus covering all the areas where U-boats had been known to operate. The *Vala* had been based on Scapa ever since August 1915, but in March 1916 Admiral Jellicoe was able to spare her, so that she came south to Milford Haven, and spent the rest of her career under Admiral Bayly. She was terribly slow—her best speed being eight knots—and of 1016 (gross) tons, or 606 (net) tons. Armed with four twelve-pounders, she was attacked by a submarine on April 21, 1917, at 7.35 in the evening, off the south Irish coast, and in reply probably hit the enemy, who then submerged. On August 19, she again left Milford to cruise between the Fastnet and Scillies, and her last reported position was much farther down the Bay of Biscay in Lat. 47, Long. 9.32 W. at 3 a.m. on the 20th. She should have come into Queenstown on the 25th, but never returned, and till after the War her end was not less mysterious than her type. To-day we know she was compelled to reveal her character, and that one of the bigger U-boats sank her in the Bay with all hands. Thus perished Commander L. A. Bernays, C.M.G., R.N., one of the toughest "hard-cases" and most fearless retired officers, who came all the way back from Canada to join up in the War.

The *Penshurst*, on the contrary, was commanded by one of the most courteous and charming English gentlemen, whose quiet, shy manner concealed an exceptionally gallant spirit. He, too, had emerged from retirement to serve afloat. Commander F. H. Grenfell, R.N., short of stature, slight of figure, one of the few officers with a beard, will always be one of the outstanding Q-ship captains of history, and his *Penshurst* will ever be remembered as a most perfect decoy. She was, to my eyes, ideal for her particular job, and a veritable box of tricks. The facility with which she changed her appearance as requisite, concealed her guns behind wind-screens and in dummy boats that could be immediately collapsed; or the thoroughness with which a tramp's slovenliness was copied—down to the crew's washing hanging from a derrick—was quite remarkable. She was of 1191 gross tons, armed with a couple of twelve-pounders and two six-pounders. Although, like *Vala*, she had for months been cruising off Scotland, it was not until the last day of November 1916 that Commander Grenfell in the English Channel bagged his first submarine, when he sank *UB* 19, that had recently torpedoed a Norwegian ship. Nor was this to be the last of her adventures.

But for the present we must leave these mystery ships, and follow a complication which of all the war theatres was unique.

CHAPTER XII

SINN FEIN AND GERMANY

It was a very bored seaman who, after much patrolling off south-west Ireland, summed up the environment as nothing but "rocks, sea, and Sinn Feiners." If this aphorism seems to exaggerate, it is the over-emphasis of a caricature rather than a false statement. Britain's time of anxiety was to be Ireland's opportunity for exultation; Britain's ultimate defeat by Germany was to mean future prosperity for Ireland. That was always uppermost in the minds of those dwellers in villages and cliff-side hamlets, remote farms and water-side communities. During the last year, when matters on the Western Front had been none too satisfactory and the submarine campaign had been taking a heavy toll of shipping, Sinn Fein activities in the west and south of Ireland gradually increased, till it was obvious to the casual observer that something was coming, a crisis maturing. Between the British naval forces and the average Irish inhabitant there was—with a few outstanding exceptions—but little fraternising, and generally a sullen politeness represented the nearest approach to friendship. Later on this coolness developed into open hostility, so that if officers or men went for a walk along a lonely country road, they might be subjected to insult and assault.

It is necessary to stress the fact that three years before the War broke out, Sinn Fein and Germany were already intriguing; that a series of articles appeared in seditious Irish newspapers, and in the Irish-American press published in the United States, urging a German–Irish Alliance in the event of trouble breaking out between Great Britain and Germany. Whilst the world was still at peace, that strange person Sir Roger Casement had already begun writing articles in this sense, and immediately after the declaration of war he, in conjunction with Kuno Meyer, some time Professor of Celtic Languages in Liverpool University, collected them into pamphlet form. Excerpts in large numbers were smuggled into Ireland from Germany and America, thus considerably adding fuel to the fire which burned determinedly. Any appeal for national freedom, and especially when addressed to ardent romantic temperaments, must always have a certain success that culminates in definite action. Little wonder, then, that this propaganda in due time brought about a clear crisis.

Casement, himself, was a romantic Irishman, but not less ill-balanced mentally; wildly impulsive, extravagantly enthusiastic, unconditionally sympathetic for the under-dog—whether of the Congo or Erin's Isle made no matter—he was above all things a complete sentimentalist. At the age of forty-eight he had retired from the British Consular Service with a Knighthood and C.M.G. This was in 1912, and now he was able to employ his whole energy on behalf of Irish Nationalism. The War had come one year sooner than he had expected, and the summer of 1914 found him in the United States, whither he had journeyed for the dual purpose of getting in close touch with Irish-American revolutionary associations and making plans with the German Ambassador, Count von Bernstorff.

Casement left America late in October (1914), and was in Berlin by the beginning of November. He crossed in the S.S. *Oscar II* by that very north route which passes near the Faroes towards the Scandinavian peninsula. Now, the *Oscar*, like certain other Danish, Norwegian, and Swedish liners, was as evasive as she was suspect. Later on they were infrequently stopped and examined for mysterious passengers by Admiral de Chair's blockade vessels; but at this date the squadron was not yet sufficiently established, so Casement had little difficulty in getting through. A few days later he cabled from the Foreign Office, Berlin, to Bernstorff:—

> Lody's identity discovered by enemy, who are greatly alarmed and taking steps to defend Ireland and possibly arrest friends. . . . Send messenger immediately to Ireland fully informed verbally. No letter (? upon) him. He should be native-born American citizen, otherwise arrest likely. Let him despatch priest here via Christiania quickly.

Lody was the notorious Carl Lody, who had been arrested on October 2 at Killarney, and was executed in the Tower of London on November 6 as a German spy. The " messenger " reached Ireland at the end of November, and the priest (John

T. Nicholson), an American of Irish birth from Philadelphia, reached Germany by January, and began work with the Irish prisoners of war. Whilst Casement was bringing pressure to bear on the latter, in order to co-operate with his plan, the big plot was maturing in America.

Kuno Meyer had crossed to New York, and on December 6, 1914, addressing a meeting of the Clan-na-Gael of Long Island, said:

"It was in the summer of 1911 that I lost all hope of peace between England and Germany. I have visited many of our prisoners' camps, and had many talks with the English and Irish among them. At a station called Lohne I fell in with a train containing Irish soldiers who were being drafted from all parts of Germany into one camp for the mysterious purpose which I have hinted at before. That an invasion both of England and Ireland will take place sooner or later I, together with all my countrymen, firmly believe."

Next followed further organisation, when in February 1915 a German spy named Albert Sander,[1] who had offices in 150 Nassau Street, New York, formed the "Friends of Peace" society, whose object was to aid Germany in securing an embargo on the exportation of United States munitions to the Allies and keep America from entering the War. This fraternity was worked in conjunction with the Clan-na-Gael. In February 1916 was being founded "The Friends of Irish Freedom" association in America, with an office also at Stockholm for maintaining close touch with the German Government. Events were now to happen rapidly.

It was on February 10, 1916, that Von Skal (of Bernstorff's Washington staff) sent a letter per S.S. *Sommelsdyk* addressed to an "agent" in Rotterdam containing an extract from John Devoy, ex-Fenian, chairman of Irish–American Revolutionary Associations, and also confidential agent between Germany and Sinn Fein. This despatch contained the following significant phrases:—

Unanimous opinion that action cannot be postponed much longer. . . . We have therefore decided to begin action on Easter Saturday.

---

[1] Sander was sentenced two years later to a couple of years' imprisonment for military enterprise in the United States against Great Britain and Ireland, and for sending spies to both these latter.

> Unless entirely new circumstances arise we must have your arms and munitions in Limerick between Good Friday and Easter Saturday. We expect German help immediately after beginning action.

On March 4 came the following cable from Foreign Office, Berlin, to German Embassy, Washington:—

> Between 20th and 23rd April, in the evening, two or three steam-trawlers could land 20,000 rifles and ten machine-guns with ammunition and explosives at Fenit Pier in Tralee Bay. Irish pilot-boat to await the trawlers at dusk, north of the Island of Inishtooskert, at the entrance of Tralee Bay, and show two green lights close to each other, at short intervals.

This was getting down to real practical details, and three weeks later it had been arranged that three trawlers with a small cargo steamer capable of carrying 1400 tons were to be sent from Germany. Beginning from April 8 Nauen wireless station was to broadcast every midnight the code word "Finn," meaning that the cargo had started as arranged, or the word "Bran" if a hitch had occurred, the wave-length being 4700 metres. Urgent messages were also being sent on April 18, 19, and 20 from America fixing the evening of Easter Day, April 23, for the delivery of arms; asking if submarines could be sent to Dublin; requesting Germany also to make both an air raid and a naval attack to coincide with the rising, followed by a landing of troops—" perhaps from an airship," was the naive Irish suggestion.

Germany, however, replied: "Sending of submarine to Dublin harbour impossible." The landing of troops was equally out of the question, though the other items will now be seen in operation. She was anxious to give proof of her sympathy with Ireland, and expected that an Irish rising would cause Britain to withdraw from the Western Front so many thousand troops for suppressing the insurrection that the World War would be materially shortened. The only question now was whether the ship carrying munitions would succeed in getting through the British blockade off north Scotland, but the safe return of the *Moewe* after raiding in the South Atlantic showed that, whilst this part of the voyage might be risky, it was not hopeless.

Very wisely the German naval authorities dispensed with

trawlers, but on March 21 selected both ship as well as commanding officer. The latter was Lieut. Karl Spindler of the Naval Reserve; the former was really the Wilson liner *Castro* (1228 tons), which at the beginning of War happened to be in a German port, and thus fell into enemy hands. She was just the ship for such a job, and must now be fitted out with hidden manholes, concealed entrances, dummy bulkheads, somewhat after the manner of our Q-ships. The same dockyard secrecy was maintained, the crew likewise were taught to discard naval smartness and copy the habits of a small merchantman's hands.

Nothing was left to chance, and with Teutonic thoroughness she shipped a cargo of piece-goods bearing shippers' marks as for Genoa or Naples. This, of course, was the "camouflage" cargo, consisting of tin baths, enamelled steel ware, window-frames, etc. They were placed above the arms and munitions, so that if the *Castro* should be stopped and examined by a blockade ship off Scotland or a patrol off Ireland, everything would seem consistent with the vessel being a Norwegian ship trading to Italy. Whilst the real freight comprised large quantities of rifles (captured from the Russians at the Masurian Lakes *débâcle*), trench tools, bombs, cartridges, surgical dressings, and practically everything that a rebel army could desire, externally she was a genuine trader with faked Norwegian logs, certificates, manifests, and even a Norwegian compass. In order to be most meticulously accurate, such items as chalked tally-marks on the hatches (usually visible aboard a vessel recently out of port) and the men's trouser buttons (betraying no German manufacture) were not forgotten.

The captors of *Castro* had changed her name to *Libau*, but before putting to sea the latter was obliterated and her Norwegian name of *Aud* was painted instead. Spindler had a number of interviews with Casement, who was about to leave Germany with two Irish companions, but nothing would induce the renegade to voyage in the *Aud*,[1] and doubtless this

[1] The *Aud* had been fitted out at Wilhelmshaven (alongside the recently returned raider *Moewe*), but passed through the Kiel Canal to Lübeck as a merchant ship about to load cargo. According to Lloyd's Register, she was built in 1911, had one deck, and was 250 ft. long by 35 ft. beam.

nervousness was connected with recollection of his trip in *Oscar II*, as also with the disconcerting fact that so recently as February 29 (1916) the German raider *Greif* had been sunk whilst trying to run the blockade. It was therefore decided that the *Aud*, with her munitions of war, should sail from Lübeck alone on April 9, bound for Fenit in Tralee Bay. Casement and his two fellow-travellers about April 12 left Kiel in *U* 22, and this submarine was to rendezvous in Tralee Bay, where Casement would be put aboard the *Aud*, after which Spindler was to act under Casement's instructions.

It may be mentioned that whilst one of these companions was an Irishman who had served with the British Army on the Western Front and been taken prisoner, the other has been officially described by the British Government as " a dismissed ordnance store conductor," "an Irish Volunteer organiser who had gone to America and thence to Germany." Spindler described him as " a thorough-paced scoundrel." The reader can therefore draw his own conclusions of Casement's choice.

Now, whilst the *Aud* and submarine are pursuing their separate voyages, let us view the situation from another angle.

It is to-day common knowledge that the British Naval Intelligence Department of the Admiralty during the War was unsurpassed for its efficiency; consequently this projected coup was not entirely a surprise. I have already hinted that those of us who were serving off southern Ireland could feel a crisis approaching. Admiral Bayly had reason for supposing that on or about St. Patrick's Day (March 17) an attempt would be made to land arms for the Irish Volunteers (Sinn Feiners), so special precautions were taken to have the coast watched. Well to seaward he placed an outer ring of sloops ready to intercept any strange vessel, whilst the coast-line and bays were patrolled by smaller craft such as armed trawlers, armed steam drifters, and small motor-yachts. Eight trawlers were stationed between Kerry Head and Mizen Head, the drifter *Golden Effort* was in Kenmare River, and my *Daisy VI* in Dunmanus Bay. These special arrangements were in force from March 16 to 18, but (as we have seen) the enemy had not quite completed his co-operative plans, so more than a month must pass. Nevertheless, a careful watch was being maintained.

During this interlude submarines were far from inactive, and they were now again coming via the Dover Straits. On April 7, for example, one of the Dover drifters saw a U-boat cut through the wire nets with ease. There was no type of vessel to which a submarine would approach so closely as a sailing ship, and for the good reason that she could not hit back. We have mentioned the case of *Ottomar*, but on March 25 the Norwegian barque *Gunn* (483 tons) was boarded by the enemy and made to jettison much of her cargo; six days later the Norwegian barque *Bell of Tonsberg* was sunk, and on April 1 the British barque *Bengairn* (2127 tons) was sunk by a submarine's gunfire 165 miles W.S.W. of the Fastnet. With these facts in mind, four small sailing craft were taken up and fitted out as decoys.

The distance at which the enemy had begun to operate away from shore patrols is notable and highly significant. The S.S. *Zent* (3890 tons) was torpedoed twenty-eight miles west of the Fastnet at 10.20 p.m. on April 5. It was a very dark night, forty-nine lives were lost, but the sloop *Lavender* was keeping such a good look-out that the cries of distressed mariners actually were heard over the inky sea. The *Lavender* stopped, assistance was rendered, and *Zent's* survivors were found clinging desperately to an upturned boat. What a situation of apparent hopelessness, tossed about the limitless ocean! What a miracle of deliverance!

But a similar activity was manifested at the opposite end of Ireland's south coast five days later. At 11 a.m. on April 10 quite a large number of steamers from Liverpool were passing Waterford, when H.M. yacht *Beryl* (commanded by a retired Admiral) on patrol sighted the two periscopes of a U-boat moving fast through the water and making for a steamer which was coming up on the armed yacht's port quarter. The *Beryl* gave chase, but the enemy submerged. Ten minutes later her periscope was seen 300 yards off, though a good shot from the steam yacht's foremost gun caused her to seek refuge in flight. A signal was made to warn the steamer, who now began to zigzag, and any attack was frustrated.

That same afternoon, however, about three o'clock the Belgian trawler *Gaby*, fishing out of Milford, when ten miles off St. Ann's Head watched a submarine come to the surface a couple of miles off, and then remain in sight for twenty minutes. The *Gaby* went out of her way to report the news to Admiral Dare in Milford, who at 6 p.m. sent the armed trawlers *Nodzu* and *Trier* to search the vicinity. Sure enough, at 7.50 p.m., when eight miles from St. Ann's Head, a submarine came to the surface. The *Nodzu's* gun was trained in the submarine's direction at the time, and fire was immediately opened. The first shot fell thirty yards short, but the second and third shells hit the submarine's deck near the conning-tower—range 200 yards. The fifth shot likewise struck the target, but shortly afterwards the breech-block jammed, and by this time the German had submerged.

Thus, even in cases where the enemy had not been sunk, at least he was sent home licking his wounds; whilst the moral effect on his crew was such that caution next time might replace enterprise. Tales of narrow escapes would be told to their opposite numbers in Kiel and Wilhelmshaven, nerves might become strained, and on a future sea occasion the sight of any patrol vessel would be the time for quickly submerging. Under these circumstances it was much safer for a U-boat to be allotted a station well out in the Atlantic, where the only danger might be a Q-ship. In this manner on April 11 was the British barque *Inverlyon* (1827 tons) sunk at 4 p.m., when 108 miles west of the Fastnet. The submarine had cleverly disguised herself with four masts, a dummy bridge and funnel, so as to represent a steamer. Nor did she need to waste a torpedo, for she kept her safe distance, and thus shelled the defenceless sailing ship. It was all so easy! And two days later the S.S. *Chic* (3037 tons) was sunk with no more difficulty forty-five miles from the Fastnet, causing the loss of her master plus eight other lives.

Thus we come to that memorable Thursday before Easter, April 20, and its complications of events well illustrate the incessant demands that were being made on our patrols. The day opened with the mortal wounding of the S.S. *Cairngowan* (4017 tons) by submarine's gunfire when sixty miles west of the Fastnet, but fortunately no lives were lost. The following account, written at the time by *Zinnia's* captain, records their rescue in fewest words. It was at 9 a.m. that the sloop's officer of the watch sighted the *Cairngowan* on her beam ends at the horizon, and shortly afterwards the conning-tower of a submarine in the middle distance, whereupon H.M.S. *Zinnia* quickened her step.

> Speed increased to full, and a zig-zag course begun. Opened fire at 8000 yards, but did not see fall of shot—due to swell and sun's glare. Gun could only be trained by bearing. A second shot was fired, and seen to fall to the left. The sub. then appeared again at about 5000 yards and dipped at once. I then saw two ships' boats. A depth-charge was fired without result near where sub. dived, and on closing the boats I was told that he was still about lying in wait. I signalled to *Bluebell* to join me.

After cruising about the spot and being joined by this other sloop,

> I then picked up the two boats of S.S. *Cairngowan* containing the master and crew: 33 all told. Hoisted one boat at our motor-boat's davits, and towed the other to Berehaven. The master stated that the sub. first fired a torpedo at him, which passed underneath. *Cairngowan* turned and ran, so sub. came to surface and shelled him. As the master could see no ship, he took to the boats only about ten minutes before we appeared on the horizon. Our first shot fell between the two boats and over the sub., so sail was hauled down from the steamer's boats lest it should attract our fire. The sub. started out to attack us, then appeared disconcerted by the zig-zag, put up his periscope near the boats, and disappeared. Crew were landed at Berehaven at 5.30 p.m. and I returned to patrol.

I have still vivid recollections of that Thursday, which was a glorious spring day with a light north-east wind. Whilst patrolling west of Berehaven the *Zinnia* passed me bound in with her survivors, and five minutes later who should come along but H.M.S. *Onslow*, the latest thing in destroyers, fresh from the Clyde. This lithe grey creature, fifty feet longer than the biggest submarine, was a great surprise, for destroyers off this coast were about as rare as waterfalls in the Sahara. What was in the wind? A few weeks later she was to distinguish herself at the Battle of Jutland, but now she had been detached by the light cruiser *Gloucester* and was bringing in a suspicious Belgian trawler to be examined in Berehaven. I was soon able to assure *Onslow's* captain about the trawler's bona fides, but what was H.M.S. *Gloucester* doing off the coast somewhere round the corner?

For answer let us watch the sequence of events from the seafaring side, since the success or failure of this great Easter Rebellion depended on maritime conditions, and it was the Royal Navy which must decide the issue. Hitherto writers, in stressing the political or military aspect, have failed to appreciate the all-important fact that Spindler's *Aud* represented the essential link, the hinge, the corner-stone, the vital help: call it what you will. Thanks to the alert patrols during preceding months, the plotters had not been able to receive those munitions which a complete and comprehensive rising demanded. It is true that in the Dublin area arms and ammunition were fairly plentiful; but in spite of houses being looted for shot-guns, and the theft of explosives from quarries or warehouses, the south and west of Ireland lacked the implements of war. The *Aud* was to supply this deficiency entirely, but she could only do so by evading the sea patrols. If once she could get alongside Fenit pier and remain undisturbed for a few hours to unload her genuine cargo, nothing would or could prevent a fiery rebellion spreading from Kerry to Cork and Cork to Dublin. How long this would continue, what would be the ultimate result on the European War, how many thousand troops must be withdrawn from France, and what schemes might be developed by Germany for invasion, there could be no telling: yet the probabilities were all too serious.

This naval side of the exciting story is now presented for the first time in its fullness before the opportunity passes. My authorities are the Commander-in-Chief himself and some of the other naval officers who played conspicuous parts during those fateful days. But, in addition to private documents, personal narratives, and conversations, I am able to rely on my own notes, written down immediately after the actual happenings. In a few short years both manuscripts and memories will have faded, so perhaps no apology is needed for giving this subject at last its rightful detail. Ireland will never cease to be a problem, and the same difficulties may be repeated by future history; but the conditions of surrounding sea and the use of ships will continue as unalterable as basic principles.

CHAPTER XIII

THE EASTER REBELLION AND THE SEA

Now, early that April an intimation had been sent to Sir Lewis Bayly from the Admiralty that a landing of arms was to be expected on the west coast for the Sinn Feiners, and that Roger Casement was believed to be on his way thither; so the Admiral informed his patrols and warned the signal stations to keep a good look-out for a steamer acting suspiciously. " We expected the danger-spot to be Fenit, near Tralee, as it was known to be a centre of Sinn Feinism; and this suspicion was intensified when news came from the police officials that a large number of motor cars from all parts of south Ireland were assembling. It was said that about 240 cars were there, and it seemed likely they had assembled to fetch arms."

On the very day that *Cairngowan* had been sunk Admiral Bayly's forces up the west coast had been temporarily strengthened by H.M.S. *Gloucester* and four destroyers of the Grand Fleet in readiness for uncertain incidents. On this day, also, did the *Aud* arrive at her destination. In her Norwegian disguise she had proceeded via the Kattegat and Skagerrak, thence up the North Sea to where the Arctic Circle intersects the meridian of Greenwich, so as to avoid the blockade patrols. Coming south-west, she was scrutinised but not boarded by one of the latter, carried on down the Atlantic to make Rockall Islet, was again scrutinised by an armed merchant cruiser though not stopped, and on the afternoon of Thursday, April 20, was near the River Shannon's mouth. She began to get ready for landing the real cargo, so must first heave overboard the false upper cargo of window-frames, tin ware, zinc buckets, and the like.

The rendezvous where *Aud* had arranged to meet Casement's submarine was one mile N.W. of Inishtooskert, an uninhabited island at the N.W. end of Tralee Bay, and here the steamer arrived by 4.15 p.m. But, to Spindler's bitter disappointment, no U-boat was in sight. According to the orders issued before leaving Germany, Spindler was to wait half an hour, and then, if the other party failed to put in appearance, the *Aud* could either run into Fenit or turn back home, as Spindler deemed advisable.

He waited, and waited. Nothing happened. No Casement. No one on Fenit pier to welcome his arrival. Complete blank! He steamed about the Bay till after dusk, displayed the prearranged green signal, but answer came there none. The sleepy place was in darkness, so finally, at 1.30 a.m., *Aud* anchored in the shadows of Inishtooskert. Spindler realised that the well-laid scheme of ships and men had gone adrift. It would be folly to run alongside the pier without Sinn Fein co-operation: he would never be allowed to unload without official interference.

The dark hours passed, dawn illumined the island; it was now 5 a.m. when the armed trawler *Setter II* (Skipper John Donaldson, R.N.R.) came alongside and boarded. This ex-fisherman was based on Galway, where the Senior Naval Officer of the patrol area including Tralee Bay was Commander F. W. Hanan, R.N. The latter tells me that although he was keeping a trawler in readiness to go out, he had expected the German steamer would not arrive till a day later.

Unfortunately, Donaldson was bluffed by Spindler and deceived by the *Aud*. In this brief engagement of wits certainly the German won. He entertained Donaldson, pretended that a breakdown of the ship's engines was the cause of anchoring, showed him the *Aud's* papers, and even removed part of the hatch from No. 2 hold. But in such a situation a skipper who has spent all his life fishing is at a disadvantage. Spindler was a smart fellow, brought up in the Merchant Service, experienced in the technicalities of ships' documents, an expert in cargoes and stowage. Such matters were outside a fisherman's cognisance, just as the handling of trawls would have been strange to Spindler. Thus, when Donaldson made a cursory examination and observed that her cargo was packed *not* in boxes, but in open crates, through which could be plainly seen the camouflage of pots and pans mentioned in the manifest, his suspicions subsided and he became satisfied of her innocence. So, after a while, he resumed his patrol, though not before he had left Spindler bewildered and despondent. The neighbourhood was surrounded by all sorts of naval vessels and (to use Spindler's[1] own words), "We had chanced into a wasps' nest and could count ourselves lucky if we got out again in the next twenty-four hours." He therefore resolved to wait under the island till dark, then get thirty miles out into the Atlantic, away from all signalling stations and steam south to Spain.

But soon after 1 p.m. Spindler had another unpleasant shock.

At the northern extremity of Tralee Bay lies Kerry Head, which also is the southern boundary of the Shannon, Loop Head being at the opposite side of the river's mouth. From the north side of Kerry Head Spindler saw a small steamer approaching at speed, having a gun on the foc's'le and wireless between her masts. This could be none other than a patrol, so the German hurriedly weighed anchor, got under way, and cleared out to the westward in something of a panic. Now, the stranger was the armed trawler *Lord Heneage*, commanded not by a skipper, but by Lieut. W. H. A. Bee, R.N.R., who had spent years in the Merchant Service. He had learnt from Loop Head signal station that a steamer was hovering about the entrance of Tralee Bay suspiciously. That was a good enough hint for this officer.

The *Lord Heneage* happened to be one of the bigger trawlers such as fish in Icelandic waters, and bows-on she might well scare the *Aud*. As the former passed Smerwick signal station a message was semaphored that the foreigner was heaving things overboard, and this confirmed Bee in his suspicions. Off he went in full chase, joined presently by *Setter II* after hailing the latter. The *Aud* was fleeing for her life and exceeding the limit of safety. "More steam!" ordered Spindler. "Captain," replied his Chief Engineer, "if we go on like this the boilers will burst. The steam is long past the red mark." She was doing two or three knots more than *Lord Heneage*, so that, whilst the latter opened fire at long range, nothing could be done to stop the fugitive heading clear of land into the wide Atlantic.

But Bee did the right thing. If unable to do the job your-

[1] See *Gun Running for Casement*, by Reserve-Lieutenant Karl Spindler. London, 1921.

self, give your friends a chance. The *Setter* had no wireless; the *Lord Heneage*, as we have remarked, possessed wireless. Several hours had by this time passed, the chase had been fruitless, so Bee sparked out a message that a suspicious vessel had been sighted west of Tearaght steering S.W. This radio was picked up at 4.30 p.m. by two sloops, H.M.S. *Zinnia* and *Bluebell*. The former was some distance farther down the coast, though *Bluebell* happened to be nearer.

At 11.30 that forenoon, whilst on my patrol, I had passed near Dursey Head a Norwegian steamship proceeding north, and on her hull were painted her national colours, as was the custom during those years. She was a quite ordinary "three-island" tramp type, yet, for some inexplicable reason, sufficiently impressed me at the time to note her in my deck log. Two days later, when *Zinnia's* captain was relating to me his adventure and describing the *Aud*, she seemed exactly and curiously like the above vessel. Not till five years later, and the publication of Spindler's narrative, did this strange coincidence become clear.

There was simultaneously a real *Aud* of Norway, and about this time she was due back from the Mediterranean outside Ireland on her way to Bergen. The false *Aud* had the lettering *AUD NORGE* and Norwegian colours painted on her side like the genuine *Aud*. Always during this voyage there existed a possibility of the two steamers meeting at sea, both looking alike down to ridiculous details, and each displaying the same bold lettering. It would have been an awkward moment for the German. But to-day as Spindler was passing the coast he unquestionably sighted my Norwegian, and it gave him a thrill. This is how he describes the incident:

> A couple of small steamers deeply laden were crawling along northwards, hugging the coast, for they were too much afraid of the German submarines to venture out on the open sea. The second one was a Norwegian—"like ourselves." The name was, on account of the distance, unreadable, but the shape of the vessel was devilishly like that of the *Aud*. I wonder if this was the real *Aud*.

At any rate, she must have been the vessel which passed me five hours earlier, for her speed was about ten knots, and at that time only fifty miles separated the two.

Meanwhile, on this memorable and strange Good Friday

the most extraordinary things had happened, and the first intimation which reached me was when passing Cahirmore signal station. The coastguard semaphored:

> Arms and ammunition found in small collapsible boat at Tralee four a.m. to-day coming to Cork.

For a few seconds it seemed just one more of those silly stories which are born every day of an Irish year. Then I wondered if the signaller in his lonely outpost was suffering from too much reading of detective fiction. The mental picture conjured up a first-rate opening chapter, and I even found myself, whilst watching the genuine Norwegian tramp-steamer, weaving an exciting romance against a background of sandy beach with mysterious men lurking inland. But who where they? Why had they left their weapons behind? And whence had a collapsible boat been launched? Perhaps the coastguard's signal was plain fact? Later on the truth was revealed, though it had to be pieced together from many sources. Here is the history.

On the Thursday night Lieut.-Commander Weisbach in *U 22* with Casement reached the Inishtooskert rendezvous, and from a distance sighted the dark outline of the anchored *Aud*. Unfortunately, the submarine people mistook this outline for a British destroyer. Finally, Casement, despairing of *Aud's* arrival, acted independently, and was landed with his two companions on the beach by means of a small collapsible boat which had been secured to the submarine's upper deck. They slept in one of those small mounds, with a hollow at the centre, locally known as a "fort." Early this Good Friday one of the natives, John M'Carthy, after coming out to pay his devotions, saw the deserted boat, wherein lay revolvers and ammunition. They were taken to the police station at Ardfert.

At 4.30 a.m. a girl named Mary Gorman saw three strangers, whose presence at this hour aroused her feminine curiosity, so she at once informed the Royal Irish Constabulary that one of the trio was a tall, black-bearded man. This was Casement, and the police were on the watch for him. They now shadowed him, but were uncertain of identification, so communicated with the Admiral at Queenstown, who at once sent an officer capable of recognising the misguided renegade. Meanwhile Casement had gone to the railway train, where this officer had no hesitation in establishing the bearded man's identity. Although he gave a false name, here was Sir Roger Casement, the traitorous ex-British official who was the prime instigator of German-supported rebellion. He tried to rid himself of his secret code, but a boy picked up the paper and gave it to the police. Another unfortunate incident! After being arrested Casement was taken to England and Bow Street Police Station. Under the ancient Statute of Treasons, dating from A.D. 1351, he was tried, convicted, and at eight o'clock of the following August 3 was hanged at Pentonville Prison. So ended his career. One of his companions escaped, but the other was arrested.

If ever an ingenious effort was muddled and mismanaged, it was in Tralee Bay. One can almost sympathise with the captains of the submarine and *Aud* for having been brought on a fruitless errand. A wireless message had been sent to the former cancelling her orders, but somehow it had not been received, and it was a ludicrous situation that both ships should actually have arrived on the same scene yet failed to make contact. To-day we know that no one at Fenit awaited the *Aud's* arrival on either Thursday or Friday: she was not expected until Saturday. But why this postponement?

Obviously before the steamer could come alongside to land her munitions, Fenit pier must be seized. The 240 motor-cars had waited in readiness to dash off as soon as loaded, but they were compelled to depart empty. Why this cancellation of plan? Three of the rebel leaders had come down from Dublin to Limerick, who were to take charge of proceedings and lead an attack that was to capture the pier. At Limerick they hired a motor-car, refused to tell the chauffeur where they wanted to go, but they said they would direct him by their map. This they did, and drove in the direction of Tralee. Having got near Fenit among some cottages, they commanded the man to take the first turning to the right, and he obeyed. Nor had he traversed more than a few yards ere disaster followed with dramatic suddenness. A mistake had been made, with fatal results; for over the edge of solid stone leapt the car, and it landed upside down in water that drowned the three leaders. When their bodies were fished out, enough weight of revolvers and cartridges was found in their pockets to have kept them from floating. Only the chauffeur was saved.

Thus a delay for landing *Aud's* munitions had been imperative, and lack of good communications had prevented Spindler (who had no wireless) from knowing the state of affairs. But the ex-Consul had been ultimately less of a help than a hindrance. As the Irish leaders some few weeks later wrote to Bernstorff, " The sending of Sir Roger Casement to Ireland was very unfortunate. . . . No one can get either in or out of Ireland now."

The collapsible boat had a somewhat rough passage before it landed on that part of the Tralee neighbourhood locally known as Ballyheighe Bay. A fresh northerly wind had piped up, slopping into the canvas craft, so that sea water was actually found with the revolvers. When the Base officer at Fenit was able to telegraph Queenstown what had been discovered, Admiral Bayly knew the *Aud* could not be far away, and wirelessed his patrols that if she were sighted they were to bring her into the nearest port for examination. His next news came from Sybil Point (south-west of Tralee Bay) that the *Lord Heneage* and *Setter* were chasing a steamer, flying the signal " Stop at once," but the steamer was taking no notice.

When at 4.30 p.m. H.M.S. *Zinnia* (Lieut.-Commander G. F. W. Wilson, R.N.) and H.M.S. *Bluebell* (Lieut. Martin A. F. Hood, R.N.) received the *Lord Heneage's* signal, they hastened towards the spot from different points of the compass. *Bluebell* sighted Spindler's ship at 5.40 p.m. still steering to the south-west, and at 6.15 p.m. caused her to stop. Th. Norwegian flag was still flying from her ensign staff, she had a black hull, two yellow masts, one funnel with black-and-white band. Captain Wilson tells me: " I met her just after *Bluebell* had arrived on the scene. The steamer proved to be a ' three-island ' tramp, apparently built for the Baltic timber trade, and a new ship. Nothing suspicious could be seen, so I ordered her to proceed, and started to shadow her pending further orders. Just as these arrangements had been made, the Admiral signalled that if S.S. *Aud* was met, she was to be sent in to Queenstown for examination. *Aud* was very slow in answering signals, and asked if I wished to see her papers; to which no reply was made, and I ordered *Bluebell* to escort her in."

Spindler realised that the game was up, and all chance of escape now impossible. Never having seen this sloop class before, he took them for "auxiliary cruisers." " All the steamers of the Channel service seemed to have been concentrated against us." (He was not so badly guessing, for bows-on these sloops did somewhat resemble the Calais–Dover ships.) " Ahead, astern, in fact all round us, we could see smoke clouds . . . we should have been caught in any case, no matter what course we had taken."

A tribute, certainly, to the perfect watch that was being kept off that coast!

But he was a tiresome fellow, and began asking questions when given orders. In vain he protested the ship was bound for Genoa. This caused quite a good laugh for months after; for why was she so far inshore if on her way to Italy? Then this sort of dialogue was signalled :—

Aud. May I proceed?
Bluebell. Wait.
Aud. Please inform me why.
Bluebell. Follow me to Queenstown. Course S. 60 E.

Spindler pretended not to understand, though to-day he admits he was trying to fool his opponent. Hood lost all patience, and now came the flash of *Bluebell's* forward gun. A shell dropped over the German's bow. " We were all stupefied for a moment by the violence of the concussion," says Spindler. He realised that he must do as he was bidden. Nothing further happened that night, and the *Aud* " came along quietly."

Next day (Saturday, April 22) at 9.25 a.m. the weather being calm and beautiful, these two vessels were off Daunt's Rock lightship and when (to be exact) 1400 yards S. 56 E. thereof—that is to say, just outside Queenstown Harbour— the *Aud* suddenly stopped engines, lowered boats, into which every German clambered, after which followed an explosion; the gun-runner bursting into flames and fragments till she sank. Spindler had used those bombs and fuses, which were to have been employed otherwise, in destroying his ship. Before so doing he had hoisted the German naval ensign at his main truck and another at his ensign staff.

The *Bluebell* stopped and picked up the total of captain, two warrant officers, nineteen petty officers and men. These twenty-two had all been drafted from patrol vessels based on Wilhelmshaven. Lieut. Hood was a young officer, but looked younger than his years. Somewhat shy, retiring, an athlete, he was in command of his first ship, and had done excellently. By firmness and vigilance he had brought the German through an anxious night, so that we can sympathise with his feelings at this final disappointment. He died not long after, but his name will ever be associated with an historic capture.

There was an amusing incident, however, which angered Spindler and caused great laughter among the British seamen. Arrived on board the *Bluebell*, Spindler was met by a " boyish-looking lieutenant," whom he requested to conduct the *Aud's* captain to the sloop's commanding officer. " For answer there was a derisive laugh from the crew." It was Lieut. Hood to whom the German was speaking!

From Queenstown the prisoners were taken by H.M.S. *Adventure* that night, and reached Milford Haven en route for Chatham. Spindler, as he admits, was treated with courtesy and kindness, given an officer's cabin. " Discipline, order, and cleanliness," he wrote, " were simply perfect on the *Adventure*." Nevertheless, Spindler left behind a bad impression at Queenstown. When the Admiral sent his barge and coxswain to fetch in this commanding officer; and the coxswain—Chief Petty Officer Wade, who had served under Sir Lewis Bayly so far back as the days that first saw H.M.S. *Lion* steaming into Berehaven—offered to help Spindler with his suit-case, the German rudely rebuffed him. Perhaps Spindler was doubtful of British honesty. Anyway, the laugh belongs to the coxswain, for the suit-case was found to be full of English golden sovereigns, and some time later after the War C.P.O. Wade followed his Admiral in retirement to take up a job in one of the big London banks!

Another of Spindler's mistakes was to imagine that the sinking of *Aud* had blocked up the entrance to Queenstown. This was a foolish conception, seeing that she foundered in fifteen fathoms (ninety feet) a mile outside. The Admiral lost no time in sending down divers, who discovered the sea-bed strewn with four-pounders, seven-pounders, rifles, machine guns, bombs, ammunition, all blown through a hole made by the explosion. Many samples were brought up, together with the two naval ensigns, of which one was framed and placed in the *Bluebell's* ward-room. The rifles, which had been deemed good enough for Sinn Feiners, were by no means modern. The butts bore the stamp and date of Orleans small arms factory, 1902. The barrels were marked with the Russian War Office arms and near the same was the word " Deutschland."

The nett result of *Aud's* failure, and Casement's capture, was to stamp out the rising which should have swept across southern Ireland, and to localise the trouble about to flare up in Dublin. But why had the blockade armed merchant cruisers off Scotland only scrutinised the *Aud* and neither boarded nor sunk her? The answer is that they were following instructions: the Navy was on the look-out for her, and wished Spindler to pass unmolested. " We knew he was coming," remarked Admiral Sir Reginald Hall, late Director of Naval Intelligence at the Admiralty, " and watched him most of the way. There was no object to be gained in sinking him in the North Sea; we wanted to make certain that he intended to carry out the object with which he was credited—namely, to carry supplies to Ireland—and this could only be proved by the arrival of the ship at her destination."

During this same month of April a seizure was made by the United States Government of certain documents at the office of Wolf von Igel, 60 Wall Street, New York, and selections were published by the American Government. From these it became clear that the " advertising agency " which von Igel had founded in the autumn of 1914 was in fact a branch of the German Foreign Office, and used for German–Irish plotting. He had done his work with thoroughness.

But if on the west of Ireland laboriously planned efforts had been ruined by precipitation and bad Staff work; if, as John Devoy, ex-Fenian and chief agent in America for communication between Sinn Fein and Germany, frankly remarked, Sinn Fein knew Casement "would meddle in his honest, but visionary, way to such an extent as to spoil things, we did not dream that he would ruin everything as he has done." On April 17 a request had been wirelessed via America to Berlin asking the Germans not to land the arms "before the night of Sunday 23rd," though both Spindler and Casement were already on the Narrow Seas, so it was too late. When Casement landed, on Good Friday, he sent messages to Dublin (by the companion who escaped), urging the leaders not to go on with the rebellion, and it was this, in addition to the report of *Aud's* suicide, which caused the Dublin leaders to postpone the beginning until Easter Monday instead of twenty-four hours earlier.

In spite of all that had happened during preceding days, the news from Dublin which reached the patrols certainly came as scarcely credible. By good fortune I happened to be due at Queenstown on Easter Tuesday for refit and boiler cleaning, so we were right in the centre of most interesting activities. As we steamed into harbour, the first noticeable sight was the patrol trawlers, with sand-bags as mantlets round their bridges, ready (if needs be) to go up the river to Cork. All mails ceased, no trains came from Dublin, every contact between there and Queenstown was cut off. In order that the British General might communicate by wireless with the outside world, Admiral Bayly sent H.M.S. *Adventure* to Kingstown; and, for the purpose of carrying mails, a destroyer was kept running from Queenstown to Milford Haven.

For Admiral Bayly this Easter Rebellion brought increased duties and responsibilities: in addition to the war with Germany, there was fighting on Irish soil, and who knew at that time what might be the next development at sea? The Admiralty[1] gave him an entirely free hand: he was on the spot—in a foreign country almost—so knew, much better than Whitehall could tell him, what had best be done. In

---

[1] Had other Government Departments taken a hint from the Admiralty, this Irish Rebellion need never have occurred; but not even the capture of *Aud* and Casement moved them. For all time the blame must rest on Mr. Augustine Birrell, nine years Chief Secretary for Ireland, who by his neglect and ill judgment ruined his own political career. But see later, page 168.

THE COMMANDER-IN-CHIEF, COAST OF IRELAND
Admiral Sir Lewis Bayly, K.C.B., K.C.M.G., C.V.O.

response to his request there were sent him (besides the *Gloucester*) the battleship *Albemarle* and 2000 marines. This 14,000-ton man-of-war, armed with four twelve-inch guns, was anchored slightly up river from Queenstown at Passage West. Instantly the story buzzed round the county that she was there to bombard Cork if the situation developed. Seeing that Cork was five miles away, and not visible, this old battleship might have found it difficult to carry out such an operation; but no one outside the Service realised this fact, and the floating threat had salutary results.

The marines had lately done service in Gallipoli, so were prepared for anything, but their arrival and quiet efficiency surprised Irishmen. One morning Queenstown woke up to find the front of Haulbowline lined with tents, gun emplacements, light guns, machine guns, the marines having occupied the spot and settled down before anyone suspected their arrival. This had an excellent effect, for most of the dockyard workmen were undoubtedly still Sinn Feiners, as indeed were Queenstown, Cork, and the neighbourhood in general with a few exceptions. It is curious to remember that this essential naval base, with stores, docks, and all the means for keeping sea warfare active, was situated in the very centre of a community which hated England and co-operated with Germany. One would have expected a sudden onslaught against Haulbowline, destroying its dock gates, setting the stores ablaze, and so on.

But it was never attempted either before or after the marines' arrival. To the Anglo-Saxon the mentality of an Irishman, with his strong idealism, his weak logic, and love of being governed, is something not easy of comprehension. That Sinn Fein men, with relatives among the insurgents, should continue to refit the sloops which captured the *Aud* seemed strangely unreasonable. Nevertheless, no acts of sabotage occurred, no disloyal demonstrations were made, no workmen's committees set up; but, in addition to normal routine, they were responsible for a brilliant achievement.

That very keen and able soldier, General Stafford, asked Admiral Bayly if the dockyard could fit him out an armoured train. The dockyard officers had never attempted such a thing before, but they set to, exercised great ingenuity, and (strangest of all) the dockyard workmen never protested, but toiled away in the most satisfactory and prompt manner. I well recollect talking one evening with a military officer who was just off to bring the train from Queenstown to Dublin. All communications having been cut for days, this was an interesting risk; but he got through, and the Dublin rebels were thus not exactly aided by their Haulbowline friends. Perhaps the high wages that were being paid at the dockyard, and the large increases periodically, may have had something to do with this lack of outward sympathy.

Although subsequent to the War the Irish burnt Admiralty House till it was a mere shell, no sort of attack occurred during the period of which we are speaking. Here were the very head-quarters, the directing brain, the confidential charts, secret telegrams and documents, the very driving force of the campaign against Germano-Irish operations; yet no ugly incident happened, and the Admiral went up and down the hill without molestation. The solitary bit of excitement was as follows.

Some of the marines had been posted at the House, and a few days later, about one o'clock in the morning, during a fog, something appeared to be moving. The marine sentry at the gate listened, heard a footstep, challenged, challenged again. Getting no answer, he fired at a moving figure very dimly seen in the fog and darkness. The gates were shut, so the footstep must be that of someone who had no right to be there. The sentry advanced and examined the corpse: the shot had gone straight to the victim's head, and death had been instantaneous.

But the body turned out to be that of a donkey, which had somehow strayed into the grounds. "It cost me two pounds," says the Admiral; "one pound to the sentry for having made such a good shot, and one pound to the old woman (who owned the animal) so that she might buy a new one." But the news quickly ran round Queenstown neighbourhood, and no one ventured to approach Admiralty House after sunset.

With the actual Rebellion in Dublin and the horrible scenes which lasted from Easter Monday, April 24, till it was suppressed on May 1; the burnings and murders; the 3000

British and Irish casualties, we are not here concerned. But on Easter Monday matters were looking very serious in the west of Ireland. The Senior Naval Officer at Galway was Commander Francis W. Hanan, R.N., who had come back from retirement and taken up this duty six months previously. Galway is, geographically, a remote corner of Europe, though the nearest port to America, and fifty miles to the north-west lies Clifden, with its important Marconi transatlantic wireless station.

On Easter Monday, Commander Hanan found himself more isolated than ever. The first suggestion of anything wrong was that all telegraphic communication was stopped. Luckily the Sinn Feiners had omitted to cut the telephone to Clifden, so the Admiralty got in touch with him by cabling to America, and this message was wirelessed back to Clifden. By a mistake, it was sent in a code which Commander Hanan could not translate, and he therefore asked for a repetition in another code. The operator at Clifden also erred by trying for hours to call up the Admiralty direct, instead of via America, and it was only by chance that an Admiralty operator heard Clifden. Thus not till late on Monday evening did the Commander learn from Whitehall that rebellion had broken out in Dublin, and serious street fighting begun.

He now informed the County Inspector of the local Royal Irish Constabulary and the Major commanding a small draft at the military barracks. The County Inspector sent out to withdraw all his men from outlying districts, and they all came in to Galway, except those in Athenry, who were cut off by a rebel force. The Commander and County Inspector consulted and decided to arrest all known disaffected persons of the district. This was done so thoroughly and easily because all the neighbouring Sinn Fein leaders had come into the town for a conference.

And here was a typically humorous Irish situation. The leaders were standing by, awaiting the signal for rebellion, but their friends had cut the line before a telegram could be sent! Therefore they must all collect in Galway to know what was going on at all! (It reminds me of an incident which happened lower down that coast before the War. A regatta was being held, and at night, after the races, a display of fireworks was to take place. These fireworks were entrusted to a man named Patrick, but somewhere about 4 p.m. Patrick got drunk, set himself and the fireworks in a state of conflagration, the display of squibs and crackers was made in full daylight, and all the money that had been subscribed so hardly became wasted.)

The most popular plan discussed was to advance on Galway from two sides, and seize the Bank of Ireland and the Railway Hotel, the latter to become a Sinn Fein base. But with the sudden arrest just mentioned, the bands of rebels from west of Galway were left leaderless, and melted away. It was a bold and courageous stroke, and the best place for the leaders was aboard one of the trawlers, where they would be safe. That night it blew hard, and a report was made that in the vicinity was a submarine. This made the trawler with her prisoners put to sea till next day, when she returned. Meanwhile (as we shall immediately observe) a sloop arrived, to which they were temporarily transferred. A little later the cruiser *Gloucester* came in, aboard which they were finally placed and taken to England. Hence arose locally the story that " the Commander has sent them to sea and drowned them, begorrah."

On Easter Tuesday news reached Galway that a force of 1200 rebels had seized the Government experimental farm near Athenry and besieged the Athenry police. " Being anxious to relieve the latter," writes Commander Hanan, " we got a railway ganger to examine the line in the ordinary way during the day, and he reported it undamaged nearly as far as Athenry. I accordingly requisitioned an engine and some trucks for the police. Just after dark they made a dash for Athenry, the County Inspector and about twenty men together with some of mine charged up the street, were sniped at (only one wounded), relieved the besieged police, and returned with them to Galway."

Of course, in such a country as Ireland, and such a distant corner as Galway, it would be impossible for tragedy to be unmixed with comedy. Commander Hanan, being himself an Irishman, was not insensible to the inevitably humorous side. " I spent the night rounding up all the motor-cars in the district. We got about twenty; and at 4 a.m., with some naval men, police and special constables, set off to scout round in the direction of Athenry. Some five miles out we were ambushed and one policeman was killed, but the party of about sixty rebels bunked, though it was afterwards reported that some had been wounded. Our special constables (who had just been enrolled) were armed with D.P.O.[1] rifles, which I had got from the military barracks. I had one myself, and fired one shot, which spat grit into my face, after which the rifle refused to function any more. Being held-up at a cross-roads, not knowing if any rebels were left, I, with one or two sailors, crawled behind a cottage and peeped over the wall, whence we could see down the side road and observe whether it was clear. But it was the police who were in occupation!

"One of the police, on sighting us, mistook our heads for the rebels, and shouted out: 'Begorrah! There the divils are!' And took two pot shots at me, the range being about twenty yards. He missed once over each of my shoulders. It had always been a controversial question as to whether the Royal Irish Constabulary, having been given rifles, should be taught how to use them. I decided the matter for myself at that moment."

Although little enough information was derived from this scouting expedition, it had become obvious that, with Dublin all aflame, developments might be expected. Commander Hanan on Tuesday had sent off a message that the rebels were marching on Galway, whereupon Admiral Bayly wirelessed through H.M.S. *Adventure* (now at Kingstown) informing the British General at Dublin. The latter, however, replied that he and his troops were surrounded, so no help could be sent.

The Army being incapable, it was for the Navy to deal further with this land situation, and late on Tuesday the Admiral sent H.M.S. *Laburnum* off to Galway "with all despatch." This sloop arrived next morning, and her captain (Lieut.-Commander William W. Hallwright,[2] R.N.)

[1] "Drill purposes only."
[2] At a later date he commanded the disguised sloop *Heather* (Q 16). A year after the Rebellion, one April morning in 1917, about breakfast time *Heather* was suddenly attacked by a submarine, whose sixth shot killed "Bill" Hallwright, a piece of shell passing through his head whilst he was on the bridge looking through the peep-hole.

went ashore to see Commander Hanan. "I asked him," relates the latter, " to be ready to help the police with her twelve-pounders if necessary, and on going back to his ship the *Laburnum* took up a position where she could cover approaches to Galway from the east. During the forenoon the police sighted some motors on the road. We had occupied the cemetery (which commanded the only eastern approach to the town), by forty police, some of my men, and a few convalescent soldiers who had been wounded whilst serving in France. The sloop now opened fire, and my signalman stationed at the cemetery informed *Laburnum* of the approaching cars."

This indirect method of firing was for the sloop's gun-layers a new experience, but only ten shots were necessary, and the effect was very great, though considerably magnified by Irish imagination. It struck terror in the rebel camp about seven miles away, and wild stories flew round the county that "hundreds" had been massacred in Galway, " guns were being landed," and all sorts of punishments were impending. But the net result of Commander Hanan's prompt pluck in having arrested thirteen of the leading trouble-makers, and the arrival of *Laburnum*, kept Galway from joining in the rebellion. The neighbourhood and town were notoriously anti-British. By superiority of numbers the people could have killed every sailor, soldier, and policeman; but now the whole rebel camp began an orderly retreat, which speedily was transformed into disgruntled gangs of sullen men trickling back to the countryside. Just as the rebels in Dublin felt they had been badly let down by Casement and Germany, so the Galway insurgents regarded now their leader.

The latter was a half-German, says Commander Hanan. " Some days later I walked out to see what damage the sloop's guns had made, and met a countryman, who told me the half-German had not been amongst the party which were fired at. ' And sure,' added the countryman, ' that's the lad the bhoys would like to be meetin' an' layin' their sticks across his back. Why, indeed? Arrah! Whin he heard your great guns banging, what did he do but " Fall in, bhoys," he sez, " bhoys, all is lost." And him hoppin' on his motor bicycle, and *off*! ' "

The thirteen ringleaders placed aboard a sloop were put down in the fore-compartment, where they were given water and ship's biscuit. Not till some days later did Commander Hanan learn of the rebels' retreat, and on this Wednesday at 1 p.m. he had wirelessed asking for 200 marines. Next day the sloop *Snowdrop* escorted the transport *Great Southern* conveying 100. H.M.S. *Gloucester* also reached Galway and landed hers. Other marines were brought by the *Great Southern* with *Snowdrop* on the following Sunday. But by May 1 the period of suspense ended, and the Dublin rebels surrendered. Of the 160 persons convicted by courts-martial, fifteen were executed, and among these was P. H. Pearse, one of the seven who had signed the Declaration proclaiming an Irish Republic. The night, before his execution, Pearse wrote a final letter adding the following postscript: " The help I expected from Germany failed: the British sank the ships."

Like many other statements emanating from Ireland, this was true only in part. We had not " sunk the ships," but the one ship had sunk herself. Moreover, the Germans definitely kept their promise of rendering support off the east of England. On Easter Monday, to coincide with the Rebellion, a Zeppelin raid was made on East Anglia. Next day another Zeppelin raid was made on Essex and Kent, whilst a German naval force of battle-cruisers, light cruisers, and destroyers bombarded Lowestoft as well as Great Yarmouth, damaging 200 houses at Lowestoft to the value of £36,000, and killing four people, besides sinking a decoy trawler.

The half-German leader of the Galway rising, and one of Casement's two companions, both escaped to America, where they were given an enthusiastic reception by Irish organisations, and began preparations for a further attempt to land arms between February 21 and 25, 1917.

After the Dublin Rebellion 3430 men and seventy-nine women were arrested, of whom 159 men and one woman were convicted, the latter being the notorious Countess Markievicz. They were sent for internment in England. The British military Commander-in-Chief at Dublin having asked for means of transportation, two Queenstown sloops were sent, and brought over the prisoners. Naturally, the naval officers tried to do what they could for the comfort of this one eccentric woman on board, but her behaviour was such that they were compelled to desist.

At that time Mr. Asquith was Prime Minister, and bearing a note from him arrived Lord Midleton, a large landowner in south Ireland. He had come over to offer any help to the busy Admiral, and the kindly gesture was greatly appreciated. On his departure he was also generous enough to leave a case of fifteen-year-old Irish whiskey, but this gift had to be enjoyed by others: the Admiral rarely touched alcohol, and from the date when Buckingham Palace went "dry" during the War, Admiralty House followed the royal example.

Next came Mr. Asquith to Dublin and Cork. The Premier having expressed a desire to stay the night at Admiralty House, his visit had to be arranged without any local manifestation of the emotions likely to cause embarrassment; so the Admiral's barge was sent with a Lieutenant in uniform eight miles up the river to Cork. Thus, whilst the crowds both at Cork and Queenstown railway stations were still waiting, Mr. Asquith was fetched, landed, met at the pier by Admiral Bayly, and driven up the hill without a sign from anyone. That evening the two distinguished men sat down and discussed recent history. "Mr. Asquith told me," says his host, "that he had been to see the Irish prisoners, had shaken hands with many, and had asked whether any of them were in want of anything; and when a man asked for a clean shirt the Prime Minister promised it should come. Mr. Asquith came down into my Operations Room, and his knowledge of ships carrying munition cargoes from the U.S.A., and the ships which I was escorting, was quite wonderful. He went back to England in the *Adventure*."

Another visitor came to call on a different mission. It was Bishop Browne, mentioned in an earlier chapter, and his duty was solemn. Among those condemned by Dublin court-martial to be shot was a foolish Irish lad aged nineteen. The Bishop had known him all his life, and was sure that the boy had been misled. Could he be reprieved? Would the Admiral try? If so, the Bishop would guarantee the youngster's good behaviour and bear his responsibility. Now, amid all the strife, the plots and intrigues, the insurrections and submarine sinkings, there is something intensely poignant about this sudden pause; something very human in the venerable prelate calling on his illustrious neighbour to plead for impulsive youth. To-day many sores have healed, many incidents done in hot blood have been forgotten like an old worn-out calendar. But the Navy, the Army, the Constabulary, immediately following Easter of 1916 were still feeling it difficult to dismiss feelings associated with anger and indignation. Under such circumstances only men of high purpose and great self-control know when to ease up on steel discipline.

But that interview was without precedent, and stern disciplinarian as the Admiral ever was, I have never found officer or man who disagreed that whenever a delinquent received what was due he likewise got the maximum of justice. Conversely, no good service was allowed to pass unnoticed, without some encouraging commendation. On the mantelpiece in the Admiral's office stood a small framed card, which must have been seen by every commanding officer, every visitor who called on business. This card contained the following words: "By the help of God I will keep the balance level." Throughout those trying four years at Queenstown and the daily multiple anxieties of persons and things, when the scales of fortune tried to go up and down, it amazed us all to see this consistent equilibrium. No matter how grave was the present, or how threatening the immediate forecast, you got no hint of it from the Admiral's manner. I watched him closely during those critical few days after Easter, and learned a lot; but, especially, how one may preserve unruffled calm when most people are storming, how "you can keep your head when all about you are losing theirs and blaming it on you."

So the Bishop went away in suspense, but with a promise that the Admiral would do his best. The best was at once done. He wrote to the military Commander-in-Chief, who also combined discipline with level thinking. The boy was let off. And if he has grown up to middle age, he owes it to the three Wise Men.

Would that there had been a similar prudence in a certain administrator. Mr. Augustine Birrell, who died in 1933, was for nine years Chief Secretary for Ireland, but his political career had been brought to a sudden disastrous conclusion owing to his blindness and hardness of hearing: blind to what was obviously oncoming, deaf to the hints which were being offered. A capable orator, a keen book-worm, he was disappointing as a man of affairs. Unchecked, he suffered the Sinn Fein movement to mature because, as he later confessed, he deemed it his duty to run even great risks for the purpose of maintaining during war time the appearance of " unbroken unanimity."

Having failed to realise the seriousness of minor events or to interpret the omens, he was taken by complete surprise when Easter arrived with the big smash. After the Rebellion had been suppressed there remained but one alternative: he tendered his resignation, and it was accepted. In his pathetic speech made before the House of Commons he compared the smoking ruins he had just left in Dublin to " my own ruins " of political hope and aspiration. But there is no doubt of his having been the unintentional cause of complicating the World War, increasing the weight of burdens already considerable, and exposing the British Isles to additional dangers. In the words of the Royal Commission which presently reported on the insurrection, Mr. Birrell was " primarily responsible " for the situation he had allowed to arise.

CHAPTER XIV

NAVAL DETECTION

FAR more entertaining than most ingenious puzzles are the mosaics of history. Having collected each fragment, each worth-while event, how strange and wonderful a pattern reveals itself in due season! By regarding the whole, rather than its component parts, we perceive not merely the big scheme of things, but surprises of sequence.

At dawn on the first Sunday of May 1916 *Zinnia* met and escorted that same Leyland liner *Huronian* which had been torpedoed and barely rescued during the previous Christmastide. It was good and encouraging to see this vessel again at sea bravely risking the enemy, yet on Monday another famous Atlantic steamer, but nearly twice the Leylander's size, came to a sad end; for the White Star *Cymric* (13,370 tons) was torpedoed on the afternoon of May 8, though she did not actually founder till early next morning. Five lives were lost.

Now, there are two notable points which here interest us. First, this sinking took place so far distant in the Atlantic as 138 miles west of the Fastnet—far beyond the patrol limits—in Long. 13.17 W. This conveyed an impression that the enemy was so shy of the inshore vigilance by sloops and smaller craft, that it would be safer to operate farther out. The obvious answer was for the patrols likewise to be placed farther out, whilst not relaxing watch on bays or other suitable places for surreptitious landing. Normally the sloops had not cruised farther west than Long. 11.30 W., and just now not merely armed trawlers, but even sloops were on duty from Galway to Sybil Point. However, with the Rebellion broken, and H.M.S. *Gloucester*, together with the Royal Marines, having departed, local dangers eased up so that armed auxiliary vessels were once more responsible for inner areas, whilst the sloops could now extend their patrols even to Long. 13.30 W.

Nevertheless, as we know to-day from our mosaic, this extension was bound to be unrewarded; for once again external authority had checked the logical sequence of affairs.

Away back on March 24 the British S.S. *Sussex*, while running between England and France, had been torpedoed by a German submarine. Inasmuch as many U.S.A. citizens happened to be on board this passenger ship, another wave of anger went reverberating. Would the Germans always be tactless and internationally shortsighted? Had the *Lusitania* lesson still not been learned? The *New York Herald* asked whether anything was to be gained by maintaining any longer "the ghastly pretence of friendly diplomatic correspondence with a Power notoriously lacking in truth and honour." Thus on April 20 America presented a note to Germany threatening to break off diplomatic relations altogether, and this caused an order whereby no U-boat was to sink a vessel before stopping her, examining her papers, besides allowing all passengers and crew to leave. Admiral Scheer realised that submarine warfare on those conditions would be impossible for his officers. They would be at the mercy of every trap-ship and many other vessels defensively armed. Scheer not unnaturally preferred to call off the campaign for the present, and recalled his U-boats by wireless, so that from May 8 till August 2 no sinkings of merchant ships by U-boats occurred off the British Isles or in the Western Approaches. The chances of hurting American susceptibilities accordingly disappeared, one more international crisis came to nothing, and the United States by a narrow margin just kept out of hostilities.

Meanwhile, the enemy became very active in the Mediterranean with his torpedoes; and in Home Waters with his minelaying by submarines—the latter being a clever way of achieving his main desire by other means. In spite of these two factors, however, Germany was still like a man compelled to fight only with his left hand, the effects of American intervention being most clearly seen from the following simple figures. Whereas in April thirty-seven British merchant ships had been sunk, this figure fell in May to twelve and in June to eleven. Then the Mediterranean sinkings in July raised the number to twenty-one, in August to twenty-two, and in September the figure reached thirty-four: yet it was not till the third week of October that the submarines came with their torpedoings even so near to Ireland as 120 miles

W.N.W. of Tory Island in the north, or thirty miles west of the Fastnet in the south. The peak (in numbers, though not quite in tonnage) was for that year attained in November, when forty-two ships were destroyed, and it was not until the following February brought its eighty-six losses, March its 103, April its 155, that the climax of the whole war happened.

The difficulty, obviously, was to know the enemy's actual strategy, to penetrate into his mind. These sudden transformations from hectic weeks of crippled ships to dull months of nothing to report were incapable then of comprehension: every day some further resumption was being awaited, and the stage was all set for the drama's continuance. Both inward- and outward-bound Atlantic traffic was kept close along the Irish coast, and long before the general employment of convoying was to be inaugurated (with such excellent success) the sloops had been doing their special convoy work. Ships with such valuable cargoes as munitions or aeroplanes from America, mails, and human lives—some distinguished personages returning from a mission to New York or Washington—were escorted through the danger zone with a sigh of relief on the part of every officer responsible. As for the Queenstown Q-ships, they were this summer cruising along the trade routes so far Atlantic-wards as Long. 17 W., as far east as the Isle of Wight, as far south as the middle of the Bay of Biscay; whilst their northern limit was not till the Hebrides.

Notwithstanding all these arrangements, the tragedy in its big scenes was being held up indefinitely and mysteriously; yet during this period the enemy was hurrying on the construction of a large submarine fleet, putting his new personnel through an intensive training for the 1917 campaign. So, for the present, the minor incidents became of major importance, till the curtain should rise on a big Act II.

One of the most surprising of these lesser episodes was concerned with the ship-rigged iron vessel *Terpsichore*, which had been built on the Mersey for Messrs. B. Wecke & Sons of Hamburg so far back as the year 1883. She was beautiful to behold, and of 1935 tons, measuring 269 feet in length. In August 1914 she happened to be at Limerick, where the

British Government seized her, and subsequently she was chartered from them by a Liverpool firm. Now, on April 15, 1916, she sailed from Halifax bound for Runcorn with a valuable cargo of timber. In those times prices were high, and £12,000 had been paid for freight. The *Terpsichore* was uninsured, but the total sum of freight, cargo, and ship amounted to £34,798.

All went well until exactly a month later she was near the Fastnet and expecting to sight the south-west Irish coast after crossing the Atlantic. This May 14 was foggy, and I happened to be patrolling near Mizen Head, noting that visibility was not more than about 300 yards. Early that afternoon came along this picturesque old-fashioned sailer, doing well with a fresh W.N.W. wind on her quarter, when she heard two bangs to the north—obviously the Old Head of Kinsale, which has an explosive fog signal giving two reports every six minutes: so she held on to her course that might bring her along the south coast towards St. George's Channel. Judge of the master's amazement when, a few miles farther, he suddenly saw looming up ahead out of the woolly mist some low-lying land, islets, and jagged rocks. Trying unsuccessfully to wear her, and expecting to hear the ugly sound of his hull being crunched, he noticed a very narrow opening between the rocks, and promptly steered for it in an almost desperate effort to cheat fate.

This opening was not more than eighty feet wide, and the ship herself measured forty-one and a half feet in beam, so that she cleared obstructions with only some six yards to spare at either side. She was doing a good seven knots, with all canvas set; and one need scarcely wonder at the captain's alarm to find *Terpsichore* rushing into Hell's mouth helplessly. A few moments later she stopped with a jerk, but most miraculously making no water; and when the fog lifted it was to reveal that she had struck the one sandy patch amid an archipelago of wicked reefs. But where had she arrived?

Actually she had never passed the Old Head of Kinsale, and was still miles short of that cape. But the two bangs?

That which she had heard was Mizen Head's fog signal, which gives two reports every seven and a half minutes, and she was to the north, instead of the south, of Cape Clear. She had run right up that bold fjord, Roaringwater Bay, into a group of uninhabited islets and reefs known as the Carthy Islands. Drawing twenty-two feet of water for'ard, she was lucky enough to have arrived towards High Water and still several days before Springs; for at Low Water Spring Tides the depths varied from fifteen to thirty feet. After the fog had cleared, news of this extraordinary predicament reached the coastguard at Schull, which is at the top of Roaringwater Bay, and he telegraphed to Queenstown. Thereupon the Admiral flashed his orders to patrol ships.

The armed yacht *Pioneer* (Lieut.-Commander W. Olphert, R.N.R.) was the first to arrive at daybreak next day. This officer, who had spent years in liners running to New Zealand, and later commanded the *Scadaun*, wasted no time in securing *Terpsichore* to the rocks by means of wires from her quarters and port bow. A few hours afterwards arrived the sloop *Sunflower* (Lieut.-Commander A. G. Leslie, R.N.), but the act of extrication was not possible till the 16th, by which time the armed drifter *Daisy VI* and the Queenstown tug *Stormcock* had been sent. It was high water about 3 p.m., and the difficulty was how to haul *Terpsichore* stern first through the narrow opening without her taking a sheer on to the rocks, before the Atlantic swell got any worse. It was a period of some anxiety as the ship floated and she began to surge and strain the wires; if the latter should snap, she would certainly become a wreck. An anchor had been laid out to the south-east from her starboard bow to hold her off, but now the tow-rope was made fast at her bows, secured along her port side till it came aft to the stern, and its end taken to the tug. No one knew that U-boat warfare had temporarily halted, and we quite expected that this flotilla of sloop, yacht, two trawlers, tug, and drifter might attract an enemy submarine; for which reason the first four were keeping guard to seaward.

The only vessel small enough to squeeze within the opening and reach the sailing-ship's bows was *Daisy*, so about 2 p.m. we entered, swung round, bow to bow, received *Terpsichore's* heavy warp, and at 2.50 p.m. the effort began.

Naval seamen on the rocks slipped the wires, the *Stormcock* from outside went slow ahead, *Daisy* at short scope kept *Terpsichore's* bows dead straight, the swell rose and fell over the reefs; but at length, after twenty-five suspenseful minutes, out came the ship of masts and yards, the stoppings were quickly cut one by one, our bow warp let go, and the tug took her in charge bow-first, anchoring her in safe water. The success was entirely due to the fine seamanship of Olphert and Leslie, though the Admiral, with his never-ceasing appreciation of any success, was kind enough to send us all a short, significant wireless message, " Well done," followed by a letter to their Lordships in Whitehall to the same effect. Months later the sum of £2000 by way of salvage was awarded among *Sunflower*, *Pioneer*, *Daisy* and *Stormcock*.

But we had been extraordinarily lucky, for soon after the *Terpsichore* anchored came another thick fog. In the morning she was towed away to sea by *Stormcock*, and eventually reached her destination, Runcorn, by May 24.

Now an entirely new phase developed when, by a curious mentality, the Germans this summer began to send an occasional submarine round the north of Scotland across the Atlantic to the United States. As seafaring achievements these few voyages rouse our admiration: as instances of political tactlessness they are hard to beat, and in effect were so much anti-German propaganda, since they brought European warfare across thousands of miles to the very doors of a neutral nation already unfavourably impressed with *untersee* operations. When it was learned that the submarine *Deutschland* was about to return from Baltimore (U.S.A.) for Europe, much thinking and studying of charts began at Queenstown. Whither bound ? For the Mediterranean ? For Germany ? If towards the latter, then she had the choice of north-about past Scotland or up the English Channel.

Admiral Bayly issued orders to six of his Q-ships, so that four should meet her about noon and have many hours of daylight—if she were making for the Mediterranean; whilst the other two (including Commander Gordon Campbell's *Farnborough*) were to intercept her should she be making either for the English Channel or round the north of Ireland. At a later date I was able to spend part of an afternoon aboard

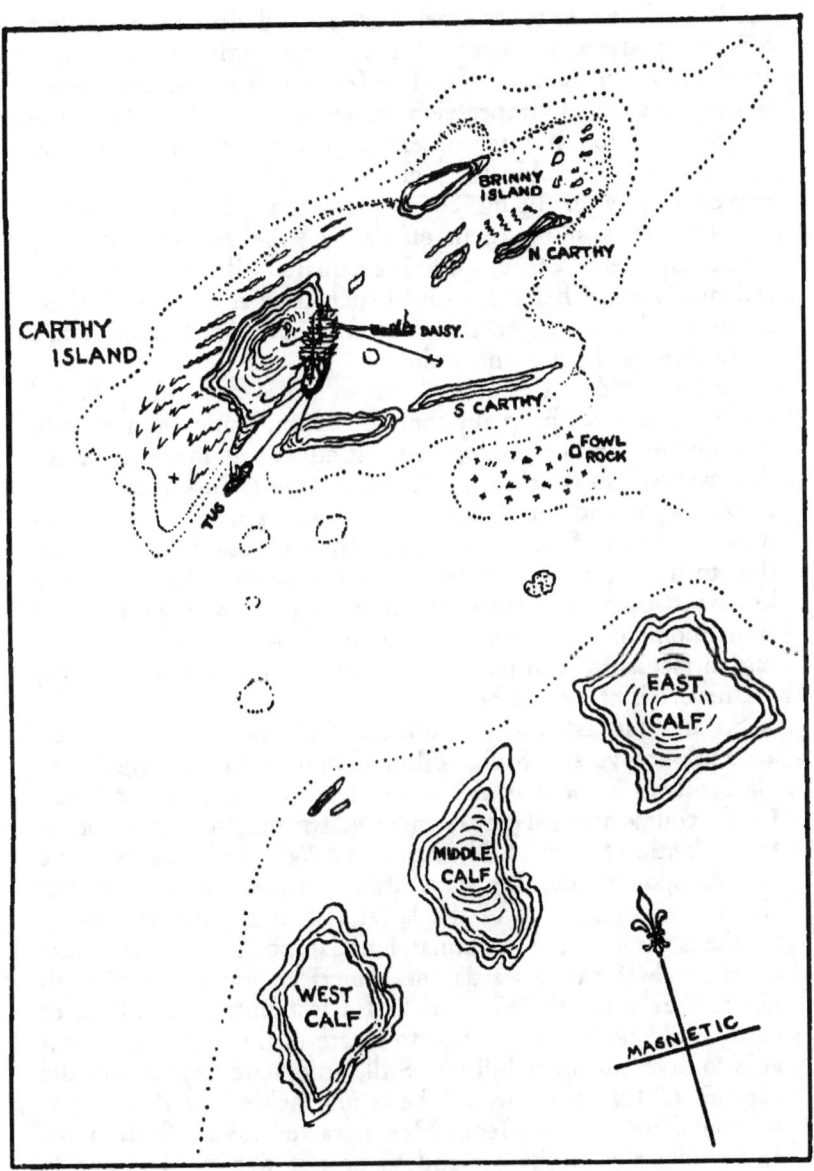

SALVING THE *TERPSICHORE*
Showing the sailing ship inside the Carthy Islands.

the *Deutschland*, to see the men's accommodation, the restricted officers' quarters, to wander through her engine-room. But, apart from the odour of bad coffee which permeated everywhere, the chief impression received was the utter discomfort and rough environment for ocean voyaging. At the end of such a double trip, no crew could be anything but nerve-worn, after being cooped up down below to escape risk of seas washing them off deck. She was so slow that monotony seems a term quite inadequate to describe the daily Atlantic lives of her men—until such time as she approached European land. From then onwards boredom became tense excitement and grim uncertainty.

Few so-called "detective" stories are so compelling as the narrative of how, by plain common sense, using the methods of induction and deduction, a great effort was made to detect this wanted submarine. We will confine ourselves to the *Farnborough*, and see what can be done as a result of enterprise. On the face of it, one might well laugh and protest that to hope for success was mere optimism. How could a low-lying craft, less than 300 feet long, be met with at the right moment and recognised upon the wavy ocean? Even big surface ships can pass each other at a few miles' distance, yet never sight each other.

So the first task was to work out the most likely track that a homeward vessel would follow if bound for the North Sea via Scotland. *Farnborough* was ordered to steer on the Great Circle course from Tory Island (N. Ireland) to a position in the Atlantic at Lat. 52 N., Long. 25 W. She was to arrive at that spot about nine days after the *Deutschland* had left Baltimore—exact date of the latter's sailing being wirelessed to the steamer—and Commander Campbell could continue to about half-way towards the American continent, though not farther than 30 W. To find a lost button in a field of corn would be less hard than to locate in the ocean a U-boat able to dive into invisibility. Still, orders are orders, and the capture of this craft would be a fine achievement, also not without a great moral effect. Her character was a little dubious, and whilst she might pretend to be not warlike, but purely a cargo-carrier, she could be signalled to stop, her captain told to come aboard with his papers, and she could be then taken as a prize. If, however, she should seek escape and begin to dive, she might be fired at.

The news finally came through that the *Deutschland* had departed from America on the 1st of August, and was expected to pass through Scottish waters (where the Northern Patrol would await her) about August 12. Four trawlers had been detached from Stornoway to cruise off the lonely Rockall Bank, whilst another couple were watching off the Faroes. On August 5 Commander Campbell left Lough Swilly in the *Farnborough*, and proceeded on a Great Circle into the Atlantic, reaching Lat. 51 N., Long. 30 W. by August 10. The average speed of the enemy could only be conjectured, but the British officer reckoned that he was about two days ahead of his rival, so turned round and at varying speeds made towards Rockall Bank (which the *Aud* during her voyage had sighted for navigational purposes). Campbell reasoned that Rockall would be a likely landmark for the submarine to verify her position after so many days at sea, and just then there were indications of a cyclone approaching, with the chance of finding improved conditions by going north.

Pass over five days, and we come to August 15. Time 8 p.m. The *Farnborough* had no sooner got soundings on Rockall Bank [1] than at 8.30 p.m. she heard on her wireless some vessel using a high Telefunken note, and five minutes later on a very low note. She made her call sign very rapidly and then this message:

" 57.29 N., 18.16 W.—N.E."

Shortly afterwards another German vessel was also heard wirelessing, and must be only a short distance away. From the above signal it was obvious that *Deutschland* was still to the westward of Rockall and heading north-eastwards, but a second submarine had been instructed to come out and assist her homecoming through British waters. So, again, it was a contest of brains and imagination, of reasoning and inference; with the turbulent green waves for environment,

---

[1] Rockall is about two hundred and fifty miles west of the Outer Hebrides, and the island itself a mere pinnacle of granite some eighty feet wide, seventy feet high. Unlit, uninhabited, it is not readily discernible in bad weather, but the uncharted reef extends a couple of miles to the eastward, and can be identified by the sudden change in soundings.

and the hope of correct judgment being justified. The *Farnborough* steered to intercept her, but saw her not; on the next day followed the homeward-bound Great Circle track for St. Kilda, and still she was not sighted; then altered course once more. Net result, nil! The *Deutschland* evaded all vigilance, and got safely back to Germany, yet indeed she was mighty fortunate. That 8.30 p.m. position, just noted, meant a distance of only 150 miles between decoy and submarine: by a mere flick of fate the two might have come together on the following day.

Still, it was just one of those failures that derive all virtue less from result than endeavour; and only two days later began another battle of intellects between a disreputable-looking old tramp and a very modern submersible. But once more was proved how much can be done by calm contemplation over an open chart.

It was August 18, again 8 p.m., but on this occasion the scene lay farther south, some thirty or forty miles west of Blacksod Bay, when *Farnborough* was steaming along to the south at her eight knots. A submarine was sighted to port, on the surface, and making to the north at nine knots. Night fell, the decoy switched on her customary steaming lights, but evidently the German was homeward bound after laying a cargo of mines, for she had no guns and wished to avoid shipping. Presently the *Farnborough* switched off lights, darkened ship, swung round and followed the enemy's northerly direction, hoping to come up with her by daylight. Hands got busy with paint-brushes, and ere long the steamer's appearance had been transformed. About 9.30 p.m. the submarine could be heard communicating by wireless with another.

Daylight returned, yet nothing was in sight, so the decoy assumed she had over-estimated the minelayer's speed, therefore course was altered to the south and east, in the hope of cutting across the track which would lead the enemy towards St. Kilda. It was now 5.30 a.m. The surmise had been correct, since three-quarters of an hour later the same submarine was sighted on the surface four and a half miles away, heading N.E. by N., but after twelve minutes the German took fright and dived. Not to be put off, the mystery ship, by steering twenty-seven minutes on such a course as should bring her immediately over the enemy's position, deemed it an opportunity for letting go a depth-charge. This was done just before 7 a.m., without visible result, yet it must have shaken up the home-goer and revealed the *Farnborough's* character.

From 7 a.m., and during the next ten hours, Campbell resumed his north-easterly course, and by careful calculation inferred that at 5.30 p.m. he was a good ten miles ahead, well out of the enemy's sight. Thereupon, being by this time to the north of Ireland, he turned ocean-wards as if he were some cargo steamer bound across the Atlantic from Liverpool or the Clyde, and at 5.50 p.m. spotted the submarine upon the horizon emitting smoke. Ten minutes later the U-boat again took fright and dived. Had she realised that this was the vessel with the depth-charges? Gradually Campbell hauled round to meet the German's direction, and for half an hour nothing happened, until the clock registered 6.39 p.m.

All of a sudden, without a speck of periscope being visible, there came from a distance of less than a thousand yards a torpedo. It missed, but the bubbles passed under *Farnborough* below her forecastle, and the decoy, pretending not to have seen the missile, maintained her course in the hope that another torpedo might follow. Speed was even reduced, but the enemy would not follow up the attack, so at 7.10 p.m., *Farnborough* changed course to the north-east for yet another attempt, and went off at full speed along the enemy's track, hoping that at dusk he might catch her as she was coming to surface for the night hours. Unfortunately, in spite of all this perseverance, the mystery ship's desire was not attained. The weather came on a typical Scotch mist with rain, but during the night the ship underwent further transformation by alterations and paint, and it was hoped an interception might be made next day off St. Kilda. Nevertheless, after a twenty-four-hours' chase over 150 miles' course the minelayer got clean away to invisibility.

Both this submarine and the *Deutschland* had illuminating reports to tell on arriving back home. The former revealed something of the deadly pertinacity belonging to trap-ships;

the latter proved that to reach American waters was entirely practicable. Therefore *U 53* (Lieut.-Commander Rose) on September 17 left Heligoland to lie off the American coast with warlike intent. Proceeding round the north side of the Shetlands, she crossed the Newfoundland Bank; on October 7 lay off Long Island Sound, and entered Newport, Rhode Island. Here (as Rose himself has stated) he remained two and a half hours, during which official visits were exchanged with the American Senior Naval Officer, and then, after this short sojourn, *U 53* made for the Nantucket Light-vessel, where she was in position the following day. Here is one of the most important focal points of the world's seaways, so he had not long to wait for victims. On this October 8 he sank no fewer than three British steamers (*Strathdene*, 4321 tons; *West Point*, 3847 tons; *Stephano*, 3449 tons); the Dutch S.S. *Blommersdyk*, and the *Chr. Knutsen*, besides molesting others.

That same night she was compelled to begin her return voyage, otherwise her fuel supply would have run out. Although Queenstown Q-ships were this month still cruising off the west coast for the dual purpose of watching out against submarines and gun-runners—since it was suspected that arms might be transferred at sea to local sailing craft—nothing happened to Rose, who passed via the Hebrides and Shetlands, coming home to Heligoland on October 28. It was very disappointing that neither of these two ocean-going submarines had been bagged, nor that other one, the *Bremen*, which failed to make her return to Germany, though the precise cause of her decease is not definitely known even after many years. Three Q-ships, however, had been sent out to waylay her, and in these boisterous autumnal days the little sloops were working as far out as 14 W. escorting, not every steamer—which would have been totally impracticable—but any with specially valuable cargoes.

It is to be noted that occasionally for weeks, because of special circumstances, some of the Queenstown Q-ships had to be sent as far away as North America, the West Indies, Mediterranean, and even the White Sea. Thus, in addition to the trio which during September steamed as decoys down the trade routes to Gibraltar and Malta, two left Queenstown on September 12. These were the *Zylpha* and the *Farnborough*, whose careers have already been introduced, but will have to be mentioned again in later pages. For the present, in watching a strange interlude we shall see that their work consisted of something more than coastal cruising.

We have observed that *Zylpha* and *Farnborough* had come to Ireland in the early pioneer days of mystery vessels, when the complete art of fitting out such unusual species had yet to be learnt. Consequently their holds were still filled with coal, whereas their later sisters were packed with timber so tightly as to be almost unsinkable. So it was decided to send them across the Atlantic, where they could discharge coal and load timber carefully stowed by experts. Within a few short weeks they should have crossed the Atlantic twice and been back in Queenstown: actually complications robbed the Admiral of their services for months. The cost of timber in that period of the War was very high, and the right kind not being available in Europe, every reason demanded that it was best for the two steamers to fetch their own cargoes.

But the *Farnborough* had orders first to call at Bermuda, where she arrived after sixteen days, discharged her welcome fuel, took in ballast, and by October 4 was at Quebec, where she received her timber. Meanwhile the *Zylpha* had crossed to Halifax direct, discharged her coal at the dockyard, and then gone up the St. Lawrence to Three Rivers (between Quebec and Montreal) for her wood. But only four days after the *Farnborough's* arrival, and by the time *Zylpha* was half laden, occurred those sensational sinkings by $U\ 53$ off Nantucket. It was feared that here was the beginning of a new campaign, and other merchant ships would be presently attacked in Canadian waters.

How fortunate, then, that these two decoys had come over just in time to perform the very work they had been doing off Ireland!

Vice-Admiral M. E. Browning was in charge of the North America and West Indies station, and he now sent *Farnborough* to patrol between Cabot Straits and Rimouski; that is to say, along the approaches towards Quebec, beginning at Newfoundland. Strange destiny, indeed, that hostilities with Germany should introduce anti-submarine tactics to the Gulf of St. Lawrence, yet this was merely one surprise after another. Of course, nothing happened, seeing that the enemy got back to Heligoland by October 28; yet the future was uncertain, and it seemed advisable to keep both decoys on the American side. But note what turned up next to increase complications. The *Farnborough* remained in that vicinity till December 10, when she finally left Sydney (Cape Breton Island) for Queenstown direct, with her buoyant cargo, that was to be found so useful on that memorable occasion two months later.

The *Zylpha*, however, was sent from Halifax on October 25 with orders to cruise about the Nantucket Shoal, thence go down to the Florida Straits, replenish at Kingston (Jamaica), and patrol the Gulf of Mexico steamer tracks leading from the Florida Straits to the ports of New Orleans, Galveston, and Tampico. Stranger than ever! Why this latest shifting of scenes?

The answer is simply that it was feared the Germans were about to molest these Mexican routes for the purpose of stopping a source of oil fuel that had never previously been more essential for every kind of War transportation. Moreover, it was alleged that a certain minor State was sheltering and abetting one enemy submarine. To-day it seems a ridiculous story, yet after the Nantucket incidents, and having regard to the vulnerability of our oil-tankers, the fears were scarcely excessive. But for the *Zylpha* it meant nearly three months of utter, eventless boredom for officers and men who had all volunteered for excitement and thrills rather than a West Indian sojourn.

And then, after this long while, the origin of such a scare was traced. Now, in Ireland one of the most annoying reports of submarines communicating with the shore had no better foundation than the vivid imagination of a young girl, daughter in a household near the sea, who had been reading lurid novels of spies and spying. Presently this fiction had become so real in her mind that she had been walking along the cliffs about 11 p.m. and saw the German sailors fetching off petrol tins. Unfortunately, these stupid lies imposed quite needless work on police and inshore patrol vessels until each canard was investigated.

So likewise in the Mexican Gulf it was elucidated that an American of German extraction had bought an old submarine from one of the South American republics. But this man happened only to be making an up-to-date War film, and no intention was ever contemplated of being more hostile than is practicable with celluloid and a lens. The suspense now eased, the *Zylpha* was able to quit Jamaica on February 25, 1917, for Bermuda, arriving at Queenstown exactly a month later. The first week of April saw her in Devonport for a refit, but on the seventeenth of that month she was thirty miles off the west coast of Ireland, when Queenstown received her message: " Submarine now shelling us." She had finished with tropical boredom and was back in the War zone: so there for a while we will leave her.

CHAPTER XV

TRAGEDY OF THE SEA

WE have just mentioned, for the first time in Irish waters, a submarine fitted to lay mines. It is not unlikely that Commander Campbell's shy enemy was *U* 78. The latter during August had made a cruise to the Bristol Channel, where she laid her dangerous black eggs on five zigzag lines between St. Goven and Helwick Light-vessels, taking bearings from Lundy Island. Such a vessel carried thirty-six mines, but only a couple of torpedoes, so it was with reluctance that she had used one of them against the *Farnborough*, and she must needs keep the other in case some better opportunity arose later.

The ambush laid did not yield results immediately, but on September 2 the 5000-ton British steamer *Kelvinia* struck one of the mines some nine miles S. by W. of Caldy Island and foundered. Thereupon the Milford trawlers began sweeping, found the mines laid in groups of threes, and at exceptional depth, the enemy's intention being to catch the deeply laden steamers arriving at one of the Bristol Channel ports with American munitions.

Now, almost simultaneously mines began to be laid off the south Irish coast, which was to place an additional burden upon the busy sloops. True, they had originally been built for mine-sweeping, and the possibility of their being sooner or later employed in that special duty was never lost sight of: they could be sent off at short notice to work in pairs and good speed, with a powerful wire hawser joining them to cut the mine-moorings adrift, so that the ugly egg-shaped bomb leapt into visibility for destruction. None the less, this fresh phase of hostilities only complicated operations, recalling the sloops from escorting and patrolling just at the time when U-boats were being multiplied and there were possibilities of some further Germano–Irish combined efforts.

Always the enemy selected the positions for his minefields with sound sense—off prominent headlands, on the steamer tracks, on the bearings of marks leading into harbours: in fact, when presently we sank his mines off the northern entrance to Valentia Harbour, I remember noting particularly that their situation was exactly in line with the two white-and-black beacons which are the marks for entering. By the fourth day of September our sweepers off Seven Heads (south Ireland) had revealed and destroyed about a score of these black perils; but the Galley Head minefield, a little farther along that coast, was not discovered until the British S.S. *Counsellor* (4958 tons) blew up. Subsequently eight " eggs " were swept up, the line (as off Seven Heads) being laid athwart the track of shipping some five miles away from the shore. Luckily not one of *Counsellor's* crew was lost, all being picked up by patrols and brought into Queenstown; but trawlers and other auxiliaries had to be placed seven miles south of the Fastnet for the purpose of warning east-bound vessels to keep at least ten miles away from the land.

In between these two sweeping duties of the sloops came belated news that the French barque *Maréchal de Villars*, many miles to the southward, had been sunk by the enemy. One more beautiful sailing ship sent to her doom! Such vessels rarely carried wireless, and their navigation was not always exact, especially after the heavens had been clouded for days. The sloop *Zinnia* must go and do her best with only the vague knowledge that the Frenchman's disaster occurred somewhere between Lat. 48 and 49 N., Long. 7 and 9 W.: that is to say, in the Bay of Biscay westward of Brest. The thought of unfortunate men rolling about in their open boat dying of cold and starvation was harassing, and every fruitless hour made all chance of finding them alive still more remote. From Tuesday afternoon till Thursday afternoon the search was continued, for most of this period zigzagging at thirteen knots; but nothing was found save large quantities of oil on the surface and many barrels bobbing in the ocean swell. Two valuable days lost with nothing to show!

One has no wish to stress the horrors of past events, yet it would not be justifiable to avoid unpleasant history. This enemy practice of leaving destitute crews to strive for their lives in a desperate gamble with death cannot be forgotten, and must never be allowed to recur. Among the worst cases was that of two old men in a fishing boat earning their subsistence west of the Scillies. A U-boat came alongside, and took everything out of her, including the old men's drinking-water. The wind chanced to be easterly, and they ran before it during three days till they reached Queenstown. Taken into hospital, they were almost insensible from exposure and thirst, their clothes as well as their boots having to be cut off. That they survived the heavy seas and cold makes one German officer's guilt no whit the less.

But strange happenings were being added to week by week, some of which have never been recorded and others only now are coming to light. On the first Saturday in this October (1916), the *Zinnia*, whilst steaming along the Irish Channel shortly before midday, sighted the American schooner *Samuel S. Thorp* behaving so curiously that investigation was imperative. On closing her and challenging, the sloop was puzzled when the schooner now hoisted her ensign upside down. Here was the signal for distress, yet no outward circumstances suggested trouble. It was too rough to board her, so for the time being the *Samuel S. Thorp* had to be kept in view. By 4 p.m. improved weather conditions allowed the sloop to lower a boat, which went alongside and found the stranger in a sad plight. She was awash to her main deck, and unable to stand up to the wind for fear of her cargo of deals taking charge. So the sloop passed a grass warp, got her in tow, and slowly they went ahead through the moonlit night, till on Sunday afternoon the schooner was safely anchored in the quiet waters of Milford Haven.

During these days, too, whilst the United States were still neutral, arose another contact with Queenstown. A steamer in Havre, bound for New York, was being loaded by German prisoners when two of them hit on a cute idea. They would hide themselves aboard till they heard the steamer's engines stop in New York, and then go ashore. Afterwards they would obtain passage in some Danish, Scandinavian, or Dutch vessel, and eventually be back in Germany as free men. Only a few days at sea from Havre! The voyage would soon end! They managed to conceal themselves in the hold satisfactorily, and now the ship was out of the English Channel plunging into big seas. Time went on, darkness succeeded daylight, they lost all count of hours and days. At last!

The sea gradually became smoother, then the engines stopped their revolutions: they had arrived. Up came the Germans out of their hiding to announce themselves on deck before all and sundry.

Now the laugh went against them. This was not New York, but Queenstown. For the steamer had met strong head winds in the Atlantic, and after battling for some days was short of coal. She accordingly put her helm hard over and ran back east into Queenstown for more fuel, and the disconsolate prisoners were taken ashore en route for an internment camp.

Before the equinoctial gales had again begun to smite Ireland's coast there arrived at Queenstown from Portsmouth a first batch of those new motor launches (M.L.'s) which were to replace the small motor yachts that carried on inner patrols. These M.L.'s had been built in New Jersey, U.S.A., Quebec, and Montreal. The pattern boat was constructed at Bayonne, New Jersey, where all fabrication work was done, the Canadian plants being used only for assembling of parts. A contract for the first fifty had been signed in April 1915, but had been increased during the following July to 550; the first lot costing £8000 each without gun, and measuring 75 feet overall. The second type was 5 feet longer and rather more expensive. Fitted with twin screws, commanded mostly by yachtsmen, with trained crews recruited from all trades, these mobile little craft, in spite of their mass production, rendered excellent service throughout the War all round the British Isles, in southern Europe, and even in West Indian waters. Built primarily for patrolling, they were employed later both for escorting convoys and for minesweeping. Admiral Bayly was so pleased with them that he soon asked the Admiralty for another dozen, realising that, in addition to their other usefulness, they would be most suitable for preventing the landing of arms along the lonely south-west and west Irish coasts.

Somehow these M.L.'s have left behind a tradition of their own. Roughly put together, with anything but yacht finish, they surprised us in a dozen different ways. They were not pleasing to the eye, and their design left much to be desired; yet, when properly handled, it was remarkable to note their seaworthiness. As the Admiral found, " They were quite wonderful at sea in weather which I should have thought quite unfit for them." Head-on, they could maintain a fifteen-knot speed during fairly heavy seas off such nasty corners as Cape Clear and Mizen Head; but their worst defect became noticeable when running before those big waves arriving from the Atlantic. Poised on a crest, these M.L.'s would do a treacherous side-slip of their own, that made one's heart miss a beat, till the ship forgot her bad behaviour and swung back on her course. For some quite indefinable reason German U-boat officers (as we now well know) regarded every M.L. with greater awe than was justified; and whilst it is true that in the Mediterranean more than one submarine was definitely sent to her doom by direct M.L. action, yet in the aggregate this new fleet won success rather by such service as continuous vigilance and incessant patrolling along the shores, sinking mines and warning steamers, as well as performing any duties which suddenly developed.

It was my experience to leave the drifter *Daisy VI* and transfer to an M.L. as senior officer of the Berehaven M.L.'s. Frankly, the change over from a stout little steamer with her tanned mizzen and lively seaworthiness seemed a sad prospect; but after a winter around the Fastnet, in one of the new eighty-footers, one had to admit that these motor craft could go through the same weather trials as any drifter. Just as the sloops and destroyers on arrival at Queenstown caused inconvenience by developing defects at the first; just as any kind of motor-propelled submarine demands considerable mechanical attention; so these M.L.'s, with their temperamental engines, their propeller-shafts which would unexpectedly break in two at sea, and certain other quaint characteristics, never ceased to be surprise ships.

Occasionally the Admiral himself would put to sea in an M.L., ostensibly for some precise purpose, though I always believe there lurked an underlying reason of testing M.L. efficiency both as to material and personnel. One day he wished to perceive with his own eyes whether that key-phrase " ready for emergency " was part of the M.L. outfit. He gave orders that one of these motor launches was to take him from Queenstown eighty miles down the coast to a spot where a torpedoed Norwegian steamer had been beached, another M.L. having been stationed near by to prevent looting.

"Before going on board," relates the Admiral, "I asked the M.L. captain whether he knew anything about internal-combustion engines such as this craft was fitted with. He said in reply that for five years he had been lecturing on the subject at Glasgow University! 'All right. Then go ahead: eighteen knots!' We sped down the coast, but when two miles short of the Norwegian our engine came to a stop and the lecturer said we might be 'a little time' before the necessary repairs were done. I answered, 'Very well—but if we are not going fifteen knots in a quarter of an hour you will remain here, and I will return to Queenstown in the patrol boat.' He shot down the engine-room hatch, leaving his cap and coat on deck. Within ten minutes we were going over twenty knots. That shows the M.L. readiness for emergencies."

But there were two quite amusing episodes which might easily have been tragedies. One dark night an over-zealous officer in one of my Berehaven flotilla was patrolling to the westward when he spotted the loom of a long, indefinite object. Convinced that at last here was that U-boat of his dreams which he must sink before war ended, he opened fire, but luckily failed to hit. The "submarine" turned out to be H.M.S. *Snowdrop*! Always I regretted this incident, since Commander George Sherston was one of my best friends, and the most courteous English gentleman. To think that a shell *might* have done him injury!

Weeks passed, and one hazy afternoon I was patrolling between the Fastnet and Mizen Head, steering to the west. I had barely turned over the bridge to my sub-lieutenant and gone below than he came running down. "We're being fired on! Shells are falling off our port side." He was right: they were plopping uncomfortably close, and in the haze there showed up a sloop's outline. Of course it was immediately obvious that she had taken our grey hull for a U-boat, and our bridge for a conning-tower. Had we turned away, or moved off, one of those shells would have hit us. The sensible plan, therefore, appeared to be to steer as we were going, and hoist our recognition flags instantly. This was done, and the shells suddenly ceased, after a few uncomfortable minutes; for they had been getting gradually so near that the next one must certainly be a hit.

The following signals were then exchanged:

Sloop: "Very sorry to have mistaken you. But how did my shells fall?"

M.L.: "Excellent for direction, but thankful they fell just short."

And then, by a kind of ironic justice, I read the sloop's name on her stern. It had eight letters—"*SNOWDROP*."

"I am still feeling rather small and very humble for having made so cruel an attempt on your noble craft," wrote her charming captain to me when he got into port. "And of course you must have realised that we were all out for blood when we started in. When a cry of 'M.L., sir,' went up, imagine our disappointment and humiliation. And then to find it was you! Of course, the humorous side was there—after the previous occasion!" So the Battle of the Fastnet was eventually celebrated over a first-rate dinner when next the two ships found themselves off duty in the same harbour.

Any seaman knows what curious pranks misty weather can play with a ship's appearance, and how her very size becomes distorted. But to a landsman this may seem less credible. I recollect the first time steaming from Queenstown en route for Berehaven, being new to the Irish station. Off Cape Clear two black objects were behaving suspiciously under the land, and at once the truth seemed to leap up with painful realism. No other ship was in sight for miles, and these were two submarines waiting off the Head for their first victim. Not being a brave man, I felt an unpleasant shiver, got the gun's crew ready, and began estimating the range, when the two objects came out from the land and revealed themselves. They were a couple of patrolling trawlers!

"These mistakes," agrees Admiral Bayly, "are very easy to understand when the weather is thick, misty, or darkish." And the experience of such a Flag Officer may be a warning to others. "One morning during manœuvres," he remembers when flying his flag in H.M.S. *Lion* before the War, "I sighted two 'enemy' submarines lying on the surface with all hands bathing. It was 4 a.m., dead calm, but a very treacherous light. I steamed straight for them, and when about 3000 yards off turned broadside-on, and put one out of action. Now the remarkable thing is that these submarines thought I was a *trawler* till I turned."

Trawler? And the *Lion* a battle-cruiser of 26,000 tons!

Similarly, in the Mediterranean, during naval manœuvres, six warships were taken for destroyers, until about three miles off. They turned out to be battleships! But perhaps the best story of all centres round the mercantile officer who was not numbered among those fortunates who became entitled to £1000 for sinking a U-boat. This is the Admiral's story:

"A cargo steamer on a foggy morning during the War saw another steamer on her port side when near the Tuskar. The second steamer had a white hull and grey upper works. But the fog made the white hull invisible, so that the mate who was on watch in the first ship saw only grey upper-works, and those quite dimly. Thinking here was a submarine, he turned to port so as to ram the 'enemy' and win the £1000. However, he made such a bad shot that the other rammed him; after which the officers and crew from the rammed ship climbed over the other's bows. They thus got to Liverpool, where they reported to their owners that their ship had been sunk in collision. The Marine Superintendent listened with interest, and then showed the captain a telegram from me, saying that one of our sloops had picked up the steamer, and towed her into Queenstown."

But now the time came for a week of anxiety, damage, disaster, and death to some of our best friends; for the last week of October 1916, with its torpedoings, fierce gales and monstrous seas, will never be forgotten by those who were serving off the coast. Like many another grand drama, the overture began quite calmly. It was Monday the 23rd, the wind at N.W., but backing, the weather fine, uncertain, though an ominous ground swell against Mizen Head clearly indicated that a bad burst could not be far away. In fact, it so happened that farther west in the Atlantic (Lat. 18 W.) was the schooner *Virgen del Socorro*, which had slipped out of Vigo with a crew of German internees who were making a brave but desperate attempt to reach Germany via the north of Scotland. Now, the weather which she experienced reached us a few hours later. On the 23rd the schooner encountered a strong gale (Force 7 to 9) between west and north-west, causing her to heave-to from six in the morning till three in the afternoon.

Submarines had been inactive for months in this part of the world. Not since the previous May had a merchant ship been torpedoed, and not since the *Farnborough's* little affair with a minelayer in August had any kind of U-boat been announced. But, all of a sudden, this Monday afternoon, came signals that a submarine had been sighted. About 1.45 p.m., when more than a hundred miles west of the Fastnet on patrol, the *Zinnia's* officer-of-the-watch reported he had seen a U-boat's conning-tower. Although the sloop's captain believed this to be a false alarm, the description seemed accurate, and he continued to cruise about the vicinity till dark. At 6 p.m. he intercepted a wireless message from the S.S. *Alexandrian* saying she was being chased by a submarine, which had torpedoed her man-of-war escort, the position being Lat. 51.26 N., Long. 13.10 W.

"I proceeded at full speed to the position," the *Zinnia's* captain tells me, " and met *Alexandrian* on the way, who said she was all right, but believed her escort had been sunk. It was now clear that the latter must be the sloop *Genista*, as she had been patrolling that area, and could no longer be called up by our wireless. We reached the given position at 10.45 p.m., and then altered course to the N.E. The night, which had hitherto been fine, now turned overcast with heavy squalls, barometer falling, wind and sea rising. We spent the night searching to leeward, weather steadily getting worse. At 1 p.m. of the following day search was abandoned, as the state of the sea precluded any chance of there being survivors, and course altered for Queenstown, in accordance with the Admiral's orders. At 9 p.m. we were running before the gale, and at 10.30 p.m. I was compelled to heave-to."

Meanwhile, the *Alexandrian's* terrible message had come into Admiralty House, Queenstown, and the Commander-in-Chief wirelessed both *Zinnia* as well as her sister *Camellia* to seek for survivors. Not content with this, and realising the very great difficulties experienced by sloops in ascertaining their position within ten miles or so, owing to continual alteration of courses and never sighting the sun on these misty days, Sir Lewis Bayly went down the hill, embarked in the *Adventure* and at 10.30 p.m. put to sea. "During the evening no news had come in, and I felt it was difficult, when continually altering course, and in such strong tides, for a sloop to know her exact position; so, if any of *Genista's* people had survived, the sloops might have missed them. The *Adventure* steered for the spot given by the *Alexandrian*, arriving there about 10 a.m. There was a strong S.S.E. wind with a tumbled sea, and we sighted wreckage with some lifeless bodies in lifebelts. The wind was steady, so that if any survivors remained they must have drifted in the same direction as the wreckage. The *Adventure* was therefore steered to the N.N.W. at fifteen knots, and at about 10.45 a.m. a Carley raft was sighted dead ahead with two live men on it, then a second with four men—all working their paddles and waving. The ship's lifeboat having been lowered, and the six sailors picked up, course was continued in the same direction, and about an hour later six more were rescued."

It was impossible to read the Burial Service over the dead bodies, as by now it was blowing a hard gale, and after searching had been completed a dozen men plucked from the threshold of death were on their way back to Queenstown. Seventy-three of their shipmates, including all officers, had perished; and with the passing of her captain—Lieut.-Commander John White, R.N.—went one of the ablest, wittiest, most lovable of human beings. His death had not been in vain, for the presence of *Genista* had saved the *Alexandrian*, which happened to be another Leyland liner bringing a valuable cargo of machinery. Three days later, some 128 miles W.N.W. of the Fastnet, the S.S. *Rowanmore* (10,320 tons) was torpedoed and sunk, by *U 57*, her master, Captain Thomas Phelan, being made prisoner, and taken to Heligoland on November 5. Now, the U-boat captain informed Phelan that he had sunk a light cruiser " 100 miles west of the Bull Rocks " at this date. The enemy then cruised in company with two other submarines on her way home. There can be no doubt as to the identity of *Genista's* vanquisher.

When one considers that even the *Alexandrian's* reckoning might have been slightly out; when one takes into consideration the uncertainty of restless sea, tides, and influence of wind, it seems a remarkable feat that, eighteen hours after being thrown into the waves, *Genista's* dozen men—mere pin-points in a desert—were actually found. As example of reward for persistence and fine navigation, this effort of the *Adventure* deserves long remembrance; but there is another consideration which raises the subject to a higher plane. It used to be a good-natured jest among the sloop sailors that the *Adventure's* crew had a jolly easy time and rarely went to sea; for which reason they nick-named her H.M.S. *Wallflower*. Such was an unthinking libel, and from the day of this miraculous rescue no such ungenerous appellations were heard again. But for the flagship, twelve more homes would have been in mourning.

Now, amid all his busy affairs and the heavy work in his office, what induced the Admiral to lay aside his papers, and telegrams, and upset routine?

"I am quite sure," he says, "that there were among the survivors some who were praying hard to be rescued, and while I was wondering whether to go or not, I was really being sent out. Nor was this the only case. A tramp steamer called the *Begum* was torpedoed about 150 miles S.W. of the Fastnet. The crew sailed in their boats to Berehaven and, as was my custom, I got the captain to lunch at Admiralty House so as to tell me about it. He said the captain of the submarine gave him the bearing and distance of Berehaven and then went away. The *Begum's* captain related that he found the wind foul and his boats could not fetch the land by two or three points, that he was not a religious man, and had not said a prayer for very many years, but that he then prayed hard for help, and not long after the wind shifted so that he and his boats got safely in."

"And," adds the Admiral, "we are sometimes helped without asking; for on a previous occasion when in command of a cruiser[1] in China I remember just sitting down to lunch having no fear or doubt of the ship's position, when I seemed to be forced to go up on the bridge. Arrived there, I found

---

[1] H.M.S. *Talbot*.

the ship steering straight for the rocks, and she was only saved from being wrecked by putting the helm hard aport and the starboard propeller full speed astern."

It was learnt from *Genista's* survivors that the torpedo struck her just under the fore-bridge, making such a large hole that the for'ard gun fell down into the mess deck. Commander White had just left the bridge and must have been killed instantly. A few seconds later there followed a second torpedo, which struck her on the quarter. Officers and men tried to clear away boats, but the ship sank in a few minutes, and only the Carley rafts got away. These were picked up between fourteen and seventeen miles off, which makes the discovery of them still more remarkable.

For, during the next five days, with scarcely any intermission, it blew one of the worst gales even for this part of the world. If I may be allowed to corroborate the statement by personal experience, I would like to remark as follows. That Tuesday morning found us patrolling off the Fastnet from 2 a.m. till 6.30 a.m., when the sea and wind were such that we had to run for Crookhaven. The Admiral always trusted his officers to take shelter or not, as they deemed best, being on the spot, and relying on each captain's judgment. But that night the gale piped up into such fury that in one of the squalls at midnight we drove ashore on the creek's eastern side, although we were riding to thirty-five fathoms of cable in two fathoms of water. Later, when a big steam yacht came in and anchored, she had to keep steaming slowly ahead to prevent dragging. A little farther round the corner by Cape Clear, in a continuation of this storm, the armed trawler *Bradford* disappeared with all hands. Two destroyers, H.M.S. *Brisk* and *Archer*, left Queenstown to meet the homecoming Cunarder *Mauretania*, but were unable to steam against the terrible seas, and ran for Berehaven. In the Irish Sea one of H.M. drifters stranded on a rock near Greenore Point, and was lost with all hands; whilst thirteen trawlers and sixty-two drifters of the Milford patrols lost their mizzen sails, broke spars or bulwarks, damaged their decks or stems; and H.M. yacht *Lady Blanche* lost her boats, in addition to her anchors and cables.

When, therefore, a letter came from the Secretary of the

Admiralty to Sir Lewis Bayly saying, " My Lords appreciate that all the survivors owe their lives entirely to the very prompt action which you took in proceeding to their rescue in H.M.S. *Adventure*, and I am to express to you their appreciation of your action," it was a very literal truth which they stressed. So, also, a valuable lesson had been learned as to the necessity of keeping rafts ready for instant release, proof of which was demonstrated a few months later when the Q-ship *Salvia* was torpedoed and sunk one morning as far out in the Atlantic as Long. 16.13 W. Her captain was taken prisoner by the submarine, but for several hours her crew, in boisterous weather and a heavy sea, were rowing about in their boats or paddling in Carley rafts. At length what resembled a tramp steamer, though was actually another Q-ship *Aubrietia* (commanded by Admiral Marx, a gallant old officer who had long since left the Service, but returned as temporary Captain R.N.R.), appeared in sight, picked up one boat, and then spent a couple of hours in what seemed a vain search, until all rafts and the other three boats were picked up with men still alive.

CHAPTER XVI

A NEW PHASE BEGINS

As the year 1916 gradually drew to its close, the situation in regard to submarine attacks had not developed favourably, and was on the eve of becoming seriously worse. Both Zeebrugge and Ostende were still wasps'-nests; but no attack against either had yet been attempted. Admiral Bayly still looked forward to a joint naval and military operation against such bases, advocating this as an essential measure to lessen the awful destruction of merchant ships. But many months were to pass ere the idea became action.

During the three months of September, October, and November no less than thirteen actions with submarines had been fought by Queenstown Q-ships, thereby showing the great value of surprise and concealment in regard to a clever foe. The Queenstown fleet at this date comprised a dozen sloops and fifteen decoys; hydrophones to be used by smaller patrol craft for detecting by ear a U-boat's engines soon began to be fitted, but a noticeable feature of the enemy's latest phase was his indirect attack on Allied shipping by destruction of neutral vessels. Of ten ships sunk off the north Cornish coast on November 30 and the following day, eight belonged to neutral nations.

Merchantmen had been so well protected by escorts along the coast that new types of German submarines, with their increased radius and improved sea-keeping qualities, were more and more tempted to seek their victims long distances from land, though occasional bursts by the minelayers varied this general policy. Not yet, however, was the Admiralty convinced that the time had come for instituting the principle of convoys as the basic protection for those valuable steamers which alone prevented starvation and ruin. And owing to the increasing demands for anti-submarine patrols, as well as minesweeping, the nation's supplies of fish food were endangered through lack of both vessels and crews. One well-known firm of owners in Cardiff, for example, possessed twenty-two steam trawlers, but the Admiralty had taken seventeen, leaving only five to keep up the Cardiff fish market;

and it was not long before three of these five were sunk by the enemy.

In addition to the twenty-seven bigger Queenstown vessels just enumerated must be mentioned the four steam (or motor) yachts, twenty-three trawlers, two drifters, seven net-drifters, and twelve M.L.'s which at this time patrolled those 200 miles from Sybil Point on the south-west to Carnsore Point at the south-east. The four old torpedo-boats kept the channel into Queenstown swept clear of any mines; but the armed trawlers, instead of being on their normal beat some three or five miles from the land, were frequently needed to escort oil-tankers and slow transports so far east as the Scillies. Now, just before the year ended there came some notable changes at the Admiralty. Sir John Jellicoe succeeded Sir Henry Jackson as First Sea Lord, and immediately inaugurated from December 18 an entirely new department known as the Anti-Submarine Division for the purpose of co-ordinating all existing measures, besides devising new ones, against the enemy's campaign. For up till then practically the entire anti-submarine warfare had been carried on by Q-ships, sloops, trawlers, and other small craft.

The new Division began to introduce Hunting Patrols of destroyers and "P"-boats;[1] to organise a system of Air Patrols round the coasts; to extend the employment of British submarines against U-boats; to develop Q-ships still more; to arm defensively most of the Mercantile Marine and supply them with apparatus for making smoke-screens; to fit armed trawlers with minesweeping gear so as to be ready for sweeping all traffic routes immediately; to endeavour to render the eastern end of the English Channel impassable to the enemy; to protect the fishing fleets. But, also, now came the first definite beginning of the time-honoured Convoy principle. In a period of many hundred years, and through many naval wars, convoys had been tried and found invaluable. Ancient Rome used to escort her corn ships from Egypt by armed

---

[1] "P-boats" were a new type, low-lying, with little top-hamper, difficult to be seen at any distance, shallow of draught, fitted with a hard steel ram. They were very handy, carried guns, and were specially designed for patrolling against U-boats, some of which they succeeded in destroying. Other "P"-boats were fitted up as Q-ships to resemble mercantile vessels.

escorts, and thus make sure of her food supply. During the Anglo-Dutch, no less than the Napoleonic, Wars, whole fleets of merchantmen were collected and conducted by men-of-war. Even during the autumn of 1914 troop transports up to as many as thirty steamers had been brought across the Indian Ocean under the protection of cruisers. Nevertheless, by some curious reasoning, and by an unhappy disregard of the lessons derived from history, the Admiralty had fought shy of using this very obvious defensive method. Cautiously it now began to be tested with regard to the coal trade across to France; but soon the system was found successful beyond all expectations, and the Convoy Section grew into a department of its own.

So, likewise, there was evolved a special section to superintend the whole minesweeping organisation in all waters. Up till then (apart from the Tory Island area) the enemy had in the Irish neighbourhood laid mines only off Seven Heads, Clonakilty Bay, Galley Head, besides the Bristol Channel; but the recently increased submarine fleet would doubtless soon put in an appearance with more of their subtle black cargoes. For, when Sir John Jellicoe went ashore from the Grand Fleet to Whitehall, it was the ending of one phase and the beginning of another. Jutland had taught Germany that victory at sea could not be hers by any contest with the Grand Fleet direct; on the other hand, Germany perceived most clearly that by intensifying and multiplying the U-boats' operations she could indirectly defeat the Grand Fleet by cutting off all essential supplies. No one visualised this future with greater apprehension than Admiral Jellicoe. It was a mere matter of simple arithmetic and time: by about July 1917, at the present rate, so many allied and neutral commercial ships would have been lost, so much tonnage of food and other commodities denied their arrival, that unfavourable peace-terms would necessarily have to be accepted.

Thus, from that time onwards, the Queenstown Command, as the western gateway to the British Isles, took on a still greater importance, whilst the appointment of Admiral Bayly was in official terms formally changed to "Commander-in-Chief Western Approaches." A curious bit of red tape still entangled certain people, even at a time of national crisis when the Allies' fate was in suspense; for, a year previously it had been Sir Lewis Bayly's own idea to change the title to a designation more appropriate to the strategical outlook, yet there came the strange reply from Whitehall that the importance of an Admiral is dependent on the size of his staff!

The Admiral promptly took the opportunity of making a long overdue series of additions. Paymaster Commander Russell, overworked to almost the limit, was given assistance by the advent of other officers; but the Admiral likewise started an Operations Staff at the House, which would materially help in conducting this war of the Western Approaches. He selected for this purpose such personnel as Commander Stopford Douglas, R.N., and Commander Godfrey Herbert, R.N., both of whom had long experience in command of Q-ships, and the latter also in submarines from their earliest days. If the whole future of this war with Germany was to rest on anti-U-boat contests, here was the type of mind which could render invaluable aid at headquarters. Presently a flotilla of minesweepers came to Queenstown under Commander G. W. H. Heaton, R.N., who took charge of that important section; and it was this officer who made the useful discovery that after recovering a German mine the latter could be made innocuous by injecting steam, which melted the explosive and caused it to run out, leaving the shell empty. Berehaven was placed under the care of Captain H. L. P. Heard, R.N., who, an Irishman himself, with property just round the corner on the Kenmare River, understood the Irish temperament.

Strange and wonderful contrasts were happening this Christmas Day 1916, both on the sea and below. Down the Bay of Biscay, for instance, U 46 was sinking British steamers and taking each master prisoner. But on Christmas night she temporarily desisted for one of the most curious festive parties ever celebrated. She submerged and sat on the sea bed in thirty fathoms. A small Christmas tree was produced, with electric lights, and presents for each member of the German crew. The commanding officer first made a speech, and then from the bright tree handed his gifts, not forgetting the unwilling British guest whose steamer had been sunk a week earlier. Even this master mariner received a packet of writing-paper and an indelible pencil. In all his sea-wanderings the former captain of the S.S. *Bayhall* had never spent Christmas under such surprising conditions.

Meanwhile, farther to the north, the sloops were having no rest. That afternoon the *Zinnia* had scarcely finished escorting the S.S. *California* when wireless orders flashed that search was to be made for the oil-tanker *Terak*, which was last seen early in the morning of the previous day with no propeller, in Long. 13 W. So the sloop had no time for peace, but only for goodwill. She searched through the night, and at 2 a.m. found the *Terak*, with the Swedish S.S. *Nordyk* standing by. The latter had tried towing, but her only hawsers had parted, so now the *Zinnia* got lines across, and at a slow four and a half knots they began to make headway. For 135 miles the sloop towed her, till safe anchorage was found in Berehaven, and then the rest of *Terak's* story was learned.

It appears that she lost her propeller sixteen days before Christmas, and just wallowed about helpless in the trough. On December 23 she was picked up by a Norwegian steamer, but the tow-rope parted after a day, so she had to be abandoned. Then arrived the Swede, who would not make a second effort after hers had failed, so the neutral was fortunate to have been brought safely through the danger zone escorted by the *Snowdrop*, though for two days *Zinnia* had been taken away from patrolling. Meanwhile, the sloop *Daffodil* had come into Haulbowline dry dock after collision with a Cork steamer, which had hit her so sharply on the starboard side as to cut her nearly in half. Three men in the engine-room were scalded to death, and it was marvellous that *Daffodil* did not sink. On the top of this came news that the *Sunflower* was undergoing repairs at Avonmouth, having likewise been in collision with a steamer.

So, taking it by and large, there had been enough anxieties, apart from enemy actions, just now; the year ending with two sloops torpedoed, and three badly damaged, as well as three more slightly injured through collisions with other vessels. But, considering that so much steaming had to be done along the trade routes at night without lights, and in many foggy days, the wonder is that so few accidents occurred.

The year 1917, which was to be so critical for all concerned, opened with two marine losses that had nothing to do with the War. The reader has observed the geographical dangers to an ocean ship making Ireland in fog or mist, after days of uncertain navigation; so in thick boisterous weather the S.S. *Nestorian*, not knowing her position, came just a little too far north, and struck the very tip of south-western Ireland at Cape Clear. She became a total wreck, though the crew were saved. Just afterwards the oil-tanker *El Toro* ran aground on Blasquet Island (off Dingle Bay). She was towed off by the two sloops *Bluebell* and *Laburnum*, but sank likewise, the crew being saved. The fact is worthy of being stressed that while both these incidents occurred in thick weather, they were also during the middle watch—that period when human nature is at its lowest, and most marine accidents happen.

On January 9 the submarines had returned, to combine with the horrible gales and heartless seas; but on this day blind fate was to play another of its odd tricks. Less than three months before, that Leyland liner *Alexandrian* had been present at the tragedy of H.M.S. *Genista*, but the steamer herself had escaped a similar destruction. Now this January morning the *Alexandrian*, undaunted by her previous experience, was again off the south-west coast twenty miles from the Fastnet. By all the laws of luck and fairness, she was due to avoid enemy's attentions for many a day, yet at 9.15 a.m. a U-boat saw her and fired a torpedo, which hit. Once more the *Alexandrian's* wireless sent out the thrilling news, and once more a sloop hurried. This time arrived the *Myosotis*, who rushed along quickly to see a periscope and a British crew in boats. Shots were fired at the periscope, which frightened the submarine from remaining. The two boats were picked up, and, most fortunately, the adventurous *Alexandrian* declined to sink. She was taken in tow by the *Bluebell*, who slowly brought her through the heavy swell all that Tuesday as well as the next day, and at ten o'clock on Thursday the Leylander just floated into Berehaven, where she had to be beached. Once more this ship had defied a submarine, and again had one of this Company's wounded vessels limped into the same harbour.[1]

[1] Compare the *Huronian*, December 28, 1915.

Meanwhile, the sloop *Myosotis* was attacked and missed, though the torpedo passed right under her; but on the following few days two more sailing ships (*Kinpurney* and the *Lilian H.*), together with four steamers (*Baron Sempill, Manchester Inventor, Nailsea Court,* and *Neuquen*), were all sent down by U-boats. It was just before 9 a.m. on the 18th that the *Manchester Inventor* (4247 tons) began to be fired on, and she had to be abandoned. Within an hour arrived the sloop *Iris*, who saw the submarine and opened fire at 8000 yards, so frightening the culprit that the latter submerged ere a second shot could be fired. Just after 10.30 a.m. the *Manchester Inventor* sank, but *Iris* now saw the submarine break surface, so went for her with shells and depth-charges, whilst next came the *Myosotis*, who took up the chase whilst her sister was rescuing the survivors. Then ambled along through that area a single-funnelled " tramp," who in actuality was Q-ship No. 12, and at one time was the sloop *Tulip*. She engaged the enemy, as did Q 14 a little later (about 2.45 p.m.), but in each case the elusive submarine slipped out of sight. And here it may be interpolated that three months later Q12 was sunk by U 62, whose commanding officer was quite deceived by her appearance for a time and considered her a well-disguised trap. Only when he saw that she had no defensive gun, and his seaman eyes noted the manner in which her Red Ensign was hoisted, were his suspicions aroused.

Once more the *Myosotis* was in the centre of excitement, and only a day after the *Manchester Inventor* episode. That afternoon the scene lay twenty-five miles W.N.W. of the Skelligs, and she was just about to escort the S.S. *Nailsea Court*, who was less than two miles off, when, without warning, the steamer received a torpedo in her side and sank. *Myosotis* picked up the crew, but the enemy barely showed herself, and then again disappeared.

Now, such instances as those of the *Alexandrian* and *Myosotis* proved the curious good or bad fortune which might pertain to any sort of ship: often a mere split second, or the length of a telescope, separated luck from disaster. Only a week later, another sloop was cruising through the dark hours when the officer on the bridge suddenly sighted, right ahead, the blurred black mass of a large oil-tanker. The night was very sombre, both ships were proceeding without lights, though a careful lookout had not been neglected. At once the sloop's officer of the watch put his helm hard-aport, went full speed ahead—well, they just cleared each other, and only just, and a miserable ending was averted by five yards.

But one event followed another; and not even in harbour, after restless, busy days at sea, could the tragedy of things be forgotten by any of us. Vividly the picture remains of that cold wintry morning when the thirty-seven unfortunates from the *Manchester Inventor* were landed and billeted at Bantry. Two of them were hospital cases—the second mate, with a shell-splinter in his leg, and one Russian, who had lost an eye, but was remarkably plucky about it, accepting his hard knock with admirable resignation. A few days pass and the scene is Berehaven. There breezed up a S.E. gale of such force that none of us could resume our patrol for two days. A sloop had come in to coal from the *Pensacola* and sent ashore stewards for food, postmen for letters, as well as libertymen. But these ratings could not be fetched off; the collier *Pensacola* dragged her anchors and drove aground on a small headland, at first in quite a good position, though soon afterwards the very high spring tide lifted her on to a ledge of rock. When the weather moderated, the sloop weighed, anchored to the S.E. and windward, got hawsers aboard, and made everything ready for towing her. As the tide fell, *Pensacola* was seen to take a fifteen-degree list, dried nearly out, and appeared somewhat hogged. Just before high water her list vanished, the sloop hove in on her cable, went slow ahead, and the collier slid safely off. It was fortunate. That night the S.E. gale burst out again, but with worse fury, so nothing could have saved her; and the *Alexandrian*, where she lay, became so battered about that the poor ship now began to break up—a cruel fate after all the peril she had escaped outside. So ended January.

Then, from February 1, 1917, began the most historical phase of the naval war. On this date Germany inaugurated her Unrestricted Submarine Campaign, and two days later the United States severed diplomatic relations with Germany, so that Count Bernstorff at length had to leave America. These three decisions were in their several ways to exercise vast influences on the political and international future, so that it would be impossible here to exaggerate their full import.

The rupture with Germany had been foreshadowed ever since the *Lusitania's* four funnels felt the inrush of Irish waters. One tactless incident after another, one unimaginative blunder following its predecessors, had gradually made impossible even the outward appearance of friendship. President Wilson had been the last man in the civilised world to be driven headlong by emotional impulse to intervene in European matters. Forbearance had, however, reached its farthest limits. At first the President hoped that an armed neutrality would suffice, though three months later—April 2—he was driven to ask Congress to declare war. And this Unrestricted Submarine Campaign was the final inspiration of that resolve. In his Flag Day address on June 14 of that year Mr. Wilson said, " It is plain enough how we were forced into the war," and added that, " the extraordinary insults and aggressions of the Imperial German Government left us no self-respecting choice but to take up arms in defence of our rights as a free people, and of our honour as a sovereign government. The military masters of Germany denied us the right to be neutral."

" Germany denied us the right to be neutral." That was the new situation, and few people had any doubt of how this must presently develop. Now, with the departure of Bernstorff there ended all subterfuges and spy trickeries, but also that means of communication between German–Irish organisations. So recently as December 31, 1916, the German wireless station at Nauen had wirelessed its Embassy at Washington that it was proposed to land two consignments each of 30,000 rifles, ten machine guns, and six million cartridges from a couple of armed disguised merchantmen, which were to reach Galway and Tralee between February 21 and 25, 1917. For the purpose Irish pilots were to reach Germany before February 6. The recognition signal was to be a white light shown three times over the ship's side.[1] But the most impudent of all

[1] These and other details of the Sinn Fein activities in regard to German and Irish intrigues carried out on American territory are for the most part derived from *Documents Relative to the Sinn Fein Movement* (Cmd. Paper 1108).

Bernstorff's messages was sent to Berlin scarcely less than a fortnight before he was handed his passport. It ran thus:

> *Washington, January* 22, 1917. I request authority to pay out $50,000 in order, as on former occasions, to influence Congress through the organisation you know, which can perhaps prevent war. I am beginning in the meantime to act accordingly. In the above circumstances a public German official declaration in favour of Ireland is highly desirable in order to gain the support of Irish influence here.

Could there be better proof of Mr. Wilson's accusation concerning the "extraordinary insults and aggressions"? Fifty thousand dollars "to influence Congress"!

Germany, at one blow, in the first week of February had thus forfeited not merely all hope of American influence at a future Conference Table, but had also made less easy than ever another Irish Rebellion. Not merely that, either. Britain's strongest weapon of all was her blockade, and the enemy felt this more deadly day after day; for which reason she sought by every means to cause such friction regarding the transportation of American cargoes as would result in a cessation of this embargo. Fortunately, the goodwill and common sense of American and British leaders continued to delay and ease any threatened crisis; but now these dangers were quickly passed.

Nearly a year after Peace was signed there sat in Berlin a most illuminating official Parliamentary Committee of Inquiry to ascertain the causes and effects of Germany's failure. The pledge had been given that this new Unrestricted Submarine Campaign would bring England to her knees within six months. What explanation had the Admirals now to offer?

Admiral von Capelle (Secretary of the German Navy from March 1916 till September 1918, and therefore during the principal War months), in explaining why there had been no speeding up of U-boat construction during the nine months immediately preceding this February 1, 1917, made the interesting admission that the urgent task of repairing damage suffered by the High Sea Fleet in the battle of Jutland imposed a heavy additional strain on the dockyards. Instead of building new U-boats, they had to patch up the big ships. Admiral von Holtzendorff, author of the "six months' pledge," had once said that the German Naval Staff hoped by this campaign to bring England to the frame of mind in which she would be ready to make peace.

Then came some remarkable evidence as to the number of U-boats available, and this has an intimate relation to the Queenstown Command. Admiral Capelle regarded the northern and southern entrances to the Irish Sea and the western approach to the English Channel as the "decisive U-boat theatres," because they were "the highways of the world's traffic." The German Admiralty had begun by dividing these waters into three patrol areas, with one boat always stationed in each. This demanded three boats to each area, since every expedition needed a month—one-third of the time being spent on the outward voyage, one-third on the station, and one-third on the voyage home. But this was further complicated by an average of two injured boats having to spend time in dock. Thus it worked out that a total of five boats to an area, or fifteen for the three decisive theatres around Ireland, was the practicable minimum.

Admiral Capelle admitted that the February Campaign was worked with not less than twenty-five and not more than forty-four U-boats at sea, though it began with only twenty, and they expected to lose an average of not more than three a month. Actually during the ensuing nine months the average was about double that estimate, which was a serious drain not merely on the construction side, but also on the personnel, comparatively few in numbers and requiring long weeks to be taught their job. It meant that one half of each month's construction went to the bottom, and the time would come when men tried to avoid service in submarines. To sum up, Admiral Koch attributed the failure to "an imperfect estimate of British endurance" on the part of the experts, whilst Admiral Capelle confessed that British counter-measures had caused such submarine losses as were never contemplated.

None of this, obviously, could be known outside Germany. But what could be done in reply to the new campaign?

The answer is—not much, except to improve and extend the means and methods already adopted. When asked at the above inquiry what were the specific British devices which prevailed over the U-boats, Admiral Koch answered that he considered these were: (1) the listening ships, (2) the fast surface craft which compelled U-boats to remain almost continuously submerged, (3) the convoy system, (4) the continual alteration in the routes for shipping. Apparently he forgot to mention decoy-ships, which equally experienced varying degrees of success; but he also omitted any reference to the British minefields in Dover Straits and the North Sea. Otherwise these four points may be accepted as a fair interpretation, and it is worthy of emphasis that they were the basic principles of all Queenstown operations. The M.L.'s were using their hydrophones more generally, some fast destroyers now came to reinforce the Command, the convoy system was about to be adopted far more extensively, and the routeing of shipping became one of the most important duties for the Operations Staff at Admiralty House. But still this shortage of destroyers was severely felt, nor would the Commander-in-Chief of the Grand Fleet suffer his flotillas to be depleted.

Thus the situation now evolved was that if America should be about to enter the War, no assistance could be more welcome, no immediate co-operation more valuable, than as many of her destroyers as she could send over to Queenstown. And this would continue to be the case even if not one single company of soldiers were to sail from the United States for England or France.

CHAPTER XVII

TORPEDOES AND MINES

FROM the list of disasters throughout February no doubt could be entertained that the enemy's new campaign was going to be mighty serious. Nor might anyone fail to notice the German plan of concentrating against the Western Approaches. The sinkings now began at 270 miles west of the Fastnet to an area 100 miles south of Ireland, and simultaneously he began laying treacherous little minefields off such useful spots as would be passed by naval traffic; for instance, off Daunt's Rock Light-vessel near Queenstown Harbour, and off Milford Haven by Skokham Island. Fortunately, the minesweeping trawlers cleared up the dangers —thanks to foresight and routine—before a ship was damaged.

It was on February 4 that the enemy indicated his versatility by coming within two miles of the shore after his victims, for that day the S.S. *Ghazee* was torpedoed without warning and had to beach herself in Clonakilty Bay. This was Sunday, and next day *Snowdrop*, with her sister *Zinnia*, began sweeping off Galley Head, but found nothing. On Tuesday at 7 a.m. these sloops resumed their clearance of an area five miles from the land. Just before 11 a.m. steamed past them the collier *Cliftonian* (4303 tons) well inside the five-miles danger-limit. The sloops signalled her a warning, but she took no heed for some minutes, when she altered course farther out. Suddenly the collier felt a bump, a violent explosion followed, a column of sea rose to a height of 250 feet, and a large hole revealed itself in her starboard side. Immediately she started settling down by the head, then drifted about during fifteen minutes, heeled to port, turned over and went down bows first, with her propeller revolving in the air to the last like a windmill.

Now, the interesting fact is that after several days' sweeping no Galley Head mines were found. But the U-boat, observing that the men-of-war were occupied on a non-existent danger field, craftily cut in, smote the collier, and would next stalk the two sloops. Water being a perfect carrier of sound, and a ship's hull being an excellent receiver, it is not surprising that, though *Zinnia* was one mile astern, the shock of *Clifton-*

ian's torpedo was felt in the sloop's engine-room. Not a man was killed or even injured, and had the enemy shown a little more spirit, the sloops were at his mercy, tethered to each other by an expanse of steel wire; another explosion against a ship's side might well be taken for more of the suspected mines. One can only suppose that this U-boat carried an inexperienced captain, who became nervous of getting foul of sweeping gear, and preferred to destroy a collier rather than a couple of small cruisers.

Certainly these submarines by no means had everything their own way. A week later *UC* 65—one of those which brought mines to Irish waters—found herself positively surrounded by the Milford net-drifters, so that the entire space right across from the Smalls to the Tuskar seemed barred. Only by submerging to a depth of 200 feet and going slow ahead did she succeed in getting clear. This was a desperate effort, which robbed the ex-fishermen of catching in their nets a big silver fish measuring more than 165 feet long. But it was the depth-charges—"wasser-bombs," as the enemy called them—which fairly scared all German crews. About this time a fishing skipper had the misfortune to be taken prisoner aboard another minelayer, *UC* 44. One forenoon she was sighted by a couple of British destroyers, who made her dive and then started dropping depth-charges, which promptly smashed all the electric-light globes and put the submarine temporarily in darkness. And there is no lack of other instances which prove that, even if the U-boat escaped structural damage, her men were permanently impressed by these explosions.

It was just chance which would decide their fate next time: they might go down for the last occasion, with sea pouring in through a hole; or they might get off with a nasty fright.

We have mentioned that excellently disguised Q-ship *Penshurst*, under the charge of her most modest Commander F. H. Grenfell, R.N., who had come back to service of a virulent kind from peaceful retirement. At the western end of the English Channel, and on the last two days of November 1916, she had been in action with German submarines, and sank the minelayer *UB* 19, taking sixteen prisoners. Then on January 14 she had a stand-up fight with *UB* 37, shelled her till she sank, and dropped depth-charges over her to make doubly sure. On February 20 *Penshurst* tackled another submarine, hit her, caused her to submerge, and again used "wasser-bombs," yet the remarkable thing is that this enemy got home, after all.

Two days passed, and the scene shifted from the English Channel to the south of Ireland, when *U* 84 was sighted on the surface. Here the *Penshurst* had no ordinary foe, but one of those very up-to-date craft which had just been evolved —230 feet long, a surface speed of sixteen and a half knots, two guns, a dozen torpedoes, and enough fuel to take her three times across the Atlantic. Altogether a formidable foe to be met by any ship at sea.

It was just before noon when the Q-ship observed her steering west, but *U* 84 likewise saw her and (as we know from German sources) took her for an oil-tanker, fired a torpedo which missed, and then stopped her by gunfire. Many things seemed to happen almost simultaneously, for eight miles away the sloop *Alyssum* was in view, escorting the S.S. *Canadian*; next a rowing-boat full of survivors came along, but a few minutes later Grenfell was looking at the hull of a 1416-tons vessel lying keel uppermost.

Only by quickly starboarding helm did *Penshurst* evade the torpedo, and by the narrow margin of fifteen feet. She then pretended to retire, thus luring on the enemy, who approached to 600 yards. The German captain (Lieut.-Commander Rohr) then demanded the ship's papers, and the usual "panic party" had "abandoned" their steamer to row off. But now the *Penshurst's* guns opened fire, hitting the submarine's conning-tower five times, exploding inside, destroying most of the apparatus, putting out the electric light over the magnetic compass, wounding an officer, and holing *U* 84 till her conning-tower became top-heavy with inrushing water.

She dived for safety, but decided to rise and fight it out on the surface, whereupon the Q-ship hit her twice more and the officer was wounded a second time. The German was using her gun when she was alarmed by what she took to be a destroyer and sped away till the *Penshurst* was out of sight. Sixteen knots against nine! But Rohr felt renewed confidence when he found the "destroyer" was the flower-class *Alyssum*, who could steam no faster than the submarine. About four that afternoon these two continued the contest, between gun and gun, until by twilight *U* 84 had retreated to invisibility.

Now, in spite of all the serious damage which *Penshurst* gave her; notwithstanding, also, two depth-charges which made the boat tremble and put out lights; besides a damaged for'ard hydroplane, main rudder, and trimming pump; this German craft did not sink. She plugged the shell-holes with the tricolour flag of the French sailing ship *Bayonne* that had been her victim five days previously, and by good fortune, combined with pluck, managed to reach Germany. There she was visited by Admiral Scheer. "I myself had occasion to inspect *U* 84 after her return from this expedition," he wrote.[1] "I realised that it was little short of a miracle that, in spite of such heavy damage, she reached home." But in the following January *U* 84 was less lucky, and she went to her doom. "Lieutenant-Commander Rohr is, unfortunately, one of the many who have not returned from their voyages," added the German Admiral.[2]

During those intervening months, however, the gallant little *Penshurst* had thrill after thrill. On July 2, 1917, she engaged another submarine, on August 19 she herself was torpedoed, but shelled the German into submergence. Help was sent, and the mystery ship was brought safely into Devonport, where she was given a gun as powerful as the enemy's, and that autumn once more put to sea. Whilst making for the southern end of the Irish Sea she was attacked on Christmas Eve by a submarine whose torpedo hit her, and whose guns next shelled her. The *Penshurst* replied, and struck the U-boat on the deck, but then arrived one of the previously mentioned P-boats. This frightened the enemy away, but at last poor old *Penshurst* had come to the end of her life, and whilst people on shore were busy with holly and mistletoe, the Q-ship, at eight o'clock that night, after two most strenuous years, went down to join Neptune's collection

---

[1] *Germany's High Sea Fleet*, p. 277.
[2] She was sunk by H.M.S. *P* 62 when patrolling between the Smalls and Tuskar.

of marine relics with the other notable wrecks. But there is some satisfaction in remembering that on Christmas Day this particular submarine—or her fellow working the district—was likewise sent to the bottom by a P-boat, never to rise again.

On February 17, 1917—that is to say, only five days before *Penshurst* just failed to sink *U* 84—Commander Campbell in the *Farnborough* off south-western Ireland was torpedoed by *U* 83, another of these newly-built super-efficient craft. Thanks to the cargo of timber (which, as we have stated, had been obtained from Canada) the ship did not immediately founder, though the engine-room soon began to fill. The enemy appeared on the surface some time after the " panic party " had " abandoned " ship, and now came Campbell's chance at 300 yards. Fire was opened, and the initial shot hit *U* 83's conning-tower, beheading her captain, and the ensuing shower of shells finally sank her, shattered to impotency. One officer and one man were picked up out of sea " thick with oil and blood."

The *Farnborough* herself was in a bad way. Assistance was summoned by wireless, and there arrived a British destroyer with the sloop *Buttercup*. The latter took her in tow, and later the sloop *Laburnum* succeeded her, though it was a trying affair with the water gaining rapidly, seas breaking over the *Farnborough's* after-deck, and a depth-charge exploding accidentally through contact with the water. The ship listed ominously, and she steered like a wild bull, yet finally she was brought that memorable night into Berehaven and beached at Mill Cove, where for many a day we all regarded her as a marvel. For this action Commander Gordon Campbell, having already won the D.S.O., was now awarded the Victoria Cross, but his old ship was played out. She was eventually patched up, and returned to the Merchant Service as a cargo-carrier. A suitable plate was later affixed, reminding all and sundry that this apparently disreputable vessel was really very much of a heroine.

In spite of these anti-submarine victories, the enemy was doing a terrible amount of injury. We have just mentioned that on February 22 Commander Grenfell sighted a boat full of survivors and then the hull of an up-turned ship. She was that fine barque *Invercauld*, yet one more of the sailing ships to be victimised, of 1416 registered tons, built of steel at Dumbarton in 1891, and there has come into my hands the captain's personal narrative of how this ship was snatched away from him.

"Shortly after daylight on the morning of February 22, when the ship was twenty-two miles S.E. of Mine Head (Ireland), 120 miles from our destination, I suddenly sighted right astern a submarine rising to the surface, distant about one and a half miles. At that time we had a light northerly wind and all sail set, the ship doing about two and a half knots. Immediately afterwards the submarine commenced shelling us; the first shot falling short, the second striking us under the port quarter, tearing through the ship's hull and causing a lot of damage." After summoning all hands on deck, sending them to boat stations and to put on lifebelts, the master luffed up into the wind, lowered boats. All this time the enemy continued firing.

But before quitting his beloved ship, the master thought of a pet in its cage and one or two articles down below. "I fetched my bird, and my bag containing the ship's papers, and passed the same into my boat, which was on the starboard side. I then took the wheel, lashed it, and suddenly saw the submarine submerging and making for our port side. It then struck me he intended to fire a torpedo into us. I went below again to try to save my chronometers, and was actually in the act of unscrewing same when the torpedo hit us amidships, blowing 150 feet out of the ship's side, sending wreckage and water 250 feet in the air. I was knocked down, and rushed to try to get out on the main deck, the ship at the same time heaving over to port until her yard-arms were in the water. All was black as night for a few minutes from wreckage and fumes. Owing to the rush of water on the main deck, I was unable to get out of the way, turned back and ran up the companion staircase on to the poop. By this time the ship was heaving over to starboard, and I jumped over the side into the sea within a yard of my own boat, being immediately picked up.

"To my astonishment, I saw the cook struggling in the water about twenty yards distant; and it appears that after I went below to try to save my chronometers, he left the boat

TORPEDOES AND MINES

and went back to try to fetch some ham which was frying. When the explosion occurred, he was blown clean through the galley door and over the ship's side, but eventually picked up unhurt. My port boat, containing twelve men, was blown 300 yards astern from the force of the explosion, and two men blown out of her, but picked up uninjured. . . . It was not until the fore and mizzen masts had been blown over the side by the enemy's shells that the poor old ship began to turn turtle, and the last I saw of her she was lying bottom up with only her keel visible.

" I had a man on a stretcher in my boat with a broken leg, a terrible gash in his head, and internal injuries, and we had great difficulty in being able to pull at all with this man laid across the thwarts."

Later on they were picked up by the S.S. *Rameses*, whence they were transferred to the sloop *Buttercup*.

" The commander of the man-of-war gave me his own private rooms and insisted on my helping myself to any of his clothes. Owing to the shock received from the torpedo, I was quite unable to sleep the whole night, and kept coming on deck every few minutes, expecting every moment to be blown up again."

A little later the survivors arrived in Queenstown, where the *Invercauld's* late master was received by the Admiral, the men were paid off, a shipless crew departing for their homes with anger and sorrow in their hearts.

From January 1917 was inaugurated a system of rescue tugs round the coast in order to help into port stricken vessels. It was a good idea, and one of the first instances happened when, on February 22, three of H.M. tugs from Falmouth came out to salve a couple of Dutch steamers which had been torpedoed by Lieut.-Commander Hersing in *U 21*. This officer was mentioned in an earlier chapter as the pioneer who went to the Mediterranean; but now he was on his way from there homewards to Wilhelmshaven. He had made an unfortunate mistake in attacking neutrals, which scarcely helped his country at a period when her neighbours were becoming rapidly apprehensive of future developments. Altogether, before long, sixty rescue tugs were stationed in Home Waters, and their efforts saved 126 vessels which had been torpedoed or mined. It is a pity such an organisation had not been started earlier in the War, yet even now there were many sad occasions when nothing could have saved a fine ship from foundering.

Just before 11 p.m. on February 25, when 160 miles west of the Fastnet, that fine Cunarder *Laconia* (18,099 tons) had a couple of torpedoes driven into her side without warning. The sloop *Laburnum* hurried to the scene and picked up most of her crew and passengers, though a dozen lives were lost this Sunday night. Next day the S.S. *Tritonia* wirelessed that she was torpedoed twenty miles west of Tearaght, and less than three hours later the *Bluebell* located her survivors, being joined that morning by *Zinnia* as well as the trawler *Lord Heneage*. *Bluebell* got the stricken ship in tow, but unfortunately a fresh S.W. breeze sprang up, and no way could be made with this enormous, helpless bulk astern; so she was headed for Smerwick Harbour (previously mentioned in connection with the *Aud*). Monday passed, the tow-rope parted, and *Zinnia* took over, but her tow-rope broke likewise. The *Bluebell* made another attempt, using her sweep wires this time, but the ship was making so much water that this steamer's crew had to be taken off at nightfall. Next, in the early hours of Wednesday one of the Q-ships took her in tow, till yet again the rope snapped. By daylight it was obvious *Tritonia* could never reach land. She had come across the Atlantic with 250 horses for the Army, and when she sank at 7.55 a.m., twenty miles short of Loop Head, she provided the pathetic sight of these unfortunate animals drowning helplessly in the Atlantic.

March was a terrible month, and indicated how deadlily, how suddenly, the new submarine campaign had got into its stride. No fewer than 283,647 tons of British merchant shipping, plus 3586 tons of fishing vessels, were destroyed —partly in the Mediterranean, the Bay of Biscay, English Channel, North Sea, and off the Orkneys; but especially off the Irish coasts, in the Bristol Channel, and Western Approaches. How long could any national marine endure such a monthly strain? The enemy's strategy was clearly to mine the inshore waters, and thus drive shipping outside, where torpedoes would await them. Thus minefields were discovered off the Old Head of Kinsale, Seven Heads, Ballycotton, Galley Head, Cape Clear, and Coningbeg lightship. The submarines were now using a type of delay release, so that the mine might not show itself for several days.

The M.L.'s, with their shallow draught, thus became of great help during their work with the sweeping sloops, or patrolling independently with vigilant eyes. I can still see in my recollection those busy spring days around the Fastnet, with the gaunt black cliffs and the rolling green seas. On the morning of Lady Day, the White Star liner *Adriatic* rushed past, escorted by a destroyer. Then about noon up rose an ugly mine near Cape Clear, and bobbed out of sight in the trough. Barely had we sunk that one, than a couple more appeared, and were disposed of just as the sea began rising to culminate in a N.W. gale.

But interesting events were now impending. On this evening occurred a strange hostile act without precedent. Around the coast some of the navigation shore lights had been put out or dimmed, but many were still working as before. However useful they might be to the enemy in fixing his position, they were essential at such spots as the Fastnet and elsewhere for the safety of our own shipping passing on their lawful occasions. German submarines had wisely never once interfered with these marks. On March 25, however, the South Arklow light-ship was boarded by a U-boat and sunk by bombs. Why? Probably because the light-vessel's crew had been seen making warning signals to the S.S. *Annan*, who was steaming south into a submarine trap.

The time had now come when British submarines were to be used against the enemy more freely. On March 10 H.M. submarine *G* 13, in north Scottish waters, torpedoed *UC* 43, and down the latter went for the last time of all, leaving nothing but a few bits of her woodwork and a square-mile patch of oil fuel. There was from the first moment no hope, for she was full of mines that were to have been laid off the south Irish coast a few days later.

Now, only five days earlier the south Irish patrols witnessed a most tantalising spectacle: six nice submarines in the same picture, yet not one of them must be touched! For H.M.S. *Adventure* was escorting them westward, and they were to be stationed temporarily in Queenstown, but ere long at Berehaven. Their numbers were *D* 3, *D* 7, *D* 8, *E* 32, *E* 54, and *H* 5. In command of this flotilla came Commander Martin E. Nasmith, who was one of the pioneers in the history of submarines, and had already won fame as well as the Victoria Cross at the Dardanelles. This very gallant and modest officer, with all his ripe experience and sound judgment, was given free control by Admiral Bayly, except that these boats were to work only in a certain restricted area, for which reason other patrols were ordered to keep out of that section. Only one of these British submarines was allowed to be out at a time, lest any regrettable mistake might occur; but the climax will be related presently.

Meanwhile the enemy's attacks were fast approaching their peak, and the escapes could be measured by inches. It was during the night of March 11 that the sloop *Alyssum* was a target for two German torpedoes, which just failed to hit. Two days later the oiler *Luciline* was being escorted by the sloop *Lavender* when a U-boat fired two missiles: one torpedo passed under the sloop's stern, but the other struck the *Luciline*. That was on Tuesday. On Friday a minefield was revealed off Galley Head, so next day sloops were sent to sweep, and whilst so employed the *Mignonette* had her bow blown off. An attempt was made to tow her stern-first, but she sank, to add one more to the many ships whose frames now rest in those tidal waters. On Sunday the *Alyssum*, whilst working also in that same field, struck another mine, and down she went too. She had been through many a perilous situation, but fate had snatched her in the end. And the net result of these two disasters was that such deep-draught vessels as sloops or trawlers could not be risked, so drifters and M.L.'s must for the present do the sweeping up until paddle steamers could reach Ireland. No lives were lost in the *Alyssum*, but the *Mignonette* had fourteen killed and her captain wounded.

In order to confuse the Queenstown patrol strategy, enemy submarines now operated both well off the land and inshore. Let the two following incidents illustrate this new phase.

On March 22 the *Zinnia* had been escorting the Norwegian oil-tanker *Malmanger* inward toward the Fastnet and had just left her. "We parted company," says the sloop's captain, "at 12.25 p.m., but, noticing that the tanker was steering rather close in, I turned ten minutes later, followed, and signalled her to keep clear of the coast. At 12.55 p.m., when five miles east of the Fastnet, she was torpedoed on her starboard side. I was then abaft her port beam one or two miles away, so closed her at full speed to pick up survivors who had left ship."

The Norwegian master said one of his crew had seen a periscope, but nevertheless *Zinnia* did not hesitate to put a party on board, take her in tow stern first at three knots with the hope of reaching Baltimore. At 4.20 p.m., when only a couple of miles still remained to be covered, the tanker dipped at the bows, the rope had to be slipped, and down she sank. At least, she did not wholly disappear till an hour later, for her bows hit the muddy sea-bottom, causing her to stand on her head, with a hundred feet of hull sticking up in the air. Then she subsided, and another neutral had perished.

A week later, and only a few miles farther east, the same sloop had a similar experience. This time she was escorting the British oil-tanker *Gafsa*. Every possible precaution was being taken aboard *Zinnia*. She was zigzagging ahead at full speed, the First Lieutenant looking out in the foretop, three men at each gun looking out ahead and astern for the earliest indication of a periscope, when suddenly the *Gafsa* received a torpedo on her starboard quarter. The time was 5.15 p.m.

"I turned," says Captain Wilson, "and when about 1000 yards south of the original position loosed two depth-charges at one-minute intervals. Then, after cruising for three-quarters of an hour, I picked up survivors, consisting of the master (Captain Burdis), thirty-one officers and men. The *Gafsa* heeled to starboard when struck, and sank by the stern. According to the survivors, the engine-room and after accommodation were completely wrecked; the Second Engineer and six men who were below were killed by the explosion, which apparently sent up the magazine, too. The ship was defensively armed with a twelve-pounder gun. No one in the *Zinnia* or the oiler saw any sign of a submarine or track of torpedo, but the short choppy sea made it difficult to have seen a periscope. About twenty feet of the bow remained sticking vertically out of the water, and this being dangerous to navigation, I sank it with three shots."

Altogether this last week in March had been an unforgettable experience, ending up with fourteen merchant vessels sent to the bottom, ten merchant-ships and patrols attacked.

CHAPTER XVIII

THE CRITICAL MONTH

As the spring sunshine returned this April to raise our spirits after another long and anxious winter, the seas began to be less persistently boisterous, and even a sudden snow blizzard made a not unwelcome change. Away went the sloops in pairs to keep the traffic channels clear, with one M.L. to starboard ready to shell the first mine that came up, and two more M.L.'s travelling ahead as seaward submarine-screen to port. In the same picture were the rugged, lonely Fastnet rock with its tall lighthouse and, beyond, the green Irish hills powdered with snow.

Was this to be the final winter? Would America come over to hasten the War's end? For most of us were kept in a condition of complete suspense, and wondered day after day what was about to evolve. The newspapers revealed little enough, censorship became more strict, and rumour took the place of genuine information. But one day on patrol certain indications fired the imagination and seemed to prophesy big forthcoming events. A large Atlantic steamship passed us near Cape Clear, flying the Stars and Stripes. She was the *St. Louis*, of the American Line, rushing east, and the most noticeable feature was one of her guns ready for action. A week later she passed west, as did also the American S.S. *Finland*, when it was noticed that each vessel was armed with three or four guns. The *St. Louis* was the very first of the United States' merchant ships to arrive thus conditioned, and from that day it became obvious an interesting announcement could not long be delayed.

Five weeks to wait!

And they were the most critical of all the weeks at sea. No less than 516,394 tons of British merchant shipping were sunk this month by enemy submarines, and in no other month of the whole War did the figures exceed 391,004 tons. During these fateful weeks U-boats reached their maximum activity off Ireland and in the Western Approaches, the enemy making a dead set on the incoming transatlantic steamers. The recent arrival of four British destroyers—*Parthian*, *Peyton*,

Narwhal, Mary Rose [1]—was a valuable addition to the Queenstown Command, nevertheless in the big scheme of things it amounted to very little. As to the mines this month, they were laid off the south Irish coasts (Coningbeg, Waterford, Daunt's Rock Light-vessel, Old Head of Kinsale); in the north off Belfast Lough, in the east off Milford and Barnstaple.

To cope with this very pressing problem, and to avoid risking such fatalities as had befallen the *Mignonette* and *Alyssum*, there reached Queenstown on April 2 a division of four new paddle minesweepers. These were the *Haldon*, *Hurst*, *Eridge*, and *Epsom*, and belonged to the "Race-meeting" class, which had been specially built during the War less for seaworthiness than to be able to do their work whilst drawing a minimum of water. They were fifteen-knot ships: draught 6 feet 9 inches. If it seemed strange for the White Ensign to be flying aboard paddle-steamers in the Atlantic, already the North Sea was accustomed to such a phenomenon. These two-funnelled "Race-meeting" vessels were of 810 tons displacement, but always there existed the danger of mines getting foul of the paddles, wherefore an improved type (all named after famous Hunts) was built with twin screws. The latter drew 7 feet, had a displacement of 750 tons as against 1250 tons of the "Flower" class single-screw sloops; but, size-for-size, with their sixteen knots speed were the nicest little ships I ever went aboard. In the "Hunt" class, as a result of much experience, the Navy finally produced the ideal minesweeper.

When the *Haldon* and her sisters now got busy along the coast, they were actually sweeping up the mines which had only just been laid by *U* 78, so that her cargo did not long continue a menace to shipping. To-day we have details of her voyage, which are worth noting. She left Germany on April 2 with thirty-six mines to be laid between Cape Clear and the Old Head of Kinsale, and got back to Heligoland on April 20—eighteen days out and home. Whilst these boats evaded all attention until the last of their black "eggs" had been released, they were free to attack when homeward bound. It was thus that *U* 78, when 145 miles W.N.W. of

[1] Not to be confused with the sloop *Rosemary*.

the Orkneys on April 13, captured and sank by her bombs the S.S. *Strathcona*, taking the master as well as two engineer officers prisoners; and the next day sank the steam trawler *Andromache*, whose skipper was also made captive.

It is debateable whether the enemy—regarding his own interests—was not overdoing his minelaying, this series of traps. Indeed, about that time Germany was seriously considering the wisdom of depositing no more off south Ireland, lest the U-boats' movements should be restricted. It was such hesitancy which brought about an illuminating sequel, though, in order to connect cause with effect, we must for a moment imagine ourselves to be off Waterford on the night of August 4, 1917.

UC 44 had come from Heligoland with eighteen mines, which she was to drop here under the cover of darkness. The time was 10 p.m.; she fixed her position by the Waterford lights, and had just begun to release through her tubes the first batch, when an overwhelming explosion disturbed the summer night. Her commanding officer, Tebbenjohanns, was shot clean out of the conning-tower and (most luckily) was picked up by a patrol vessel about two hours later. Now the enemy had been too zealous. Unknown to Tebbenjohanns, a minefield had already been laid by a previous visitor! Admiral Bayly presently sent down divers, who noticed that the conning-tower hatch remained open, and half her mines were still in the tubes. Salvage operations followed, and this enemy submarine was brought into port to be dried out for a complete inspection. Her log-book yielded some valuable information.

Sea-luck is very curious in its phases and variations. Some ships throughout the whole War continued to dodge dangers with impunity; others had experiences quite different. It was so with respect to certain steamship lines. Not content with having torpedoed the *Huronian* at one date, robbed the *Alexandrian* of her escort on another, and then on a still later occasion maimed the *Alexandrian* fatally, a submarine on April 4, 1917, must destroy a third Leyland Liner. This happened off the Skelligs (west Ireland) at night time, and during the forty minutes preceding midnight the S.S. *Canadian* (9309 tons) was torpedoed no less than four times. Un fortunately, her master lost his life, but within two hours the sloop *Snowdrop* found the crew and rescued them.

Pass over a fortnight, and we see the impossibility of patrol vessels fulfilling all and every demand that during such a crisis was being made by shipping. This story begins on Monday (16th) at 1 p.m. The *Zinnia* met the oiler *Aral* and escorted her. Next the S.S. *Cranmore* was taken under protection, but at 10.40 p.m. she had to be left, for the S.S. *Queen Mary* was calling up help, having been torpedoed 180 miles west of the Fastnet. After steaming at full speed for three hours, the *Zinnia* reached the given position, cruised about, saw nothing, but kept flashing a light occasionally. Still nothing happened. At dawn, however, were revealed the *Queen Mary's* boats rowing about. There had been nine lives lost, and the survivors who were picked up said they had observed the sloop's flashing lights, yet feared to reply, thinking it was the submarine come back to take the master prisoner.

Now, exactly while this conversation was proceeding, another S.O.S. called forth. It came from the S.S. *Kish*, reporting that she was steaming at ten knots, chased by a submarine, so the sloop hurried off again, and on the way passed the woeful sight of the *Queen Mary*, still afloat with her decks awash. Just before 7 a.m. the *Kish* was found all safe and escorted for two hours, when the S.S. *Cairnhill* wirelessed that she in turn was being chased and shelled by the enemy. Therefore, leaving the *Kish* for a while, Commander Wilson made off to intercept the *Cairnhill*, who came steaming south. Nor had the warship been gone more than half an hour when the *Kish* was torpedoed with the loss of six lives, thus compelling *Zinnia* to return. Survivors were picked up, and the Q-ship *Viola* came to help. The *Cairnhill* met her fate too, and her master went as prisoner.

It was now time to escort a transport, but in less than a quarter of an hour the submarine showed herself. The latter was wily, and knew her job; for, whilst *Zinnia* endeavoured to intercept, the enemy cautiously kept out of gun range till she finally dived. A depth-charge was dropped over her, but with no good result, and for the rest of this day till nearly midnight the sloop protected the S.S. *Irishman* through the danger zone. Wednesday forenoon came, and showed the destroyer *Peyton* in company with the S.S. *Rhydwen*, which had been damaged by torpedo. The destroyer was flying the signal, " Submarine in the vicinity," and about an hour later *Zinnia* caught sight of a conning-tower five miles away. But the enemy had become cautious by now, so dived at once and went after other victims. Before Wednesday had passed a torpedo darted towards the S.S. *Clan Sinclair*, though it fortunately missed. Attack next came by gunfire, but the *Clan Sinclair* happened to be armed defensively and returned the fire, thus escaping.

In the meantime two more steamers were sent to the bottom this same Wednesday, and all within a few miles; whilst at 2.15 p.m. the *Rhydwen* turned turtle, to disappear for ever. On Thursday morning *Zinnia* steamed up Bantry Bay to land Captain Gilmore, his thirty-four officers and men from *Queen Mary*, who had certainly spent the three most thrilling days in all their existence. Most of the crew were Chinese, who behaved admirably. When the steamer received her torpedo, one of these Orientals down below tried to escape by way of a stokehold ventilator. Unfortunately his body got jambed, so that he could move neither up nor down. Then someone lowered a rope, to which he held on desperately with one hand and his teeth. It needed a good deal of force and heaving, till at last he was extricated with the loss of four teeth, but his life still to be lived. No other man from the engine-room had been saved.

Next day the *Zinnia* came into Berehaven to coal and stand off. As we were " chummy ships," and it happened to be our day in port likewise, we lay alongside for the night, and were entertained with a first-hand narration of these fresh excitements. The week ended with eighteen merchant ships sunk, nine attacked, and eight men-of-war engaged. A worse week never was known in Irish waters.

The following Thursday morning was beautiful, sunlit, spring-like; more suitable for yachting than for hostilities. The sea sparkled, the wind kept light; everything looked peaceful and pleasant—which was exactly the opposite of reality. For the British nation had reached one of its biggest historical crises. If the situation remained hidden from public awareness, it tormented those who were in authority. The enemy seemed to have seized victory in his hands, and to be running off with it.

It was April 26, and at seven that morning we had picked up, during our patrol, an east-bound oil-tanker off Brow Head, escorted her round the danger corner past the Fastnet and Cape Clear till abreast of Baltimore—the limit of our area. During the next hour and a half we were examining the Baltimore fishing fleet, whose crews, by reason of their pronounced Sinn Fein sympathies, had long been under grave suspicion, when an east-bound collier semaphored us: " Do you know that there is a steamer being attacked by something off Brow Head ? "

Full speed ahead! We began at fifteen knots, worked up to eighteen, signalled the Fastnet lighthouse men en route, and at the end of twenty-two miles came up with a steamer of 4470 tons—no way on her, lying idle with empty davits, ship low in the water—so low that on going alongside I stepped straight on to her steel deck. Not a soul aboard. Not a sound except the gurgling of the sea swishing across as she rolled to the swell. Expecting to find someone wounded and dying, I kept shouting, and entered the officers' cabins; but already the water covered the floors. No one there. Outside I stooped to pick up bits of steel splinters. Gracious! The submarine must have showered his shells. She gave an ugly lurch, behaved like some dull, drunken creature. Scarcely a ship any longer.

Immediately there now arrived the sloop *Snowdrop*, her crew's faces black as negro minstrels'; for she happened to be coaling in Berehaven when the signal came through from Brow Head. She had slipped and proceeded within seventeen minutes. Almost simultaneously there joined us what I took for a tramp steamer, until she thought she saw a periscope and began steaming round furiously, hoisting at the same time a very new White Ensign. It then became obvious that she was a Q-ship.

But the enemy had been frightened away, though gun-crews were all standing by expectant for a long while. The steamer turned out to be the *Quantock*, which had just arrived from North America with a valuable cargo of timber. Commander Sherston now took charge, sent me down to semaphore Brow Head signal station, who told us how a U-boat had attacked by gunfire, and that all hands from the steamer had landed from their boats the other side of Mizen Head. They were quite safe: no one killed. So the next job was to try to save the *Quantock*, which seemed unlikely to be successful.

It was a coincidence that we should meet the *Snowdrop* at the very spot where she had once nearly sunk us in mistake for a submarine, but her captain now put a couple of his officers with a salvage party aboard the sinking steamer and summoned me on the bridge to assist in the navigation. At first he was in favour of beaching her just round the corner in Crookhaven; but these two years had made me familiar with every creek and rock of that south-west coast, and I knew the *Quantock* was drawing so much water as to make her block up Crookhaven entrance for weeks to come. And Sherston was kind enough to agree with this opinion.

So it was decided to make for Berehaven; the tow-rope tautened, other patrol craft collected round us as an anti-submarine screen, and away we started. For the rest of that day *Quantock* did the wildest things, refusing to be controlled by those right aft at the hand-steering gear. Then she would remain quite steady for a minute till she took a mad tack to starboard and suddenly went about on the other tack like a racing yacht quick in stays. We had only thirty miles to go, and were fortunate to find a smooth sea; yet it took us eight fatiguing hours. The worst bit was coaxing her to behave nicely through the narrow opening of Berehaven's boom defence. Long after dark we anchored her in safety, and she just floated till then; for by this time she had dropped so deeply that at low water she was touching bottom. Only her timber kept her from foundering off Brow Head, and this is one more proof that a hull so packed will always defy the enemy for hours. When we learned that the total value of ship and cargo amounted to about £250,000, and called to mind the King's Regulations, more than one officer made a rapid bit of calculation, and decided that on the lowest scale his share of salvage money would increase the pleasure of post-War existence. But, of course, there was a " catch " in it. The lawyers remembered that the *Quantock* had been chartered by the Government, so the salvage regulation didn't hold good, and we got nothing—except a most interesting and exciting eight hours.

But that submarine skipper lost the chance of his life. Why did he run away? Why ever did he fail to come back and try a long-distance shot? Our cavalcade proceeded at only four knots all the way up to Berehaven, and he could have bagged sloop as well as steamer. Perhaps the grey *Snowdrop's* coal-faced gun's crew made him think twice?

At the end of this ever-memorable month—just four days later—followed an amazing finale. If the U-boats were now at the height of their success and must presently begin slowly to decline, even so were the Q-ships just about to wane. But this April 30 could not pass before $Q\ 21$—otherwise the three-masted schooner *Prize*—performed one of the most dramatic feats in all decoy operations.

The *Prize* had a curious history. In the first week of August 1914 I happened to be yachting down the English Channel, and to have anchored in Falmouth harbour. Here the cruise came to a sudden stop, for the great European War immediately broke out, and nothing could leave the port. But one morning we found a newly-arrived neighbour anchored a few yards away, with the White Ensign hoisted over German colours. Her name was the *Else*, and within the first four or five hours after declaration of war she had been captured at the western mouth of the English Channel.

Built of steel and iron, in 1901, at Westerbrock, she was registered at Leer in Germany. She measured 112 feet 6 inches long, with 100 net tonnage, and was the very first prize to be captured from Germany. Subsequently this schooner was put up for auction and bought by the Marine Navigation Company of London. In November 1916 the Admiralty was looking about for a suitable decoy ship with two auxiliary motors and sails. The *Else* happened to be lying at Swansea, and her owners, for obvious reasons, had changed her name to *First Prize*. She now seemed just the craft for Q-ship work; the Admiralty took her over, but the Company's Managing Director Mr. (now Sir William) Garthwaite, waived all payment for hire, and patriotically lent her to the Navy free of charge.

She was then fitted with a couple of twelve-pounder guns cleverly concealed on her deck, her name was shortened to *Prize* but officially to *Q* 21, and in command of her went Lieut. W. E. Sanders, R.N.R., a very brave sailorman from New Zealand. On April 26 she left Milford to cruise off south-western Ireland, and at 8.35 on the evening of April 30 was in Lat. 49.44 N., Long., 11.42 W., the weather that evening being clear, spring-like, with a light N.N.E. wind, calm sea, and excellent visibility. Under all sail she was heading to the north-west, doing about two knots, when a couple of miles away on her port beam appeared a great submarine, 225 feet long, with a couple of guns.

The latter was *U* 93, which had left Emden for her maiden trip in the Atlantic on Friday April 13 (Friday the thirteenth!). She carried thirty-seven officers and men under Lieut.-Commander Freiherr Spiegel von und zu Peckelsheim. The other two submarines working the Irish war-theatre at this time, whose operations we have just watched, were *U* 43 and *U* 67, but Spiegel had come out to relieve the former. On April 25 *U* 43 was attacking the British S.S. *Swanmore*, when the submarine's engines suddenly and temporarily broke down; whereupon *U* 43 called up *U* 93, who torpedoed *Swanmore* without any warning some 230 miles W.N.W. of the Fastnet, causing the loss of eleven lives. Altogether Spiegel sank eleven merchant steamers, took five prisoners from three of them, had completed a very successful week on his station, and was now about to go home, being also anxious to reach Berlin in time for the races that were to be held during the second week of May, when two of his horses were running. But now he sighted this poor little schooner, so why not make the eleven victories into a round dozen, and then carry on?

At three miles' range he opened fire with his four-inch gun, and invited on deck to witness this easy conquest all his own men who could be spared. The *Prize* immediately sounded her alarm gongs. Sanders and Skipper Mead, R.N.R., were concealed inside the steel companion-cover amidships, six hands were visible on deck, but the rest were hiding under the bulwarks or crawling to action-stations, whilst Lieut. W. D. Beaton, R.N.R., in charge of the guns, lay by the foremast with his ear to a voice-pipe leading from Sanders' observation post.

Prize was now luffed up into the wind, the "panic party" of six hands under another skipper, W. H. Brewer, R.N.R., launched the boat and "abandoned ship." The U-boat, however, maintained a deliberate fire, to make sure the schooner was genuinely deserted, and one of these shells put one auxiliary motor clean out of action, wounding the stoker petty officer in charge, whilst a second shot shattered the wireless room and wounded the operator.

Closer yet closer drew the big enemy from astern, whilst Sanders and Mead, through small slits in the plating, watched and waited. Twenty minutes of unbearable suspense! The submarine now came so near as to foul the schooner's patent-log line and wrench the fitting from its screws. Excellent! For now Spiegel starboarded and came on to the schooner's port quarter, which—at last—enabled the *Prize's* guns to bear. So "Down false screens!" "Up White Ensign." "Range seventy yards. Open fire!" The hatchway slid back and a gun rose into position, deckhouses collapsed, and within two seconds the first British shells jumped forth.

Spiegel saw his error as the White Ensign ran up, and in time to hit the schooner twice again, wounding one more man. Angrily the German next at full speed tried to ram the sailing ship, but when too late realised she was not inside his turning circle, wherefore he reversed his helm and tried to escape. It was now that the trap-ship's after-gun fired a shell which struck the submarine's foremost gun, blowing it to atoms and annihilating the gun's crew. Seeing that Spiegel was heading away, Sanders rang down for full speed, but one engine was disabled, and the other, after driving the ship for a hundred yards, died on him.

Moreover, the wind had died likewise.

Meanwhile the schooner's after-gun hit the submarine's conning-tower, demolishing that, whilst a Lewis gun raked the surviving Germans on the after-deck. Another shell brought such damage to Spiegel's engine-room that *U* 93 stopped at the end of 500 yards and slewed round broadside on to *Prize*. No more survivors were visible, but as shot after shot went home, the submarine slowly settled down, the red glare of internal conflagration being visible in the rents of her hull. After the thirty-sixth shell, and four minutes after the action began, *U* 93 vanished below the surface.

The last shot had knocked Spiegel into the water, together with his navigating warrant officer and an engine-room petty officer. Sanders then ordered his "panic party" to rescue these in the fast-falling darkness. They were taken on board. Spiegel, however, behaved as an officer and a gentleman. Giving his word of honour not to make any attempt at escape, his parole was accepted. He promised that he and his men would render every assistance to save the sinking ship. The navigating warrant officer now dressed the wounds of Sanders' unfortunates, whilst the engine-room petty officer went below and helped his British opposite number to start one motor. Just before midnight, with all sail and one working engine, the *Prize* shaped a course to the north-east for Ireland, and on the afternoon of May 2 sighted the coast, being finally picked up by Lieut. Hannah, R.N.V.R., in M.L. 161, who towed her from five miles west of the Old Head of Kinsale into harbour.

From Kinsale a drifter towed the schooner with her three prisoners to Milford. On the way thither was sighted a German minelayer, so *Prize's* nerve-tried crew went to action stations again. For a whole hour the two rivals steered on a parallel course, but finally the enemy drew ahead and disappeared. She had not yet deposited her cargo.

For this brilliant victory on the night of April 30 Sanders was awarded the Victoria Cross and promoted; Beaton was given a D.S.O., the two skippers each a D.S.C., and every member of the ship's company a Distinguished Service Medal.

But here is the amazing sequel.

U 93 was hit in her starboard fuel tank, where the oil got on fire. She was terribly knocked about, unable to dive properly, unable to summon help by her ruined wireless; yet her Sub-Lieutenant Ziegler, with three wounded and one killed, leaving behind the trio taken captives, managed to plug the holes, to get back on the surface during the darkness, to carry on right round Ireland and Scotland, then down the North Sea and so to Germany, where *U* 93 miraculously arrived on May 9. In itself it was a brave and marvellous achievement, but still more wonderful when we think of her voyaging all those miles and through the numerous patrols without being able to dive. This officer rightly won promotion, and *U* 93 was duly repaired; but on January 7 of the following year was sent to the bottom by the S.S. *Braeneil*. The War ended, Spiegel went home, many months after the races he should have attended. One day I was surprised to receive a letter from him. He had written an account of his experiences in his U-boat. He described the life as "Purgatory." I can well believe that German submarines made life something different from one grand sweet song.

Nevertheless, it was a theme with variations.

Pass over a few months, and we can observe the sequel. Of course Sanders' ship after that breathless incident was duly reported, and in detail described to other submarine officers of the German Navy. In August 1917 Lieut.-Commander Steinhauer was bringing *UB* 48 on her maiden voyage via the north of Scotland and N.W. Ireland bound for Cattaro, where she was destined to arrive in the Adriatic on September 2. Steinhauer was a young man, full of daring, smart, cold as steel, efficient, quite sure of his own ability, dignified, perhaps even somewhat self-complacent, yet a fine naval officer. With the exception of his Chief Engineer, all his crew were taken from German merchant ships; so that it is very certain every strange vessel would be carefully and accurately scrutinised. Bluff would be difficult.

On her way out *UB* 48 did not hesitate to sink whatever trading ships crossed her path, or to take the master prisoner. When 100 miles W.N.W. from the Butt of Lewis (Scotland) she captured a British steamer, *Roanoke* (4803 tons), and took captive her master. That was on August 12, the steamer being destroyed by bombs. Captain W. H. Williams, the master, tells me that before abandoning ship he adopted the ruse of "disguising myself by making good use of soot, which caused contemptuous grins at the unkempt state I was in." Three exciting and adventurous weeks did Captain Williams spend in the belly of this submarine from Scottish waters to the Adriatic, and then was sent to Germany for many months' internment. "After my return home I

CAPTAIN OF THE GERMAN SUBMARINE *UB* 48
Lieut.-Commander Steinhauer, who sank the Q-ship *Prize*.

carefully watched the movements of the surrender of the German Navy, U-boats, etc., with the intention of making a personal visit to the port where this submarine was to be delivered, and to have the pleasure of returning the grin." But Steinhauer was one of those ten who scuttled their boats at Pola or Cattaro.

However, to resume our story, on August 15, disguised as a Swede, the *Prize* had gone forth from the north of Ireland into the Atlantic, accompanied by the British submarine *D* 6. That afternoon, just after four o'clock, she sighted *UB* 48 coming down from the north, and signalled *D* 6, though the latter could not see the enemy for some time, owing to the amount of sea that was running. The schooner began to be shelled, then hoisted the White Ensign and returned the fire, claiming to have registered a hit at 200 yards range.

But again we see how tough were these new boats; for she was not seriously injured, but Steinhauer, with his callous determination and cool courage, kept just out of sight, and waited for the sun to go down on his wrath. The opportunity came after midnight, for we must realise that while under these conditions a submarine's periscope would be invisible, the white sails of a slow schooner would afford the most perfect target. Two torpedoes were fired, the first of which missed, but she carried ten altogether, and the second hit, causing a terrible explosion. At 1.30 a.m. the ex-German ship, with her brave British crew, went down in Lat. 56.3 N., Long. 10.6 W. At 5.35 a.m. *D* 6 unsuccessfully attacked, in approximately the same position, this identical enemy, and next day returned to Buncrana with the doleful tidings. The loss of Sanders and his men will not readily be forgotten, and on a later date Lord Jellicoe unveiled his memorial in New Zealand.

During the whole War the enemy lost exactly 199 submarines from different causes, as the memorial column at Kiel records. Of this total only eleven were sunk by Q-ships, which may seem extraordinarily few, having regard to the glamour which belongs to these decoys. But it must be added that the greater portion of such successes pertained to those mystery vessels which derived from Queenstown—the home and school of these craft—and it is estimated that about ninety more enemy submarines were damaged by the Q-ships' gunfire.

Life aboard a trap-ship, whether under sail or steam, was nothing but a sheer gamble with death. No one knew when dullness would in a twinkling of the eye be transformed to a contest with all the excitement possible. When on April 30, 1917, the ex-sloop *Tulip* (Q 12) was sunk in Lat. 52.40 N., Long. 14.20 W., her eight survivors were picked up by the destroyer *Mary Rose*, but Commander Lewis of the decoy was taken prisoner. He was well treated aboard $U\,62$, and a few years after the War invited his host over to England from Germany, who came accompanied by his wife. A courteous gesture, indeed, but considerable comment was roused; and it will need many years for the public to forget such things as happened at sea and under. So, too, the Q-ship *Chagford* had scarcely been commissioned and started out from Buncrana (N.W. Ireland) on August 2 than she was torpedoed and sunk on August 7 in Lat. 57.41 N., Long. 10.17 W.

But we can end this particular phase with a very slick story. We introduced above those first British submarines which came to Queenstown under the command of Captain Nasmith, who was in H.M.S. *Vulcan*, their mother ship. The flotilla now comprised six of the E class, two of the H class, and six of the D class. Let us go out into the Atlantic 180 miles north-west of the Fastnet in $E\,54$. It is May Day, 1917.

At 3.40 in the afternoon she heard an under-water explosion, and then observed the British S.S. *San Urbano* (6458 tons) stopped, and down by the head. That was a very obvious clue, so the E-boat hurried towards her, and when three and a half miles off dived, till an hour later she sighted $U\,81$ on the surface making towards the steamer also. At five o'clock, when still 1500 yards distant, the enemy altered course to pass round the steamer's stern, whereupon $E\,54$ altered course to pass round the steamer's bows. On reaching the latter, $E\,54$ proceeded to attack at 5.11, and fired both tubes at a range of 400 yards. One torpedo hit the enemy between conning-tower and bow, the other torpedo struck between conning-tower and stern. The affair was all over at once, for $U\,81$ immediately sank, though half a minute later a third explosion occurred. Seven survivors came to the surface, including the German captain, who was saved by one of the British submarine's officers jumping overboard with a line. The rescue was just in time, for the U-boat skipper had been injured, and would certainly have gone whither he was sending the *San Urbano*.

But here was a most dramatic situation, tense, and full of uncertainty; for if the *San Urbano* without any warning had lost four men, what could be more surprising than that her assailant should, with equal suddenness, have lost nearly all hers? In fact, the survivors in their boats took a lot of persuading that this second submarine was British, so that Lieut.-Commander Robert H. T. Raikes, R.N., had to go after the boats and compel them to come in. Then, and not till then, were the steamer's people glad. Meanwhile, the seven Germans were none too happy, and one of them wished to inform Commander Raikes that another U-boat was cruising about in the neighbourhood below surface; so *E 54* might go up—or down—any minute. Fortunately, all went well. Raikes brought his craft and his mixed crowd of guests east into Queenstown. It was late when he arrived and everyone had retired to bed, but the Admiral wished to hear all about it, so up the hill went Raikes to Admiralty House. It was 1 a.m.; the Admiral was a pipe-smoker, Raikes longed for a cigarette, so there the Commander-in-Chief and the submarine commander sat on the kitchen table, whilst the latter smoked cigarettes that belonged to the Admiral's valet. Through the blue clouds, and in the stillness of early morn, was related this strange episode of the sea.

CHAPTER XIX

HAIL, COLUMBIA!

NOTHING could have been quieter and less spectacular than the way the American Naval Forces unostentatiously steamed into the Great War. Unheralded by the press, they just slid across the Atlantic, arrived, reported for duty, refuelled, and went forth on patrol. Having regard to its great historical importance, and its enormous influence on future events afloat, this unannounced phenomenon was rivalled only by the silent mode in which the British Expeditionary Force had crossed to France nearly three years before.

Nevertheless, to those who could interpret the meaning of things, it was very evident what was about to happen. Captain J. K. Taussig, U.S.N. (destined presently to lead the first American warships into British waters) has recorded [1] that " We of the fleet had felt for some time that war was inevitable. When diplomatic relations were severed in February, the fleet was in West Indian waters, carrying on the usual winter manœuvres. The Commander-in-Chief immediately took all necessary precautions to guard against surprise attacks by submarines. Outposts, pickets, and patrols were established. The ships were darkened at night. During the passage to Hampton Roads the fleet proceeded cautiously by an unfrequented route. A screen of destroyers surrounded the big fighting ships. From Hampton Roads it moved up the Chesapeake to the mouth of the York River. Here Base 2 was established. A boom was thrown across the river."

But these were purely defensive measures, and as yet no evidence was forthcoming of any offensive action. " From what little we had heard concerning anti-submarine operations, it was known that the destroyers were the best antidote for the poisoning. It was therefore disheartening to think we were destined for nothing more than to guard our battleships at home and to patrol our coast." Captain Taussig was in command of the destroyer *Wadsworth*, and senior officer of the Eighth Division, Destroyer Force. Let us leave him for a moment. The *Wadsworth* had been detailed to run mails

[1] *United States Naval Institute Proceedings*, XLVIII. 12.

between Base 2 and Hampton Roads, where she anchored every night: in fact, it was all so peaceful that Captain Taussig's duties allowed him frequently to go ashore and enjoy his family's society at Norfolk. One night he was about to attend a dance, an automobile waited outside the house; he was just departing when the telephone rang. "*Wadsworth* to sail at daylight for New York, to fit out for distant service." She left at 5.30 a.m., April 13, 1917, and off Cape Henry the five destroyers *Conyngham*, *Porter*, *McDougal*, *Davis* and *Wainwright* joined him.

Strange coincidence that the setting for a most memorable phase in Anglo-American history should have been chosen by fate in this fashion! One April day, just over three centuries ago, three ships from England had sailed past a promontory at the end of their four-months' voyage into Chesapeake Bay and anchored off Kecoughtan. It was the expedition bringing the famous Captain John Smith and the first settlers of Virginia. The promontory was named Cape Henry in honour of King James I's elder son, and Kecoughtan became Hampton. That channel which passes Cape Henry saw, indeed, the very beginnings of the American nation and the dawn of Western civilisation, as also (by a curious sequence) it was to witness, in the *Deutschland's* arrival, the first submarine that ever came from Europe to America. And, to complete the list, it was off Cape Henry that in 1928 the airship *Graf Zeppelin* first made the American coast, after being as many days on the passage from Germany as John Smith had been months sailing from England. Thus, when *Wadsworth* steamed off that spring morning, she was unconsciously inaugurating one more of those colourful chapters which connect the early seventeenth century with our own contrasting age.

In the weeks that immediately followed Bernstorff's departure from America, so much had been decided upon in secret concerning much which was of tremendous import that even before Captain Taussig received his sudden orders, a telegram from the Navy Department broke the serenity of the Naval War College at Newport. Here presided Rear-Admiral W. S. Sims, learned in naval history and the works of Mahan, a great student of strategy, a clear thinker, but likewise a man of action and marked independence of character. It was now late in March, and he was summoned to Washington immediately, but (as Admiral Sims has himself related in his own story) " to come as unostentatiously as possible, to keep my movements secret, and to this end I was not to appear at the Navy Department, but to telephone the Secretary as soon as I arrived."

From that moment events happened swiftly. Mr. Secretary Daniels wished Admiral Sims to leave at once for London, get in touch with the British Admiralty, and formulate plans for co-operation in the War; yet to proceed without rousing any suspicions. The Admiral was still to remain ostensibly President of the War College, his family to continue living in the official residence, and he must travel under an assumed name. Thus, only a few days after this remarkable interview, two officers in plain clothes went aboard the American liner *New York*. Instead of " Admiral S. W. Sims," there appeared on the passenger-list a " Mr. S. W. Davidson." As his aide there accompanied him Commander Babcock, but he passed as " Mr. J. V. Richardson."

It was on Easter Monday, April 9, that the *New York* reached the Mersey, but the ending to that voyage was not without some little excitement. On March 24 a bunch of German mines had been found at the Mersey entrance, another batch four days later, and yet another on April 7. Although proceedings were taken to sweep certain channels clear, it happened that the *New York* now struck a mine on the north side of Mersey Bar Light-vessel, which seemed an ungracious welcome to a willing guest. The weather was far from good, a strong wind blowing with showers of snow. Soon after four that afternoon the S.S. *Tynwald*, with mails and 600 passengers, had left Douglas, Isle of Man, for Liverpool, and when about four miles off the Bar Light-vessel sighted the *New York*, evidently in distress, with a cloud of smoke issuing from her side. The *Tynwald's* captain therefore went to her assistance; the American lowered lifeboats and, in spite of a lumpy sea, the transatlantic passengers, including Admiral Sims and Commander Babcock, were transferred, being duly landed on Liverpool landing-stage. The mine had made a hole in the liner's side " large enough to take a full-sized horse and cart," yet the tugs managed to bring her into dock, although the fore compartments were full of water.

A special train was waiting in Liverpool, and Admiral Sims was brought safely to London, where the First Sea Lord, Admiral Jellicoe, revealed the real but discomforting truth of the submarine situation. Under the present conditions it looked as if the limit of British sea endurance would be reached by November, unless the U-boat problem were controlled. For it must again be stressed that this April coincided with the peak of Germany's big onslaught against our shipping, and Britain contained enough food to last not more than two months: certain proof at once of an island nation's weakness, and of her utter dependence on the safety of her sea communications that just now were in gravest peril. Although at the time it was deemed prudent by those in high authority to minimise the true crisis, and keep the public mind mollified, yet to-day it can be admitted that never in her long history was Great Britain in such jeopardy as during the terrible month of April 1917.

Fortunately, Jellicoe and Sims were old friends, and that connoted frankness from the outset. All the cards of the game were laid face uppermost, nothing was hidden; the two Admirals tackled the problem with unity of mind. Question: What was the best known means of fighting the U-boat? Answer: Destroyers. So, as Admiral Sims has stated, " A few days after reaching London I cabled the Navy Department to send immediately all our destroyers and all the light surface craft which we could assemble, to the vital spot in the submarine campaign—Queenstown."

"In April I was sent for by the Admiralty," Admiral Bayly informs me, " and they told me that in May some United States destroyers were coming over to help us. They would be put under my orders, and the Admiralty hoped I would be 'nice' to them. I was introduced at the Admiralty to Admiral Sims. On my way back to Queenstown I wondered how to be 'nice' to them, and finally decided to treat them exactly the same as I treated the British."

Now, we left Captain Taussig's destroyers at New York. From there they soon went to Boston, and hurriedly prepared to take on board not merely fuel and provisions, but also spare parts, fittings and equipment such as normally would have been carried for them by their mother ship. In fact, so much gear was put down below that instead of the usual 1000 tons, each destroyer displaced 1400 tons. Never before had destroyers been sent across the Atlantic unaccompanied by larger vessels, and even now their captains were kept ignorant as to their destination. Mediterranean? North Sea? It might be either—or further. Not till April 23 did the Navy Department receive Admiral Sims' cablegram designating Queenstown as the destroyers' base, but even this was kept secret from Captain Taussig till he was at sea.

This need for the most extreme caution was not exaggerated. German spies under Captain Boy-Ed, the German Naval Attaché at Washington, and also under Count Bernstorff, had been clever, cunning, and remarkably dangerous. But whilst the former had been recalled as long since as November 1915, at the demand of Mr. Lansing, United States Secretary of State, and the latter had also recently been compelled to go, yet there existed plenty of enemy agents still. Perhaps they might learn by devious channels that these destroyers were bound for Queenstown? Doubtless Germany would then hurry a submarine across to lay mines at the entrance to Queenstown harbour?

In the afternoon of April 24 these six previously mentioned pioneers one by one slipped from Boston without ceremony or benefit of publicity, with only a handful of people on the docks as casual spectators, and a few womenfolk, whose intuitive minds guessed what others had no solid information of concerning the destined objective. For once in a generation the American press were done out of a first-class "scoop." That morning a secret envelope had reached Captain Taussig with instructions to take his force till he reached a position fifty miles east of Cape Cod, Massachusetts, when he was to open an enclosed second letter containing sealed orders.

After clearing Boston harbour, the Eighth Division formed in column and steamed at fifteen knots. At midnight Taussig opened the second envelope and read the following:

> The British Admiralty have requested the co-operation of a division of American destroyers in the protection of commerce near the coasts of Great Britain and France. Your mission is to assist naval operations

of Entente Powers in every way possible. Proceed to Queenstown, Ireland. Report to Senior British Naval Officer present, and thereafter co-operate fully with the British Navy. . . . When within radio communication of the British Naval Forces off Ireland, call " G.C.K." and inform the Vice-Admiral at Queenstown of your position, course and speed.

Just before quitting they had read in the newspapers that thrilling narrative of what had happened in the Dover Straits on the night of April 20–21: how six German destroyers had made a raid, how they had been encountered by the British flotilla-leaders *Broke* and *Swift* in one of the hottest engagements; how Commander E. R. G. R. Evans of the *Broke* had rammed one destroyer, and helped to sink a second; how the old boarding tactics of a bygone age had even been used with advantage. It was the latest bit of War news and, for impressiveness, could not have come at a better moment: for the *Broke–Swift* episode continued to be discussed all the way across, and from the first remained a source of inspiration for American destroyers.

The days and nights passed, bad weather was encountered, a good deal of discomfort had to be endured, and the destroyers rolled so that for many meals the mess tables could not be spread, but those people with any appetites at all ate off their laps. On May 2 the sea began to go down, and during the following forenoon wireless contact was made with the Queenstown destroyer *Parthian*, though she was not seen; but on May 4, soon after midday, another Queenstown destroyer, *Mary Rose*, came in visual touch. She had been sent by Admiral Bayly, and now a flutter of coloured bunting showed from her yard-arm. It was a signal by International Code.

" Welcome to the American Colours," it read.

" Thank you. We are glad of your company," answered the *Wadsworth*.

And from that moment was enacted an episode which the British Admiralty did not hesitate to name an " historic occasion." Perhaps there lay far more meaning in that expression than officialdom imagined at the time. It was a unique day in the story of civilisation, not merely because here could be seen in terms of ships and men the pact of two great nations to defeat Germany's tyranny of the seas; but because it connected up with events dusty through age. The arrival of Taussig's fine division, with their four funnels and tall masts, their angular bridges and long lean hulls, has been called "The Return of the *Mayflower*"; but it was that and much more besides.

Whilst the *Wadsworth* and her healthy sisters had taken their departure from that same Cape Cod which the "leaking unwholesome ship"[1] *Mayflower* sighted only after many days, and spent another six weeks "for want of experience" before they found "a place they liked to dwell on," yet originally (let us not forget) Taussig's flotilla had come up from Virginia and Hampton Roads. Thus the imagination could behold, this balmy sun-brightened May afternoon, not merely the *Mayflower*, but those three vessels of John Smith's expedition *Susan Constant*, *God Speed*, *Discovery*, whose united tonnage was about one quarter of *Wadsworth's*. By one of those happy turns of circumstance not only New England, but Virginia —the two oldest Anglo-American plantations—had been intimately associated with an unparalleled gesture. It was the expression of two English-speaking people in plainest dialogue, capable of being comprehended by every Teutonic mind.

By a fortunate chance which was appreciated, and has never been forgotten, I happened to be at Queenstown for this occasion. We had, at the time when the *New York* passed, been busy sinking mines within half a dozen miles of where *Lusitania* foundered. It was beastly weather, and the mines were not easy to see as they bobbed and rose, but we managed to finish the lot, and presently the time came to enter Queenstown, where we were due for refit and leave. The usual kind invitation to dine at Admiralty House was accepted with alacrity, and one heard with joy that the American destroyers were about to arrive; that the Admiralty—with incredible disregard for all precedent—were sending a man with a cinema camera to photograph their incoming; that Sir Lewis Bayly—notwithstanding his lifelong hatred of anything to do with publicity in any form whatsoever—had been requested to appear in the picture. That is to say, the American captains

[1] As Captain John Smith called her.

were to be filmed in the act of shaking hands with the Admiral at the threshold of Admiralty House as he formally welcomed them to Queenstown.

Orders, of course, were orders. But I do well recollect the Admiral saying over his dinner-table that this request had not stipulated his face should be turned towards the camera. Wherefore, if I may anticipate, whilst this historic film duly took in the ships arriving, the officers being received, you will find little record of the Commander-in-Chief except from a back view.

Secretly, in the recesses of my private thoughts, I envied those whose duty it would be to go out of Queenstown and meet these first American forces. The Admiral has, in the generosity of his appreciation, been kind enough to state: " I was very glad, as a recognition of what the M.L.'s had done, that I was able to send an M.L. to lead the first U.S. destroyers into Queenstown harbour. They really were splendid; always ready, never complaining." By the merest luck of my craft chancing to be in harbour then, and my being the senior M.L. present, the lot fell on us to take part in this ceremony. As passengers this May 4—three days before the anniversary of *Lusitania's* loss—there came with us Captain E. R. G. R. Evans, just promoted after his *Broke* engagement with the Germans; and Commander Babcock, U.S.N. (previously mentioned), Admiral Sims' Secretary, and five British naval officers who were to pilot in the destroyers.

We cruised about off the Daunt's Rock Light-vessel over an oily swell, and then out of the haze in line ahead steamed *Wadsworth* with her division. We had barely signalled her to stop, got alongside her, and put Captain Evans on board, than a few cables to the southward up went a couple of violent explosions; for the Commander-in-Chief had suspected the enemy might have cognisance of this arrival. A submarine had actually plastered the approaches with mines, only a few hours before, but now the trawlers had discovered the " eggs " and were sweeping them up. It seemed a poor sort of welcome to those who had just come across the sea, yet, as one of the American commanders remarked a few hours later, when we foregathered in the Royal Cork Yacht Club, " Those mines certainly told us we're in the war zone." I have since wondered if that submarine did hang about to report the definite arrival of America's first warships, and to note whether the mines had their intended effect. It has also been a subject for thought that had this minelayer torpedoed *M.L.* 181, and taken prisoners the two officers sent by Admiral Sims, together with " Evans of the *Broke* " (for whose capture it was commonly reported there was a high price), this submarine might have won half a dozen Iron Crosses on her return home.

The *Mary Rose* did not survive many months. She was transferred to the North Sea, and on October 17 was part of the escort bringing a west-bound convoy of British, Belgian, Scandinavian, and Danish ships towards Lerwick. On a typical cold, grey morning of bad visibility two three-funnelled German cruisers appeared out of the mist and sank her by a shower of shells.

MAY 4, 1917
H.M.M.L. 181 going out to meet the first American destroyers off Queenstown.

MAKING HISTORY
Admiral Bayly's flag being lowered at Queenstown, and the flag of Admiral Sims being hoisted.

CHAPTER XX

THE RIGHT SPIRIT

WHEN the six American captains wended their way up the hill, they had en route been warned that the Commander-in-Chief was a man of few words, who would waste no more time than necessary over any proceedings which did not have a direct bearing on defeat of the enemy. None the less, their introduction brought with it considerable surprise, and the following dialogue is now so famous on both sides of the Atlantic that it deserves to be set down.

When Captain Taussig was presented to Admiral Bayly, perhaps it was hardly surprising if the former would have been quite ready to hear some such expression as "Hands across the sea.... Hope you had a pleasant voyage.... Glad to welcome you in Queenstown...." But of such remarks there was a significant absence. It might delay the anti-submarine operations! After shaking hands, the Admiral immediately inquired:

"Captain Taussig, at what time will your ships be ready for sea?"

"Ready as soon as we have fuelled, sir," came the perfect response.

"Do you require any repairs?"

"No, sir."

"Any stores?"

"No, sir. Each vessel has enough on board to last seventy days."

"You will take four days rest," concluded the Admiral. "Good afternoon."

That night, however, all six captains dined at Admiralty House, and four were invited to remain and sleep, "so as to get a good rest after your long journey." There was little talk of the War until next morning, when all six captains met the Admiral in his office and got down to business. The Commander-in-Chief's opening sentence was short and highly characteristic:

"Gentlemen," he addressed, "the Admiralty are afraid I shall be rude to you. I shan't if you do your work; I shall if you don't. Now here is the situation at present, and this is what I expect of you...." Then followed general instructions and advice as how to conduct tactics against German submarines.

It was exactly this plain, direct speaking, without any superfluity or useless effort, which made a deep and lasting impression. Commander (now Captain) Zogbaum of the *Davis* tells me: " I have always thought that Admiral Bayly's frankness in his opening remarks laid the foundation stone of the fine spirit which was ever present in the Queenstown Command throughout the War." Another officer who came over in a later division says: " The speech of Admiral Bayly to commanding officers, upon their arrival, in which he placed our duties in order of importance as: first, sinking of submarines; second, protection of shipping; and lastly, the saving of human life, made a great impression."

Whilst the *Broke* was being repaired in an English dockyard, Captain Evans was lent as liaison officer, went out on patrol aboard the *Wadsworth*, and his experiences as a destroyer officer were much appreciated. So, too, for a while went British signal ratings, whilst instruction was received in regard to the use of depth-charges. The tall topmasts were housed at once during those initial four days in port, so as to decrease the distance of visibility from the enemy. In order to lessen a destroyer's draught—thereby perhaps saving her in a minefield—all excess stores and equipment were landed at Haulbowline Dockyard.

Between the arrival of the first and second divisions of American destroyers, the *Davis* had been out and come back. On the second day of her patrol she sighted two boats some 300 miles from nearest land, and picked up the captain with twenty-two men of a British ship that had been torpedoed five days previously and left to starve. When found they had some water and half a biscuit a-piece. The *Davis* received permission at the end of a week to land them in Queenstown, where the survivors were looked after by an organisation for which Miss Voysey was responsible. Then the Admiral told the *Davis* to wait a while, and in half an hour his green barge came alongside with a basket of fresh eggs and vegetables, together with his compliments. It was this kindly, human

GETTING READY FOR SEA
American destroyers at Queenstown.

DEPTH CHARGES
Arranged on board American destroyer in readiness for immediate use.

consideration which till the very end of hostilities welded that bond of affection between American personnel and British Commander-in-Chief.

From now onwards, at short intervals, transatlantic destroyers kept arriving in divisions, till Queenstown's spacious harbour presented a remarkable sight. There were two types, of which the "*Wadsworths*," with their 1100-ton displacement and 315 feet length, had a speed of thirty knots. The smaller or "flivver" class were of 750 tons. As each batch arrived, they were sent to sea for five days so as to get acquainted with the local coastline and Ireland's south-west harbours. The utility of having a British signalman aboard during the first month may well be illustrated by the two following amusing incidents.

Once, when in Liverpool, a U.S. destroyer was sent a signal by semaphore from the sloop *Snowdrop*, whose captain invited the destroyer's captain to dinner. The U.S. signalman got the first letters of *Snowdrop* correctly, but missed the next five. The signal thus reached his captain that the S.N.O. "requested his presence at dinner," etc. Now, S.N.O. always signified "Senior Naval Officer"; and at Liverpool the S.N.O. happened to live ashore. When, therefore, the hungry American arrived at the house and found himself quite unexpected, the mistake was realised, but finally he dined aboard the *Snowdrop* without being any the worse.

So also a U.S. destroyer was steaming up the Irish Sea about 1 a.m. when she sighted a British destroyer steaming in the opposite direction. The latter signalled that she had a number of survivors aboard from a torpedoed ship. Thinking that the British destroyer meant that he wanted help to carry some of these people, the American replied that he would come alongside, though (as he explained at a later date) he did not think it a very safe proposition with so much sea running. However, since the Englishman had made a suggestion, well, why not try?

When this signal reached the Englishman he was heard to remark that whilst it seemed a risky manœuvre to perform at night in such a sea, he would not refuse the American's suggestion; so the latter came alongside, a number of people were removed, and, remarkable to relate, no damage occurred to either vessel—proof of the fine seamanship which distinguished both.

The numbers to which all these British and American units now increased might well have worried many a Senior Officer. Merely to keep these vessels out on steady patrol was an achievement. Their engines had to be maintained efficient, fuel and stores were always being consumed, unexpected accidents would upset carefully designed programmes, yet it all turned out a great triumph over difficulties. By the late summer of 1917 the Queenstown Fleet had grown so marvellously as to comprise thirty-five American destroyers, seven H.M. sloops, eight minesweeping sloops, nine Q-ships, together with the ever-ready H.M.S. *Adventure*: total sixty vessels. But additional to all these were the trawlers, drifters, and M.L.'s. Thus, within two years the importance of this base had been magnified beyond all imagining, yet still more vessels were to swell the list. In those wonderful days, when Great Britain and America seemed to have pooled their wealth, their resources, their ships and their men, everything was done on such a big scale that one lost the sense of values. About every ten days during the early summer a destroyer division would arrive. Each vessel would secure to her buoy, each captain would land to report that he had crossed the Atlantic, and almost immediately he would be patrolling outside. It was all like the moving pictures: events followed so quickly, situations succeeded each other so rapidly, that no time was left to think.

From the first Admiral Bayly's tact and common sense made it impossible for any friction to occur. He made it quite clear that officers and crews of both nations were to be treated exactly alike. When more than one ship happened to be at sea together, the senior officer was to take charge, no matter whether he were American or British; no matter whether his ship were big or little. If it were necessary to hold a Court of Inquiry relative to an accident where a ship of either nationality had been involved, he decided that the first Court should consist of: Senior officer, British; second officer, United States; junior officer, British. The second Court was to have: Senior officer, United States; second officer, British; junior officer, United States. The third Court

ACROSS THE ATLANTIC
U.S. Destroyer *Sampson* en route from America to Queenstown, May 1917.

CONVOY INWARD BOUND

was to be as in the first, the fourth as in the second, and so on.

In order to prevent delays, as also to give more rest to officers and men, the same regulation in regard to defect lists was laid down for the U.S. destroyers. Thus, a ship coming in from her patrol signalled whilst entering harbour whether she wanted to go alongside mother ship, or to oil, or coal, or if she needed attention for special repairs, and so on. Thus, during the two days in port any troublesome auxiliary engine could be put to right while the ship's company was taking a stand-easy before going out on another strenuous five-day spell.

It was not immediately possible for Admiral Sims to accept the Commander-in-Chief's invitation and come over to Admiralty House; for the King desired to see the U.S. Admiral at Windsor. But about the middle of May opportunity would surely present itself for the two experts to meet in Queenstown and get down to a firm understanding. Already things had begun to shape well. Even on May 8 Admiral Sims wrote to Admiral Bayly:—

> You will, I am sure, find our officers more than willing to carry out your orders and instructions, and to co-operate with your forces as completely as their present inexperience in this peculiar warfare will permit.
> My aide, Lieut.-Commander Babcock, reports them enthusiastically grateful over the reception you have given them and anxious to be of the maximum service to the common cause.

And in reply Admiral Bayly again emphasised the unity of Queenstown Command:—

> I do not consider that I am in charge of two different kinds of destroyers, or that there is any reason to make a difference. We are all one here, and an order is sent out to such destroyer as is in any particular place, whether she is American or English.
> I have told the captains of your destroyers, as I tell ours, that the way to prevent misunderstandings, doubts, etc., is, when they come in here, to come and see me. It is an old plan of mine that I have always found useful, whether with captains or lieuts. in command; I am always here, and my business is to help them.

And Captain Evans, after a fortnight with the Queenstown ships, went away to England with many a story to tell of strenuous effort. Healthy rivalry is a fine incentive. In those days somehow it happened that the press always managed to keep before the public a reminder of the excellent work which was being done by the Dover Patrol. So rarely was even a mention made of the Irish coast that we all felt a mild jealousy at this slight. Perhaps it was merely the old story of out of sight therefore out of mind? We were off the civilised map, and few came to Ireland willingly. So there arose no little pleasure when Captain Evans candidly remarked to Admiral Bayly: "I had quite made up my mind that the Dover Patrol did more sea time and running than in any other command. However, I take off my hat to your ships. . . . I hope some day that I may have the honour to serve under you, sir."

Six or seven years previously I had first seen Evans as a keen, young lieutenant standing by at the hoisting of the White Ensign aboard Captain Scott's Expedition ship *Terra Nova*, when she was starting from London for the Antarctic. To-day he is an Admiral with a brilliant career behind him, but it is with the Dover Patrol that his name will ever be associated. And here I would apologise for giving another personal recollection.

Coming back from a few days' leave in London just after that memorable May 4, and seeing a private view of the Admiralty film which was presently to convince all and sundry that America had entered the naval war with her amazing energy, it so happened that Admiral Sims and his aide were travelling to Queenstown by the same route. On board the Holyhead steamer Commander Babcock was kind enough to present me to the Admiral, and we breakfasted together in the Kingstown train. Throughout that journey I felt a great admiration for this distinguished naval officer, with the clear bright eyes and pointed grey beard, the tall stature and extraordinary independence of character; when the train drew into the Queenstown platform, and I watched Admiral Bayly shaking hands, I wondered how it would be possible for two such determined personalities to work together.

History and biography prove over and over again what strange coincidences may be created. Now, not merely in disposition, but also in careers, Admiral Bayly and Admiral

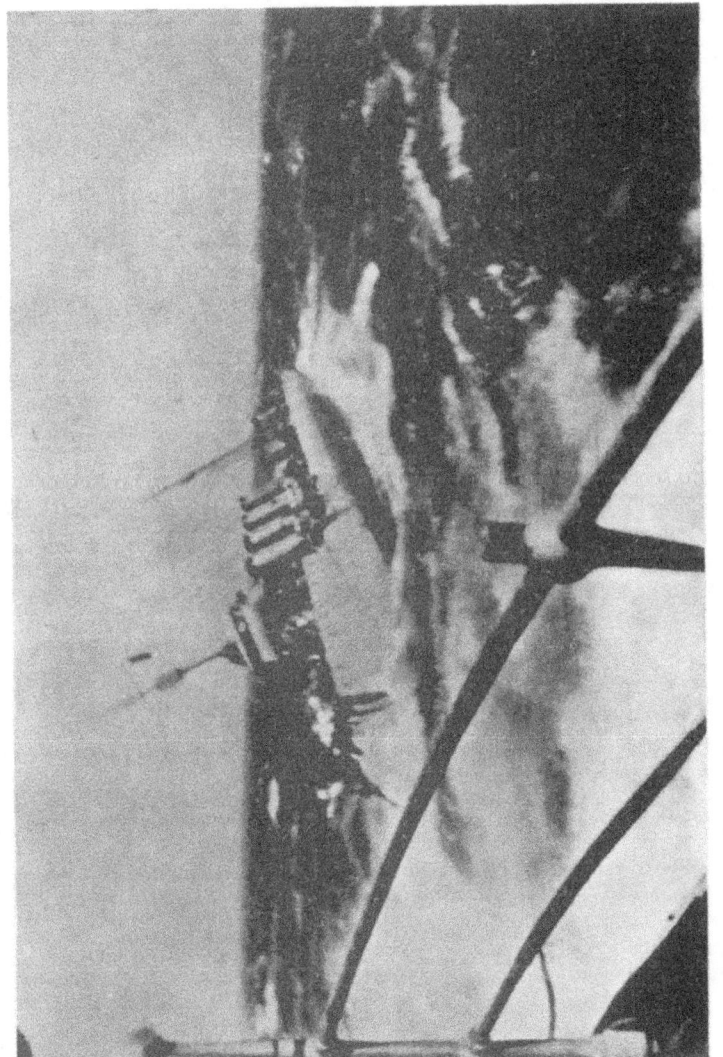

ON CONVOY DUTY
American destroyer in heavy weather.

Sims had been pursuing almost parallel courses. The former was father of the British destroyers (as we have seen); but the latter was not less responsible for having made the American destroyer force what it then was. If the former had held the Command of the Royal Naval War College in England, the latter had been once President of the Naval War College in the United States. Each combined with the characteristics of a man of action those of a student in naval history. Both had exhibited an outspoken attitude in regard to Departmental opinion with a freedom and courage that might have wrecked their careers, had their abilities and determination been less significant. Withal, each Admiral was imbued with a deep religious instinct, the great driving force which carried them on through one difficulty after another; so that, in short, either of these very modern and up-to-date Flag Officers might have been brother to Blake or in the Cromwellian Navy.

But from the very day when the two Admirals up at the House got to know each other, to see into each other's mind, victory in the Queenstown area was assured: two minds with the single thought of combating the submarine menace and preventing starvation from dictating a premature peace. "We are all one here," was the spirit which emanated from "topsides" down to the water below, through every ship, every wardroom and foc'sle in a general pull-together principle —every one of those thousands of men hauling on the same rope, in a united resolve to keep going till the end. And after Admiral Sims had returned to London, whilst it was still the month of May, came the most absolute proof to the world that this allied co-operation was something beyond all belief.

For close on two years Admiral Bayly had been working "double-tides" without any sort of break, but with every kind of worry that one in high command could face. The U-boat campaign had been, and still continued, the major anxiety. To receive telegrams every hour of the day that one more fine steamer had gone to the bottom, to read the painful successive stories of men adrift in open boats perishing for food and warmth, and then to have had the extraneous duty of defeating the Irish Rebellion—all this had been an immense nervous and mental strain. Still, he would now take only the inside of a week as holiday, and he would spend it within Ireland, motoring to some quiet corner in the west.

But who could carry on his work—operations, control of all those ships and men? Be ready for the sudden developments and emergencies that were sure to arise?

It was then that Admiral Bayly made a decision which had no sort of precedent in naval history, but was in keeping with his bold independence of outlook. He sat down and sent this letter to Admiral Sims :—

> I have a suggestion. If I go on leave from June 18th to 23rd, would you like to run the show from here in my absence? I should like it (and you are the only man of whom I could truthfully say that). Your fellows would like it, and it would have a good effect all round. If you agree, go and see the First Sea Lord, and we will arrange it between us without any frills. We both look forward to your return. You will, of course, live *here* while I am away.

The reply came back at once from Admiral Sims in these terms :—

> Your letter reached me yesterday evening. It was the surprise of my life. I will not attempt to express my appreciation of the honour you have done me, or my gratification for the confidence your suggestion implies. . . . I shall be more than glad to act as your representative.

The Admiralty welcomed this suggestion. Sir Lewis Bayly with his niece went off for a motor-tour, and as one Admiral's flag with a red cross was lowered at Admiralty House, up went another with white stars. A new page in the World War had been written. But, best of all, this incident proclaimed *urbi et orbi* in splendid symbolism an unsuspected agreement. The moral effect was felt till after the Armistice, and the Irish were impressed—even if they did now for a period spread the delicious rumour that the two Admirals had quarrelled, and that Sir Lewis had gone off in anger, leaving Admiral Sims to do what he liked!

During his first visit to Admiralty House in mid-May, and whilst dinner was in progress, conversation was suddenly interrupted by the sound of explosions. Once again a division of destroyers was arriving from America, and once again German spies had acquired news of their coming. It is remarkable that on almost every occasion the approaches to Queenstown harbour were mined the previous night. Now, before the end of May, there came over the mother ship *Melville*, followed on June 12 by the *Dixie*. Mines had also been laid for their reception. " In the latter case," Admiral Bayly tells me, " the mines must have been laid very late the night before, or very early the next morning, for the channel was swept during the evening until dark. It was known how valuable a ship was the *Dixie*, and special precautions had been taken to ensure her safety. Fitted with every kind of machine that could be useful to a destroyer, together with a large consignment of spare stores, she was expected to arrive at 8 a.m. No mines had been revealed by dark, but that morning at six o'clock one was discovered, and then some more. I signalled *Dixie* to remain at sea till the channel was swept, but to my horror, whilst dressing, I saw her with her destroyers entering the mined zone. There was nothing for me to do but hope for the best. Afterwards I found the signal only reached her when she was in mid-channel, and her commanding officer (Captain Pringle) wisely decided to go on into the harbour instead of turning round, and because it was high water he saved his ship."

In regard to the internal economy and disciplinary matters affecting the American forces, Admiral Bayly declined to deal. He left that in the capable hands of Captain J. R. Poinsett Pringle, for whom a great admiration was quickly developed. " Pringle is splendid," wrote the Commander-in-Chief to Admiral Sims early in July, and a week later Captain Pringle became Admiral Bayly's Chief of Staff. The *Melville* had come over under Captain H. B. Price, with Captain Pringle in the *Dixie*. As the former was the bigger ship, and Captain Pringle was the senior United States officer, it was decided now for these to change commands. For all administrative matters, such as repairs, maintenance, stores, personnel, discipline, the destroyers received their orders from Captain Pringle. In all other respects, such as when to go out of harbour and what operations were to be carried on at sea, orders came from Admiral Bayly.

" It will help him and help me," foresaw the latter in making the suggestion that this officer become Chief of Staff, "and will strengthen the bonds that hold us all together." That closeness of co-operation was certainly most happily achieved. It was the first occasion that a naval officer of another nation had ever found his name printed in our Navy List for such an appointment. Pringle was just the man for this not easy and very responsible job, and he did wonders. Delicate points requiring careful handling kept cropping up, yet Pringle never failed to handle these minor crises and save the Commander-in-Chief from unnecessary worry. This is how Admiral Bayly thinks of him :—

"It is no exaggeration to say that the good feeling between the two Services was very largely due to him. A first-rate seaman, of perfect tact and unfailing good humour, he laid down two principles which he faithfully followed, viz. to use his exertions for ensuring that every person and every ship under him was ready to do the utmost in carrying out my orders; and to prevent any kind of friction between the two nations. I am very proud to say that he was one of the greatest friends I have ever had. And his death, just as he had been appointed Chief of Naval Operations at Washington in 1932, was a very heavy blow to me and the United States Navy."

The morning after coming in from sea, every commanding officer, American or British, went up to see the Admiral, who wished to hear what they had done on patrol; but the American captains had to call on Captain Pringle first. "If they had a growl or a complaint, he put them in a good humour before they came to me." One day there had been picked up a piece of wood that had been the signal-board of a German submarine. This board Admiral Bayly placed against the bulkhead of the mother ship *Melville*, exactly opposite to her main gangway, and on it had been inscribed in big brass letters the two words "PULL TOGETHER." That motto could not fail to be noticed many times a day by everyone coming aboard, and not merely was it remembered, but it has since taken a more artistic form, as a later chapter will explain.

It must never be forgotten that whilst Britons serving out of Irish ports felt as visitors in a strange land, at least their homes were only across the Irish Sea. In a few cases British naval wives temporarily settled in Queenstown. Very different

U.S. NAVAL MEN'S CLUB, QUEENSTOWN

was it for the Americans, who could never return across the Atlantic for months at a time when women were not allowed to come over the ocean. Of course the walled-in " Sloop Garden," with its tennis-court, was now shared by American commanding officers; there existed a private entrance from the road, tea was arranged for them in an arbour, and so on. There was a certain amount of social life in the port, with golf and even an occasional dance; but the informal centre of the latest naval intelligence continued at the Royal Cork Yacht Club. If, then, the Americans who had come over to help us had for the time being no homes save their ships, the real problem was how to cater for the crews, and for a while it remained unsolved.

But immediately after the arrival of *Melville* steps began to be taken for providing them with a club. A number of American business men in London subscribed over £4000, and with this money a building was leased, whilst additional huts were erected. Finally, on August 25, 1917, the U.S. Sailors' Club at Queenstown was opened, and filled up a real need. It contained a stage, kitchen, restaurant, canteen, billiards-room, library, dormitory, and shower baths. The management was run by the *Melville*; films, musical and dramatic entertainments becoming very popular; so that in every way both the happiness and morale of the men were being looked after.

After a long fight the Admiral succeeded in getting the British Military removed from Haulbowline Island, where they had been for many years. It was now possible for the Navy to take entire control. By the seamen of the sloops, trawlers, and other British vessels, a hut was very much to be desired where they could meet, read the papers, and have their club. But no money was available. Thereupon the Y.M.C.A. generously offered to erect the hut, though this created a certain criticism among a community largely Roman Catholic. Finally the Admiral again called on his neighbour Bishop Browne; a friendly conversation did wonders, and the Bishop gave his permission, provided no proselytising was attempted; so this useful scheme went through satisfactorily.

Now, at first, after their arrival, American seamen used to spend some of their leave hours by taking train to Cork, rather than remain among the dismal unattractiveness of Queenstown. They had plenty of money to spend, they spent it liberally, and partly for this reason the local girls were glad to see them. Let it be said at once that if " every girl loves a sailor," no sailor ashore for a spell would find a more moral type of womanhood than these Irish girls, with their pretty wit and pleasant accent. Quite a large number of them eventually chose husbands among the destroyer crews. In the early days you would find U.S. sailors walking along the streets of Cork with a girl on each arm, and perhaps a third bringing up the rear hopefully. This went on for some time, but the young men of the city could endure jealousy no longer, and fights became frequent, till ultimately there raged quite a small battle between Americans and Irish. The U.S. sailors were planning a big revenge for their next visit, and it was common knowledge that bloodshed would have ensued had not the Admiral forthwith issued an order forbidding anyone in either Navy to approach within three miles of Cork.

Now, when that city was put out of bounds, it meant a loss to the tradesmen of several thousand pounds a week; wherefore the Lord Mayor of Cork and seven other citizens were appointed to wait on the Admiral, who consented to receive the deputation, provided that only one acted as spokesman. They arrived up the hill on October 23, 1917, and Sir Lewis invited Captain Pringle to be present at the interview. It was a memorable event, and it is still talked about; but, in order to get the full value of its humour, one must imagine a strong persuasive Irish brogue pitted against the chilly taciturnity of a much-occupied officer wasting valuable minutes on a fruitless endeavour.

The Mayor began by reading an apology for " the unseemly and disgraceful conduct " in attacking American sailors, and then asked that the Admiral " permit the sailors of the U.S. Navy to renew their visits to Cork." There ensued a slight pause, when the following questions were put and answered:

Admiral: Does this memorial include a request for British sailors to be allowed to re-visit Cork?

Lord Mayor: Yes.

Admiral: Are the persons responsible for this most regrettable conduct still in Cork, and at large?
Lord Mayor: Yes.
Admiral: Is the notice that appeared in the papers, requesting respectable people to be indoors by 8 p.m., still in force?
Lord Mayor: Yes, it is still in force.
Admiral: Does the Lord Mayor guarantee that the British and United States sailors will not again be insulted or attacked in the streets of Cork? Does he speak in the name of all the inhabitants?
Lord Mayor: No. He cannot guarantee it.
Admiral: Was the riot in Cork, after the Convention left, expected? If so, why were not steps taken to stop it? If not, it may happen again?
Lord Mayor: It was not expected, and it may happen again.
Admiral: Is there a possibility of the King, the British flag, or the United States' flag being hissed, or otherwise treated with contempt at cinematographs or elsewhere in Cork?
Lord Mayor: I am unable to say.
Admiral: Is it true that Sinn Fein Volunteers assembled in Cork last Sunday, contrary to the law?
Lord Mayor: Yes.
Admiral: Then the order will not be rescinded.
There followed a whispered conversation between Mayor and leading tradesmen, after which the former asked whether the order might be in force only after 4 p.m.
" What you mean," corrected the Admiral in acid tones, " is ' Can the U.S. men spend money in the shops, and then leave Cork just as they are beginning to enjoy themselves?' Reply—No."
The disappointed deputation filed out, descended the hill. At the foot the Lord Mayor met a friend, who was waiting to hear the result.
" Well, and did you get what you wanted? "
" I did not indeed," answered the Mayor. " But by the grace of God I left through the door, and not by the window."

CHAPTER XXI

A MAN'S LIFE

DURING the latter half of May that big inlet at the north of Ireland, Lough Swilly, with its facility of navigation, its proximity to the Atlantic, and its loneliness from the world in general, became an important base of Q-ships. Rear-Admiral Miller was appointed to look after northern Ireland, and Buncrana took on a new importance. As convoys were now to become one of the most essential means of thwarting the enemy, thirteen so-called convoy-sloops were to be based here. They were curious craft, with a single funnel, mast amidships, and stem shaped to resemble the stern. When complete with dazzle painting, these vessels were supposed to fool the spectator as to which way they were going; but such may be dismissed as rather excessive optimism, and we know from German U-boat officers that the camouflaging of ships (which this summer began to be undertaken widely) not merely caused no annoyance to the enemy, but was much ridiculed.

That spring three useful little steamers of about 1200 tons had been taken up to serve as Queenstown Q-ships, each armed with one four-inch and two twelve-pounders. Of these vessels we may mention the *Paxton* (alias $Q\ 25$). U-boat captains had now become very suspicious of trap-ships, and the days of decoys' usefulness were passing. The *Paxton* was plodding along on Sunday, May 20, when she was sunk by a submarine, being then so far away as 14 W. in Lat. 51.50. Both Lieut.-Commander G. O. Hewett, R.N., and Engineer Sub-Lieut. J. W. Johnson, R.N., were taken prisoners.

Now, this incident shows alike the vigilance and caution of the enemy and the ultra-ingenuity already demanded of a successful mystery commander. The U-boat saw *Paxton* grinding out her eight knots, took up a safe position from a distance, and began shelling. Then the steamer played the usual tactics of pretending to run away, making much smoke, yet really slowing down to lure the submarine within range. But finally the shells fell around so seriously that Hewett opened fire with his stern gun, whereupon the German sheered off—though apparently she continued to watch through her periscope. Hewett, believing the U-boat had guessed *Paxton* to be a trap, set his crew to repaint the ship's side and transform outward appearance. The enemy looked on with interest, and when the disguise was finished suddenly hit her with a torpedo, followed by a second. It all happened so quickly that no time was available for sending forth an S.O.S.

The marvellous fact is that survivors were picked up. The *Wadsworth* had barely settled down to patrolling these waters, there had passed less than three weeks since she arrived across the Atlantic, and now it was 9 p.m., just getting dusk, when Captain Taussig's officer-of-the-watch sighted in the lonely wilderness of waves and sky a small boat with a sail. Then the sail disappeared. Ah! The Admiral had warned them of that trick! U-boats were up to all sorts of disguises also. Full speed ahead to ram! The *Wadsworth* made straight for the object, but found it actually was a boat with three officers and eight men, who had lowered sail on sighting the destroyer. Dressed as mercantile seafarers, they were soon climbing on board, after having been tossed about since the previous afternoon. Among them was Lieut. G. MacGregor, R.N.R., who, in being blown over the side by that second torpedo, had received an ugly cut across his eye. There were another boat and a raft still missing, for which the *Wadsworth* proceeded to search at daylight. It was now blowing hard, with a nasty sea, so that one cannot be surprised nothing was seen. After a week, however, some more survivors were rescued by a trawler and taken into that north-west Irish harbour Killybegs, whilst four others were picked up by an American steamer, who brought them to Manchester. The irony is that whilst the *Wadsworth* had not seen them in the trough, the missing men had twice sighted the destroyer's masts.

But, in spite of such a loss as that of the *Paxton*, Q-ships had not yet finished their voyaging. Once again Commander Gordon Campbell essayed his skill and courage, this time in a 2817-ton collier armed with five guns and even a couple of torpedo-tubes. Her name as a mystery ship was the *Pargust*, and at 8 a.m. on June 7 she was off south-west Ireland in Lat. 51.50, Long. 11.50 W. when a torpedo rushed from an invisible enemy and struck the steamer amidships, making a huge hole, filling the boiler-room with water and blowing the starboard lifeboat into the air. The normal "panic party" then did their job, and at 8.15 a periscope was sighted. Less than twenty minutes later up bobbed *UC* 29, about fifty yards away, with a rating on deck shouting directions to Campbell's boats, and then semaphoring.

Three terribly tense minutes of suspense ticked by, and now the submarine was in such a position that all *Pargust's* guns could bear, and the enemy received a full surprise. The first shot from the four-inch hit the conning-tower and knocked off both periscopes, but next came a veritable downpour of shells, hitting beautifully. The submarine listed to port, Germans came rushing out of a hatch, oil squirted from her side, and now could be seen part of her crew holding up their hands in surrender, waving. Campbell ordered "Cease fire!", but immediately *UC* 29 tried to get away at fair speed, so fire had to be reopened and went on till 8.40 a.m., when an explosion took place for'ard, she fell over on her side, tilted up her bow, and finally disappeared stern first.

The *Pargust's* "panic party" then rescued a German Reserve sub-lieutenant and an engineer petty officer, from whom it was learnt that *UC* 29 had left Heligoland on May 25 with a crew of thirty-one, including three for training purposes, and expected to return about June 19. She had sunk a couple of sailing ships, had fired at a British destroyer, but this torpedo passed underneath. The third had penetrated *Pargust*, whose fire had killed the German captain. The Reserve officer with two men had gone on deck to open fire with their gun, but it was blowing a fresh southerly breeze, and all were washed off before reaching the gun.

At 9.30 a.m. *Pargust*, who had one stoker petty officer killed and an engineer sub-lieutenant wounded, wirelessed that she herself was totally disabled and required immediate assistance. The message was intercepted by the two sloops *Zinnia* and *Crocus*, the former reaching *Pargust* at 1 p.m., and the second ten minutes earlier. The *Crocus* got the stricken ship in tow, whilst *Zinnia* lowered a boat and fetched off the two prisoners. Lieutenant Hans Bruhn of Hamburg spoke English, but would give no information; Petty Officer Franz Tailla, a Saxon, had little English, but spoke freely. Presently the American destroyer *Cushing* steamed up and escorted. *Crocus* brought *Pargust* safely into Queenstown, and *Zinnia* resumed her patrol, two days later picked up three boats from one torpedoed ship and shortly afterwards the crew of a second. A total of sixty-three men were thus taken on board. " Great care had to be taken to keep them apart from the two prisoners " (Captain Wilson informs me), as considerable feeling was clearly manifested. Next day all guests were landed at Queenstown. That was Sunday, June 10, and the week had been fairly busy even for this area!

Next day, however, during the dark hours, came the first of several collisions in which American destroyers were to be victims. The sloop *Laburnum* ran into the newly-arrived U.S. *Jenkins*, and a Court of Inquiry followed. Meanwhile, on this same Monday, 11th, yet another Q-ship tragedy was being enacted in the Atlantic, for exceptional submarine energy was being displayed at this time in a desperate attempt to smash up British shipping. We mentioned in an earlier chapter the mystery ship *Zylpha*, whose Captain, Lieut.-Commander " Jock " McLeod, had once been a " hard-case " destroyer skipper before he ran his ship over one of our minefields and was blown up. He then took to Q-ship work for a quiet life, and, being something of a wag, framed and hung up in his cabin for decorative effect the letter of censure which the Admiralty had sent him for losing the destroyer.

Now, McLeod was both a brave officer and a great " wangler." On April 17 that year the *Zylpha* had been in action with a U-boat off south-western Ireland, and, by a curious fluke, the enemy's torpedo suddenly swerved, missing *Zylpha* by ten feet. Then " Fritz " (who knew his job) came to the surface at 5000 yards and began pumping in shells from a safe distance. Commander Cowap (who was then her first lieutenant) tells me the German " showed us some remarkably fine shooting," the steamer's decks being littered with splinters, and " we opened the valve of the escape steam pipe in order to encourage him to believe he had scored a hit." Finally, as he would come no nearer,

McLeod opened fire after two and a half hours of suppressed excitement, and the ninth or tenth round apparently damaged the submarine, for a flash and large cloud of black smoke were seen on her after-deck. She then made off *on the surface* at fifteen knots and, in spite of sending extra men down into *Zylpha's* stokehold and every rivet of her boilers weeping under the pressure of steam, the Q-ship could not catch her.

Fortunately the *Zylpha* had suffered no casualties, and the hull had been hit only by a shell which failed to explode. It went through the side and buried itself in her wooden cargo. "What we need," determined McLeod, "is an additional, but larger gun with a range long enough to engage 'Fritz' at his shyest." Arrived in Queenstown, he set to work, but the difficulty was where to place the gun. It was decided that amidships would give the greatest arc of fire, though this would mean the ship's lifeboats would have to be removed for'ard and two smaller boats scrapped. The next thing was to obtain Admiral Bayly's approval. One morning the famous green barge came alongside *Zylpha's* gangway, the Admiral stepped aboard, and the captain explained what he proposed doing.

Instantly the Commander-in-Chief placed his finger on the weak spot.

"Yes, McLeod. But, suppose at some future date you want to leave the ship in earnest? Suppose you really do sink? You are going to be two boats short, and the possibilities are that your lifeboats will have been scuppered as well by that time."

"Jock" bit his lip, shuffled uneasily, and muttered something about "having to take a chance," but he was very disappointed.

Then, looking him straight in the face, the Admiral pondered a moment.

"All right. Go ahead. Put your gun where you want it. If anything happens, I suppose you'll rely on me to help you out. I will do the best I can for you."

So the gun was placed, the *Zylpha* went to sea, and on June 11 she was about 200 miles from the coast, heading out into the Atlantic. The weather was fine, with very little wind or sea, and the time was just after 8 a.m. Cowap had been keeping the morning watch (four till eight) and had just been relieved by the navigator.

But let the former tell this story in his own words :—

"I was a few minutes late leaving the bridge, as I had some short conversation with the navigator. I went forward as usual, had just finished apportioning the work to the crew when there was a tremendous crash on the port side of the ship, in the wake of the engine-room. I suppose a certain amount of time must have elapsed, but my next recollection is that I was standing half-way up the ladder leading to the upper deck, with two or three men almost on top of me, shouting at the full stretch of my lungs for the men to get to their stations. The whole incident was instinctive on all our parts, and once we had collected our wits the men went off to their stations at the double, leaving me to find my way to my own, which was now in charge of the midship gun. I had to pass along the port shelter deck, through the engine-room and into the engineers' mess-room, and it took me quite a time, for chaos reigned in the vicinity. The decks and shell plating were blown in all directions, and as I passed the bathroom, I could see one end of the bath driven inches deep into the wooden planking of the deck-head. I could not help reflecting that I had missed a messy end by being a bit late for my bath that morning.

"The sight in the engine-room was most discouraging; water was rising there at the rate of feet a minute, in fact it was over the cylinder tops of the engine within ten minutes of our being torpedoed. There was no doubt about it, we had 'copped it' properly, in our most vulnerable spot.

"At length I arrived at the mess-room. The ammunition party were standing about with several boxes of charges and a number of projectiles. On the deck above, through the manhole, I could see the gun's crew clustered around their gun. I called out to ask if everyone was at their station, and someone replied that the gunlayer was missing. Just as I was about to question one of the ammunition party, a muffled voice from the manhole which led to the magazine down below, said, 'Here I am, sir; I think we'll have enough rounds now, but I thought we'd better make sure, before she sinks too low in the water.' He handed up another box of charges and clambered through the manhole after it. He was wet through to the armpits, and had been scrambling around in the black darkness, hauling out ammunition, carrying it a considerable distance along a narrow passage, and handing it to the ammunition party in the mess-room, not knowing from minute to minute if the ship was going to sink. I think it was one of the coolest pieces of bravery I ever witnessed, and it also showed great initiative, for we had comparatively few rounds of ready-use ammunition at the gun, which, had we gone into action, would have only lasted a few minutes.

"While this was going on in the mess-room, things were happening outside. The submarine that had torpedoed us made no sign, and not even her periscope was seen either before or after she hit us. The probabilities are that she kept in the wake of the sun, and the glare on the sea made the periscope invisible to the officer-of-the-watch and the lookouts.

"After about five minutes, with the panic party racing around the decks to the boats, turning them out and preparing to lower them, they were ordered to 'Abandon ship.' We could hear the clatter and the shouts of the men lowering the lifeboats, and they pulled away from the ship, and waited on the beam, two or three hundred yards away, ostensibly to see the last of her.

"Minutes went by, the old ship groaned and moaned as she settled down in the water, and for a time we thought she really would sink under us. However, she steadied up eventually, and we knew that the buoyancy of the timber in the flooded holds was taking effect. Still the time went on; every five minutes seemed an hour, the bright sun sent streaks through the cracks in the gun-house, the sea lapped against the ship's side.

"Every now and again the ship would give a shudder, and all was peace. After about ninety minutes of this a voice from the bridge through the gun voice-pipe said, 'There she is; but she seems to be steaming away from us.' Another half-hour went by and 'action stations' were dismissed. The captain had watched the submarine steam out of sight, after she had surfaced several thousand yards from us.

Q-SHIP *ZYLPHA*
"Panic Party" about to "abandon" ship.

Q-SHIP *ZYLPHA*
"Panic Party" return to stricken ship.

"This was not our idea of how the game should be played at all, but the initiative always lay with Fritz, and one can't play with a chap who simply 'strafes' one and then clears out. All that remained for us to do was to send out a bleat for assistance and try to get the ship into port.

"There was no steam to drive the dynamo for the wireless: we had a small emergency set, but that had a radius of only about fifty miles, and also a very short life. However, we got off our message to another ship, who relayed it to Queenstown. The 'panic party' was recalled to the ship and we took stock of ourselves.

"The old ship appeared to be in a bad way: the torpedo had hit her full in the engine-room, killing one man, a watch-keeping engineer. The water-tight bulkhead between the engine-room and No. 3 hold was fractured, and the hold full of water. The bulkhead door between the boiler-room and the bunker was jammed and could not be closed, consequently there was free access for the water to run from the engine-room into No. 2 hold, via the bunker, until it was stopped by the water-tight bulkhead between Nos. 1 and 2 holds. In short, the ship was full of water from the afterpart of No. 1 hold to the forward part of No. 4 hold. A sounding of the wells in No. 4 showed three feet of water, which indicated a leak in No. 4 bulkhead. Against this, there was the buoyancy of No. 1 hold, the fore-peak, the wood in No. 3 hold and the buoyancy of No. 4 hold, if we could keep the water down. At this time, the stern had settled several feet, but the ship seemed to be holding her own.

"We rigged the hand-pumps as quickly as possible, put the men into watches, and kept the pumps going continuously. After a couple of hours, we found, to our delight, that we were gaining on the water a little, so it appeared that the leak in No. 4 bulkhead was not very serious. In the meanwhile, three gun-crews were kept under cover, in case the submarine should change his mind and return. The after-gun was not manned, as she had only a few rounds of ready use ammunition available, and by this time the magazine was under water.

"I may say now that neither our old friend nor any other

submarine showed itself again: our fight from then on was against a much more implacable enemy, the sea.

"Preparations were made for towing if help arrived, and a bright lookout was kept for submarines and approaching vessels.

"Along in the afternoon smoke was seen, and a destroyer appeared in answer to our message. She was the U.S.S. *Warrington*, and very pleased we were to see her. She zigzagged around us and signalled to ask if we wanted to abandon ship; if not, she would stand by until help arrived. This gave the captain an idea; we wanted to get the ship into port, if it was humanly possible; on the other hand, it was useless jeopardising the lives of a number of men who were doing no good on board. The engine-room ratings were of no value, as there was no means of raising steam, also there were a number of other ratings we could dispense with. So we sent about half the crew away in the lifeboat and put them on board *Warrington*. The chief engineer and chief stoker petty officer almost mutinied when they were ordered away, and the captain eventually allowed them to stay behind. The men who did go were not at all keen, but they realised, I think, that they could do no good on board.

"Towards evening the wind freshened and a long swell set up, which made the ship roll considerably. With our depleted crew, all hands took their spell at the pumps—officers and men—and throughout the night we continued pumping. A lot of gear had been brought out of the wardroom and the officers' cabins aft, as by this time there was a foot of water on the deck there. Among the salvage was the ward-room gramophone with two records, 'Mighty Like a Rose' and 'The Eton Boat-Song.' These were ground out the whole night long, on No. 3 hatch, to cheer up those at the pumps. To this day, whenever I hear either of those tunes, my mind goes back to the scene of *Zylpha* slowly sinking, with the men clustered around the pumps and the sound of the wind in the rigging.

"Daylight found us with a fresh breeze, a dirty-looking sky, and quite a big sea running. The ship was perceptibly lower in the water aft, and at times seas were breaking over the poop: the after-deck was awash the whole time.

FIGHTING FATE

Q-ship *Zylpha* is being kept afloat by hand pumps. An improvised sail is moving her. In the background is U.S. Destroyer *Warrington*.

Q-SHIP *ZYLPHA*

Showing officers after four days without a wash.

"It was now my turn to have a brain-wave: I had left sail about three years before this date, and it is the ambition of every properly constituted sailing-ship man to sail a steamer. 'Here,' thought I, 'is my chance.' We got everyone we could spare, routed out tarpaulins, awnings, any canvas-gear to be found, and contrived sails out of them. The stitches were 'homeward bound' ones, and as sails, I suppose, they would have broken a yachtsman's heart. But they held the wind, steadied the ship considerably, and if one looked very hard indeed at the water overside, one could see the ship going ahead. It is said that one can see the hour-hand of a clock move if one looks hard enough. I imagine that perhaps we might have been good for three or four knots, in that breeze, had the ship not been three-quarters full of water and drawing thirty feet aft with about twelve forward.

"All this time we were receiving frequent signals from *Warrington*, and we knew that several ships were looking for us. The visibility was not too good, but we were hoping that any minute a tug would pick us up. In the afternoon *Warrington* signalled that she must leave us, as she was running out of fuel and had to return to Queenstown. We did not feel particularly happy when she made a final turn around us, gave us a valedictory toot on her whistle and streaked for home, but there was nothing to be done about it.

"Another problem presented itself about this time: we found that we had no fresh water. The water used in the galley came from a small tank, and this in turn was filled, by means of a tap, from a large tank situated above the deck. The stewards who were doing the cooking had been using water from the small tank all this time, and when it was empty they turned the tap to fill it again and nothing happened. It transpired that the explosion had fractured a pipe running to the bathroom below, and the water had run out from the large tank. Our only other fresh-water supply was in the after-peak, and at first there seemed to be no means of getting at it, as we had no pump. Very luckily, however, the filling pipe led from the poop deck, and by lowering down a small dipper on a string, we were able to bring up about a quarter of a pint of water at a time. It was a laborious business, filling buckets in this way, as seas were constantly breaking over the poop and the after-deck was well awash. But we had to have water, and four men persisted at the job until the galley tank was filled again.

"As darkness fell, we abandoned the pumping; the ship was still settling aft and the leak in the bulkhead getting worse. The sea was quite high by this time, and on several occasions we were washed away from the pumps. During the night it blew a moderate gale with a heavy sea; the ship was rolling and straining heavily. We had revised our routine after *Warrington* had left us, and the plan was that if we were attacked, two gun-crews should remain by the ship and the 'panic party' would consist of the remainder.

"After abandoning the pumps, everyone except the captain, officer on watch and lookouts looked for a dry spot and slept the sleep of the just. We were all pretty well done in, as there had been little or no sleep the night before, and everyone had been going all out, wet through, most of the time. It was this evening that the captain sent a message to be relayed to Queenstown, to the effect that we were under sail, making a knot and a half, giving our position, and saying that all was well. It was a pleasant lie, but at any rate we were drifting towards the coast with the westerly gale, and it showed that we still had our tails up.

"The next morning life looked rather grim: the gale still continued and the sea was very high. Our foresail had blown to ribbons during the night and the mainsail was split. The poop-deck was about level with the water, and the after-deck was a-wash to the rails. The motor-boat, which was lashed on the after-deck, had broken adrift, washed around for a while, and eventually had been taken overboard by a particularly heavy sea.

"Our worst trouble, however, was the fear the shelter deck, in the wake of the bunkers and No. 2 hold, would burst with the pressure of water beneath, and that the water would flow forward along the shelter deck and down No. 1 hold, which was still intact. Already there was a considerable amount of water in the shelter deck, due to some of the hatches at No. 2 hatchway having been forced out of place, and it was the sound of the water washing around the shelter deck that drew my attention to the state of affairs. It was a

Q-SHIP *ZYLPHA*
The doomed steamer is settled down aft. Notice improvised sails.

Q-SHIP *ZYLPHA*
Damage aft as a result of action with U-boat.

fearsome business, going down below decks, at first: not a great deal of water had got through, but in the darkness, with the noise of the flooded holds and the deck heaving beneath one's feet, it made one catch one's breath. However, one can get used to most things, and after a few minutes it was not so bad. We got a working party together and quickly replaced the hatches and 'tommed' them down. The iron deck itself was working up and down in a most alarming manner, and it seemed as though it might burst at any minute. We opened No. 1 hatch and robbed it of some balks of timber; these we jammed between the shelter-deck and the deck beams above, and hammered them tight with sledge-hammers. It was a long and tedious job, working by the light of oil-lamps, and it was evening before we had finished.

"The night passed uneventfully, and towards morning the wind and sea decreased considerably. All this time we could hear ships calling us up by wireless and asking for our position, and we were in the exasperating position of not being able to answer them, as our emergency wireless batteries had given out.

"About noon the next day our long-looked-for assistance arrived. A ship was sighted making towards us at full speed, and very shortly afterwards ranged alongside. She proved to be H.M. Sloop *Daffodil*, sent from Queenstown on receipt of our first message asking for help. We quickly picked up her hawser, shackled it to our cable, which had been prepared for towing, and in a few minutes were under way, bound for Berehaven in Bantry Bay. Our relief may be imagined, and our luck seemed to have turned; for the weather cleared up, and it was now a beautiful day, with little wind and a long swell, which did not cause us any trouble. Very luckily, too, the hand-steering position was under the bridge, and not on the poop, as is the case with most ships, so we were able to steer the ship and keep astern of our tug with ease.

"Our troubles, we felt, were over, and for the first time after some days we really had hopes of getting the ship into port. There was nothing we could do, now that we were in tow, so we sat in the captain's cabin, played bridge, drank

Navy rum—our own wine locker aft was twenty feet under water, by this time—speculated on our chances of getting the old hooker repaired, and the amount of leave she was good for, whilst in dockyard hands.

"During the afternoon a destroyer was sighted, making for us at full speed, then another, then a sloop, then several trawlers and two tugs. They formed an escort around us until it looked as though the old *Zylpha* was the Royal Yacht and a review was in progress. They had been sent out to find us, and, having found us, they escorted us. Apparently, everything that would float and could be spared had been sent to our assistance on receipt of our message, and had it not been for the bad weather intervening, we should have been picked up days before.

"The Admiral had kept his promise.

"After a while, as they received their orders, our escort dispersed, with the exception of one tug, which stood by in case we needed assistance quickly. For the remainder of the day and all that night we continued towing. It was like heaven to be able to get a few hours of undisturbed rest and sleep. The following morning we increased speed a little, and shortly after noon we could see the land looming up, although a long way off. The ship by this time was in a very bad way indeed, and it was obvious that if we were going to get her into port we must do so quickly, or she would founder. The constant rolling during the gale had weakened her a lot, and the heavy tow was helping to complete the work. We signalled to *Daffodil* for more speed, crossed our fingers and laid bets with each other if she would 'make it' or not.

"By the afternoon the after-deck and poop were completely under water and seas were washing around the galley door, which was forward of the engine-room, on the upper deck. We had dinner early that evening, as the steward came along and said that he couldn't guarantee a hot meal much longer: the water threatened to put out his galley fire. How those two men managed to provide food for us all is a marvel to me. After the first day there was always a cooked meal ready if one had time to eat it, and hot coffee was to be had at any time. What this meant to us, who were nearly always wet through, can be imagined. It could not have helped them greatly to have the galley packed with clothes we were trying to dry, as we had very little to change into.

"About eight o'clock that evening the ship gave a tremendous lurch, settled a little, and then steadied with a list of about twenty degrees to port. At the same time the steering gear carried away, the ship took a long sheer away from *Daffodil* and the towing hawser parted. She was settling rapidly now, and in a few minutes the water was abreast of No. 2 hatch on the upper deck. The tug, seeing that we were in trouble, came as close to us as he dared, and the captain ordered him to go forward and give us his hawser. We had just got on to the forecastle to take it from him when there was another lurch and a crack, which meant that No. 1 bulkhead had at last given way. It was obvious by this time that our ship was doomed, so we waded to the bridge and lowered the lifeboat. We hadn't far to lower it, as, with the list, it was nearly in the water already.

"The crew got into the boat and pulled over to the tug, returning for the captain and myself. Still McLeod refused to leave his ship, and we sat on the boat-deck for over half an hour, watching the water creep higher and higher, and cursing the luck that we hadn't been able to hang out for just a few more hours, when we should have been able to beach her in Bantry Bay.

"The lifeboat was standing by close to the ship, and at last, when it was apparent that there was no hope whatever, the boat was called alongside, the captain got into it after me and we boarded the tug. *Daffodil* meanwhile was standing by, ready to do anything possible, but when he saw us finally abandon *Zylpha*, he left us. He had done a good piece of work in towing us all that distance, and it was hard lines for him that he hadn't succeeded in getting the ship to port.

"For another twenty minutes the ship gradually sank, then there was another crack, and she went down stern first until about thirty feet of her bow was sticking out vertically above the water. Still she would not sink, and for over half an hour she remained in that position. At last, very gradually, she started to settle and disappeared.

"So ended *Zylpha*: she had been torpedoed on the morning of June 11, and, having drifted, had been towed upwards of 200 miles, till she sank off the Skellig Rock, on the night of June 15.

"Little more remains to be told. The tug took us into Bantry, where we arrived the next morning. It was a good sight to see the green hills in the summer sunlight and to know that our troubles were behind us. I think it had crossed some of our minds during the preceding few days that that particular shade of green was one which we were not very likely to see again. The thought had certainly occurred to me, in any case. From Bantry we went to Queenstown by train, reported to the Senior Officer in Charge, and the men were drafted off to barracks to be kitted up and await disposal.

"As for the officers, Trembeth, a young watch-keeping sub-lieutenant, was appointed to another 'Q' ship almost immediately, and within three weeks was lost in her, with all hands. Rainey, another watch-keeper, turned over to Auten as his First Lieutenant in H.M.S. *Heather*, another 'Q' ship. The others commissioned a brand new 'Q' ship, with McLeod in command; the majority of the ratings went back with him also."

"I really do think," wrote Admiral Bayly to Admiral Sims at this time, "that I have the finest brand of people under me that ever man was blessed with: all I have to do is to tell them to go on, and then not interfere." It was this mutual respect and confidence between Commander-in-Chief and his thousands of Anglo-Americans which made Queenstown such a wonderfully inspiring centre, and everyone worked or risked his life till the last breath. In truth, there was plenty of discouragement for all—from the Admiral right down to the rawest recruit. Only a few days later—June 20—the Q-ship *Salvia* (Q 15) was sunk at 9 a.m. well off the coast in Lat. 52.17 N., Long. 16.13 W. Her captain was Lieut.-Commander Wybrants Olphert, R.N.R., whom we last saw present at the salvage of *Terpsichore*.[1] He had been longer on the Irish station than almost any officer, and commanded various types of vessels. That day, however, he was taken

[1] See Chapter XIV.

prisoner, though not even captivity prevented him from working on behalf of his country, and he managed to send valuable information back to England. How? Well, if you happen to be a pipe-smoker and lay down your pipe casually for the right person to pick up; and, if you have taken the trouble to roll up a bit of thin paper in the stem; it is wonderful what a lot of news can be transmitted.

The 26th of June, 1917, will ever be a memorable date, for that day the first U.S.A. troops were landed in France with safety, thus defying the enemy's worst threats and proving that the Atlantic approaches to Europe were not entirely dominated by him. If it be true that wars are won not by navies, but by armies, then this landing of so many thousands of soldiers was the beginning of Germany's end. Six transports had come over, escorted by the two American destroyers *Wilkes* and *Fanning*. To meet them went out six more American Queenstown destroyers, *Cushing, Cassin, O'Brien, Jacob Jones, Ericsson*, and *Conyngham*, who brought them into St. Nazaire, up the Loire, after affording protection during the final three days.

One of the amazing successes of this latter part of the War at sea was the development of convoys from the particular to the general; from the escort of troop-ships to that of other vessels. Those critics who had refused to accept the lessons of history, to profit by well-proved results in the past, now began to realise their mistake. Just as in classical times the Roman Fleet convoyed their corn-ships, or in the Middle Ages the Hanseatic League sailed their merchantmen under protection against pirates, or in the sixteenth century the Spanish treasure-ships were escorted from the West Indies, or the same principle was effectually tried during the Anglo-Dutch wars of the seventeenth, and the Anglo-French wars of the eighteenth centuries—so at long last, in spite of some prejudicial opposition on the part of certain master mariners who naturally hated the idea of station-keeping and being herded in fleets, the convoy system now inevitably had to be accepted.

It was natural enough that masters of merchant ships, with clean tickets, most careful all their sea-lives to avoid risk of collision, should not relish this new departure. As a secondary consideration, they equally objected to forfeiting their freedom of movement and to being under naval discipline. I have spoken to many masters on this subject, both during and after the War, but it would be difficult nowadays to find one who denied that this system more than justified any inconvenience. Ask any U-boat captain to-day, and he will admit (as some of the ablest have done in print) that not even the Q-ships were dreaded so much as the convoys, with their destroyers ahead, on either side, astern, ready to ram at the first suspicion of a periscope or to turn a calm sea into violent upheaval by a generous use of depth-charges loosed every twenty seconds at three differing depths. Even that brilliant Commander Hersing, mentioned earlier in this book, recorded the fright he had in these circumstances. "For five hours," he concluded his account, "we had been pestered by those blasted depth bombs. How we managed to dodge them all is a mystery."

Thus we now get what may be termed purest military reasoning. The Western Front was to be the decisive theatre of the War, but more troops were needed by the Allies. America was ready with her men, yet a safe sea method of transportation must first be guaranteed. The unofficial Queenstown convoys had indicated a secure means, but this connoted a very large force of highly mobile escorts. But now that three dozen American destroyers were over here, and many more were being built, one could begin to see both the fight on land being won and the U-boat campaign losing its sting. Here was the very opposite of a vicious circle, and all this while the British blockade was sapping the physical, no less than the moral, ability of Germany to resist. By reason of his knowledge as a student of naval history, Admiral Sims foresaw the value of convoys, emphasised to Admiral Jellicoe (at that time First Sea Lord) their value, and before the end of May the system had been adopted. On July 21 Admiral Sims states he was able to report to Washington his assurance that "the system will defeat the submarine campaign if applied generally and in time."

The actual escort became essential only when the transports arrived about three days west of France. The risk of meeting with an occasional raider such as the *Moewe*, or an ocean submarine, west of 200 or 300 miles from Ireland was possible but remote; and, in any case, there must be a limit to the wear and tear of destroyers and crews. But whenever possible a convoy setting out from America was escorted all the way by such destroyers as were due for the voyage to Queenstown, which could easily be reached after seeing the steamers safe up the Loire.

By gradual, rather than sudden, modification the old-time principle of patrol was now giving way to the more scientific method of a two-fold nature: (1) defending merchant ships by convoying, (2) hunting the submarine by means of hydrophones, radio-compass, and giving the enemy no rest, rather than casually waiting for the latter to show himself. In order to give an actual record of an early example with regard to (1) the following narrative of the Fourth Troop Convoy sailing from America to France under the care of destroyers intended for Queenstown may here be cited. I am indebted to Ensign A. G. Berry of the *Shaw* for giving this lively account :—

"On June 17, 1917, the *Shaw, Ammen, Parker, Fanning,* and *Terry* steamed down the North River to Tomkinsville and joined the Fourth Troop Convoy bound for 'somewhere in France.' We had no idea of our ultimate destination. The troop-ships were the *St. Louis, Hancock, Montanan, Dakotan,* and *El Occidente.* At noon of the same day, we got under way and, steaming out of the harbour, headed east. Due to the slowness of the *Hancock,* the speed of the convoy was restricted to about ten knots. Immediately a zigzag was adopted, in which all ships joined, the destroyers employing the same zigzag as the troop ships.

"As the shore lines of New York and New Jersey slowly faded from view, we all wondered what was to be in store for us. The orders from Admiral Gleaves were very strict—no lights were allowed, no radios to be used unless absolutely necessary, and no rubbish was to be dropped overboard except at specified times, when all such stuff was heaved over at once. Any suspicious disturbance in the water was to be fired upon immediately, investigation to be made later.

"The weather was perfect—blue sky by day and stars by

night, no wind and practically no motion. We zigzagged by day and by night. Our position was on the left flank of the convoy alongside of the *Montanan*. About the second day out we held target practice on some boxes, with fairly good results. This being our first war, our main feelings were curiosity more than anything else.

"One very dark night we were steaming along about seventy-five yards on the port beam of the *Montanan*, keeping position on her dim form in the darkness, when suddenly, without any warning, she changed course and came charging down on us. The officer of the deck gave a frightened toot on our whistle, jammed our rudder hard left, and rang up full speed. We just avoided her by a few yards. Shortly after this we settled down again, the officer of the deck roundly cursing the *Montanan* and keeping a very wary watch on her after this. The *Montanan* had been showing a light every night on her port side near the bridge, and we had so informed her. This, together with the fact that she had almost rammed us, coupled with our uncertain state of mind, made us very suspicious. We were thinking of German agents, spies and everything else very freely, as we were very 'green' in those days.

"During the days following, several times a day, the quiet was disturbed by firing from some of the ships, and each time everyone jumped to his station, hoping it was the enemy, only to be disappointed. On the way over the *Terry* salted up, and had to drop back and return to New York. About half-way over the ocean escort returned to New York, leaving the *Shaw*, *Parker*, and *Fanning* to protect the convoy.

"The following day we sighted the oiler *Maumee*, which had been floating about in mid-Atlantic waiting for us. We dropped out of formation, went alongside and took on fuel, together with some fresh provisions, which were very much needed, and rejoined the escort. The other two destroyers followed suit in turn. The *Maumee* then returned to the United States, and we felt at last that we were alone and really in the War.

"As the War Zone was reached, the tension was increased. From stories that we had been reading before leaving the United States, we pictured submarines about every couple of miles all over the ocean, and the account of the *Broke–Swift* action with German destroyers was fresh in our minds. We even went so far as to organise a boarding party, armed with cutlasses, meat-axes, crowbars—anything and everything to be ready to beat off the Germans, should they appear. We carried no depth-charges in those days except two small 100-pound depth-charges (U.S.) furnished us, which we had to save for a sure shot, as we could not afford to waste them.

"One morning we passed a floating mine close aboard. This gave us something to talk about and broke up the dull routine. We still did not know where we were bound, but from our course we supposed it to be L'Orient or St. Nazaire off Belle Isle. Three days out we started to look for the United States destroyers which were to join us. Finally they appeared as specks on the horizon, which grew larger and larger until we could see them charging down on us with a 'bone' in their teeth plainly visible. These were the real things! They had been over for a month or more, and were veterans. They dashed in and out between various ships at full speed in a very business-like fashion, and took their allotted stations in the convoy. Finally the leader hoisted a signal, 'Welcome to the War Zone,' and we felt that we were really there at last.

"Although they were the same class destroyers as ourselves, they looked very different. Their masts had been cut down to make for low visibility, their paint was old, and the men about the decks were dressed like pirates; but they did look ready for business, and we envied them. We at once noticed they did not zigzag with the troop-ships, but did an independent zigzag of their own, dashing back and forth at high speed, but always maintaining position. We took the hint, abandoned our old-fashioned tactics, and followed their lead.

"The last day and night the tension increased. Everyone was on his toes; we stood watch and watch, and expected to see submarines by the dozen. The silence was frequently broken by scattered shots from the troop-ships at objects in the water, which may have been only waves, but not a submarine seen.

"Finally the morning of the 1st of July dawned, and with it the low coast-line of France. We were almost there.

Two French light cruisers came out, joined us, and guided us into Quiberon Bay. On the way in a small French motor launch came tearing out in front of the *Shaw*, got under our fore foot, forced us to change course frequently to avoid ramming her. There was a French officer on deck, who was jumping up and down, waving his arms and spouting French at a great rate. As nobody understood him, we just thought he was a nuisance, and enjoyed the show. Seeing that we paid no attention to him, he got so mad he threw his hat on the deck and jumped on it. After we had anchored in Quiberon Bay, we found that this active French officer had been trying to warn us off a mine-field, which we had carelessly passed over, with no damage, due to our shallow draught.

"The next morning we got under way at high tide and steamed for St. Nazaire. We passed many small French fishing-boats with sails of many colours, and finally arrived at the dock. When passing the *Seattle*, Admiral Gleaves' flagship, we dressed up for the first time, got all the men into 'blue'—that is, those on the side nearest the flagship—and made a neat seamanlike appearance when passing the Admiral. On tying up at the dock, the French populace was in a state of frenzy at the sight of thousands of American troops. The German prisoners, who were on the docks cleaning up, did not look so pleased."

CHAPTER XXII

DEATH AND DELIVERANCE

OF course it was inevitable that occasional accidents and narrow shaves should take place even in the best-organised convoys; although they comprised large numbers of units, they took on a generic character of their own, so that escorting sloops or destroyers found that one convoy would be nervy, the next convoy would be well-disciplined and give no trouble, whilst a third would need considerable shepherding. The stragglers, the loiterers, or those who got lost, were a danger to the fleet as well as themselves; but this story (for which I am indebted to Captain F. W. Hanan, R.N., Senior Naval Officer of Galway) is the most amusing instance likely to be remembered.

" One day a Spanish ship wandered into Galway Bay, in broad daylight, fine weather, and piled herself hard and fast on the Margaretta shoal, midway between the two buoys marking its extremities. I went out to get her off, and during a pause in the operations remarked to the captain, ' I suppose, Captain, you had no charts of the Bay, or you would have noticed this shoal?'

" He spoke excellent English, and replied thus:

" ' Señor, I have many charts, but I did not look at any. I come from America, I am intended to go to France, I lose the convoy, I continue my voyage, I come to this country. It is not France: I do not know what country it is. How, Señor, can I look at the chart of a place, when I do not know the name?'

" This astounding reply will probably seem to you so ludicrous as to be almost unbelievable, but I did not laugh, either then or later. For this captain was a most magnificent figure of a man, immaculately dressed, who bore himself with the traditional Spanish grace and poise. He had also the traditional Spanish air—that mixture of pride and courtesy which is inadequately described in English as ' perfect breeding.' He delivered his statement with an air of complete detachment, as though stating a logical syllogism—as, in fact, he was.

"Picture to yourself the position. His ship, with some 7000 tons of valuable cargo, hard aground on a dangerous shoal—by the grace of God she had struck the only sandy spot and from the bridge we could see the rocks a couple of boats' lengths away—yet he showed no trace of anxiety. By his own statement he was *two hundred miles* out in his reckoning, and as completely lost as ever was Columbus. On his return home he would probably forfeit his job and his master's ticket; nevertheless he continued quite unperturbed."

But there were in those days some callous U-boat captains off the coast. On the last day of July $U\,44$ torpedoed and sank the S.S. *Belgian Prince*, 175 miles N.W. of Tory Island, taking the master prisoner. With survivors on her deck, she did not hesitate to dive, and altogether thirty-nine lives were lost from that steamer. Five days later this submarine sank the Q-ship *Chagford*. $U\,44$ was on her way back to Germany, but had been so damaged by the mystery vessel as to be unable to dive except for short periods. Disguised as a trawler, she was on August 12 sighted by H.M.S. *Oracle*, who shelled and then rammed her, sending her down for the last time into destruction.

We mentioned above the destroyer *Parker*, which came over with the Fourth Troop Convoy. On August 3 she was off the west Irish coast in Long. 15.10 W. when she heard the British S.S. *Newby Hall* wirelessing "S.O.S." The *Parker* sped towards her at twenty-five knots, sighted her with a nasty list to port, and ascertained that the submarine had dived six miles to the N.N.W. It was now 4.10 p.m. She remained unseen until 6.50 p.m., when the U-boat appeared bearing north. She was chased, but dived when *Parker* was within 8000 yards of her. Nothing dismayed, the destroyer held on, noticed a very clearly defined oil track, followed it down to the end, and saw the submarine showing below the *Parker's* bridge. Two depth-charges were dropped, whose explosions were followed by a third.

Now this was one of those difficult instances where it could not be accepted with absolute certainty that an enemy had been vanquished. There came to the surface air bubbles, oil bubbles, a heavy scum of oil, particles of cork: yet, in spite of this evidence, we shall never know exactly how much injury was done. As one American officer neatly put it, " The British Admiralty were so conservative, they would never give you credit for having sunk a submarine unless you brought in a floating monkey-wrench picked up." But the interesting and illuminating fact is that Lieut.-Commander Halsey Powell, commanding officer of the *Parker*, had at least caused her serious damage. On that day, and two days previously, the submarine had been heard (through a certain source) making her call-sign—" FAJ "—which enabled her presence and position to be fixed; but from the time that *Parker* so cleverly and persistently attacked she was not heard again.

This must be mentioned as one of the occasions for which the British Admiralty were anxious to award decorations for distinguished service, but the American Navy Board's regulation did not allow this wish to be fulfilled.[1]

Commander Powell again distinguished himself the following February in connection with a fine rescue of survivors from the Union-Castle liner *Glenart Castle*, a hospital ship, torpedoed ten miles west of Lundy Island; and after the War, on November 11, 1920, he received from the President of the United States the Distinguished Service Medal " for exceptionally meritorious service."

Fine ships as they were, these American destroyers had a big turning circle. For this reason, and also because so many vessels of all sorts were rushing about the sea in thick weather as well as clear, steaming through the dark hours without lights, it was only to be expected that collisions would occur. Sometimes also accidents happened whilst manœuvring over the tide in the crowded channel of Queenstown harbour. Between August and December the *Drayton* was in collision with a steamer, the *Cummings* with the tug *Flying Spray*; whilst one night at 9.40, when steaming at ten knots, the *Zinnia's* officer of the watch suddenly sighted a darkened ship on the port bow, switched on lights, but the

[1] The Admiralty were equally desirous at the end of this year of showing their appreciation for services rendered by the following American destroyers: *Wadsworth, Benham, Conyngham, Fanning* and *Nicholson*.

crash came. Here was the destroyer *Benham*, which at first appeared to be sinking. With considerable difficulty, owing to the darkness and a now twisted bow, *Zinnia* got alongside, took off most of the American crew, and before midnight was towing the *Benham*, though almost awash aft, to Queenstown entrance. Luckily both arrived safely, though *Benham* had been cut down to her keel. It was found that no one could be blamed, but officers and men of both ships were congratulated by the Admiral for having behaved remarkably well, though it had been a very near thing.

A few nights later the British paddle minesweeper *Eridge* was going out of harbour to clear a channel when she ran into the *Wadsworth* lying at a buoy; and in November the *Wainwright* had to re-enter port after colliding with the S.S. *Chicago City*. Meanwhile the British paddle minesweeper *Haldon* was badly damaged by striking a mine aft. One man was killed, but they managed to beach the ship near Dunmore. Admittedly there were many hair-raising experiences for the ships in convoy steaming on dark nights, yet for some time the difficulty was to persuade them—for their own safety against submarines—*not* to show any sort of light and to refrain from signalling.

Before the " official " convoy system was introduced, the Queenstown Forces used to work their own method, as follows. The destroyer or sloop on the westerly patrol would gather together all east-coming merchantmen, communicate with the neighbouring patrols to the north, south, and east, and then quite a respectable escort protected them before the latter were turned over to the in-shore patrols, who would bring them along the south Irish coast. Captain (then Commander) Zogbaum, U.S.N., says:

" There were mixed escorts of British and American ships. Whoever happened to be the senior took command of the escort, and I know of no case in which he did not receive the loyal support of the captains of ships in his escort of the other country. There is one case I should like to recall as an example of co-operation. Commander Sherston of the sloop *Snowdrop* volunteered to make up a vacancy in my escort when we were very hard pressed, late in 1917. He

BARELY AFLOAT

U.S. Destroyer *Benham* brought alongside *Melville* and *McDougall* in Queenstown Harbour after collision with H.M.S. *Zinnia*.

MOTHER AND DAUGHTERS

U.S. Depot Ship *Melville* and three U.S. destroyers in Queenstown Harbour.

was senior to me, but waived seniority in this case, he being a slower ship, the rest being destroyers. His advice and assistance during that particular trip, which happened to be with what we called 'a nervous convoy,' was of infinite value, and never did he indicate that he would have done things differently, had he been in command—even if he thought so. I know of no case in Allied warfare that has a precedent for this, and only mention it as an indication of the close co-operation between the ships and personnel of the two services."

In truth, Germany was in the position of a hard-pressed gambler who has lost nearly all his wealth and sees disaster ahead. She had counted on winning quickly by intensive and expensive methods. Inexperienced officers and half-trained crews were trying the impossible task of doing what U-boat pioneers could no longer perform. In Flanders, at least, the German Submarine Flotilla was known as the Suicide Fleet. Despondency and desperation were ruining naval morale, and in August of this 1917 came the first serious manifestation when mutiny broke out in the High Sea Fleet for a while. The will to win was already weakening. Not merely that, but by mid-August over half a million more shipping tonnage had been entering United Kingdom ports than the average of the last few months.

This was not to mean that the War could be regarded as ended, or that matters might be taken easily. Indeed, there was ever an expectation that the enemy, in his ultimate disappointment, might spring some heavy surprise. Of what nature? Well, the temptation in a contest is always to go one better than your adversary. Just as submarines may yield to destroyers, so destroyers may be overcome by cruisers. The loss of *Mary Rose* in the Scandinavian convoy is a perfect example. Now, all those invaluable Atlantic convoys, whether bringing each time thousands more troops or thousands of commodity-tons, were to the enemy a most irritating bait. The temptation to send out against them a squadron of raiders—disguised or otherwise—was such that some day the escorting destroyers might first be overcome suddenly, and then their convoy one by one.

Actually another twelve months passed before this possibility seemed so real as to demand counter-measures.

Meanwhile, the Queenstown Forces were providing some of the most thrilling episodes in an area where excitement could scarcely be reckoned a stranger. First came Gordon Campbell's crowning Q-ship achievement. Already a post-captain, with the V.C., a D.S.O. and a bar to the latter, he sallied forth to sink more submarines. We have noted that his last decoy, the *Pargust*, had been badly injured when on June 7 he sank the minelayer *UC* 29. The latter had only three torpedoes when she left Germany, and was free to use them after releasing her mines. It was the third torpedo which hit *Pargust*, the first having sunk an Italian barque, and the second having failed to hit a destroyer. Among the mines laid by *UC* 29 good fortune permitted my ship to sink four. We found one off Brow Head on June 4, and three excellently placed at the entrance to Valentia Harbour (Dingle Bay) on June 12. Altogether this submarine's voyage had not much assisted her country's cause.

But now, on August 6, in another disguised collier named the *Dunraven*, but with his same gallant crew, Campbell went out into the Atlantic, and on August 8 was in the Bay of Biscay, some 130 miles west of Ushant. Zigzagging, and pretending to be a defensively-armed British merchantman, he was shelled at a distance of 5000 yards by a submarine whose commander knew the war game from A to Z. Campbell returned the fire with his defensive gun (a two-and-a-half pounder), played the usual decoy tactics, including an exhibition of "panic"; but this time his people endured shells, explosions, and a raging conflagration such as seemed barely credible for human men to suffer calmly. His mainstay—the four-inch gun, with its crew, was blown into the air, German four-inch shells deluged the *Dunraven*, the poop became red hot, with the possibility of her magazine going up any minute. Nevertheless, in this awful moment Captain Campbell wirelessed an approaching man-of-war to keep away. He still hoped to have one real chance.

The action had begun shortly after 11 a.m. Later the enemy submerged. At 2.30 p.m. she was on the surface astern, where none of *Dunraven's* guns could bear. But

CAPTAIN (NOW ADMIRAL) GORDON CAMPBELL, V.C., D.S.O., R.N.
One of the most famous mystery-ship captains.

HER LAST AGONY
Q-ship *Dunraven* awash and about to sink.

twenty minutes later she had dived again with periscope showing, and then Campbell fired two torpedoes. The first passed just ahead of the periscope, the second just astern. Realising that the enemy had observed the second and would now " go all out " to annihilate the obvious " trap-ship," Campbell wirelessed at length for urgent assistance. Nor had he long to wait. First came the U.S.S. *Noma* (who actually saw the periscope and fired on it), then the two British destroyers *Attack* and *Christopher* arrived. But *Dunraven* was in a bad way, the poop completely gutted, all her four depth-charges as well as her ammunition having exploded to complete a perfect hell. The medical officers from *Noma* and *Christopher* came off to tend the wounded, of whom a couple were in a serious condition, so *Noma* took them aboard for operations and hurried them eastward to Brest.

That evening *Christopher* began towing *Dunraven* in a brave attempt to save her from foundering, but the poor ship was far gone, and would not steer. Of course an ugly sea made things worse; the stern went down, waves rolled over her, yet stoically Captain Campbell stuck to her for another twenty-four hours, when he transferred sixty of his crew to the trawler *Foss*, who had now met him. At 9 p.m. two tugs arrived and took over the towing, but at 1.30 a.m. of August 10 the drama ended. In spite of the darkness and heavy sea, *Christopher* got alongside, rescued Campbell with his remaining heroes, and then, almost immediately, *Dunraven* went down stern first, showing a few feet of her bows. Loth to die, she floated derelict for over an hour, till the *Christopher* shelled and depth-charged her lest there be a new danger to shipping.

Of this glorious fight His Majesty the King remarked that " Greater bravery than was shown by all officers and men on this occasion can hardly be conceived." He awarded Campbell a second bar to his D.S.O., besides conferring on one officer and one petty officer the Victoria Cross. That was at once the summit and the conclusion of Captain Campbell's Q-ship experiences, and next we find him back in naval uniform, but in command of Admiral Bayly's flagship *Active*, which succeeded *Adventure* at Queenstown.

We last saw Lieut.-Commander S. H. Simpson, R.N.,

commanding the sloop *Jessamine*. In May 1917 he had transferred to the Q-ship *Cullist* (1030 tons), and on July 13 was between the Irish and French coasts down the Bay of Biscay. It was an ideal summer's day, the sea as smooth as glass, the *Cullist's* officers and men off duty enjoying the restful sunshine, when all of a sudden, about 2 p.m., the alarm gongs sounded for action stations. As if from nowhere there came into view—but astern—a small sailing craft some four miles away. Curious phenomenon! For visibility was perfect! Could she have flopped from the clouds into this middle distance? Glasses were focussed, but then . . . immediately down came the sail and flash went the stranger's gun.

Submarine, sure enough! *Cullist* slowed, let herself be straddled, and for one hectic hour silently offered herself as a splendid target, during which the U-boat fired some seventy-seven rounds. To lure the German on, *Cullist* lit imitation fires, but the enemy's shells fell so close as to keep the steamer's decks wet and extinguish the fires. Everything now was in readiness, the stage was set for a contest of wits, the submarine had only to be encouraged a little further and she would get that which she asked. To the *Cullist's* crew her gunnery seemed despicable: one hour, seventy-seven shells, never a hit! Encourage her to come closer! End of Scene I.

Scene II. Coming towards them now was descried a steamer, who, seeing the *Cullist's* predicament, wirelessed (with the most charitable intentions) that help be hastened to this latitude and longitude; with the result that twenty minutes later, to Simpson's everlasting annoyance, two destroyers were galloping over the smooth surface. Now or never! The warships' masts were becoming too quickly visible. Untimely interference and unwanted aid! The enemy was 3000 yards away, so *Cullist* relinquished disguise and opened fire. The first salvo fell short, the second went over, but subsequent shots hit the U-boat. Just for'ard of his conning-town on the deck one shell flashed and burnt for some time, but suddenly the German took his departure in flight, diving at a steep angle.

"We then proceeded," says Captain Simpson, " over the spot where he was last seen, marked by a large expanse of oil, and dropped two depth-charges in case he was still alive. By this time H.M.S. *Christopher* and *Cockatrice* had arrived, and inquired what was the matter. They were directed to continue their patrol," concludes the narrative.

Was the submarine sunk?

Well, there were no "monkey-wrenches" floating around. Bright red flames, rising higher than the conning-tower, had certainly been seen where *Cullist's* shells hit. The corpse of a man in blue dungarees, floating face uppermost, was also observed by three of *Cullist's* crew. Captain Simpson even lowered buckets and took a sample of the rising oil. Pretty interesting evidence? But no "monkey-wrenches." So the Admiralty could not accept this as convincing proof of total loss, but they agreed she must have been seriously damaged, and awarded *Cullist's* captain the D.S.O., with a D.S.C. to a couple of other officers.

Pass over a few months, and shift the war-theatre up the Irish Sea. Captain Simpson has been kind enough to write me his account of how the *Cullist* met her painful end:

"On February 11, 1918, H.M.S. *Cullist* was cruising on a southerly course about thirty miles S.W. of the Isle of Man. The weather was overcast, with moderate visibility and sea slight. Just after the hands had turned to after dinner, about 1.20, I was talking to the first lieutenant on deck at the foot of the main mast, when he suddenly remarked, 'What's that?' at the same time pointing to an ominous streak of air bubbles in the sea distant about 200 yards. Instantly I recognised the wake of a torpedo, which was approaching at an angle of about 120° with the ship's course, and made a dash for the bridge to put the helm hard a starboard, hoping that if the course could have been altered in time the torpedo might have just grazed past the ship. However, my intentions were not to be realised.

"As I was running along the boat deck, and yelling to the officer of the watch, the torpedo exploded in the engine-room immediately beneath me, with the result that I must have turned a few somersaults in the air, while the ship went on without me, for I was stunned by the explosion; and when I regained consciousness found myself being washed overboard by the water thrown up from the torpedo, and lying on the same part of the deck from where I had first sighted the track of the torpedo, beside the main mast.

"To reach this position in such short time I had cleared not only the water-tanks and railings on the boat deck, but also the topping-lifts of the double main derricks in the course of my flight. The place where I found myself lying and looking at the ship's side had been railings only a few moments before, till the torpedo had removed them. However, I gradually realised the situation, and dragged myself inboard (in no little pain from a damaged shoulder), and made my way to the bridge. As I passed the spot where I met the torpedo, I could hear through the engine-room skylight the noise of the engines, which were only just revolving.

"By the time I got to the ladder leading to the bridge, the situation looked none too hopeful. The ship was listing heavily to starboard, and her stern was just settling under water. Of the two boats which were carried, the starboard one had been wrecked by the torpedo, and the port one had swung inboard and was leaning against the funnel—an impossible position from which to get it into the sea. Consequently it was quickly realised that the ship could not float much longer, so the order was given to 'Abandon ship, every man for himself.'

"There were two large improvised rafts carried on Nos. 2 and 3 holds, constructed of several layers of stout timber, with provisions and water especially for such an occasion, which it was felt would inevitably occur.

"It was a standing order if a torpedo struck the ship all hands were immediately to go quietly to their action stations, which had been done. When the order had been passed to the gun's crews to abandon ship (I was subsequently told) they refused to do so, imagining that as a result of my injury I was giving in too soon. Unfortunately, these gallant men perished with the ship.

"As the ship was sinking, all men on deck were directed to launch the raft on No. 2 hold—that on No. 3 had been blown overboard by the torpedo. While I was assisting the work on the forward raft on No. 2 hold, a sea came over me and took me down with the ship. It may be of interest to record the thoughts that pass through one's mind when on the verge of death. As it was getting darker and darker while I was sinking, I was gasping for air and drinking quantities of sea water. I suddenly remembered that when I was in Colombo in 1904 a nigger had told me my fortune, and had predicted that when I was aged thirty (*i.e.* 1914) I should be in a 'Great War' (his words) 'wounded twice' (I had been wounded in two places a few minutes before) and 'come out of it alive.' My last thoughts before losing consciousness were, 'What a liar that fellow was at Colombo; my end has come quicker than I expected.'

"When I regained consciousness, I found myself on the surface of the sea, with water pouring out of my mouth, so that I was unable to speak for a few moments. Immediately I heard a voice from behind me (from the officer of the watch) saying, 'Look out, Sir, submarine behind you.' I looked round quickly, and saw the enemy submarine on the surface, approaching the wreckage, among which I was floating together with several other survivors. The submarine came so close that when he went astern with his engines I went under again in the wash of his propellers.

"As soon as I got on the surface I heard the captain of the submarine ask, 'Ver is de Kapitaan?' Our officer of the watch saved my life by replying, 'The captain has been killed.' The captain of the submarine then examined us through his glasses, shook his fist at us, and called us 'The damned English swine.' Two of our survivors were then hauled on board the submarine, one forward and one aft, where they were apparently cross-examined. The submarine, which was a large one with two guns, then trained the after-gun on two or three survivors who had climbed on to one of our rafts a few yards distant: orders were evidently next given not to fire, as the gun was trained fore and aft, and the submarine dived with our two survivors on board and left us. Before the submarine left we got a last sight of the *Cullist* about 300 to 400 yards away, floating vertically, with about 100 feet of the keel showing, till a loud explosion occurred on board (probably the boilers bursting) and she disappeared from sight suddenly.

"Our survivors on the raft then paddled among the wreckage, sorted out the living from the dead and hauled us on to the raft. Eventually nearly all the survivors were got on the raft, and a few over were taken in tow on a Carley float. Fortunately, we had all had a good dinner before this catastrophe occurred, but, as bad luck would have it, the raft which had carried provisions was upside down, so none of the food could be reached. It must now have been about 2 p.m., and we saw smoke on the horizon, so decided it would not be long before we should be picked up. Reassurance was also got from the thought that the routine signal to be sent at 3 p.m. daily to the C.-in-C. giving our position, course and speed would be missed, so it wouldn't be long before a search would be made for us.

"Consequently, instead of feeling down-hearted, we were very thankful to be alive with every prospect of an early rescue and we started a 'sing-song' of popular airs, with arms around each other in order to stabilise the raft, which was well under water. There were several disappointments during the afternoon when ships were reported approaching, but they evidently didn't see us, even though we had hoisted a shirt on an oar. After sunset some of the weaker souls started getting thirsty and faint-hearted. An order was promptly given that anyone drinking sea water would be thrown overboard. The prospect of keeping these men's spirits cheery with fourteen hours of darkness in the present situation was not comforting. A prayer was offered for an early rescue, and hymns, such as 'Nearer my God to Thee,' 'Abide with Me,' 'Jesu, Lover of my Soul,' etc., were sung, which all had a good effect, as the cold and hunger were beginning to be felt more generally. In the middle of the hymn 'Sun of my Soul,' a voice shouted, 'Ship in sight.' As it had gone sunset some time, and visibility was only about 200 yards or more, we all looked round, and saw a trawler (which turned out to be the *James Green*) uncovering her gun. We immediately sang 'It's a Long Way to Tipperary' as a recognition signal, and kept it up till the trawler got alongside. The trawler stated that we looked like the conning-tower of a submarine, and she was just going to ram us, for she did not hear our hymn. Once on board the trawler we were given dry clothes, hot food, and were eventually landed at Kingstown, where we were met about midnight by the Commodore himself (Admiral John Denison), who (as always) was kindness personified.

"So ended 11th February, 1918."

CHAPTER XXIII

PLUCK AND ENTERPRISE

By the late summer of 1917 Germany, in her efforts against Atlantic convoys, was sending out ocean-keeping cruiser-submarines such as *U* 151. Whilst these had the one disadvantage of being slow to submerge, they possessed the double ability of being both a light cruiser on the surface and a vessel that could disappear for nearly fifty miles without showing herself. Such a vessel was over 200 feet long, and if her maximum surface speed was only nine knots, at least she could cruise at six knots for nearly 16,000 miles; which is to say that she could have gone half-way round the world. If only Germany had possessed a few bases, or fuelling stations, or could have relied upon the good friendship of some neutral, this part of the campaign might have been more serious. All the same, they did quite enough harm to inadequately protected convoys—as, for example, coming up from Gibraltar. In war it is not practicable to be strong everywhere, and the North American convoys both received and required the principal escort. Besides carrying ten torpedoes, the " U-151 " class was heavily armed with two guns of 5·9-inch, two twenty-two pounders, and a machine-gun.

Pretty tough problem for the best of Q-ships to tackle!

However, there would seem to have been either some inefficient staff work at German Headquarters, or gross carelessness on the part of certain submarine officers. Surely the worst sin for a minelayer is that she should be mined? The reader will remember our citing *UC* 44, who arrived off Waterford to lay an ambush, but was destroyed in a minefield on August 4, 1917. Behold *UC* 42 repeating this performance by sinking to her grave on her own mines near Daunt's Rock Light-vessel, outside Queenstown—the date being September 10. Two bad cases in just over a month.

The following month two of my friends drove over to Waterford to have a look at *UC* 44, now hauled up on the beach in Dunmore Cove. There still remained a skull and an offensive odour. It was noticed that besides her mines she carried three torpedoes. All hands apparently slept on spring bunks, and when the explosion took place the watch below must have been killed in their sleep, for in some cases the bodies were found still wrapped in their blankets. Part of the submarine had been blown right off, and a torpedo in the stern tube broken in half. Later on she was again taken out to sea, and our depth-charges experimented with, so as to ascertain their effects on the enemy. Some illuminating and very encouraging results were afforded; and ere long, instead of destroyers or sloops carrying a mere handful, they were supplied with several hundreds of depth-charges, which could be used in the most liberal and devastating manner throughout a wide circle.

September had still further surprises. Sunday the 9th was a calm day. The Queenstown sloop *Myosotis* (Commander W. C. O'G. Cochrane, R.N.) was returning from convoy duty, zigzagging at thirteen and a half knots. It was forenoon, and all hands were aft at church. Without any warning the wake of a torpedo was seen approaching about 200 yards away abaft the beam, and ere the ship could be turned she was hit on the starboard quarter. This detonated all her depth-charges, blew her stern off, killed three men, and seriously wounded an officer. But the *Myosotis* did not sink, and she was afterwards picked up by the sloop *Bluebell*, who towed her into Devonport.

Commander Cochrane was one of my friends—we had spent many days in company minesweeping that spring as far east as Old Head of Kinsale—and I still remember a very kind congratulatory signal he made us off that cape on one lively occasion. It was hard luck that, after all his experiences among mines, a torpedo should get him; but please note what followed. In November he left Devonport as commanding officer of the Q-ship *Candytuft*, together with a convoy for Gibraltar, the *Candytuft* being disguised as a tramp steamer. On November 8, off Cape St. Vincent, she had a dispute with a German submarine, who sent a shell into Commander Cochrane's cabin, where it exploded under his bunk, wrecking also the ship's wireless and steering-gear. Three shots were sent in reply, but the enemy disappeared.

Candytuft put into Gibraltar for repairs, and then left with the S.S. *Tremayne* for Malta on November 16. Two days later, off Cape Sigli, a submarine fired one torpedo, which missed the *Tremayne*, but struck *Candytuft* on the starboard quarter, blowing off the stern exactly as in *Myosotis*. But this time all the officers were killed except Cochrane and two others, of whom one received mortal wounds. Then the U-boat came back, struck this time for'ard of the bridge, and up went Cochrane in the air. As he was coming down some wreckage hit his head, knocked him inboard, and he staggered off the bridge, stunned but alive. Finally the ship drifted on to the sandy African shore with bow and stern missing, but a French armed trawler took off the survivors. Life is full of curious contrasts. Commander Cochrane was one of the quietest and most placid men, yet within a few short weeks he went through more excitements than befall a hundred lives. And the last I heard of him was that he was living in a remote corner of England, where simple peace dominated.

That by way of interlude.

During the final summer days of 1917, Germany's more experienced submarine skippers were making a strenuous effort to keep the campaign going, and the same efficient plan continued of maintaining well-tried officers in the area they knew so well. Now U 88 was a modern type, with two guns, ten torpedoes, and a surface speed of fifteen and a half knots. It happened that on September 17 the Q-ship *Stonecrop* (Commander M. B. R. Blackwood, R.N.) was some distance south-west of Ireland in Lat. 49.42, Long. 13.18 W., when a submarine appeared on the surface, and at 4.43 p.m. opened fire with both her guns. The *Stonecrop* was a vessel of 1680 tons, and pretended to run away, but lured the enemy to come nearer. She carried out also the usual " stunts "— lit her smoke apparatus (to make it seem that the ship was on fire), and " abandoned ship." The enemy now submerged and made a careful inspection of *Stonecrop* through the periscope, but at last surfaced. A distance of only 600 yards separated the rivals, and at 6.10 p.m. Commander Blackwood attacked with his four-inch and howitzers, the fourth shot hitting the submarine's conning-tower, causing a terrible explosion, splitting the conning-tower. Seven more shells consecutively registered hits.

Clearly she was vanquished by this time, disappeared stern first, but one-quarter of a minute later, with a heavy list, rose to the surface. Evidently she was trying to surrender, but the conning-tower had been damaged by the Q-ship's fourth shell and would not open. Thus did *U* 88 go to her doom.

The very next day, at 12.30 p.m., *Stonecrop* and her people took part in a drama that makes even a Greek tragedy to seem commonplace. The Q-ship was roughly 150 miles south-west of the Fastnet when she received a torpedo from another submarine and began to settle down by the head. Unfortunately, the explosion had killed five men, besides wrecking wheel-house, voice-pipes, and wireless. At first *Stonecrop* did the regulation pretence of " abandon ship," and Commander Blackwood hoped to get a chance of using his torpedo, for now a periscope was sighted; but the ship began to sink quickly, and at 2.30 p.m. was almost standing on her head, so she had to be abandoned genuinely. Owing to one boat having been smashed in the explosion, there was accommodation in the remaining boats for only forty-four men, but twenty-three (including Lieutenant N. F. Smiles, R.N.R.) managed to climb on some floating timbers. Amid all this the submarine surfaced and came alongside a boat that was under the charge of Lieutenant A. J. Booth, R.N.R. The U-boat was not new, and her paint was rusted. She demanded name of ship, whence and whither bound. The survivors of a Mystery vessel were daily taught what to say, and now they answered *Menonia*, 3000 tons, Baltimore for Liverpool. Thus satisfied, the enemy made off.

Smiles was first lieutenant, and his conduct is an amazing example of pluck, patience, enterprise, and good leadership, such as could scarce be excelled in the annals of seafaring. The planks were now collected by the boats, and under his supervision were lashed into a crude raft. At 6 p.m. Lieutenant Booth in one boat was ordered to sail off in the direction of Berehaven before the south-westerly wind and summon assistance; for there had been no chance of sending out an S.O.S. Throughout that afternoon Smiles—perfect example of self-help—toiled about in the water fixing up this impossible ocean raft, and finished his job as night came on.

Like a true captain, Blackwood in the second boat stood by and hoisted a light. But the breeze freshened, and before dawn the raft and boat had separated. Realising the pathos of such a situation, he tried to find his shipmates, but the boat's crew were so chilled that they could not row against the wind. Finally the attempt had to be given up, he hoisted sail and made towards the Irish land, off which they were picked up by a passing steamer. The first boat, under Booth, with one other officer and twenty men, was rescued by one of the M.L.'s. Meanwhile, patrol vessels were sent forth to search for the others, but after two days the task had to be abandoned as hopeless.

Now was evidenced the magnificent seamanhood of Smiles. At daylight he and his twenty-two companions looked out on to a lonely sunrise and a wilderness of waves. Nothing in sight. On the makeshift raft their supplies consisted of drinking water, three gallons; biscuits, one tin. He decided to make a fair wind of the problem, rigged an oar and a piece of canvas, sailed eastwards till dark, when the treacherous breeze veered to N.N.W., that would blow them down the Bay of Biscay; which was hard luck. But the sea became so bad that sail had to be lowered, and about 10 p.m. a cruel wave washed them all off the raft. Back they climbed, to find one gallon of water and all the biscuits missing.

They had now one and a half gallons of water and nothing else, so Smiles took charge, put his party on a tiny ration, and thus passed September 19. Parched with thirst, one of the men foolishly drank sea-water, and their leader now gave them a serious warning. During the 20th some of the party disregarded this caution, and two went mad at night and threw themselves overboard. To increase their sufferings the rest twice sighted American destroyers steaming about, but the latter could not perceive this blob on the ocean. Nor is there any wonder. Then, about five miles away, moved a vessel which seemed to be a three-funnel light cruiser, but the sea was so rough that it took the wretched men all their time to avoid being swept off, and no signal could be made.

On the 21st two more men succumbed. Next day died Engineer-Lieutenant Ayres, R.N.R., and five men. At 10 p.m. Smiles sighted the Fastnet lighthouse to the north-east. An hour later two more men perished. Sunday the 23rd arrived, and about dawn Smiles disconnected part of the raft, sending four men away in one half, while the other six remained in the second portion. They kept company till 2.50 p.m. that afternoon, when the sloop *Zinnia* came along from Queenstown. The two surviving officers and eight men were rescued off the coast in Lat. 51.16 N., Long. 9.24 W. Having been blown about, continually wet, and practically starving ever since Tuesday afternoon, they were now in a precarious condition, with legs and feet fearfully swollen, and their minds unhinged. Captain Wilson tells me that the rafts were "of a most primitive construction," yet, thanks to Smiles, he had brought some of his party past death into deliverance. No time was now wasted, the *Zinnia* hurried off to the north, and landed them the same evening in Bantry, where they were given every attention. For their victory over the enemy, Commander Blackwood was awarded the D.S.O., whilst Lieutenant Smiles, Lieutenant Booth and two other officers received a D.S.C.—but what decoration could ever make up for the unspeakable suspense and anguish of those five days? However, on the second Tuesday following, *Zinnia* was in time to prevent a recurrence of such a trial.

At 2.45 in the early morning the S.S. *Pikepool* informed the sloop (then escorting a convoy) that a boat had been passed with some men in it. *Zinnia* went back, searched, and found a dory containing five French fishermen, whose sailing craft had been shelled the preceding day by a submarine. They were lucky to have been saved further suffering; for at least they possessed a boat, whereas the *Stonecrop's* tiny raft merely consisted of four smaller barrels with planks, and other planks as paddles, whilst the larger portion was just a lash-up of deals about 12 feet by 8 feet. And these were on the verge of breaking asunder. In all his multifarious experiences during the War few were so pathetic to *Zinnia's* captain as the last sight of *Stonecrop's* crew—"these brave men who had made such a gallant fight for life lying in their stretchers and trying to express their gratitude for what little we had been able to do for them."

The sea is a most merciless master to serve. Hear the

yarn of the rescue tug *Flying Falcon*, which on September 25, in company with the tug *Milewater*, left Lough Swilly under sealed orders, that were to be opened off Fanad Head. Here the tugs arrived, and it was learned that at 7 a.m. the following day they were to meet an east-bound convoy in charge of the sloop *Primrose*; but ere the rendezvous could be reached there was piping up an autumnal gale with a nasty cross sea. The convoy was met at 9 a.m., *Flying Falcon* being directed to take station in the rear, and *Milewater* likewise. About midnight the gale increased with the full Atlantic chorus howling, and off Oversay Light, Islay, a tremendous wave broke over the *Flying Falcon*, which swept away the top of the companion, and much water got down below. The tug lay on her beam ends and wirelessed for help, but now came a second sea, which washed her towing hawser overboard and fouled the propeller, stopping her engines. For a while she lay in the trough of the waves as if she were about to roll completely over. Next the coal in her bunkers shifted. With two of her fires out, her propeller jammed, and apparently sinking, her master ordered the port boat to be launched; but in so essaying a huge sea washed five hands, master, together with the boat, over the side. Three of them struggled back, three were drowned.

Hopelessly the *Flying Falcon* drifted shorewards, but her crew trimmed her bunkers, so that after half an hour she was a little more upright, and the engineers even got their machinery to revolve. Cruel fate! By this time she was so near the beach that the master had to let go both anchors. There she held for two doubtful hours, when the cables snapped and she drove ashore—fortunately on a sandy bottom, the crew being taken off by the rocket apparatus.

CHAPTER XXIV

DESTROYERS AND *U* 58

It was in September that Admiral Bayly issued the following memorandum to all his Queenstown ships :—

> The Commander-in-Chief wishes to congratulate Commanding Officers on the ability, quickness of decision, and willingness which they have shown in their duties of attacking submarines and protecting trade. These duties have been new to all, and have had to be learned from the beginning, and the greatest credit is due for the results.
>
> The winter is now approaching, and with storms and thick weather the enemy shows an intention to strike harder and more often; but I feel perfect confidence in those who are working with me that we shall wear him down and utterly defeat him in the face of all difficulties. It has been an asset of the greatest value that the two navies have worked together with such perfect confidence in each other and with that friendship which mutual respect alone can produce.

Thus encouraged, all hands settled down for another trying winter; since from late September till at least April Irish weather at sea is not pleasurable. Actually Germany was busy preparing new boats and new crews for a fresh effort that began with the new year.

So also more destroyers and additional personnel were coming over from America. Just as British amateur yachtsmen had in the early months of the War volunteered for service afloat, so now a number of keen young American gentlemen this summer had undergone a concentrated training at Annapolis till the middle of September, and then shipped across to join Queenstown as Reserve officers. By the second week in October they were already out on patrol aboard the destroyers, and doing fine work. Happily they kept diaries, and, still more fortunately, more than one temporary officer was able to be present almost immediately at very memorable occasions. Such personal records, set down at the time, are the very material for history, and I appreciate the opportunity that some have been placed at my disposal.

To Mr. H. W. Dwight Rudd of Boston fell an experience as Reserve officer which was unique in the late War and could scarcely be surpassed. For three separate reasons.

U.S.S. *CASSIN*
Reaches port after losing her stern by being torpedoed.

U.S.S. *SHAW*
After being in collision with the S.S. *Aquitania*.

Having just put to sea on his initial cruise, his ship was torpedoed at once, and he was thus aboard the first American man-of-war to become the enemy's victim. One month later he was serving in another destroyer, which barely got outside harbour than she was receiving surrender from the first U-boat crew to be conquered by American naval forces. Straight from Annapolis to the Danger Zone's centre, and being present at more startling events in one month than were witnessed by most seafarers during four years of hostilities!

Now, the *Cassin* had been one of the earliest destroyers to arrive from America. Her captain was Lieut.-Commander W. N. Vernou, a very able officer (now an Admiral). She had done months of excellent work out of Queenstown, and to this day her late skipper remembers picking up a certain east-bound convoy. "I remarked to my executive officer that the convoy was splendidly handled, and that they manœuvred just like ships of the regular Navy. After several exchanges of signals with the commodore of the convoy relative to its handling, I received a signal from the latter asking if I was taking all responsibility for the convoy out of his hands. I do not recollect my exact reply, but it was to the effect that the responsibility was mine, though his co-operation would be greatly appreciated. I had gathered the impression that the commodore was always a Merchant captain of long experience, and upon dispersing the convoy several days later off the Smalls, I sent him a signal congratulating him on his good work. You can imagine my surprise and mortification when, upon my return to Queenstown, I discovered that this commodore was a retired British Admiral!"

But, on October 15, 1917, perceive the *Cassin* early in the morning off down Queenstown harbour. This is how Ensign Dwight Rudd describes that day, which he regards as " the longest, most thrilling, and most fortunate " imaginable:

" I turned out at 5.30: went up on the bridge and watched the skipper take his ship down the harbour and out to sea. He sure could handle her; and this helps. Being new at the game, I was on the bridge most of the time to learn what I could. We steamed out at fifteen knots to ten miles south of Mine Head, and there had target practice, firing some ninety rounds.

"Just after we had finished lunch, and while we were sitting around the ward-room, the officer of the deck (Lieut. Angroll) reported sighting a submarine two points on the port bow about three miles away. The captain rushed to the bridge, and I followed. 'Fritz' had submerged, so we changed course and ran towards that point. The look-out in foretop had first seen the Hun, and both the quartermaster and Mr. Angroll looked at her cruising on the surface. When we got to about where we thought she had submerged, we changed course again, and at that moment (1.58 p.m.) the captain shouted, 'We've been torpedoed. There it is.' I saw the torpedo making tremendous speed towards us directly amidships on the port side. Without any hesitation the captain gave, 'Hard left! Emergency full speed ahead!' and so I am here to write about it. 'General quarters' was sounded at once. I started down the ladder after Lieut. McClaren to my station. I could still see the thing coming, and it was an even bet whether or not it would hit or miss, when *blam*! and there was no doubt. It had struck about fifteen feet from the stern on the port side. Before I could get to the fourth stack there was a second violent explosion, which proved to be the depth-charges. The men who had been in the after-compartments were getting up on deck, and at a glance I could see that some were badly injured. As the after-gun was completely shot away, I took station near the waist-guns. All hands were at battle-stations, and everyone made himself a look-out. The ship started to make circles to starboard, forced around by the overhang on that side. The stern fell off in large masses, and soon the starboard engine would not turn over, so, running on port engine and with a virtual right rudder, we turned short. At about 2.40 the submarine was sighted coming to the surface, broad on the port beam. I saw his periscope and a little of his conning-tower. We fired four shots, and he ducked after the second. A vigilant watch was kept by all hands, because there was little doubt in our minds that 'Fritz' would come up any minute to let us have another 'tin fish.' Why he did not, I shall never know.

U.S.S. *FANNING*
Here seen camouflaged. This was the destroyer which defeated *U* 58.

FOUR-FUNNELLED AMERICAN DESTROYER
Based on Queenstown.

"At the time we were torpedoed there was another destroyer in sight, but for some reason or other we could not get a flag signal or a searchlight signal to her, and our radio had been carried away. The radio gang turned-to at once to rig up a set and, by some clever improvising, got off a message just one hour after we were hit. The destroyer got us. Much joy! Luckily an antenna, consisting of a single wire rigged for experimental purposes, among other things had saved us. In another hour the destroyer stood by us.

"A muster, taken immediately, showed one man missing— by name Osmund Kelly Ingram. He had been swabbing out the after-gun, had seen the torpedo coming, and had run aft (the captain believed) to release the depth-charges, but he was a trifle too late. The injured were cared for in the wardroom and two put into the life-boats. The most serious case consisted of a broken ankle.

"A careful watch was kept, as we fully expected to be hit again, and by this time we were drifting about perfectly helpless: not even turning over now. The next four hours were hell, especially the two from dusk to dark, but 'Fritz' did not show up. The *Porter*, which stood by, relayed our radio messages, and if all went right we would have assistance by 7.30 or eight o'clock. About nine the British sloop *Jessamine* showed up, and sent signal she could not take us in tow till daylight. Shortly afterwards H.M.S. *Tamarisk* stood by, and tried the rest of the night to get us in tow. She vainly attempted to float a line to us, but we drifted faster than the buoy, so no luck. Finally she lowered a boat and carried over a heaving line to us. We sent back a 'messenger' and our eight-inch hawser, with the result that we were in tow after about an hour. The line finally parted. Again she brought over a line and sent us her eleven-inch hawser, which parted at once. It must be realised that the sea was nasty and the night black.

"The hours dragged on, but finally at daylight the trawler *Heron* came alongside, gave us her cable, and thereby kept us off Hook Point, which was scarcely half a mile away. About eight o'clock we were in tow of three trawlers making about three knots towards Queenstown, distance sixty miles, when H.M.S. *Snowdrop* came alongside, and said she was ordered to take us in tow. After some pretty work in ship-handling she got us a line and we got under way at about seven knots. Meantime eight ships had gathered and were escorting us. Nevertheless, no one felt exactly calm about the situation until we turned at Daunt Lightship and made into the harbour. At the nets we were turned over to three tugs, who docked us about eight o'clock in the basin at Haulbowline Dockyard. The damage had taken thirty feet off our stern and flooded three compartments. Such a forty hours I do not want to spend again for some time. They put us in dry dock, and of course many visitors and Boards came to inspect us. In fact, we caused quite a stir, as we are literally the first American man-of-war against which the enemy has registered a hit."

The miracle is that a score of men in the three wrecked after-compartments escaped with only minor injuries. One was asleep in his bunk, only a few feet for'ard of the torpedo's point of impact. Four frames were disrupted immediately alongside him, yet he managed to make his way through each of the three compartments, climb the ladder to the main deck in a state of unconsciousness, and did not regain consciousness till he had gone for'ard to the fourth funnel. It was a further twist of fortune that the *Cassin* was hit at all. Had the torpedo functioned properly, the missile would have missed, but actually it broached twice and turned to the left both times.

The *Cassin* was then laid up in dockyard hands for months, so Mr. Rudd was transferred to the American destroyer *Nicholson* (Commander Berrien). On Saturday, November 17, a convoy of eight merchantmen was leaving Queenstown escorted by the *Nicholson*, *Fanning*, four other American destroyers, H.M.S. *Zinnia*, and the Q-ship *Viola*. It was now 4.10 p.m., the scene seven miles south of Daunt's Lightvessel, and the convoy forming up for the voyage, with *Fanning* on the port quarter. Put baldly, the facts are thus. The *Fanning* caught sight of a periscope 400 yards away on the port bow, heading across, so the destroyer increased to twenty knots, followed by *Nicholson*. The periscope disappeared, just as the enemy was preparing his attack, but *Fanning* dropped a depth-charge, whereupon a conning-tower

U 58

She is partly submerged. Notice one gun forward and one aft.

came to the surface stern first between her and the convoy, some 500 yards from where the depth-charge had been dropped.

Nicholson now dropped a depth-charge alongside the submarine, turned to port, and fired three shots whilst turning. The submarine's bow came up rapidly, she righted herself, but was noticed to be down by the head. *Fanning* then fired three shots from the bow gun, and the German crew lost no time, but came on deck, and at 4.28 surrendered, hands above their heads, calling out " Kamerad! Kamerad!" For the other six escorting vessels this was a thrilling moment. Their duty was to remain with the convoy, yet they could not open fire for fear of hitting friends. Officers in the *Conyngham* watching this breathless drama kept on asking, " Why don't they ram her?" but they could not see that *Fanning* was now going alongside to pick up the prisoners, covered by *Nicholson*.

A line was got to the submarine, with the intention of towing her, but two of the Germans just then disappeared down the conning-tower and remained below for a minute scuttling the boat. At 4.38 the line was let go, the submarine sank for the last time, her crew jumped into the water and swam to the *Fanning*. She was *U 58* (217 feet long, fifteen knots speed on the surface, nine knots submerged, armed with one 4.1-inch and one twenty-two pounder, plus ten torpedoes), and had come from Wilhelmshaven, not via the north of Scotland, but through the Dover Straits, which she negotiated at 2 a.m. on November 14, well over towards the French coast. She had operated off the Irish station previously, though this was her new captain's first trip aboard her, arriving off Queenstown on the evening of November 16. The next afternoon he had seen the convoy emerging, and was about to fire a torpedo when the excellent vigilance of *Fanning* ruined his career. Her depth-charge wrecked the submarine's motors, her diving gear and oil-leads. She then sank to the preposterous depth of 278 feet, and was out of control. She blew her ballast tanks, and was coming to the surface when the *Nicholson* dropped her bomb, which caused further damage. Thus, whilst her hull—marvellous to relate —was not crumpled by the pressure, she was wrecked internally, and this again proved that the combination of fast destroyers with keen lookout and reliable depth-charges was the finest offensive against the enemy's weakening campaign.

Fanning (Lieut. A. S. Carpender, U.S.N.) was certainly a proud ship that day, and the signal which she wirelessed into the Commander-in-Chief was such that every officer for all the war years had longed to have the chance of sending:

> Dropped depth-charge on enemy submarine. Submarine surrendered. Returning to Queenstown with forty prisoners.

And on the way in, whilst the thirty-six men were being looked after by the American sailors, the four officers were being messed in the *Fanning's* ward-room. A German officer asked an American if he would give him a clean shirt, so that a proper appearance might be made on arrival. The American had the mind of a business man and agreed—on terms. He would exchange a shirt for the other's Iron Cross. Result: transaction carried out with mutual satisfaction.

But these guests were not entertained in Queenstown long, and on the evening of next day were conveyed to Pembroke by the *Snowdrop*. Here is the eye-witness account written by Mr. Rudd of the *Nicholson*:—

"On November 17th, 1917, we sailed at eleven o'clock in order to be outside near Daunt Light at twelve. As soon as we got down the harbour, we began to get radio signals reporting submarines all round. We steamed back and forth, waiting for the merchantmen to come out. About this time we got a radio saying the trawlers had dropped a depth mine on a submarine two miles east of Daunt at nine-thirty this morning. We saw them still patrolling the vicinity.

"The chief and I had just come off watch at four o'clock, when, as we sat in the ward-room, we felt the ship speed up and we ran out on deck. There seemed to be nothing exciting going on, so we went back inside. I had just sat down when 'General quarters' sounded. I could hear the forward gun-crew going to their stations on the deck above. I was on deck in a jiffy, just in time to look ahead and see a tremendous explosion close astern of one of the destroyers a few hundred yards ahead of us. It took a second to comprehend that they had sighted a submarine and had dropped a depth-charge.

DEPTH-CHARGE WINS!
The German submarine *U 58* rises to the surface and surrenders.

We manœuvred over close to her, and in a minute we saw two periscopes come to the surface, then a little of the nose. It appeared as though they were labouring to get her awash. Then she disappeared. She seemed to be well in position to fire a torpedo at one of the merchantmen, but none appeared. Then up she came a little more, till we could see her conning-tower and some of her deck.

"By this time we were close alongside her—so close that some said we brushed her with our starboard fenders. At any rate, from the bridge I looked over right down upon the Hun. I could easily have dropped a pebble on her deck. As we slid by her we were preparing to let go our depth-charge. This we did as she was about under our whale-boat. A trifle too soon, for it discharged astern of her. Meanwhile the *Fanning*, who was the lucky destroyer to get her, had circled, and when we got clear we circled around her. In perhaps three minutes after we dropped our mine the decks of 'Fritz' were awash.

"Out came the first Hun I, or anybody present, had seen in the War. I shall never forget the sight of that man as he ran frantically up and down the deck, his hands over his head. He, anyway, had surrendered; there was little doubt of that. Bees from out a hive had nothing on the crew of that submarine. They simply poured out of those hatches, until the deck was black with them. There looked to be thirty or forty of the—well, Germans. Our skipper had signalled *Fanning* to take prisoners. They pulled up alongside; I personally and others (I found afterwards) had the feeling that something was yet to happen while the *Fanning* was alongside, and something did—the submarine sank; but that was not what I expected. We stood off about 100 yards distant and watched what never happened before, and may never again. It took less time than it takes to say it for those Deutschmen to dive overboard and scramble up the side of that destroyer. This they did before she sank. An exchange of signals told us they had thirty-nine prisoners. One Hun had been seen to jump overboard just after he had come up on deck, so we circled about in an effort to find him, but no luck at all.

"The whole procedure was so much more exciting than this description makes it, that it is funny. Our guns were all manned, our torpedoes ready to fire, our machine-guns all set, and a bunch of men equipped with small arms in case we should take the prisoners. Our after-gun did get off two shots. The crew were so anxious to get started it was damn hard not to have them. But there was the slight possibility of its being a Britisher, and the captain showed wonderful judgment in not doing any more than was necessary to make the thing sure. To the *Fanning* went the credit and distinction of being the first American ship, without the question of a doubt, to get a submarine and take any prisoners at all. A wonderful piece of work from first to last.

"At any rate, I had then been present at two 'first' occasions: On the *Cassin* when the Huns drew first blood against an American man-of-war, and, secondly, when an American man-of-war got the first Hun prisoners. And thirty-nine we got. We proceeded on our convoy, the *Fanning* returning. I have little doubt that those were the happiest living Germans to-day. It showed also to me the fact that they are getting to the point where they were perfectly willing to surrender, for it took little time to decide.

"They were well treated in *Fanning*—so well, in fact, that after they got aboard and settled down they all began to sing. They were put aboard the *Melville*, where each was placed under a separate sentry, and there they stayed Saturday night. Many spoke English very well, and told a good deal of interest. It was the captain's first cruise on that boat, though he had been on submarines of other types for some time. The warrant machinist had been in submarines for three years.

"The shortage of leather in Germany was shown by the fact that most of the crew wore shoes with part-leather and part-canvas tops and wooden soles. They spoke of the shortage of oil in Germany. All gave the impression that they were forced into the submarine service, and all seemed glad to get out as they had, especially to fall into the hands of the Americans. In fact, all seemed to think they would not have surrendered to the 'Limies.' All were crestfallen when they were turned over to the British for imprisonment.

"The explosion of the *Fanning's* mine, they said, seemed at first to have done no harm, but it soon developed that the diving gear had been completely disabled, and the boat made two unintentional dives to a depth of 250 feet. They were in

"KAMERAD! KAMERAD!"
Crew of U 58 on deck surrendering to U.S. Destroyer *Fanning*.

too deep water to lie on bottom to repair, so there was nothing but to surrender or suicide. She was the *U 58*, almost a sister boat of *U 53*, which came to the United States before the War. Our skipper got a complimentary letter about our small part in the capture."

The truth that *U 58* had voyaged through the Dover Straits was an unpleasant confirmation that the barrage there existed in theory rather than in efficiency. From now onwards the net-obstruction plan was regarded as a failure, and a new scheme of employing reliable mines was launched on November 21. This colossal task demanded months, and barely reached completion when the War ended; yet even during its various stages of being laid this intensive minefield kept destroying one submarine after another, till the Folkestone–Grisnez area developed into a veritable suicides' leap, and the long voyage round Scotland became preferable to U-boat officers.

Sundry important developments also were going on at Queenstown. Whilst the *Adventure*, with Captain Hyde, was being succeeded by the light cruiser *Active*, and Captain Campbell, some of the first American destroyer captains were now leaving Queenstown for America in order to bring back the newly-built craft as soon as steaming-trials were over. Thus, for a while departed Commanders Taussig, Vernou, and Johnson. But such was the attachment which had grown up between them and their Commander-in-Chief up the Hill that, loving their work, hating to be separated from this station, they looked forward to a speedy return. "Uncle Lewis," with all his stern discipline and insistence on any task being well done, had been to them something more than their Admiral. Many of them went to him with their private troubles for advice, and, however busy, he was always found approachable.

"We who have been fortunate enough to have you as our Commander-in-Chief," wrote one officer in farewell, "cannot fail to profit by the example of your devotion to duty, by your character, and high professional attainments. Nor can I ever forget the unfailing consideration that you have always shown toward me and my brother officers. You have made us feel that we are serving under the same flag."

It was another officer who privately expressed his regret at leaving Queenstown in more humorous terms. " I hate having to go to X——, for the lid is on tight, and there are a bunch of old stiffs always sneaking around trying to catch one doing something that he shouldn't. The Senior Officer there has Moses lashed to the mast: Moses wrote only ten commandments, whilst this guy has a hundred-and-ten, with more coming. They hate the life out of us Irish boats, while we reciprocate quite as cordially."

Among the zealous American officers was one who had worked and worked till he needed a rest, but refused to know it. Admiral Bayly sent for him, told him he had been working too hard, and that he must take some leave. The indefatigable officer protested, called to mind the amount of work in hand, and so on. The Admiral was fond of him, wanted him back, but knew that a few days' rest and recreation in London were necessary. Few words could be wasted. " The train leaves at four this afternoon. I have notified Admiral Sims that you will call on him next Tuesday in London. Good day!" The officer obeyed, and returned to his job later entirely benefited.

That autumn, too, arrangements were being made for the United States to have a Q-ship of their own based on Queenstown, and Naval Training Barracks were organised ashore for the American crews who were to replace those sent home to commission the new destroyers. But there was one visitor who at first received anything but a warm welcome. Throughout his service career Admiral Bayly had shown a firm dislike for any sort of publicity, and his attitude towards the press was similar to Lord Kitchener's.

One day there arrived at Queenstown from London, armed with a letter of introduction from the Admiralty Chief Censor, Mr. Ralph D. Paine of the *New York Evening Post*, expectant to be granted every facility of visiting the various ships. But this is how that distinguished journalist described his experience.

After " climbing the narrow, cobbled streets of that Queenstown hill," he entered the Admiral's office, " which was cold and bare. Upon the walls were huge charts of the Irish Sea and the Western Ocean, dotted with tiny flags to indicate the

SALVING A SUBMARINE
UC 44 brought into Waterford after being blown up by mines.

GERMAN SUBMARINE PRISONER
Aboard U.S.S. *Melville* after being picked up by U.S.S. *Fanning* from *U* 58.

positions of troop and cargo convoys and the courses of the divisions of far-flung American and British destroyer escorts. There was no other furniture than the flat-topped desk and the chair behind it, in which sat a grizzled, elderly man in a well-worn blue uniform." At the entrance of the American correspondent he did not look up from his desk, but finished writing a letter. There was an odd illusion that the temperature of the room was falling. Soon it reached freezing point. The visitor felt like rubbing his ears or blowing on his fingers. After several years Admiral Sir Lewis Bayly raised his eyes and said in a voice from which the icicles hung:

"What can I do for you, Mr. Paine?"

"My errand is to describe the work of the American destroyers, sir, and I was instructed to report to you."

"Oh, indeed! . . . Your Admiralty permit allows you to 'mingle freely' with the officers and ratings, I believe. That means in port, of course. I have no objection to that."

The journalist protested it would not be worth his while staying in Queenstown to meet the crews on shore. He wanted to go to sea. "Do I understand you to say there is no chance of that?"

Admiral Sir Lewis Bayly picked up his pen and signed a document or two before he said:

"This war is not a pastime, Mr. Paine. Good afternoon."

Later on came an invitation to dine at Admiralty House, chill was supplanted by warmth, a friendship was inaugurated, Paine went for a trip in the *O'Brien*, and on his return from sea the Commander-in-Chief not merely sent for him to stay at Admiralty House, but placed the green barge at his disposal for trips round the harbour. By the time Paine finished his articles, he was writing [1] superlatives about "one of the kindliest men I have ever known."

Now, during November there seemed quite a possibility that another Irish Rebellion was imminent; for some time communications had been passing between the Sinn Feiners and certain of their sympathisers across the Atlantic. The messenger had been a man named Thomas Walsh of the Clan-na-Gael, who that year sailed backwards and forwards between New York and Liverpool in such liners as the *Baltic*,

[1] *Roads of Adventure.*

Celtic, and *Lapland*, but he was arrested on November 3. Two days later the Queenstown soldiers were confined to barracks in readiness for fresh trouble. Out in country places men would be seen marching in Sinn Fein uniform with their banner, contrary to the law, but the new Irish crisis had not yet come.

Much more to the point at the moment was the renewal of bad weather and an occasional deadly attack by submarines. One Monday the *O'Brien* put to sea, found it so bad that she had to come in again, but, in doing so, rolled over forty-four degrees. Worse was to follow a little later. First of all, the *Cassin* had to be sent from Queenstown to Newport, Mon., for her repairs, having been delayed by quarantine after the death of her doctor. On the last day of November she was taken in tow by the rescue tug *Flying Foam*, escorted by the sloops *Snowdrop* and *Zinnia*. The destroyer had been temporarily patched up, and fitted with a jury rudder, but that night wind and sea increased so that the tug could no longer control her. Next morning the *Zinnia* tried to get hold of her, but after some hours the attempt had to be given up. The *Cassin* rolled alarmingly, but eventually *Flying Foam* succeeded in getting the destroyer on her course again, and only after two days—speed four knots—did she reach her destination.

Barely was the *Cassin* made safe than the American destroyer *Jacob Jones* was smitten with trouble. She had been escorting a convoy together with the *Nicholson*, and they were returning in company to Queenstown, when *Jacob Jones* requested permission to do target practice, which the *Nicholson* approved. This was at 9 a.m. Now, about 4.30 p.m., having finished her shooting, she was rejoining the flotilla at thirteen knots when a torpedo appeared, approaching from 800 yards off towards the starboard beam. It could not be avoided, and the enemy had struck her just abaft the engine-room, in such a place that two compartments were flooded immediately. She began to sink by the stern, and when the depth-charges on the after deck reached the designed pressure they detonated, injured or killed many of the men, blowing the whale-boat to bits and everyone in it. Altogether more than sixty lives were lost, and she went down in ten minutes. This incident happened some forty miles S.W. of the Scillies.

PERIL BY SEA
Top: Tramp steamer torpedoed and sinking rapidly.
Middle: U.S.S. *Cassin*, after temporary repairs, now at sea with a jury rudder.
Bottom: U.S. destroyer picking up survivors from torpedoed ship seen in distance.

Half an hour passed, and the cautious submarine returned, picking up two prisoners and leaving the rest. A motor dory remained and three rafts. The former was picked up the same night by a merchant steamer who used her wireless, and then the sloop *Camellia* began to search, finding next morning the rafts with twenty-five survivors. Many died of exposure during the night. Lieut.-Commander David Bagley, captain of the destroyer, was saved, but one of his officers had to be listed as missing. A few days later the German press news announced that *Jacob Jones* had been sunk by $U\ 53$. Extraordinary coincidence! For the reader will not have forgotten that this was the submarine which some months previously had arrived in the United States harbour of Newport, Rhode Island.

But now came days of foulest weather, and such casual attacks on warships as if the enemy were now devoting his attention to those stray meetings as well as the old ambition of starving by blockade. During Sunday, December 16, the glass fell rapidly, and by the forenoon it was blowing a heavy gale from N.N.E. with a blizzard of snow. These American destroyers, true to type, could certainly roll, and on one occasion the *Nicholson* heeled fifty-six degrees to port, but to-day the *Ammen* even lost one of her funnels overboard in a very heavy sea. The gale did not ease up till Tuesday evening. Commander Roger Williams, U.S.N., in the destroyer *Duncan*, considered it "the worst I have experienced in a destroyer," and had to heave-to, making steerage way. Both the *Trippe* and *Jarvis*, destroyers, lost men overboard, whilst their sister *Cummings* had three funnels battered out of shape. Nearly every ship carried away boats. As to the British destroyer *Achates*, she was escorted into Devonport with no bridge, and only one funnel left.

At Queenstown Captain H. B. Price of the *Dixie* achieved a very fine bit of work. When he learnt of the *Ammen's* accident, he got busy on the drawings, set his people on the job, with the result that when she came into Queenstown two days later she found a new funnel ready awaiting her. The three American destroyers *Wilkes*, *O'Brien*, and *Parker* on that Sunday were all patrolling in the Irish Sea, when about 9.30 a.m. (being then some twenty miles W.S.W. of the Smalls), a submarine was sighted eight miles away on the surface, but promptly dived. A concerted hunt then took place by all three destroyers, and at 2 p.m. a wireless message was intercepted from a trawler (seen earlier in the day) that "Fritz" was again on the surface. The *O'Brien* altered course, at twenty-two knots sped towards the position mentioned, and an hour later the same trawler reported having been in action with the U-boat.

Half an hour passed, and the *O'Brien* observed a vessel coming down from the north. Mr. Junius S. Morgan (now Commodore of the New York Yacht Club) was then serving in the *O'Brien*, and has given me these details, written down at the time: "At 3.55 p.m., when I began turning over the deck to Poe, she was about one and a half miles away. At 4 p.m., almost exactly, I happened to look at her, and saw a tremendous column of water, smoke, and steam come up from her. We immediately went to 'General quarters,' and began circling around her. She seemed to be on fire forward, and we saw boats put off from her. On our second turn around we saw the submarine break water twice, and dropped a depth-charge right over it. Meanwhile the *Parker* had joined us, and continued circling us while we picked up survivors. She turned out to be the Q-ship *Arbutus*, and we took on board about seventy-five survivors. Her captain and navigator stayed on the ship, but the other officers came aboard, and also the crew, bringing about six wounded men. Except for their doctor, whose leg was crushed, these were all cases of burns from the steam."

They were landed by the *O'Brien* in Milford Haven. Two tugs presently took charge of the *Arbutus* and towed her from 10.20 p.m., but at 2.50 a.m. an explosion occurred in the damaged ship, and immediately afterwards the hawsers parted. The vicinity was searched in the darkness, but a violent gale sprang up, and *Arbutus* was never seen again. Nor were those two gallant officers who had stoically remained and declined to leave. Lest their memory should perish, may their names be set down for all time: Commander C. H. Oxlade, R.D., R.N.R., and Lieut. Charles Stewart, R.N.R.

Throughout that night the westerly gale blew with great force from the west, veering to N.N.W., and even N.N.E., with

THE GREAT STORM

Taking it over the side aboard U.S.S. *Ammen*, December 1917.

THE GREAT STORM

The arrow shows whence her No. 2 funnel was lost overboard from U.S.S. *Ammen* in December 1917.

a terrible sea. "I was wakened from a sound sleep about 7 a.m.," adds Mr. Morgan, "by a loud bump and crash. I thought we had been torpedoed, but found it was caused by the seas. A terrific gale blowing from the N.N.W., and the ship barely making steerage way into it. Wind blowing 60 m.p.h. and tearing the tops from the waves, so that seeing was impossible at any distance over a hundred yards. Poe stood watch with me, and at about 2 p.m. the seas became less violent, when we began to get somewhat under the lee of Ireland. By four o'clock (or a bit after) the weather began to moderate, and we set our course toward Queenstown, where we anchored at midnight. Weather terribly cold, and all hands extremely tired, but glad to be in. The experience was one I am not likely soon to forget, and I do not expect much more excitement has occurred at any time during the past two days. These boats are extraordinarily good at sea, and will apparently come through anything without much difficulty."

For days this blow was the subject of discussion—until a worse breeze followed at Christmastide. And this was the time when that mammoth liner *Leviathan* (ex-German *Vaterland*) was due to arrive from America with 8000 soldiers. Admiral Bayly took the greatest trouble to have her met and escorted by a special selection of American destroyers commanded by the ablest U.S. captains, and great secrecy was maintained. It was quite probable that the enemy would make every effort to lie in wait and torpedo. This was the first detachment of American troops to be voyaging for England, and the responsibility of seeing her through the Danger Zone can well be imagined. Supposing she had been sunk, with the loss of at least several hundred men, consider the outcry that would have been raised! But how difficult would have been the next transport's coming! And meanwhile the armies in France would have had to wait still longer for this invaluable help from the West.

The six chosen destroyers were the *Allen, Wilkes, Downes, McDougal, Wainwright,* and *O'Brien,* all under the care of Lieut.-Commander S. W. Bryant, U.S.N. (to-day Admiral and Chief of Naval Operations in the Navy Department, Washington).[1] They were to leave Queenstown on the even-

[1] Correction.—Bryant is now Rear Admiral

ing of December 18, meet *Leviathan* at a certain rendezvous, and a wide berth of seven miles was to be given to all shipping. A Liverpool pilot was carried in the *Allen* to be put aboard, weather permitting. Actually three rendezvous were given: one off S.W. Ireland, one off the south, and one off the Tuskar. The weather was thick, and she was not found at the first, so the destroyers went to the second, and she was not there either. Luckily, having a superior speed, the escort did find her at the third, and got her safely into the Mersey. But the *Leviathan's* captain received considerable criticism, and after returning home from that trip was relieved of his command. It was essential that troop convoy commanders should attend most strictly to regulations in those days of submarine peril: otherwise some ghastly catastrophe would have occurred.

This was, indeed, one of those occasions when the Admiral went out himself in his flagship. How the destroyers fared may be appreciated from the lively account by Mr. Junius S. Morgan, but other officers at the time chronicled the experience no less forcibly.

" We ran into a hard blow from the N.N.E., and spent the day and night rolling around. The weather after that was very poor: hard winds, mostly from the N.N.E., which made us roll badly. Impossible to stand up without holding on to something all the time, and life extremely uncomfortable. No signs of the *Leviathan*, and we spent two entire days patrolling back and forth outside at 17° W., with the sea piling up all the time, promising a pleasant run home. Finally on the 22nd she showed up, and at about 8 a.m. we started for home in the teeth of a No. 7 wind and sea: seventeen knots was our speed, and we had to increase it to eighteen or nineteen at times to keep up. Down below it seemed as if the entire ship would be pulled in two. She was bending and springing all the time, and the green seas were coming over the forecastle in a way that threatened to smash in the decks, but we stuck at it and came through pretty well, considering.

" By night our chart house was bent in, the forecastle gun out of commission, most of the ammunition had gone out of the racks, the machine-gun stands were bent and the deck

SINKING OF THE UNITED STATES STEAMER *COVINGTON*

AMERICAN TRANSPORT
One of the big liners converted for trooping and escorted by U.S. destroyers.

was leaking. In my room the ceiling was badly bent down and the bulkheads strained. About 8.15 p.m., just after I had gone on the bridge, a sea carried away our bridge ladder, but it was lashed, so that we still had means to get up and down. The sea was easing by that time, and we were able to make twenty knots, but about midnight we lost the convoy, which must have changed course. Next morning we were in smooth water and running full speed to catch up with the convoy, which we succeeded in doing by about noon. We patrolled on our port beam at twenty-two knots, and after an uneventful day arrived off Liverpool, too late for her to go in, so we all anchored and formed a beautiful target for all the submarines out of Germany."

It was a relief to everyone that this valuable convoy at last went safely up the Mersey, and that gales, submarines, and mines had made no difference. Less than a month before —November 28—the Mersey Bar examination ship had been less fortunate. She hit a German mine, and with her were lost no fewer than twenty-eight pilots. A terrible tragedy! Now, after this there seemed to be some delay when a convoy was leaving Liverpool. Each ship was bound by local regulations to take a pilot out, but they had to be dropped at the Bar, and this was a long process, especially in rough weather. It meant delay and crowding at this important spot, then the convoy got out of formation, and the escorts were at their wits' ends to protect the ships. Protests were made, but the destroyer captains felt that somehow neither the Port authorities nor the pilots appreciated the seriousness of this waiting about.

"On one occasion," writes Admiral Zogbaum, U.S.N.,[1] "when things had got pretty serious, I had lunch with the convoy commodore before sailing. He agreed to the following scheme. One hour after the first ship of the convoy had reached the Bar, the escort commander was to signal that he considered it highly dangerous to keep the convoy stopped with the leading ships proceeding on their course. He suggested that the convoy was to proceed at once, taking the pilots with them, if time did not allow their disembarkation.

[1] He was in command of the U.S. destroyer *Davis*.

This scheme was duly carried out, the ships waited but one hour, and those six who had not disembarked their pilots took them along to New York, Halifax and other western ports. After that incident we had no further trouble. There were always sufficient pilot boats at the Bar, and the interval between pilots was reduced to a few minutes."

One may add that all this anxiety on the part of escorts was more than justified. Even if the *Leviathan* managed to pass through the Irish Sea, we now know that *U* 87 was in that area; that on December 24 she sank the Q-ship *Penshurst*, but was herself sunk on Christmas Day by H.M.S. *P 56*.

We hinted just now at the advent of an American Q-ship. This suggestion emanated from Admiral Sims. At first it was intended to use Captain Campbell's former mystery vessel the *Pargust*, but she would not be ready for many weeks, so finally the *Arvonian* was chosen. She had three four-inch guns besides four eighteen-inch torpedo-tubes, and Commander D. C. Hanrahan became the fortunate Q-ship skipper. Essentially a fighting man, a fine leader, with a very level and cool head, this officer was the senior American destroyer captain at Queenstown, and at that time commanded the *Cushing*. No happier selection could have been made for this special job.

Originally the *Arvonian* (2794 tons) was to have been manned by the crew of the torpedoed Q-ship *Chagford* (previously mentioned), but at the end of November 1917 she was paid off and Commander Hanrahan commissioned her. In her was summed up all that had been learnt concerning decoy work. With her perfect gunnery arrangements and disguises, her additional twelve-pounders, her tilting mountings, her searchlight and emergency wireless set, her boats, and even a motor-boat, she was the ideal mystery-ship. At Christmas came Admiral Sims to stay with the Commander-in-Chief, and two days later the *Arvonian*, having changed her name to *Santee*, left Queenstown. Nor had she been out of harbour five hours before, by the greatest piece of bad luck, this cloudy moonlight night she was torpedoed by a submarine. It is a pity that the enemy was in such a hurry to rush off, for all the normal stunts were played, and, with

THE AMERICAN MYSTERY SHIP *SANTEE*
Top: Captain D. C. Hanrahan, U.S.N., and his officers disguised as belonging to the Mercantile Marine.
Middle: The *Santee* just before leaving Queenstown.
Bottom: A few hours later, after being torpedoed.

perfect discipline, the *Santee's* gun-crews waited five hours patiently for " Fritz " to bob up.

Nothing doing! So Commander Hanrahan wirelessed Admiral Bayly, who sent out a tug, and, escorted by four U.S. destroyers as well as two sloops, the *Santee* at 1 a.m. began her return to Queenstown, where she safely arrived. Here she was detained for some time, till finally she went to Devonport for repairs, and eventually became the British Q-ship *Bendish*. She suffered by having only a nine-knots speed, and also that her service began just at the period when Q-ships had long since started their decline. Tonnage was wanted in those anxious times for many purposes, but Admiral Bayly believed that a bigger type of vessel—such as a Blue Funnel liner, with a speed of fifteen knots, capable of carrying six six-inch guns, the deck cabins being used as screens to conceal these guns, could have been excellently employed if sent to steam in the south Atlantic as a trap for the new German cruiser-submarines.

That area, however, does not come within our present study.

CHAPTER XXV

DOWN TO THE DEPTHS

IF the reader has marvelled that German submarines were able to make long voyages, it must not be forgotten that British submarines voyaged to the Dardanelles, and that American submarines crossed the Atlantic. Seven of the latter, numbered *AL* 1, *AL* 2, *AL* 3, *AL* 4, *AL* 9, *AL* 10, and *AL* 11, left the United States early in December 1917 and proceeded via Bermuda and the Azores, encountering heavy weather. They were in company with the U.S. tug *Genesee* and other surface vessels, who towed them part of the way, though sometimes the weather was far too rough, and the boats had to use their own engines instead.

Crossing the ocean in winter was equally trying for enemy or ally. The U-boats had no pleasant journeying, and these American craft suffered continuous hardship. Heavy seas came down the conning-tower on occasions, fittings were carried away, tow lines would part, eating a meal was most difficult, the whole flotilla would be compelled to heave-to; and in general from Newport, Rhode Island, to the Irish coast it was just so many weeks of discomfort.

All things come to an end, and on the evening of January 27 four of these submarines arrived at Queenstown, the other three reaching Berehaven direct. It was decided that the seven were to carry out patrol duty against the enemy, and to be based on Bantry Bay, where eventually (after training under Captain M. E. Nasmith, V.C., R.N.) they were to relieve the British submarines. The American patrol began on March 6, with three and sometimes four units out on their beat simultaneously, and this went on till October 21, when all submarine patrols off Ireland were discontinued. That they passed through some thrilling experiences during these seven months will be seen from the following, and it may at once be stated that the mere suspicion of a British or American submarine being in the neighbourhood was enough to keep a U-boat's crew in one long suspense of fear, so that the Germans were more concerned with their own safety than attacking. The combination of these keen young American

DEPTH CHARGE
Being let go from an American destroyer.

WHAT A TORPEDO DOES
Hole in U.S.S. *Santee*'s side after being hit by a U-boat

officers with Captain Nasmith's unrivalled practical experience since the earliest days of under-water craft, and the lessons learned by him in the Dardanelles, now worked out excellently.

AL 4 on March 20, 1918, was on the surface patrolling off the south coast of Ireland to the westward of Queenstown, when, at about 4 p.m., an object was sighted which was at first thought to be Fastnet Light. The object was discovered to be a ship, that almost immediately turned away at high speed. A sail could now be made out to resemble a submarine, and *AL* 4 proceeded to head for it at full speed in an endeavour to gain an attacking position before submerging. At 4.45 about two feet of brown periscope were sighted 300 yards on the starboard bow. *AL* 4 turned with hard-over rudder, and passed over the spot where the periscope had been sighted, in an attempt to ram. The submarine dived, and the sound of the enemy's propellers could be quite plainly heard throughout the vessel without the aid of listening devices. The sounds were first picked up astern, and the *AL* 4 swung about so as to bring the sounds abeam, as, in that relative position, more accurate bearings could be obtained. Having got satisfactory bearings, *AL* 4 was swung about so as to intercept the enemy and ram.

As the boat was swinging to the new course, a distinct jar was felt throughout its length, and Lieut. G. Hulings, at his station at the torpedo tubes in the forward compartment, stated that a shock of considerable intensity was felt. No further collision was noted, and the propeller sounds were gradually lost without contact again being established. There is little doubt that the two vessels collided under-water. The relative mass of submerged submarines in a state approaching neutral buoyancy is very small, so that damage done one to another in such collisions is rarely of any importance. The *AL* 4 suffered no damage in this case.

Towards the latter part of this month, the *AL* 9 (Lieut. P. T. Wright) was at her patrol billet off Lundy Island in the surface condition. It was a bright night, but for the greater part of it the moon was generally obscured by masses of drifting clouds. At about 3 a.m., however, there was a rift in the clouds and a vessel was sighted in the moonlight. The vessel was on the port quarter at a range of 400 to 500 yards, and, at first, appeared to be a drifter with its steadying sail set aft. The supposed drifter must have sighted *AL* 9, for it swung off sharply to port. It was then made out to be a German submarine with a gun forward and a triangular sail set aft. The enemy dived before the *AL* 9 could bring its tubes to bear for a torpedo shot. *AL* 9 dived also and followed the enemy, by using the listening gear, for over an hour. At times *AL* 9 seemed quite close to the German, and prepared to ram, but finally the enemy zig-zagged at high speed, and eventually escaped.

The *AL* 4 again had also contact with an enemy submarine during the early morning hours of April 12, while darkness still prevailed. The sea was rough, but the visibility good. *AL* 4 was on its patrol station, under way on one engine and charging batteries with the other. As was the custom, two torpedo tubes were ready for firing, with the torpedo watch at their stations.

Suddenly a U-boat was made out almost dead ahead in the act of surfacing, and not more than 1000 yards distant. The action had to be quick, and not a second wasted, or the enemy would be lost in the darkness.

Lieut. Hancock judged that the enemy was making a fairly high speed (on account of the amount of bow wave it carried), estimated the course, applied a deflection angle, swung his boat, fired one torpedo and steered to ram. The torpedo was seen to make a straight run and barely missed ahead. As the German surfaced, the conning-tower hatch was thrown open and an officer was seen to emerge on the double. He apparently sighted *AL* 4 at once, and immediately scrambled back in the conning-tower and the vessel dived. She had been so close aboard at this time that the German officer was heard to shout "Ach Gott!", followed by some order as he disappeared down the conning-tower hatch.

AL 4 barely missed ramming the U-boat, who succeeded in submerging sufficiently before *AL* 4 actually passed so near over the German, that the bubbles from its ballast-tank vents could be seen boiling all about the American. This brief but exciting contact is typical of the startling suddenness with which situations developed after hours and days of monotonous patrol. But here is another instance.

While proceeding on the surface and charging batteries on its patrol station during bright moonlight at about 5 a.m. on April 24, *AL* 4 again made a contact. A German submarine was distinctly seen on the surface in the moon's path at a range of about 1000 yards on the port bow, and heading directly for the American. Almost at once the enemy changed course, so as to present his full port side to *AL* 4, and commenced to dive, having, no doubt, sighted its opponent. *AL* 4 fired a torpedo, and a trail of bubbles was seen to pass just forward of the enemy's conning-tower. Missed!

Two nights later, at about midnight, was sighted a vessel in the path of the moon that must unquestionably be a German. *AL* 4 was not in a firing position, and consequently the stranger was soon lost to view. As the vessel, however, was making very little speed, it seemed as if she were occupying a station, and would most likely reverse course in a short time. Hancock decided that the best chance of re-establishing contact probably lay in remaining where he then was. The assumption proved correct, and not very long afterwards the stranger was again sighted on the reverse course, proceeding as before.

AL 4 was now in an excellent firing position, and discharged two torpedoes at an estimated range of 1000 to 2000 yards. They were seen to leave the tubes in a normal manner, settle down to good straight runs, but great was the consternation a few seconds later when a torpedo was sighted heading for the American submarine, and too close aboard for anything to be done about it.

The torpedo struck *AL* 4 well forward on the port side, but for some reason failed to explode, being thrown off its course by the impact; yet it must have had a truly remarkable steering-gear, for the gyro brought the torpedo right back to its course and it again struck *AL* 4. This persistent torpedo repeated the procedure, until it finally cleared the stern and was lost to view.

For some time Hancock thought his craft had been hit by one of its own missiles running erratically; but reports eventually indicated that the torpedo had been fired by a British " P "-boat, which, on account of the striking similarity of its silhouette to those of the German U-boats, had been taken for an enemy. But it was a case of mutual mistaken identity, as the " P "-boat had thought that the *AL* 4 was a German, and other American submarines also had remarkable adventures on this station, as, for example, *AL* 11 (Lieut. A. C. Bennett).

On May 11 at 3.10 p.m. she was on submerged patrol in the southern approach to St. George's Channel (Lat. 51.32 N., Long. 6.32 W.) when, on her port quarter, she sighted a U-boat proceeding on the surface at a range of about 6000 yards. *AL* 11 made an excellent approach, using a very slow speed in order to avoid detection. The range had been closed to 900 yards and two torpedoes were fired. The first was seen to broach, and the second one settled down to a good straight run, but when the torpedoes were about 200 yards from the German a violent explosion occurred in their track. The enemy dived, was not again seen through the periscope, or heard on the listening devices, for it is believed that the initial broaching of the first torpedo caused the latter to lose distance, so as to be overhauled and torpedoed by the second one.

On May 18 *AL* 4 had an experience which almost resulted in the loss of boat and all hands. She was submerged on patrol station off Berehaven with the regular watch set. At 8.40 a.m. the boat was running at a depth of twenty-five feet, and a speed of two knots, when it became apparent that she was slightly heavy. The officer of the watch gave the order to " blow " the adjusting tank. This held only about 1500 lbs. of water, being used for fine regulation of ballast and also as a safety tank, built to withstand a higher pressure than the other tanks of the boat.

It may be explained that levers operating flood valves of the various ballast tanks were grouped together. Removed from them a short distance were the water-gauges for the tanks. It was the custom for one man to operate the air-blowing system, another the flood valves, and for a third to observe and report the action within the tanks as indicated by the water-gauges.

Now, when the order was given to " blow," the man at the air manifold put an air-pressure on the adjusting tank, while another man observed the gauge for the tank—as was proper. Unfortunately, the man at the valves operated the lever of the flood valve belonging to a different and much larger tank. As a result, no water was expelled from the adjusting tank, and a large quantity was admitted to the other tank to aggravate the already too-heavy condition of the boat.

The error was soon discovered, but not until the boat was out of control, and going down fast, in spite of the motors doing full speed and the diving rudders set at hard " rise." The commanding officer, Lieut. Hancock, happened to be in the officers' quarters, but as soon as he heard the motors speed up and felt the boat take a sharp angle, he knew that something was amiss. He rushed to the control-room in time to see the indicator on the depth-gauge pass 150 feet, and shortly afterwards the boat struck bottom at a depth of 294 feet—ninety-four feet beyond the test depth of the boat! Had she been operating in deeper water, undoubtedly she would have continued her dive to a depth when her hull would have been crumpled.

Since the air pressure required at 294 feet to expel water in the ballast-tanks against the outside sea pressure was greater than the tanks were designed to withstand, an attempt was made to pump them by means of the regular motor-driven pump. But the load on the pump became so great that the circuit-breaker in the electric line to the motor tripped, and continued tripping. The pump barrels were sprung by the excessive pressure and began leaking badly, as did the flanges of the water lines and the discharge connections to the hull. So much water was being taken on board in this manner that the pump had to be stopped.

An attempt was then made to use the small trimming pump, but the fuses in the electric circuit " blew " as fast as they were renewed, and the effort had to be likewise abandoned. By this time small leaks were developing throughout the many sea connections in the engine-room, and both stern tube bearings were leaking a considerable amount of water, despite the fact that the glands had been set up hard.

Not knowing how long the boat would be held fast on the ocean's bottom, nor how great the need for a supply of compressed air might eventually become to support life, Lieut.

Hancock then decided to recompress the air that was being vented from the adjusting tank.

The water level in the engine-room was now climbing at an accelerated rate closer and closer to the main motors. If the motors were flooded, they could not be used for any purpose. Each pound of leakage meant that the boat would be just that much more difficult to raise. The situation was rapidly becoming hopeless. Hancock coolly surveyed their condition and prospects, then decided that the boat could only be brought to the surface by one last desperate measure.

The navigation chart showed the depth of water to be fifty fathoms, with a soft mud bottom. The boat could therefore be skidded along the bottom by using the main motors on the propellers with little likelihood of damaging either the propellers or the hull. There was just a possibility that by so doing sufficient speed might be worked up to give the diving rudders lifting power, and also it might break the " suction " of the mud bottom. On the other hand, it must be remembered that it was essential the vessel should be able to use her propellers when on the surface, and also that, should a large rock be struck while skidding on the bottom, her plating would be dented and distorted. Were this to happen, the " strength section " of the boat would be destroyed, and she would be weakened to such an extent that she would very likely crumple.

Lieut. Hancock accepted the risks. An air pressure of 145 lbs. was put on the forward trimming-tank, the diving rudders were set at " rise," and full speed was ordered on the motors.

The forward trimming tank had been built to withstand a pressure of 88 lbs. per square inch, and in now putting the pressure of 145 lbs. on the tank, there was grave danger of rupturing its bulkhead, separating it from the torpedo compartment. Should this occur, the boat would surely be lost with all hands.

When the order for full speed on the motors was given, the chief electrician took the motor-control station, started the motors, and as they speeded up, held the circuit breakers " in " with his hands, heedless of the arc-ing and flaming of the contacts.

Up rose the bow to an angle of three degrees, but the boat still remained in the mud. Then she gathered way and, as more water was expelled from the trimming tank, she took an angle of six degrees, when suddenly she broke free. A rapid ascent to the surface was made, assisted by the blowing of other tanks forward, the boat taking an angle of fifty degrees on the ascent. She had been on the bottom for one hour and ten minutes, and the water remained only three inches from the main motors when she was freed.

It may be mentioned that, on the next periodic high-pressure test of the adjusting tank, this tank ruptured. Examination showed that the strains of her deep dive had changed the contour of her bottom from a concave to convex shape!

Such narrow escapes are the portion of all submarine officers, irrespective of nationality; just as some brave souls seem to go from one peril to another. One might have imagined that Lieut. Lewis Hancock, after his experience in *AL* 4, would have been content in future peace-time existence to carry on a quieter routine. Alas! This gallant gentleman is no more. Instead of going down below the sea, he elected to soar aloft in the dirigible *Shenandoah*; and when she found disaster in August 1925, Hancock lost his life.

Finally, let us tell the story of *AL* 2, who in the evening of July 10, 1918, was proceeding from her patrol billet to her base up Bantry Bay. When fifteen miles south of the Fastnet —that ever-notorious zone—she sighted a curious object resembling a buoy, and altered course to investigate. Five minutes later a severe explosion shook *AL* 2, and a large column of water was thrown into the air, eighty yards away. Immediately after its subsidence *AL* 2 was surprised to see about six feet of periscope in the disturbed water, so dived and tried to ram; but the enemy passed and escaped so narrowly that his propellers could be heard through the hull. By listening on her special instrument, *AL* 2 now heard two submarines: one to the north, and one to the south. The former was evidently running her engines at high speed, and it was she whose periscope had been observed. The one to the south was running at moderate speed.

The American next went in chase of the U-boat hurrying north, but after twenty-five minutes, the latter stopped, and soon afterwards the one in the south began calling to her, but could get no reply. Nothing further was heard of the northern submarine, who was *UB 65*, and at 7.20 p.m. the southern submarine ceased calling. Now, we know definitely that *UB 65* was lost then and there, but we shall never learn by what means. She was a craft of 121 feet long, with a surface speed of only eight and a half knots and, submerged, she could not do more than six knots for an hour. She carried four torpedoes. Whether she hit a mine, whether some internal explosion took place, cannot be stated explicitly; but the accident must have been serious, and her situation made no happier when suddenly she heard the engines of *AL* 2. So, down on the sea-bed where lay many a U-boat victim, rolled that steel German coffin with its crew of men gasping desperately till unconsciousness came charitably to console them in their last sleep. Gaunt and forbidding rises the Fastnet Rock, with its lighthouse shedding its illumination to guide shipping; but to me it seems to burn as a perpetual light over the many sailor-men who lost their lives because of a Kaiser's envy and malice.

CHAPTER XXVI

A BAND OF BROTHERS

SOMEHOW Germany must have heard via the Azores all about the American Submarine Flotilla and its destination, for on the night before their arrival in Queenstown Harbour the enemy very considerately mined the port's approaches. Still, it was not such a bad day, this 26th of January; for three German submarines were destroyed in twenty-four hours. One was *U 84*, at the hands of another P-boat. Just after four o'clock in the morning—that hour when most collisions occur, and human nature is at its weakest, as Napoleon knew so well—H.M.S. *P 62* was zigzagging between the Tuskar and Smalls across the Irish Sea when she sighted the enemy, made for him, but before the latter had time to dive, rammed him good and heartily at right angles. Now, the P-boats had been designed specially for ramming, and this one was travelling at seventeen knots. She smote the submarine just abaft the conning-tower and was brought up all standing in the darkness of night. A magnificent occasion! Down disappeared *U 84*, and when dawn came it showed a sea smooth, with large quantities of oil; but a depth-charge, set at 200 feet, was dropped as a final full stop.

Meanwhile, had Nelson been able to pay a visit to Queenstown, as Admiral Mayo from America in December had been, and Admiral Jellicoe (now freed from the cares of Admiralty) came in February—both of them to see and admire the fine co-operative spirit—the hero of Trafalgar would not have failed to notice a " band of brothers " still grappling with the one big problem in the same eager unity. Commander Roger Williams, U.S.N., then captain of the destroyer *Duncan*, tells me another instance of this when, in company with two other American destroyers, the two sloops *Zinnia* and *Bluebell*, together with the British Q-ship *Aubrietia*, they were standing out to meet a convoy that was approaching under the care of Rear-Admiral F. H. Henderson, C.M.G. The latter wirelessed his noon position, but owing to the rain and fog had not been able to get sights for three days in the Atlantic.

Commander Williams, who was in charge of the escort, says: "My navigating officer, Calvin Cobb, was born and brought up on the Maine coast, and had a natural affinity for fog, and in such circumstances was particularly able. At 4 p.m. in a fog we ran straight into the big convoy, *Duncan* being bows on to the *Carrigan Head* (Admiral Henderson's flagship—a former Q-ship). The Admiral signalled: 'You did very well to find us.' When later *Duncan* ran up under his stern and threw dispatches aboard, he signalled, 'Another smart performance.' Of course, finding the convoy so easily was a piece of good luck, but these two lovely signals made me completely happy, and I still feel most grateful to Admiral Henderson for his thoughtful generosity in passing a little praise at the end of a day on which I had been tortured with the fear of missing my first big merchant convoy."

Band of brothers? This same Commander Williams had an amusing experience of how that expression can be perverted. By anticipation let me add that after the War there was founded a Queenstown Association of British and American Naval Officers who served under Sir Lewis Bayly. Once a year we met and dined together in London; once a year a similar dinner took place in America. Now, the guest of honour in London—the date was several years after the Armistice—happened to be Roger Williams, who, at the time when the invitation by telegram had been sent him, was visiting Germany. He had retired and become Vice-President of a well-known American shipbuilding company, and for business reasons was temporarily at one of the big German shipbuilding yards.

Someone called him up on the telephone to announce the telegram.

"Open and read it to me, please."

When he returned to the works' office he was met by a man who said:

"Excuse me, Commander; just now I happened to be standing by and overheard the message in your telegram. Would you tell me, please, what is this Queenstown Association?"

"A band of officers who were serving afloat during the War off Queenstown."

"THEY COULD ROLL!"
U.S. destroyer from Queenstown patrolling in bad weather.

"Then," asked the other—and with perfect seriousness—"do you think I might be eligible for membership?"

"Why?"

"Because I, too, served in those waters. I was captain of a U-boat."

By the end of February 1918 the Queenstown Forces consisted of thirty-five destroyers, thirty being always ready for service (which in itself was a triumph of organisation); and twelve sloops. What with escorting troop convoys, merchant convoys, mail steamers, hunting submarines and rescuing survivors, they were kept as busy as the inshore patrols or the minesweepers. Well may we nowadays smile at the question that was put in 1920 by the Berlin Parliamentary Committee of Inquiry to the German Admiral Koch—" How was it that only one transport conveying American troops to France was sunk by submarine agency?" The reader has already seen the answer for himself. But about thirty U-boats during February were operating in the English Channel, the Irish Sea, and the Western Approaches, so that the problem was still acute. Good Staff work enabled us to know with reasonable certainty where they were to be found, and the improved method of scouting—searching-hunting, in lieu of the sentry-beat system, was giving the enemy no peace. The unrestricted employment of depth-charges likewise shook him up both physically and figuratively.

What this was like we know from Lieut.-Commander (now Captain) Bernard Acworth, R.N., then in command of H.M. submarine *L* 2. The United States destroyers *Paulding*, *Davis*, and *Trippe* on February 29, 1918, mistook her for a U-boat, fired at her, causing her to dive to 90 feet, and even 200 feet. Then came the first depth-charge, which exploded and jambed the submarine's after-hydroplanes, so that she dived 300 feet and struck the seabed. Four more frightful explosions followed, but by great skill and coolness Acworth managed to bring his boat to the surface, there to receive a hot fire from three destroyers at 1000 yards—one shell striking just abaft the conning-tower. Of course it was a great disappointment for the destroyers, and a miracle of deliverance for *L* 2, who wasted no time in making the recognition signals and waving the White Ensign. Only then did firing cease after a very efficient attack.

But not every ship of every convoy in every voyage could possibly hope to evade misfortune. On February 5 that year *UB* 77 had come north after operating off Berehaven to try her luck in the North Channel, and in spite of being hampered by destroyers as well as other patrols, took up her position seven miles north of Rathlin Island lighthouse, in which area *U* 97 happened to be operating. At 4.30 p.m. the two met and exchanged remarks, but at 5.5 p.m. *UB* 77 sighted a convoy eastward bound strongly guarded by destroyers, speed twelve knots. Lieut.-Commander Meyer of *UB* 77 was an able officer, determined to get in his attack before the light departed, and with considerable difficulty managed to torpedo the largest ship of this convoy. At 7.40 he fired, to hit her just abaft the second funnel, and after one minute ten seconds heard the result of his two torpedoes. He had sent death to the Anchor Liner *Tuscania* (14,348 tons) at a range of 1300 yards. She hoisted two white mast-head lights, fell by the stern, and foundered with the loss of forty-four people. One week later, however, H.M.S. *Roxburgh* chanced to be in this area. The time was 11.20 p.m., she was steaming at eight knots past the north of Ireland (Lat. 55.38 N., Long. 7.32 W.) when Lieut.-Commander A. R. Smithwick, R.N., the officer of the watch, sighted *U* 89 150 yards away. The weather had been foggy, but ten minutes previously it had somewhat cleared, and the night was very dark.

Quick as thought, Smithwick starboarded and made straight for the enemy, from whom rose the frightened cries of men about to receive their punishment. Then the *Roxburgh*, with her speed and 10,850 tons, struck the U-boat, and more cries arose, together with a flash and explosion. The shock and noise were terrific, and the cruiser was temporarily brought up by the collision. Then one portion of the submarine passed aft along the port side to disappear, whilst two pieces of metal were afterwards recovered from the *Roxburgh's* bow. No survivors were taken, but Smithwick received a D.S.O. for having destroyed *U* 89.

Next month came yet a third notable incident off the north of Ireland; for this alternative approach to United Kingdom ports quite naturally tempted the enemy. This time the exact position was Lat. 55.49 N., Long. 8.06 W., and the hour 9.30 a.m., March 15. The two British destroyers *Moresby* and *Michael* were patrolling through this spot when the S.S. *Amazon* (10,037 tons) was sighted outward bound, but twenty minutes later she was heard sending an S.O.S., and just after ten o'clock was seen to be very low in the water, so that she sank within fifteen minutes thirty miles N. by W. of Malin Head. *Moresby* picked up the survivors, dropped four depth-charges, and left *Michael* to continue the hunt.

Now, this time the submarine was *U* 110, one of those powerful craft 225 feet long, with two guns and a surface speed of sixteen and a half knots. She was making her third cruise, having left Wilhelmshaven on February 26 under Commander Kroll. After torpedoing *Amazon* and sighting a British destroyer, she dived to 131 feet, and remained submerged for an hour; but six depth-charges shook her violently, caused her diving gear to be damaged. She now descended to over 300 feet, at which depth the pressure caused a serious leak. She was thus compelled to rise rapidly to the surface, and at 11.19 a.m. the *Michael* observed her five miles away. By this time *Moresby* had returned. Fire was opened on the enemy, whose Sub-Lieut. Busch was killed while in the conning-tower. Commander Kroll assembled his men on deck with life-saving waistcoats, and they began to jump into the water, but at 11.45 she was just below the surface when a shell from *Michael* hit and caused a tremendous explosion. Thinking there were two submarines about, both destroyers were cruising at high speed, when one of the latter ran over the partially submerged *U* 110, which thus went down finally with her captain and most of her crew. Ten survivors out of the forty-three were picked up, and they were found (as had long been expected) to be very young and very inexperienced. Clearly Germany was getting to the end of her resources as regards submarine personnel.

Eleven days later H.M.S. *P* 51, in the Milford area at 8.30 p.m., sighted *U* 61, made towards her at thirteen knots, increased to full speed, and was just about to ram when the steering gear broke down. Shortly afterwards, however, the submarine was again sighted as she hurried away to the north. She was chased, compelled to dive, after which the P-boat dropped depth-charges which blew much wreckage into the air. Ten minutes later three more shocks were felt, when considerable quantities of oil appeared and one large air bubble burst on the surface. That was the last of *U 61*.

These were critical days. It is now history that a German raid on the east coast of England was likely, and the time came for the flotilla of British submarines to be moved away from Ireland to Portsmouth. A plan for landing arms in Ireland was ripening, and Germany now was waiting only the opportunity. Indeed, on April 12 she landed one of her agents in Ireland from a submarine, but he was arrested. This time it was intended to bring munitions from Cuxhaven to the west of Ireland in U-boats, which were to arrive in May. The truth is that Germany, both economically and from a military aspect, was getting into such a situation that she could not carry on much longer: a decision must be obtained, and now she made preparations for the biggest gamble of all. During this April she began to lay the first of those mine-groups off the east Scottish coast which, when completed, were to form the perfect ambush for the Grand Fleet. It was a long job, since each submarine could carry not more than thirty-four mines a trip; but the strategy was discovered, and the mines were regularly swept up soon after being laid, yet the enemy still continued plodding away in delightful unawareness. Mines this month were also laid off the Lough Swilly approaches, to entrap convoy escorts.

In her desperation were evidenced still more and more the inexperience and lack of morale on the part of her submarine crews. No class of men during the long war years toiled and endured more splendidly than those rough hardy fishermen who had come with their drifters or trawlers into the great contest. With often wooden hulls, but always slow speed and slight armament, they had never wavered. In Dover Straits their brothers were about to reap a glorious harvest, driving submarines headlong down to the unsuspected minefield specially laid for that purpose. And now on April 17 at last those drifters of the North Channel between Fair Head and the Mull of Cantyre were to have their wish.

It was 5.25 p.m., and the exact position was Lat. 55.13 N.,

ON PATROL
Drifter communicating by semaphore.

PATROL DRIFTER
Looking aft, showing gun.

Long. 5.15 W., when the drifter *Pilot Me* (Skipper A. Walker, R.N.R.) sighted a periscope, and began dropping depth-charges over the course which the submarine was steering. Result: enemy so damaged that she rose to the surface after twenty minutes, for half a minute, when several drifters with their guns had the joy of showing how well fishermen could shoot. " Fritz " disappeared stern first, but a drifter named *Young Fred* chased and dropped a couple of well-placed depth-charges right over her, causing such a fierce explosion that the other drifters thought the *Young Fred* had gone. Not a bit of it! It was *UB* 82 who had gone to destruction, and the articles now picked up included such interesting souvenirs as woodwork fittings, two seamen's caps and cap ribbons bearing their owners' names and " IV Unterseeboot Flotilla." The Admiralty was satisfied, and awarded £1000 between the *Pilot Me* and *Young Fred*.

These little vessels were based on Larne, whither had come as Senior Naval Officer Commodore [1] Carpendale, who for some time had been Admiral Bayly's flag-captain at Queenstown. He had not long to wait for another and still more interesting occasion. It was the last day of April, and the time 2.45 a.m., when one of his drifters, *Coreopsis* (Lieut. P. S. Peat, R.N.R.), whilst patrolling, sighted *UB* 85 off the Maidens (which are to the north-east of Larne). The drifter, of course, went full speed, hitting her with the first and third shots, and then fired signals as well as sending out wireless messages that he was in action. Owing to the darkness and swell, accurate shooting was difficult; but Peat kept hard at it in spite of the German having at least double the armament. Incredible to relate, rather than make a good fight of it and blow *Coreopsis* out of the water, *UB* 85 just after 3 a.m. stopped, fired a Véry light, and her crew shouted in unison, " I will surrender," " We are your prisoners."

It was like the fulfilment of a wonderful dream.

But Peat could not believe it all: there must be a trick. And he blazed away at the German's conspicuous gun. Still no response, so *Coreopsis* stood by and waited with gun trained, and at 4 a.m. other patrol craft began to arrive. The enemy

[1] Afterwards Vice-Admiral Sir Charles Carpendale, who became one of the officials in the British Broadcasting Corporation, London.

crew were now allowed one by one to jump in the water and be picked up by the *Coreopsis'* small boat, which made four trips, whilst the drifter *Valorous'* boat made two trips. Finally, with three German officers and twenty-four men in the former, and nine in the latter, they returned to Larne. At 4.30 a.m. Lieut.-Commander Krech, captain of the submarine, had opened valves and sunk her, but when asked by Peat, " Why did you not attack me ? " Krech answered in broken English : " I had been down two days. My crew were all ill with gas. I could not submerge, as my conning-tower was damaged ; and as I saw you still firing, and saw other ships, what was the use ? "

She had left Heligoland a fortnight before, and for a week had been operating in the North Channel. Krech had been a most unsuccessful officer, having fired six torpedoes at merchantmen and missed them all. His crew were mostly raw, but such had been patrols' vigilance during the last few days that *UB 85* had been kept submerged almost continually. In short, the whole ship's company were fed up, and had no will to win. One more proof that the German morale was cracking. However, Peat was awarded the D.S.O., whilst £1000 came to be divided between him and his men.

But already the sinking of submarines had become fashionable in the waters around Ireland. Let us come some distance farther south into the St. George's Channel. The date is April 23, and the time fifteen minutes before noon. The U.S. destroyer *Cushing* sighted (in Lat. 51.29 N., Long. 6.23 W.) a well-defined oil track and ten minutes later began dropping depth-charges (set for 150 feet deep) every ten seconds, whilst speeding at twenty knots. Now by rights this submarine belonged to *Cushing*, who remained cruising about for half an hour, but nothing of the enemy was apparent beyond that oil. Bad luck ! The War was like that : a small and narrow margin separated victory from disappointment.

In much the same neighbourhood (Lat. 51.59 N., Long. 6.26 W.), at 1.45 a.m. of April 25, the Queenstown sloop *Jessamine*, which had been so busy for two and a half years, had her great chance. Half a mile away on a smooth moonlit sea was an unmistakable submarine lying on the surface, stopped. Full speed ahead! The officer of the watch, Lieut. Marshal Reay, R.N.R., rang the alarm bell and made to ram her. The enemy was keeping a bad lookout and saw her plight too late, altered course and began to dive. But by now the *Jessamine* was passing close to her and dropped four depth-charges, then swung to port and fired a shot at the disturbance in the water.

Cries for help rent the night, and after a short interval the sloop picked up a man. Large quantities of oil were welling up, two more depth-charges were released, and this was the end of *U* 104, another biggish craft of 210 feet, with a couple of guns. She had been split open by the second depth-charge, but though *Jessamine* remained about till daylight, no more survivors were observed. Engine-room Artificer Karl Eschenberg, aged twenty-two, had been carried up by the escaping air, and told the interesting story that his submarine had come via Scotland, west and south of Ireland, into the Irish Sea, where she had made two unsuccessful attempts to torpedo the Holyhead–Kingstown mail steamers. He also related the incident of *Cushing* having attacked her at noon two days previously. So Commander S. A. Geary-Hill, R.N., Captain of *Jessamine*, won his D.S.O., whilst Lieut. Reay was also decorated.

CHAPTER XXVII

OLYMPIC AND *U* 103

AFTER the United States had entered the War, there came from Europe anxious and distinguished men who advised the building of 110-feet patrol vessels. These were to displace about sixty tons, propelled by gasolene engines, with a speed of sixteen knots, and to carry a three-inch gun. The programme included 350 craft, which were to be known as Submarine-Chasers. A great improvement on our M.L.'s, they were excellent sea-boats, and at economical speed had an endurance of 1500 miles. Fitted with scientific listening-devices, they were given a newly perfected radiophone for intercommunication of five miles, and carried a crew of two officers and twenty-one men.

It was decided to send two squadrons for Queenstown, though their departure was delayed a couple of months by the arrival off the American coast of *U* 151 in May 1918: an obvious attempt of the enemy to prevent the United States from transporting any further troops or allowing any more warships to come over. There could be no better proof of the submarine-chasers' seaworthiness than the determination to cross the Atlantic on their own bottoms rather than on a steamer's deck. Nor can we fail to admire the grit and ability of those amateur crews who came in them. This plucky effort has never received its full praise, but it indicated what can be done with flotillas of small ships, provided the personnel are the right sort.

Leaving the American coast in June and Bermuda on July 7, the convoy comprised yachts and some chasers intended for France. On July 20 they reached the Azores, whence they departed for Brest. A week after leaving the French port they were in Plymouth, and a fortnight later Queenstown saw thirty chasers based there under Captain A. J. Hepburn, U.S.N. They were operated later from Berehaven, Wexford, and Holyhead, and at Queenstown co-operated with the United States Air Force, about which we shall speak later. These little vessels were used essentially as an offensive, hunting force, rather than for the protection of shipping. Actual operations did not begin till September 20, but they managed to put in some useful attacks and to harry the enemy determinedly.

By the courtesy of Mr. C. Blake Pitt of Baltimore, who came over with this Queenstown contingent, as an ensign commanding Submarine-Chaser 206, I am able to give the following account of how they fared from the Azores into Brest. Other chasers were despatched to various parts of Europe, and still more would have come over in time for service, but the arrival of *UC* 156 off the American coast on July 19 was a German threat which succeeded to the extent of creating additional delay.

" After leaving Ponta Delgada, the Azores Islands, we proceeded to Brest, France, being fuelled on the way by the tanker *Arethusa*, alongside which we would have to proceed each morning at daybreak and take on gasolene while under way; which was a considerable job, considering the rough sea and the fact that it was very difficult to proceed parallel with the tanker, which fuelled four chasers at once. If one were not very careful, the chaser would be smashed into the side of the steel tanker, or else would yaw away from it, so that the towing-line and the gasolene hose would part.

" On a thick foggy morning of August 5, 1918, we arrived at the entrance to Brest Harbour about 4 a.m. The convoy consisted of U.S.S. *Buffalo* (Captain Tozer commanding); U.S.S. *Bridgeport* (Captain Jessop commanding); U.S.S. *H.M. Whitney*, towing an army scow; three or four French tugs, and thirty-six submarine-chasers. We were steaming in columns four abreast, but owing to the narrowness of the entrance to the harbour of Brest, we changed formation into columns of two abreast; and naturally, with all these ships in a rough sea on a foggy morning, there was more or less confusion in changing formation. Just at that time a German submarine, which was nicknamed *Penmarch Pete*, owing to its having cruised around Penmarch Point as its basis of operations and having torpedoed several ships off that point, came up and fired a torpedo at the U.S.S. *Bridgeport*. This torpedo missed, passing about twenty-five yards astern. If it had happened to hit her, I would not now be writing this account, because the entire double bottoms of the *Bridgeport* were filled with T.N.T., which she was carrying across for depth-bombs and the like.

"Immediately the periscope was sighted, all the ships in the convoy, including the chasers, spread out in a fan-shape manner and began dropping depth-bombs. The French tugs, who apparently had difficulty in keeping up with the convoy on the way across, and were being continually signalled by the commanding officer to close up, now passed us like a house on fire, making us look as if we were tied to a post. Their stacks were belching smoke and flame as they proceeded at full speed into Brest.

"The submarine-chaser directly ahead of me let go three depth-charges at once, one off the stern and two out of the Y-gun. These depth-bombs were set to explode when they reached a depth of about ninety feet, and knowing that they would go off practically immediately underneath my ship, I gave the command, 'Hard over left rudder, full speed ahead,' in order to get away from the force of the explosion. All our men had been called to battle-stations by our Klaxon signal. Our cook, a negro, who enlisted at Charleston, S.C., was at his battle station on the stern, ready with a big butcher-knife to cut the rope lashings which held our depth-charges on the rack. He was all dressed up in life-jacket and cowhide sea-boots, and, as we made the sharp left turn at high speed, the stern settled in the water, the ship listed, the depth-bombs exploded, and at the same time a wave broke over the stern, washing the cook overboard, butcher knife and all.

"With the fog, rough sea, and the general excitement, some of the boys on the other submarine-chasers mistook his head (which was just awash) for a periscope, so they let go at him with machine-gun bullets and prepared their three-inch guns for action. After signalling frantically, blowing the whistle, and ringing the bell with no effect, I ran in between the cook and the line of fire, stood by to pick him up, and with one engine going ahead, one going astern so that the chaser could be easily manœuvred, I picked him up in about five or ten minutes after he went overboard. This negro cook was hauled aboard, and I asked him, 'How did you like it out there?' He answered with ready humour, 'I didn't mind it, Captain; but I didn't like those boys shooting at me.' Then, on seeing his assistant, the mess boy, Roy Johnson, a negro lad of about eighteen years old, standing on the deck and sort of blubbering from excitement, he said to him quickly, 'Hey, boy, what's the matter with you? Here I've been overboard getting fish for breakfast and you ain't even got them dishes washed yet; get down there in that galley and finish up them dishes.'

"These depth-bombs exploded practically underneath our keel, and the force of the explosion was such that it lifted the chaser quite a bit out of the water. The boys in the engine-room, which was located amidships, right on the keel, swore that they saw the hull bending in. One boy, who came from the hill district in Georgia and had never seen the sea before, and I doubt whether he had ever seen a ship previously, stayed out of the engine-room for some little while afterwards. His eyes looked like two holes burned in a blanket. I was standing on the hatch in the pilot house at the time the depth bombs exploded, and this hatch was on hinges. It just lifted me right off the deck. There was no harm done, as the main force of the explosion was downward. However, it was said later that the chasers ruined the French channel buoys, mistaking them for periscopes."

It was on May 4, 1918, the anniversary of the arrival of the first United States' warships in Queenstown, that Admiral Bayly issued a much-appreciated memorandum congratulating their officers and men on their " skill, energy and unfailing good nature." " To command you is an honour, to work with you is a pleasure, and to know you is to know the best traits of the Anglo-Saxon race." And then the pace quickened again. Compared with that of events in 1915, it now seemed breathless, with surprise closely pursuing wonder. The converted *Deutschland*, which had begun to sink shipping off the American coast, was of no permanent value, though of spectacular notoriety. What did matter very seriously to the enemy lay in the fact that during April and May the destruction of Germany's submarines averaged two a week, which was a heavy blow when one remembers that Admiral von Capelle in January 1917 had informed the Reichstag that U-boat losses might average two or three a month. We were already bleeding her to death.

For this reason, with sound sense, and in order to assist her armies, she essayed to find the elusive convoys carrying their thousands of American troops. Now, in May the White Star *Olympic*, full of soldiers and marines, had to be escorted by American destroyers up to the Lizard, when British men-of-war were to take over. She was duly met on the 11th in the Atlantic by *Davis*, *O'Brien*, *Conyngham* and *Porter*, and all went well till the early hours of the following morning, when still forty-three miles short of the Lizard. The convoy was zigzagging at twenty to twenty-two knots through a dark but very clear night, with a light N.E. wind and slight sea. This is the thrilling account of Lieut.-Commander A. T. Emerson, U.S.N., who at that time was a junior officer aboard the *Davis*, senior ship in the escort :—

"At 3.50 the next morning, as we were getting along to the Lizard, the *Olympic* suddenly let fly with one of her bow guns ; a minute later two shots were fired from her stern ones. We immediately circled to see what the trouble was, and soon after saw a steady light astern. Headed up for same, but found nothing, so started to rejoin, when a couple of rockets went up, so we turned again and went to general quarters. I was asleep, and got on the bridge just in time to see another one go up. We let go a few stars, to try to illuminate the water, but could see nothing, when suddenly someone commenced blinking at us from ahead. The message came very slowly. 'Please . . . please . . . please . . . take us up.' We thought it must be survivors, and cleared away both searchlights, for it was still dark as pitch. A moment later, a black mass, low in the water just to starboard, with a big oil-slick trailing behind it, headed towards us. We turned a searchlight on it, and there was a big Hun submarine, making slow way through the water, with her conning-tower black with men, her bow well up, and her whole stern submerged.

"We stopped, ran by, and backed down on her, stopping when about fifty yards away. I made a leap down the ladder, ran to my room, and buckled on my Colt, and told the gun-crew as I came out to get rifles out of the passage-way. Then I ran aft, just as we got word to lower away the whaleboat. I jumped in, and we dropped into the water. The submarine was by this time on the port quarter, and just as we hit the water, she stuck her bow nearly straight into the air, and went down. All the men on her tumbled off like little bugs, and came tearing through the water for us. I never saw anyone swim so fast in my life. Before I could get clear of the ship, half a dozen of them had reached the boat, and we pulled them in. I then got clear, and pulled forward, where there was another bunch. Three of them were clutching at the guard-rail, but went down before I could get there. One had a new cap, with bright gold letters on the ribbon, but it drifted away and I couldn't reach it.

"Under the forecastle I took up three more, one with a heaving line fast around him, and the other two hanging on to the forward deck hose that the gun-crew had thrown over from above. We then pulled around the bow, to pick up those that had fallen off as the submarine went by. As we came up, we had let go two Carley floats from the ship. One was empty, but the other had half a dozen Germans, one of whom was the captain, standing square in the middle. As he saw me coming, he took off his cap and threw it overboard. I wasn't bothering with him though, for there were half a dozen more in the water, and the whaleboat was nearly full by this time. Just as I had picked up the last one, who was warmly attired in a jumper and life-preserver, I looked around and saw the dory coming after me. It was high time, for we had about twenty-five men in the boat, and every big sea was slopping water over the gunwale. I pulled back to the ship, ran alongside, and shoved the Huns out, while the dory took the two Carley floats in tow. Then I pulled around to port and hooked on, after a long and hard fight, for there was quite a little sea running for us, and the ship was rolling quite a bit. We got some pretty good bangs while hoisting, but finally got clear. The next time I go in a whaleboat, though, I shall pick my crew. Nagler, the ship's cook, was the best oarsmen in the boat.

"As fast as the Huns came aboard, each one was searched and sent forward. None of them had any arms, but the first officer had a pocket full of 6-mm. automatic pistol cartridges. When they started to search the engineer officer he jumped up and shouted, 'Ich bin offizier.' Macaulay, the gunner's mate who was doing it, told him that he didn't give a polite damn if he was. Then Scherer went to lead him forward. As they got by one of the cowls Scherer grabbed him by the arm, whereupon he clutched the rim of the cowl with both hands, shouting that he was an officer. He probably thought that he was going to be thrown over the side. They were all in pretty good shape, except a couple who were well exhausted, but a little whisky soon brought them round. Shame to waste it on them, though. There were thirty-one men, including a warrant navigator; three officers and the captain.[1] The fourth officer and eight men were lost.

"We stripped them all, as we came to them, taking off their wet clothes and giving them dry ones, and incidentally searching them at the same time. After the excitement had somewhat subsided we had a little breakfast, and gave our guests some. It was funny to watch them. No one would touch anything until the captain had helped himself. He and the first officer tried hard to show that they were quite accustomed to plenty of bacon, butter, sugar and coffee, by eating only small portions; but when the engineer got a chance he simply shovelled the chow away. Put his butter on a quarter of an inch thick, and the other one followed suit.

"Zeller, one of our quartermasters, who comes from Milwaukee, was brought up, and we tried to get a little dope out of them, but the skipper was as uncommunicative as a clam, and of course the others followed his lead. They all pretended at first that they could speak no English, but before long they all became as fluent as I am. Strange how fast these Huns can learn! Or perhaps it was our excellent instruction—and cigarettes! We found a lot of letters and papers on them, including their original sailing orders, with a sketch showing the arrangement of the destroyer escort, and all, very similar to our own type. They were signed by Captain Boy-Ed, and the last paragraph was: 'These orders are to be destroyed as soon as the manœuvre is completed.'

"There were eleven of them that came out together from Wilhelmshaven on May 2nd, protected by a destroyer escort until well at sea. They were all numbered in the hundreds, the highest being 196, so there must be a lot of new ones. Ours was the U 103, and she was about 800 or 1000 tons. One of the prisoners had two post-card photos of her, showing her with two long guns, evidently four-inch. This was taken in Heligoland.

[1] See Appendix B.

"She had been waiting for the *Olympic*, and there were two others with her, in line. The captain admitted that he had made a mistake by trying to attack on the surface, and seemed greatly cut up over that and the loss of his ship. They were only 500 metres ahead of the *Olympic*, a little on the bow, when she opened fire, and the submarine submerged without firing his torpedoes. He claimed to have gone down thirty metres, but either he was wrong, or the suction of the screws pulled him up again; for the big fellow hit him and ripped his hull open just abaft the conning-tower. She floated for nearly twenty minutes before she went down though, probably due to the air imprisoned in the forward part of the hull.

" If we had not been so prompt, they would all have been lost, for the water was bitterly cold. One bird I picked up had no pants on, and another one in the Carley float was the same, and both were nearly paralysed. We had given orders to search them as they came aboard, but Reichart asked me how in the devil they could be searched when they had no clothes on. The others were well dressed, with leather porpoise-hide coats and pants, and the officers had good shoes, though a few of the men had wooden-soled sabots. They said that food was pretty scarce in Germany, though, and one man used to save his rations to take part of them to his family when on leave.

" Nearly all of them were between twenty and thirty, and of average physique, though there was one kid only fourteen or so, and they seemed quite well nourished, though the way that some of them passed out seems to point to a weakened stamina. They all could certainly yell, though. I never heard anyone make so much racket in my life, and a few even kept it up after we had pulled them into the boats. As we passed the submarine, they were all holding their hands up, and shouting ' Kamerad, Kamerad, save, save.' But as soon as we had pulled them in, they just flopped in the bottom of the boat, and would not even help pull their comrades in, until we made them. One big husky bird caught on to an oar, though, and nearly pulled the whole other side of the boat around. As soon as I saw him do that, I went back in the sternsheets and kept one hand near my pistol. Two were in the bottom, and I stood on them for several minutes before I knew it. They didn't seem to mind, so I just stayed there.

"Just before she went down, one of the Huns got hold of the big horseshoe-shaped life-buoy, and tried to get away with it, but two others grabbed him, and were pounding him for all they were worth when she took the last plunge. Our after gun-crew were trained on them all the time.

"After breakfast, we gave them things to read, and I noticed one reading with great interest the articles in the *World's Work* about the German spy system. We showed the captain a picture of the sinking of the *U 58* by the *Fanning*, and he looked at it for five minutes without a word, then turned to Scherer and said, ' I hope you did not get a picture of my boat.' I carefully assured him that it was much too dark.

"He knew about the Zeebrugge[1] affair, and said, ' But you did not block the channel.' He also said, ' We knew that you were not English when you threw the life-preservers,' meaning the Carley floats. They were also very anxious to know if they would be taken to the States, and kept there, but seemed much reassured when we told them that they would.

"We had sent the *O'Brien* radio orders to proceed on with the convoy, and she had turned the *Olympic* over to the Devonport boats, and rejoined us. We sent the *Conyngham* and *Porter* on to Berehaven, and the other two of us started back. About 7 a.m. I sighted a thick oil-slick, and we went for one end, while the *O'Brien* took the other, dropping forty-eight depth-charges between us, and causing a lot of fresh oil to come up. A sea-plane came buzzing up, and we circled for half an hour, but saw nothing, except the fresh oil rising. Before starting to drop them, I sent word down to watch the prisoners. When the first one went, they all jumped up, and one started to come through the door into No. 2 compartment, but the guard shoved him back. The officers all started, and every one looked up at the clock, then at each other. I am confident that we had run across one of the others of their bunch, but of course we will never know. All the sailors below said ' Wasser bombe '! When they went aft they all looked at our rack of depth-charges, and seemed much impressed. They had been given the impres-

---

[1] The Zeebrugge blocking operation took place on the night of April 22-23, 1918.

sion at home that they were only about the size of a football. The captain said that our depth-charges did not bother him much, as he could submerge far enough beneath them to be safe. Moral: three-hundred-foot depth-charges instead of 150-foot ones.

"We arrived in Queenstown about 6 p.m. the 13th, and went alongside the oiler at the oil-jetty. Everybody in Haulbowline was there, looking at the Huns, and several of the staff came over The Colonel in charge of intelligence came and had a little heart-to-heart talk with the officers. We only stayed in about an hour, and were sent out again with the *Downes* to escort a tramp around to Milford Haven, where we would turn over the Huns to the British. We pulled in there safely the next morning, and anchored. Two drifters, with about forty soldiers on each, came out, one on each side, and drew up to the gangway, all the soldiers with fixed bayonets, and apparently expecting a battle. There was a subaltern as personal escort for each of the Hun officers, and a Tommy on each side of each sailor. One grey-whiskered old sergeant grabbed one of them, shook his fist in his face, and then winked up at us with a most expressive grin. The Hun captain, before he left, thanked our skipper for his treatment of himself and crew, in a very decent way. Just the same, we were very glad to see them all go, for their skipper was a rat-faced bird that I wouldn't trust ten feet from me."

History plays many strange pranks, but surely it was quite a curious coincidence that *U* 103 should have been sucked into the screw current of *Olympic*, and the submarine's hull along the port side been thus ripped open. The *Olympic*, of all ships in the world! Why? Well, only two years before the War this mammoth liner had been in collision with H.M.S. *Hawke*, and considerable discussion then followed as to whether *Olympic* by suction had drawn the smaller vessel so near as to hit.

But for the *Davis* there awaited a further thrill only a few days later, and the incident so dramatically described suggests the suspense as well as the uncertainties of those memorable days. Men were keyed up to expect the unexpected, and to regard the unusual as normal. Commander Emerson continues :—

"On the 19th, as we were peacefully sailing along, Macaulay saw a periscope about 500 yards ahead, so we went for it and gave her eight depth-charges. No apparent results. That afternoon I saw another one, and greeted him with six. The whole ocean is full of them. Right after I had come off watch, Scherer reported to the captain that there was a suspicious large ship ahead, running at high speed, possibly a raider. We all hopped up on the bridge pretty pronto, and soon made her out to be a battleship. Probably British, but who knows? We went to general quarters, and headed for her. Gave her the challenge several times, but no result.

"'What ship?'

"No answer. Then I yelled down to Dumke, my chief water-tender, to get steam on the two forward boilers, which were full of water. They had steam up on them in ten minutes, where it usually takes at least half an hour. They were lit before the stack-covers were off, and one man stood in the stack, out of sight in the dense smoke, and pulled at them.

"At 10,000 yards the strange ship swung round, showing us her broadside. We were making twenty-five now, and passed the old *Zinnia*, who had been up ahead. As we surged by, she blinked over at us, 'Did you get her name?' We had not, nor could we make out her colours, though she had some flying. There was a long glassy swell, and the spray covered her forecastle at each plunge, while we, running before it, skidded around like a Ford on wet asphalt.

"'Range 8000, stand by starboard tubes, angle 343.' 'Range 6000.'

"All the men were standing by the guns, their eyes popping out as she lifted out of the swell and showed us four huge turrets, none pointing towards us, thank God—*yet*. She was making full twenty knots. Finally Awtrey turned to the skipper, 'We'll last one broadside, perhaps, sir?' Hardly had he got the words out, than the quartermaster sang out, 'Flying British colours, sir.' We again asked, 'What ship?' and the answer came back '*Resolution*.' By this time we were within 4000 yards, and none of her six-inch guns was pointing at us. We ran on to less than 1000 yards, then swung hard left, paralleled her course, with six torpedoes trained on her, and signalled 'Please answer our challenge.'

"HEAVE AWAY!"
U.S.S. *Conyngham* passing orders to H.M.S. *Cochrane*.

TORPEDOED OIL-TANKER
Holed on the starboard bow, the steamer is about to sink.

" And she did. There would be no more war to-day. 'Secure.' And we ran on back to the *Duke*, who was having a race with the tramps to see which one could go the slowest without actually stopping, and told her the dope.

" That night the *Hardy* and the Devonport boats joined up, and we split, *McCall* taking the *Duke* on to Devonport, the *Sterett* and *Fanning* taking the *Besoeki* and an oiler to Queenstown, while the rest of us went on with eleven merchantmen for Brest. We arrived off Ushant at 2 a.m., and after getting by a submarine (that the *Heather* laid a couple of eggs on), promptly ran into a thick fog. We succeeded in getting the convoy into column in the fog, though the Lord only knows how they ever did it without all getting rammed. Everyone had all lights on and the whistles going full blast, but could see nothing. At daylight the fog lifted, and the French torpedo-boats took over the convoy. We started back home at twenty, but immediately ran back into the fog, which held all the way to the Scillies, when it lifted again. We hit her up then, and got in by 7 p.m., in time to have a peaceful dinner, and the others came straggling in afterwards.

" The *Conyngham* piled up on the beach just west of Kinsale that morning. She had been out with a troop-convoy, salted up, and was coming home from sixteen West, running twenty knots in the fog, when she sighted the cliffs dead ahead not 500 yards away. She immediately went full speed astern, but still was making eight or ten knots ahead when she hit. Fortunately the beach was almost a forty-five degrees slope, and she only crumpled up her forefoot, flooding the forward trimming tank, but not damaging the bottom. She remained on the beach until the tide (which fortunately was flooding) came in enough for her to back off, then she steamed around to Queenstown at fifteen knots, and into the Rushbrooke dry-dock for fifteen days, for refit. The *Burrows* was rammed in the Irish Sea in the same fog ; then, to make things sure, rammed a tramp steamer, and went to Liverpool. Eight boats out of commission altogether! What chance is there for a poor hard-working Bath boat these days ?

" No chance at all. Out you go! Up the Irish Sea to hunt for three days. Anyhow that is better than running around in fifteen West."

CHAPTER XXVIII

UP THE IRISH SEA

MANY records had been broken during the last three years, and all sorts of precedents were being created week by week. But no sooner had one become accustomed to a new routine, a fresh type of ship, a different phase, than the trend of events would cause some sudden modification.

The importance of rushing American troops over to France direct had increased till it was of major consideration; but equally the responsibility for their safe conduct, regardless of all Germany's submarines, had become immense. Never could the possibility, even the probability, of a sunken transport be banished from the minds of Admiral Bayly, Admiral Sims, or Washington. The narrow escapes, the occasional visit of a U-boat across the Atlantic, the steady loss of merchant tonnage, all were a constant reminder of big risks undertaken. The best possible dispositions were in force to prevent disaster, meticulous arrangements were worked out for every mile of the route, the most careful considerations given to escorts and rendezvous; yet no human effort could guarantee absolute safety, and peril could not wholly be eliminated. The *Olympic* episode had illustrated this truth.

But in view of present conditions it was decided that, as the number of troop convoys and single-ship transports had become so great, and a much heavier strain had been imposed on the American destroyers, it would be advisable to base some of the latter on Brest, whence they might be utilised for escorting outward-bound steamers each time the destroyers went forth to bring in the troopers. Thus, with regret on the part of both Admiral Bayly and the officers themselves, eleven steamed from Queenstown to the French port by the middle of June.

Before their departure, Admiral Bayly went to sea and flew his flag thrice aboard American ships, and the sight must have caused even the gulls to pause in their hovering. Such a phenomenon was unique in all naval annals. How the incident happened has been related to me by one of the officers of the *Trippe* :—

"It was nine o'clock in the evening, the big red sun was just setting behind Old Head of Kinsale, off which the *Lusitania* had been sunk, and Queenstown presented a very comforting appearance.

"Permission to enter was granted, but with it came another signal: 'How long before you can be ready for getting under way? Urgent.' The captain glanced at the signal, asked the engineer officer how much oil we had, and sent back the answer: 'Immediately.'

"Next came the signal: 'Admiral will come aboard in outer harbour at 9.40.' What could this urgent mission mean? We hurried alongside the oiler and took on as much oil as we had time for.

"It was known that the Admiral had planned for some time to take a trip in an American destroyer under his command, both to compare the American with the British type of ship, and to keep in touch with the life and duties of the men under him. But there seemed little chance of our ever taking such a notable passenger. We were only a 'flivver'—a 742-ton destroyer, while most of the destroyers at Queenstown were 1000-tonners, and there were three of the newest type—so-called 'flush-deckers,' of approximately 1400 tons.

"All the pre-war destroyers, classed as 'flivvers,' and '1000-tonners' had high bows back to the break of the forecastle, where there was an eight-foot drop to the main deck. From here aft the ship was low and appeared to hug the water. The new type of destroyer had no such drop, but just a gradual decline from the bow to the stern; hence the title 'flush-decker,' making the ship much higher amidships, and consequently drier in a heavy sea.

"Although we considered our class the equal of any in fighting submarines and in sea-going qualities, it was hardly probable that the Admiral would select a little 'flivver,' with her small uncomfortable quarters, when he might travel in luxury on one of our fine new 'flush-deckers.' 'They were not destroyers anyway,' we felt; 'they were light cruisers.'

"On one occasion the Admiral arranged to take a short run over to England on one of the 'flush-deckers.' The ship was notified two days in advance and extensive preparations were made for his visit. To the outsider practically all work on a destroyer consists in slapping on paint, scraping it off, and then applying fresh coats. One can never walk the crowded decks without running into fresh paint somewhere. Scraping and painting were done with a vengeance for the Admiral's benefit. Then urgent sailing orders were received at the last minute, and Admiral Bayly's trip was postponed for some more urgent duty.

"About a week later one of the '1000-tonners' was informed she would probably take the Admiral over to England in two or three days. Again scrapers and paint brushes were applied in anticipation of the voyage. The evening for sailing arrived, and the ship shone like a private yacht. While steaming in the outer harbour to await the Admiral it was discovered she was rapidly salting up her boilers; a mechanical catastrophe there was no way of foretelling, and one which would require several hours to remedy. Until it was remedied, no fast steaming was possible; thus she was out of the question.

"Admiral Bayly was very anxious to attend a conference at Holyhead, Wales, the following morning. Only a destroyer could get him there in time. One destroyer was in dry-dock, two were having boiler-cleaning alongside the mother ship, *Melville* and *Dixie* respectively, whilst the rest of the Queenstown flotilla were out on convoy duty. It was one of the busy periods when troops were being hurried to France at the rate of 250,000 a month, and the destroyers must escort them all; so not much time was spent in port.

"Fortunately we had taken in oil at Liverpool, and the last two days had been comparatively calm, so were cleaned up in fine shape. With our reply of 'Immediately' the Admiral decided that was the ship for him, thus the little *John Trippe* came to be the American destroyer to carry the distinguished British Admiral and fly his flag.

"At 9.30 p.m. the *Trippe* proceeded to the outer harbour; at 9.40 the Admiral came aboard, and his flag was hoisted to the main-top. He must be in Holyhead at 8 a.m., and at twenty-two knots speed we set our course for Wales. The Admiral slept way forward in the captain's cabin, almost in the eyes of the ship. In anything but a dead calm this location was far from comfortable. At sea the captain always slept in the emergency cabin on the bridge. New officers were assigned his cabin as a luxury for their first trip out. If they could stand the motion here they were admitted 'sea-going,' and nothing else would 'faze' them.

"It was not to try the Admiral out that he was offered the cabin, but simply because this was the largest room in the ship.

"On turning out for the morning watch, it was pitch dark, but the stars were shining brightly. No sign of daylight yet. We were still gliding through a dead calm sea at twenty-two knots. Relieving the deck when it was so dark one couldn't see a hundred feet over the bow of the ship, and having the life of the third ranking man of the British Navy in your hands was a novel experience to most of us. The darkness was not unusual, but heretofore we had always entertained the comforting feeling that if we did ram a ship, the latter would doubtless be the one to sink and we should simply crumple our bow. Now the crumpling of the bow meant the crumpling of the Admiral! But at least a submarine had little chance at us with this darkness and speed.

"Everyone on the bridge was awake to their responsibilities, and all eyes were straining to pierce the darkness ahead. Standing on one side of the bridge was a quartermaster who had an uncanny way of sighting ships in the night long before they came within the range of an ordinary vision. Over in the port wing was a look-out, who the day before had picked up smoke on the horizon with his naked eye fully three minutes before any one else was able to detect it with glasses. He was crouched down, only his head showing over the rail, and an exaggerated squint on his face, apparently sound asleep; yet one had but to come in line with his two bead-like eyes to realise sleep had not captured them yet.

"It began to grow light about 5.30 a.m., and we were due to pick up land soon after six. With the coming of dawn all breathed more easily, for at least danger of collision was over. And risk of collision in the Irish Sea, where more shipping goes on than in any other sea near its size, and no ships carried lights, was a very real peril. The great number of collisions and resulting sinkings are proof enough of this. I must confess I was glad to have the morning watch with only two hours of darkness, instead of the middle-guard with four long black hours.

"We arrived at Holyhead, anchoring about five minutes

after eight. We blamed the morning fog for making us five minutes late, but I doubt if the Boston and Maine express would have done better on a run of equal length. As we steamed around the breakwater and into Holyhead Harbour we felt very grand indeed. And why shouldn't we? A little American destroyer, the Stars and Stripes at our gaff, and a British Admiral's flag at our main-top. It was like the triumphal entry of some great monarch into a city, all the ships appreciating our importance. A boat shoved off from H.M.S. *Patrol*, the senior of the Irish Sea Patrol, and Captain Gordon Campbell, V.C., D.S.O., R.N., of Q-boat renown, came alongside on a visit to our Admiral.

"The conference over, shortly before noon we were under way again, this time for Milford Haven. The Admiral wished to arrive there at 4 p.m., spend the evening, and return to Queenstown by 8 a.m. the following morning. During our journey we found the Admiral to be a very human person, in spite of his gold lace. Battleship formalities were, of course, impossible, and the Admiral was simply one of the officers.

"Among the destroyer flotilla it became a fairly well-established custom never to take a bath at sea. One had to be ready at any time to answer the general alarm and rush to 'battle stations.' Also the fate of two men in the destroyer *Jacob Jones* when she was torpedoed showed the wisdom of wearing heavy clothes always during the ever-present possibility of finding oneself in the cold sea. These two men were taking a shower at the time, went overboard as they were, and only survived one half-hour; whereas many others withstood the exposure for over twelve hours, and were eventually saved. As one officer said, men went back to the old custom of taking a bath every Saturday night, and if you were at sea on Saturday you were out of luck. In this respect nobody broke our regulations. We had a shower which alternately ran steam and ice water. There was no happy medium. No one had ever used this shower without scalding himself on first attempt.

"The commissary steward 'Jerry' certainly lived up to his already enviable reputation, and we were in the midst of an elaborate 'Memorial Day' banquet of planked steak when word came down over the voice-tube from the bridge, 'Blimp on port-bow signals she sees submarine.' The general

[*Courtesy of Messrs. Cochrane & Sons, Ltd.*

H.M.S. *KILFREE*
One of the double ended patrol vessels.

A RARE SIGHT
Admiral Bayly flying his flag at sea aboard an American destroyer.

alarm sounded, the banquet was forgotten, and all hands rushed to their battle stations. The blimp, a type of British airship, was quite close to the surface, and pointing her nose down at a sharp angle to designate the location of the submarine. Emergency full speed was rung up, the whole ship seemed to leap ahead, and the water flew out from under the stern as the speed increased. At thirty knots it did not take long to arrive under the blimp, where we began laying a barrage of depth-charges. As we circled the spot at high speed, one ' can ' containing 300 lbs. of ' T.N.T.' was slipped over the stern every ten seconds.

"Our passenger was on the bridge, and the captain later said the Admiral's eye sparkled as each depth-charge went off, shaking the ship, and throwing up a mountain of water, and his smile became broader with every explosion.

" It was an impressive sight looking over the stern towards the blimp, which was about seventy-five feet above the surface, with almost a continuous line of eruptions gradually drawing away from it in a semi-circle. The spray would hardly settle from one explosion when another charge would draw the surface of the water taut like the hide on a drum, and then break forth in a fountain. As we returned under the blimp, thick bubbles of oil and air were still rising to the surface, where the first few ' cans ' had gone off. Let us hope we'd destroyed one ! But many times the clever Hun would simply blow out an oil tank to deceive the attacker, so the Admiralty never gave credit for a submarine unless absolute proof was forthcoming. Although we had probably at least damaged an enemy, the Admiralty report would read, 'No apparent results.'

" The blimp remained to patrol in the vicinity, while we proceeded to Milford Haven. The remainder of the trip was uneventful. Shortly after dawn the following morning we passed close aboard an open life-boat, only to see another mark of the fiendishness of submarine warfare: one dead body stretched across the middle thwart. Doubtless the last trace of an unarmed schooner or barque, sunk by gun-fire.

" We returned to Queenstown at 8 a.m., after a most enjoyable trip. A number of destroyers had returned from convoy duty, and so, as we steamed up between the buoys, we felt ourselves the envy of all the American ships. The green barge, already out in the stream waiting for us, quickly came alongside, taking away our guest, and as we hauled down his flag, the red-crossed flag of Admiral Bayly was again hoisted at the white flagstaff on the hill.

"About an hour later we received a signal from Commander-in-Chief's office. '*Trippe* will not sail until June 4, if avoidable.' Four days in port!! Why couldn't we be the Admiral's flagship all the time, if it meant four days ashore after every trip?"

In June began the custom of sending in convoy empty troop transports returning to North America. They were collected at Southend on the Thames, and at Liverpool, sailing about every sixteen days. This obviously increased the strain of escorting through the danger zone; nor was the problem made any the easier when, on June 3, occurred the first instance of mines being found off the United States coast; the American oil-tanker *Herbert L. Pratt* thus receiving damage two and a half miles S.E. of Overfalls Light-vessel, Delaware Bay. Mines were also discovered in other spots, and the U.S. tug *Waltham* in this manner met her end. The capture of eleven United States steamers and sailing vessels in the West Atlantic by the converted *Deutschland* type of submarine that month was not merely another precedent, but one more awkward reminder of Germany's persistence. If by these threats to American shipping she could delay the troop transports for even a few weeks, that submarine's long voyage would have been amply worth while.

But there came a nasty blow when the converted liner *Patia* was torpedoed whilst being escorted by the American destroyers *Trippe* and *Wilkes*, the exact position of the disaster being Lat. 50.57 N., Long. 5.19 W., or in the approaches to the Bristol Channel: that is to say, within only a few miles of the port to which she was bound. The time was 2.26 p.m. Here is the story as witnessed by an American naval officer:

"It was the 13th day of June, 1918—a glorious afternoon at sea, with the fresh south-west wind blowing just strongly enough to colour the blue surface of the water with a few white caps here and there. We were zigzagging back and forth about 800 yards on the port bow of the British auxiliary cruiser *Patia*. On the starboard bow about 1000 yards away was another destroyer. It was one of those bright and cheerful afternoons which made one feel life at sea in war-time was not such a hardship as many people imagined.

"Three days before we had set out from Queenstown in a division of eight destroyers, had gone out to 15° W. Longitude, met a large convoy of thirty-five merchant ships, and escorted them in almost to the Scilly Islands. H.M.S. *Patia* was the ocean escort of this convoy from the 'States.' Although she was an auxiliary cruiser, even she was loaded with cargo, and was carrying enough meat and sugar to feed one million soldiers in France for one day.

"This very morning the convoy had split up. Eight British destroyers had taken over the ships bound for English Channel ports; six of the American destroyers were escorting the remainder of the convoy to Brest and Bordeaux; while the *Patia* and two American destroyers headed up toward the Bristol Channel, their destination being Avonmouth.

"We were just entering the Bristol Channel, and had only about 100 miles to go before we should be through the danger zone with another duty done. Fifteen minutes earlier the *Patia* had increased speed from 12·5 to 13 knots, and ceased zigzagging preparatory to changing the base course. It had been several months since the *Patia* had visited England, and the men were already counting the hours before they would be in 'Blighty' again.

"Suddenly our whole ship shivered, and there was a violent explosion like the firing of a depth-charge close aboard; only sharper, louder, and a more crackling noise. Dense yellow smoke was pouring from the hold of the *Patia*, and a great burst of flame shot up as high as the mast. At the same time the figure of a man was seen to rise from the gun-deck aft, slowly turning somersaults, and describing an arc through the air, catapulted overboard by the explosion.

"'Both engines ahead full—Hard right rudder' were the commands given. The captain immediately took over the deck; the depth-charges were set at 'Fire,' ready to drop on signal, and all hands were at their battle stations. No one had seen the submarine, but it was obvious the torpedo had been fired from the starboard side, and must have been fairly close to make such a perfect hit.

"We were cutting close across the stern of the *Patia*. 'Stand by the depth-charge signal,' the captain called, 'we'll start laying a ten-second barrage just abeam of that piece of wreckage. He probably dived straight ahead, and that ought to get him.' (There was a piece of wreckage on our starboard bow, just about where the ship had been, when struck.) 'Belay that signal—there's a man on the wreckage.' And there, sure enough, was one lone, pitiful figure on what looked like a door, clinging with one hand, frantically waving the other and screaming at the top of his lungs. This was the poor man who had been on watch at the after-gun when the torpedo struck and was hurled overboard. We couldn't drop a can [1] directly under him, but as soon as we were clear, the captain said, 'Let her have it,' and we did.

"The other destroyer had also swung back, and together we laid a heavy pattern of charges around a wide radius. The Hun couldn't be far away and, from the amount of oil and bubbles that was brought to the surface in one spot, he was either fooling us or we had surprised him.

"'She's done for,' some one cried, as we swung back toward the *Patia*. She was listing quite badly to starboard and settling aft. Her stern was almost awash. She appeared like some stricken animal with its hind leg broken, limping along, pitifully dragging the injured limb after it. She was gradually veering her course to starboard and losing headway.

"The life-boats were lowered smartly, and were all clear of the ship eighteen minutes after she was struck. By this time she had lost all headway. The list was very decided, and she was settling rapidly. As the stern went down the bow came up, as if pivoting amidships. A few men could still be seen running wildly about the decks, having failed to get away in the lifeboats and apparently unable to swim. They all had life-vests on, and finally we saw three of them brave the water, and, after some splashing and kicking, reach the nearest lifeboat. The stern was now well under water, and the final plunge might come any minute. The remaining six or eight men had just jumped into the water, and were bravely striking out for the lifeboats, when there was another terrific explosion. Two depth-charges on the stern of the *Patia*, set for 'Fire,' had reached the required depth and gone off. Several were snuffed out by the explosion. The last to jump had decided too late, and both men and wreckage were thrown high into the air.

[1] Slang for depth-charge.

"The sight which now met our eyes was almost unbelievable. The bow gradually rose higher and higher, as if a line were pulling it right up to Heaven. You felt as if you were at some thrilling drama—it seemed so impossible and unnatural, and you felt so helpless to do anything. At last the bow was raised perpendicularly to the water, over 100 feet in the air, the foremast parallel to the water. She hesitated in this position just long enough for us to take in the whole picture and sum it up. A great big, fine ship of 8000 tons standing right on end only a few hundred yards away from us.

"A few minutes ago, alive and unsuspecting, cheerfully and gracefully making her way along—almost at the end of her journey—bringing meat for one million men for one day, and sugar and flour. Bang—and it was all over! A poor smitten animal, gradually weaker and weaker, she collapsed in one spot, throwing her nose high into the air, apparently rising, and extending herself toward Heaven, lingering in this position for several seconds, half her body still putting up a fight, while the other half had succumbed. In five minutes she would be no more—a dozen life-boats filled with men, and a little wreckage, all that would be left of her.

"She began to settle, sliding down, stern first,—not hurriedly, nor jerkily, but smoothly and easily, as if a firm hand were directing her course to the bottom, as indeed there was. When about thirty feet of her bow was still showing, and the foremast just level with the water, she hesitated again, as if her stern was resting on bottom. Then came one violent shake, a last brave gasp for breath, all beneath the surface seemed to collapse, she glided swiftly out of sight. A slight whirlpool, and she was gone.

"What a spectacle! What a tragedy! It gave one a thrill, but as the ship stood on end and started down there was a feeling of depression that came over us. I felt as if I should remove my cap and stand at attention—like at a funeral, as in truth it was. On looking around, I discovered others, likewise, had bared their heads. Here we were 'lying-to' waiting to pick up survivors, a perfect mark for a submarine; but I'll venture to say there were not five men in our ship, or even in the life-boats, able to see this ship go down, who were thinking of a submarine. Every eye was riveted on the doomed *Patia*. One officer called to his men to 'keep a sharp look-out for a periscope,' and the men turned as if offended at having their attention distracted. It seemed like insulting a dying man to turn away at such a time. The impressive sadness of the sight is beyond description.

"It was all over so quickly, and no one saw the cause of it all. She didn't have a chance from the start. Twenty-five minutes after she was struck, the *Patia* disappeared. There wasn't much to be done, although, since we were there, the results were not as horrible as they otherwise might have been. We 'lay to' while the boats came alongside with survivors and the other destroyer circled us to afford protection. It didn't take us long to look like a ferry-boat and hospital. We picked up 240 men, including thirteen badly wounded, who were cared for in our ward-room. One of our most esteemed passengers was a large police dog, 'Bobs,' named after Lord Roberts. One of the officers had almost lost his life in going back to save this dog, but they delayed lowering the life-boat; they wouldn't leave without 'Bobs,' and 'Bobs' was saved.

"After cruising around for about forty-five minutes and dropping a few more cans, we left the scene. Except for a little débris the Lord cleans up His battlefields at sea pretty thoroughly, as also He conceals the foe. At a speed of twenty-seven knots we were in Milford Haven in three hours.

"It was a very good opportunity to see the British seamen under trying conditions, and they certainly showed up wonderfully. Instead of talking of the narrow escape they'd had, the hardships they'd been through, and their tough luck, these men, who only a few minutes ago had been almost shaking hands with death, were cheerful and unselfish. They were very grateful to us for all we were doing for them, as if we were doing anything more than was to be expected. Who wouldn't do it for them? We simply gave them food and dry clothes. Our little galley got busy, and in a short time the commissary steward was serving chicken salad sandwiches and hot coffee to all. The American coffee and white bread impressed them particularly. The British Navy was not as fortunate as the American in always having plenty of white bread.

"The other chief topic of conversation was how they would spend their ten days 'Torpedoed leave.' In the British Navy every time a man is in a torpedoed ship he automatically gets ten days' leave, and ten days' leave looked very good to these men. They were human, after all—why worry about the past, in days when one never knew what the morrow would bring?

"We arrived at Milford Haven at 6.45 p.m. A tug came out and took off the wounded, rushing them in to the hospital, and another large tug came alongside to take off the remainder. The captain was the last to go. He was a tall, fine-looking man. Not one word of complaint had he uttered, or sought the least sympathy over the loss of his vessel. All his time was spent in caring for the wounded and making his men comfortable. He was now wearing an old U.S. Navy cap one of our officers had given him, as his own was lost. As he stepped over into the tug he said in an hesitating, almost childish tone, referring to the cap, ' You don't mind if I keep this—do you?—I'd sort of like it—to remember you by.'

"Most of us have heard some good cheering at the Harvard Stadium, and the Yale Bowl, and some of us have heard the American troops in the transports cheer the destroyers as they steam by going into Liverpool or Brest, having safely escorted the convoy through the danger zone; but I never had the thrills go up and down my back in quite the same way as they did this quiet evening in the Welsh port, when the four-striper R.N. captain, with water still running off his clothes, and wearing the U.S. Navy cap, stepped out before his remaining officers and men, and led a cheer for us, as we shoved off. It was only three good rah's—but the last one was a long one, hats were off, and those ' Limeys ' certainly got into it. I, for one, shall never forget it.

"Sixty minutes after entering Milford Haven harbour we were steaming out again past the lighthouse on the headland. We had landed the survivors, the ward-room was transformed from a hospital, running in blood and filled with bandaged victims, into a respectable dining saloon, and the *Trippe* was again shipshape.

"We were under way for Brest, France, where we were scheduled to escort an out-bound convoy on the following morning, and we must hurry in order to take in oil before the convoy sailed, but we were not likely soon to forget our experiences of June 13."

CHAPTER XXIX

RESCUE SHIPS

THROUGHOUT this summer of bitter contest, when the last rounds were being fought out, the enemy was able to inflict no little suffering on non-combatants. A protracted case was that of the British S.S. *Ausonia* (Commander R. Capper, D.S.C., R.N.R.), which was torpedoed without warning on May 30, 1918, causing the loss of forty-four lives. Now, the remarkable feature is that this happened 620 miles west of the Fastnet, so that any chance of survivors being saved was remote.

Eight days later the *Zinnia* was still searching for them, when at 5.15 a.m. she found a lifeboat, twelve and a half miles south of the Bull Lighthouse, containing Commander Capper, the stewardess, and twenty men, including an eighteen-year youth with both legs broken. The master related that *Ausonia* had been sunk at 5.58 p.m., seven boats had left the ship, but two had parted company the same night. Five had kept together until the afternoon of June 5, when a north-westerly gale separated them.

Commander Capper was an officer of the highest attainments, a fine seaman, a first-class leader and organiser. Aboard the *Ausonia*, boat-drill had been regularly carried out, "Abandon Ship" stations practised, boats kept ready with provisions. His own boat, when found, was already badly strained and leaking, though all the officers and men in it spoke with admiration of Capper's skill and courage. But for his leadership the five boats with 108 people would not have completed their long voyage of nearly 600 miles.

For ten days he had no sleep whatsoever. Ten days!—nevertheless, still in full possession of his faculties and able to give the probable position of his other boats. Three were picked up by the patrol H.M.S. *Safeguard*, and the sloop *Camellia* found the fifth boat twenty-one miles to the south-west of where Captain Capper had been picked up. She contained a score of unhappy men, of whom one also had both legs broken. Bad enough to suffer such injuries on shore, with doctors and hospitals at hand; but for two men thus afflicted to be tossed about in open boats at the mercy of Atlantic waves appals the imagination. And before the new month was over—on June 27—another submarine 116 miles west of the Fastnet, with absolutely no warning, torpedoed the 11,423-tons hospital ship *Llandovery Castle*, thereby sending 146 helpless people to death. The culprit was Lieut.-Commander Helmut Patzig of *U* 86.

But in spite of these horrors, gallant seafarers of both nations carried on, and the flow of American troops across to France had now attained enormous figures: 250,000 a month being landed. And herein was another death-blow to the German cause. As against this, Germany possessed, by the beginning of July, fourteen submarines based on Brunsbüttel, eighteen based on Heligoland and Wilhelmshaven, fifteen built or building at Wilhelmshaven, twelve at Emden, ten of the big cruiser-submarines (*U* 135, etc.) at Kiel, twenty of the UB's and UC's in Flanders; or a total of sixty-nine; but additional to the above were thirty-three comprising the Mediterranean Flotilla based on Pola and Cattaro. This month, also, *U* 20, who had sunk the *Lusitania*, continued to operate off the Irish coast. Those veterans Lieut.-Commander Förstmann in *U* 39, and Lieut.-Commander Schneider in *U* 24 were also working this area. Thanks to the improved Dover Straits obstructions, these submarines still preferred to come even to the Scillies via Fair Island, St. Kilda, and southwest Ireland.

On July 24 Queenstown was visited by the First Lord of the Admiralty (Sir Eric Geddes), together with Mr. Franklin Roosevelt, destined a few years later to become President of the United States. All was pomp and ceremony—officers in full dress with swords, the band playing—when these two personages came alongside the *Melville* in the Commander in-Chief's green barge. In those days, when everyone was doing his bit, when many had laid aside a distinguished citizen career to become uniform and pull their full weight, there inevitably ensued more than one amusing meeting.

Mr. Alexander Forbes, a scientist of the Harvard Medical

School, has given me a delicious account of that day. In the previous February he had become a temporary naval officer as expert in wireless, on his friend Mr. Roosevelt's advice. To-day he chanced to be in dungarees when his old school friend inspected the *Melville*. "Presently the procession appeared coming aft from the bow, very grand, Captain Pringle (Chief of Staff), Captain Price (of the *Dixie*), Commodore Martin-Leake (who had succeeded Commodore Carpendale), and some other naval magnates, resplendent with their swords clashing. I braved the austere frown of Captain Price and stood near as they approached. Suddenly Franklin Roosevelt saw me and exclaimed: 'Hallo, Alex! I didn't know you were here'; came back up the ladder to shake hands and have a bit of chat. The resulting confusion to the procession was a treat. The mighty men didn't know whether to go on down the ladder without him, or to wait while he talked with the dirty boob. Finally, when he found he must visit the bakery, he said, 'Come along down.' So I joined the grand procession, dungarees and all. On the deck below he took me up and introduced me to Sir Eric. It was a proud moment when I wrecked the morals of the Admiral's flagship by shaking hands with the First Lord in my dirty dungarees."

So also Admiral Wemyss, First Sea Lord, came over to inspect. Suave of manner, agile with his monocle, he was, in the average American sailor's imagination, the typical British officer as depicted in a thousand novels and plays. In addition to the British Naval Forces, by the end of June there were in European waters 7467 officers and men of the United States Naval Forces, of whom more than half belonged to the destroyers, tugs, and mother ships. The rest were in training barracks; attached to the Base Hospital, Torpedo Repair Station, the Submarine Detachment; or serving at the five Air Stations. The latter comprised Queenstown, Lough Foyle, Wexford, Whiddy Island, and Castletownbere on Bantry Bay. Apart from the above and the recreation facilities, was an important supply depot for anticipating the destroyers' and other warships' needs of provisions, clothing; and this included the cold storage of some 600 tons. The American hospital was commenced at the end of May 1918, when the buildings

INSPECTING U.S.S. *MELVILLE*
Admiral Sir Rosslyn Wemyss, First Sea Lord, walking with Captain J. R. Poinsett Pringle, U.S.N.

ABOARD AN AMERICAN DESTROYER
The First Sea Lord being received by the destroyer's captain.

were staked out, but a month later they were practically finished.

On March 5 the first shipload of building material arrived from America for erecting quarters at Whiddy Island, Wexford, and Lough Foyle, but already several days previously the American flag had been hoisted over the U.S. Naval Air Station at Queenstown and elsewhere. Actual flying operations were delayed owing to the necessity for training all pilots at Queenstown for the other Irish stations, and the first patrol was made on the last day of September. Thus, by the time most things were in an advanced state of organisation the Armistice came. During this period the wake of a submarine had been bombed, several convoys escorted, and over 11,000 miles patrolled; and had the War continued a little longer this efficient arm, working in close conjunction with the submarine-chasers, would have been able to harry the enemy with thoroughness.

But that which impressed the mind was the self-supporting character of the American naval organisation. The *Melville* and *Dixie* could be relied upon for most minor repairs: though after such incidents as collisions it usually meant that the destroyer was sent to a Birkenhead shipyard. With the exception of small quantities of fresh meat and vegetables, all the provisions used by these forces at Queenstown had been shipped across the Atlantic. From first to last (*i.e.* May 1917 till October 1918) this meant the arrival of nearly seventeen million lbs. of food. At a time when food shortage had become acute in the British Isles, it was providential that our naval allies could—so to say—feed and clothe themselves from their own homeland. In short, the Queenstown of pre-War days was like a mere sleepy village compared with the doubly busy base in the last year of hostilities. It was, in fact, the centre for two Navies co-operating in a war but lightly linked to that contest proceeding in the North Sea. As the weeks sped by, these western operations became still more Anglo-American, not merely in respect of personnel, material, and supply, but because the quickest way to bring peace was to protect troop convoys into port.

The thoroughness of transatlantic aid was completed before the end of August by the arrival of the biggest units of all. So far we have noted destroyers in large numbers, submarines, submarine-chasers, supply-ships, tugs, aircraft. But now came some American battleships to south-west Ireland. This division of six reached Berehaven on August 23, and they brought with them six months' stores, excepting fresh provisions. Thus they, also, were self-supporting. But for what purpose had these battleships come over?

The answer is quite simple: they were the logical result of the convoy system. Now that the protection by destroyers and other men-of-war was generally defeating the submarine, it was expected that sooner or later Germany would send out either raiders or battle-cruisers to defeat the present escorts. Therefore a couple of battleships—excellently placed at Berehaven close to the Atlantic, with an easy exit at each end of the fjord—would be invaluable to come out and meet the incoming military transports. They could stay to fight the enemy's surface vessels, whilst the convoy sought safety in flight. Had the War lasted a little longer, it is highly probable that as a brave gesture such an attack might have been attempted. Other raiders,[1] taking advantage of the northern mists and long nights, had successfully got round northern Europe from Germany into the Atlantic, and returned home. The *Moewe*, let us remember, ran the gauntlet each way twice. Now, in the middle of this last October, a sudden scare reached the authorities that three large vessels of a mysterious nature were steaming across the North Sea, and it was thought they might be bound out to fall upon the convoys. For this reason, hurried orders came sending the Berehaven battleships to the Atlantic, but the North Sea rumour had no substance, and no crisis ripened. The enemy was much more interested in concentrating seven of his submarines off Brest, which, of course, was sound strategy: though why, in those uncertain days, he never sent through the Dover Straits by night a division of battle-cruisers to wipe out some big convoy near Ushant seems difficult to explain on any grounds other than lack of initiative or weakened morale. There was one convoy at the end of August this year consisting of forty-one ships! What a target! And

[1] For instances see my books *The Sea Raiders*, and *The Big Blockade*.

FIRST SEA LORD AND CHIEF OF STAFF
Admiral Sir Rosslyn Wemyss, K.C.B., C.M.G., and Captain J. R. Poinsett Pringle, U.S.N., at Queenstown, 1918.

how terrible would have been the depressing effect on the Allies had this merchant fleet been wiped out!

By midsummer the opportunities for Q-ships had shifted from Irish waters to the neighbourhood of the Azores and Gibraltar, with the exception that a chance might be found in the English Channel. On July 30 this year was to be seen a small coasting steamer about twenty-five miles S.W. of the Start jogging along at seven and a half knots. Actually she was the Q-ship *Stockforce*, under the command of Lieut. Harold Auten, D.S.C., R.N.R., who had served under Admiral Bayly some time in the *Zylpha*. Now, just before 5 p.m. a torpedo struck her, completely wrecking the fore-part of the ship, including the bridge, wounding several officers and men. The "panic party" did their stuff as normal, the wounded were got below and tended by the surgeon, but the ship was settling down, and his duties were extremely hazardous, no less than difficult.

Auten watched the submarine appear and make a close inspection, till at 5.40 p.m. the enemy provided a longed-for opportunity, being then 300 yards on the steamer's beam; whereupon both four-inch guns opened fire, carrying away the German's wireless as well as one of his periscopes, besides partly demolishing the conning-tower and hurling a sailor into the air. Next the U-boat was torn open and more of her crew were blown into space. From both guns shell after shell deluged the enemy, till she sank by the stern, leaving a quantity of debris on the water. As to the *Stockforce* herself, she was doomed, although her captain went full speed ahead in an effort to beach her on the nearest land. The wounded were transferred to a couple of trawlers about 6.30 p.m., and then came a couple of torpedo-boats; but at 9.20 p.m. the decoy finally sank.

For this engagement Auten was awarded the Victoria Cross, and decorations were given to his officers. Both they and their captain were appointed to another collier, *Suffolk Coast*, which had barely been fitted out in the most complete Q-ship manner at Queenstown than hostilities with Germany were suspended; so that with the passing of *Stockforce* was concluded the brief but historic period of decoy tactics. Even had the War continued, it is doubtful whether their usefulness could any longer have existed; for the enemy by this date had developed his counter-measures pretty thoroughly.

So now the time came round once more for the gales, and with October there arrived likewise some thrilling events. It was on the 9th, about 6 a.m., that the American destroyer *Shaw* was escorting the big Cunarder *Aquitania* along the English Channel, and the following (written by *Shaw's* commanding officer) is so clear a narrative that no elaboration could be needed.

"The *Shaw* was zigzagging at twenty-seven knots on the port bow of the *Aquitania*, which vessel was making slightly over twenty-two knots. The *Shaw* was in position 1000 yards or more broad on the port bow of the *Aquitania*, and heading on a course approximately 35° converging to the course of the *Aquitania* when the order was given 'Left Rudder' to begin a left leg of our zigzag. The helmsman attempted to put the helm over, and immediately reported that he could not, as the wheel would not move, but had stuck at about 15° right rudder. There was a moderate following sea. The ship started to swing at high speed towards the *Aquitania*, and it was perceived at once that a collision was imminent. My immediate concern was to avoid if possible, and make every effort to prevent ramming and possibly sinking the *Aquitania* and my subsequent actions were thus governed. The engine telegraphs were accordingly rung for emergency speed astern and I blew three blasts on the whistle, sounded the siren, and ordered the general alarm rung, which was done. In the meantime, and during a very appreciable interval, certainly a minute or more, the *Shaw* and the *Aquitania* rushed one upon the other. From the bridge I looked over our side to see if our speed had appreciably diminished, and noted that we were still making great speed through the water. The *Aquitania* struck me on the starboard bow at the forward edge of the bridge at an angle converging about 45° from ahead to the line of the keel of the *Shaw*. My bow was literally shaved off, the *Aquitania* passing between the two sections of this ship. The *Shaw* then scraped her port side along the port side of the *Aquitania*, our lifeboat at the port davits was smashed, and a big gash, about 20 feet by 4 feet, was cut in our side above the water-line in the forward boiler-room. There was a tremendous flash of sparks at the moment of impact, and while the *Aquitania* was going through us. This immediately ignited all the oil in the forward bunkers, and what was left of the forepart of the ship, including the bridge, was soon in flames.

"In my judgment, had the *Shaw* been continued at full speed, as the other alternative in this situation with rudder jammed right, we would have turned more sharply to the right, and we would have struck the *Aquitania* fairly amidships at tremendous speed, which would probably have resulted in her loss and appalling loss of life.

"The *Duncan* and *Kimberly* at once stood over to our assistance. Word was given *Kimberly* and *Duncan* to stand by my then floating bow to rescue men there. I ordered the forward magazine flooded, and Lieut.-Commander Van L. Kirkman, Ensigns Edward C. Riley and Ross A. Dierdorff, went through the flame in an attempt to gain the charthouse, where the floodcocks were located. They were unable, however, to accomplish this. The crew was then ordered to gather in the after part of the ship, as my immediate concern was the probability of an explosion in the forward magazine. How this explosion was averted I cannot at this time say. Had this magazine blown up, it undoubtedly would have ruptured the forward boiler-room and cofferdam bulkheads, which I believe would have caused the loss of the *Shaw*. Depth-charges were ordered put on safety, after-magazine flooded, all ammunition about the deck thrown overboard, and life-rafts put in the water. The *Duncan* was then signalled to come alongside, which was accomplished on our starboard quarter in a moderate sea in an extremely seamanlike and commendable manner. All men were got off the ship except fourteen men and six officers.

"I directed the *Duncan* to shove off and stand by me. We then turned to see what could be done to save the ship, in case the forward magazine did not go, or even in case it did. The engine-room and after boiler-room appeared to be intact, and orders were given to attempt to get up steam again. Steam had fallen to about thirty or forty lbs. I wished to get a steam jet on the fire that was raging forward, and also felt that I could use my engines. Steam was raised in what seemed a very short time, and a jet of steam sent into the forward fuel tanks through the steam connection. It had been noted when the crew was gathered aft previously that the mainmast had snapped off and fallen over the starboard counter, and the wreckage with stays, etc., fouled the starboard screw and rudder. An effort was made to clear the wreckage, while the crew was gathered aft, without success. After the majority of the crew had left the *Shaw*, a working party was told off to plug the gash in our port side abreast the forward boiler-room. This was done very expeditiously and efficiently with mattresses and other odds and ends scattered about the deck, the whole being secured by boards on the outside, held in place by lines leading through the side of the ship into the boiler-room. Another party was told off to dump overboard remnants of ammunition forward. During all this time an intense fire was raging forward, and the four-inch ammunition around the charthouse was going off, as well as the small-arms ammunition in the wardroom passage-way, which was in flames.

"We next tried to clear the wreckage which fouled our starboard screw, and it was discovered that the mast in some manner had found its way between the forks of the strut, and was jammed there at about the middle point of the mast. We triced up the after end of the mast to clear the propeller and cut some of the stays, etc. Our efforts to dislodge the mast were unavailing at this time. The steering engine was examined, and it was found that the set screw of the collar on differential gear had worked loose, and the engine jammed, so that the rudder remained in right position about 15°. This defect was repaired in a short while, the after-steering gear tested and found to be working. By this time it was reported to me that both engines could turn over and, the fire forward having somewhat abated, I concluded to attempt to make port under my own steam. Accordingly, the *Kimberly* was signalled to lead me to the nearest port, and we would follow; so we started ahead slowly with the port engine. All lashings on the mast over the starboard side were then ordered cut, and in about twenty minutes the mast cleared and floated astern. Our colours were recovered from the water and hoisted to a spar. The two Y guns, No. 4 4-inch gun and the two after torpedo tubes were prepared for firing. The starboard engine was started ahead slow, and without very much difficulty, except in steering, the ship followed the *Kimberly*, at about five knots, to entrance of Portland Harbour, where we arrived at about 1.30 p.m. Tugs met us at the entrance, but could not come alongside of me due to heavy seas, until the *Shaw* passed through the net.

"Upon arrival alongside dock, representatives of the dockyard came on board. We looked over the ship, and it was concluded to board up the gash in our side at the forward boiler-room and hoist out the foremast, which somehow had remained standing. These were the only temporary repairs deemed necessary to put the ship in condition to proceed escorted to dockyard under her own steam."

Now, on the day after several lives were lost through this accident there occurred in the Irish Sea a deliberate tragedy which shocked Ireland, Europe, and America. At 9.50 a.m. the Kingstown–Holyhead mail and passenger steamer *Leinster* was two miles S.E. of the Kish Light-vessel—that is to say, comparatively near the Irish coast—when she was torpedoed with the loss of 176 lives, including that of her master. It was in this ship that thousands of Queenstown officers and men had been accustomed to travel when going on leave, so that day an American officer, Captain Cone, happened to be one of the passengers. He was severely injured, but not immediately. After the torpedo struck, he offered his services to the master, and was assigned the duty of getting women and children into the boats. Then a second torpedo hit the disabled steamer abreast of where he stood, blowing him into the air, breaking one leg badly, and so injuring the opposite ankle that he was unable to stand.

When the *Leinster* sank, Captain Cone himself rolled into the water, got hold of a raft, yet had not the strength to haul himself on board, but had the presence of mind to lash his elbows to the raft, and then lost consciousness. Two sailors later got on to this raft, took charge of him, and afterwards put him aboard a patrol vessel. Two hours had he spent on the former, and then several more elapsed before he reached hospital.

It seems scarcely credible that any civilised nation should, among the last of her operations at sea, have perpetrated such an attack; yet we have seen in a previous chapter that at least one other submarine had been trying to sink these very cross-channel steamers. Nor was the *Lusitania* affair more disgraceful in principle.

In brighter contrast, let us watch the battle between men and the sea: instead of Hunnish brutality, let us follow a grand drama of bravery and sacrifice. Some of the pluckiest unknown achievements afloat are done by comparatively small tugs; but few records exist except of those exploits belonging to war days. At Queenstown were based such British tugs as the *Stormcock* and *Warrior*; such American tugs as the *Genesee* and *Sonoma*. They combined the duties of patrol and rescue. The *Sonoma*, for example, was assigned the south Irish coast from the Tuskar to the Fastnet, being kept in readiness to aid any distressed vessel in the eastern Atlantic, Irish Sea, and English Channel as well. She was only 185 feet long, with low freeboard. When loaded with coal, as was usual, she had a pretty rough time in heavy seas; but Lieutenant James S. Trayer, U.S.N., her captain, won considerable admiration at Queenstown in both Navies for his seamanship and courage.

The following story begins at noon of October 8, 1918, when *Sonoma*, lying at anchor in Queenstown Harbour, received orders to coal and proceed to the assistance of the British S.S. *Huntscliffe*, which was in distress a very long way out into the Atlantic—Lat. 51.22 N., Long. 26.50 W. This steamer seemed destined for adventure. Less than a month before she had been chased by a submarine in the Atlantic, but escaped through the use of a defensive gun; yet now her cargo of grain had shifted, and she had been abandoned at sea since the previous day.

Within three hours the *Sonoma* had taken in enough coal, and was outside Queenstown smashing into a heavy westerly gale with a rough sea. It meant steaming most of four days through this sort of unpleasantness, but by midnight of the 11th she picked up a wireless from the armed auxiliary cruiser

Teutonic, which had been standing by the *Huntscliffe*. At 6 a.m. next morning *Sonoma* reached the given position, but the weather was thick, and in spite of cruising about for some hours nothing could be seen. At 3 p.m. the *Teutonic* could wait no longer, and wirelessed that she was proceeding on her voyage because of a submarine's proximity. But still the *Sonoma* kept up the search; and often enough the given position was some distance from the correct spot. Absence of sights on passage, and then the effect of wind, would be responsible for the intervening mileage.

Throughout that day in the wild Atlantic, with a southwest gale blowing all the time, *Sonoma* went on seeking, and at 4.10 a.m. of the 13th the look-out saw something vague in the darkness. Presently this was found to be the deserted *Huntscliffe*, with a dangerous list, and it looked as if she would roll over any moment. At the best she was a menace to all the shipping that crossed the Atlantic, but with the heavy sea running no attempt could be made to board her. Trayer therefore stood by, in the hope that the weather would ease up before long.

Meanwhile Admiral Bayly sent out from Queenstown two of his sloops. At 8 a.m. on the 11th, *Zinnia* and *Jessamine* slipped, and began battling with the gale, which had now got round to N.W., and on passage picked up a wireless message for help from a steamer only fifty miles short of *Huntscliffe's* given position. It looked as if "Fritz" were having a fine harvest.

At noon of the 13th, the two sloops, together with the American tug *Genesee*, found *Huntscliffe*, not in her supposed position, but in Lat. 51.19 N., Long. 21.47 W.—that is to say, much farther east. In spite of the bad weather, the *Jessamine* decided to send a boat with a working party and board the *Huntscliffe* in order to get the *Sonoma's* hawser secured. The first attempt was unfortunate, as in lowering the boat some one let go the after fall, though luckily both men and boat were recovered. It was a ticklish business lowering away and shoving off without being smashed against the sloop's side, but at the second attempt they succeeded, and clambered aboard the grain ship. It was then discovered that more men were required to heave in the hawser, so at 3 p.m. *Zinnia* lowered her whaler.

The whaler had great difficulty in getting alongside *Huntscliffe*, whose lee gunwale (except amidships) rolled under water and would have completely wrecked the boat. The latter was very well handled, and her crew got aboard the steamer amidships; but the boat could not lie alongside in that swell, so had to be cast adrift. It then capsized, and the *Zinnia*, whilst endeavouring to salve, sat on it. The short afternoon wore on; both *Sonoma* and *Genesee* had failed to get their lines fast, and now the sloops' boat-crews were recalled. The carrying out of this order was not easy. One of the *Huntscliffe's* lifeboats, after considerable danger, was lowered (one davit being found cracked), and the men picked up by *Jessamine*, who then cast the boat adrift.

Presently, the sea having moderated, this lifeboat was picked up by *Sonoma*, who now sent a volunteer crew aboard the grain steamer and secured a hawser after forty-five minutes; but the boarding party had a difficult return, being forced to swim, as no boat could go alongside.

Later on, the hawser parted, and renewed efforts were made. So things went on till shortly before 6.30 on the morning of the 17th, when *Huntscliffe* finally sank, after all those heartbreaking days. The *Genesee* developed boiler trouble, and had to be towed home by *Sonoma*, but no further incident occurred. Both tugs had done extremely well, and towed the *Huntscliffe* 282 miles before the final plunge. They well deserved the commendation afterwards received from the Admiralty. The weather was the roughest encountered by these tugs throughout their stay in Europe, and it was really bad luck that the steamer did not allow herself to be brought home.

"The sighting of the *Huntscliffe* was a piece of luck," Lieutenant Trayer tells me. "We usually, on searches for disabled vessels, discovered them many miles from their assumed position. This vessel was found before dawn in thick weather. It had been abandoned then about three days. It had drifted many miles to the eastward. The morning the *Huntscliffe* was found, the writer had just come on duty for the 4 to 8 a.m. watch, which he always stood with the Chief Quartermaster at sea. Having lost lots of sleep, and also having drunk considerable coffee, I was not normal. Just after relieving the deck, I took my position on the port side of the upper bridge. The Chief Quartermaster took his station on the starboard side. We had a working agreement that if I should go to the port or starboard side of the bridge, he would take position on the opposite side. I thought I saw a black object ahead, but being so dull-witted, I considered I was seeing things, so crossed over to the starboard side. The Chief Quartermaster crossed over to the port side, and he was not there a moment before he said, 'Captain, I think I see a black object ahead.' 'Hard right,' I shouted to the helmsman below in the pilot-house, for I knew it was the object that was seen just a few moments before by myself, and just in time we cleared the *Huntscliffe*.

"At dawn this fine vessel was a terrible sight to see, her lee rail almost awash, and looking as though she would roll over with every wave she was riding.

"The rescue of the members of our crew that had secured the *Sonoma's* hawser to the *Huntscliffe* was a thriller. The tug was manœuvred with the hawser over the stern, and had to be turned quickly through 180° to effect the rescue of the men in the water. The *Sonoma's* whale-boat proved too slow, as darkness was rapidly setting in.

"The details leading up to this rescue were as follows: The life-boat's crew of the *Jessamine*, after attempting to secure the *Sonoma's* hawser to the *Huntscliffe*, returned to the *Jessamine* in one of the *Huntscliffe's* boats. Their own boat, which was used in boarding, was wrecked in going alongside the *Huntscliffe*. After the *Jessamine's* life-boat crew got back safely to their vessel, they cast the *Huntscliffe* boat adrift. The *Sonoma* steamed over to this boat, placed a crew in it, and sent it to the *Huntscliffe*. The crew reached the *Huntscliffe* safely, but the boat was wrecked alongside. After the hawser was secured, the *Sonoma* men had to be taken off the *Huntscliffe*. The *Sonoma* lowered a whale-boat successfully with the use of oil. The coxswain of this boat was the chief boatswain's mate, and he received orders in detail as to how to effect the rescue. The substance of these orders was, to lay off a boat's length from the *Huntscliffe*, and caution the men on that vessel to jump overboard, *one at a time*, and swim to the whale-boat, when it would pick them up. The whale-boat carried out orders, but the first man that jumped overboard from the *Huntscliffe* and swam to the whale-boat had such an easy time of it that the rest of the men thought it was easy, and so disobeyed orders, and all jumped overboard at the same time, thinking they would have no trouble in swimming to the whale-boat.

"There were twelve men in the water, and the whale-boat was making slow work of picking them up. Night was rapidly approaching. I realised that we were going to have some one missing if it was left to the whale-boat to accomplish. The tug must help; so decided to turn the tug about and go to leeward of the men in the water, and pick them up from the decks of the *Sonoma* as they drifted down to leeward. This was a very difficult manœuvre to make in so short a time, but it proved a success. Ten men and one officer were rescued by the tug. The last man, Kearney, the chief gunner's mate, was quite an elderly man. Although he volunteered for the life-boat, he could not swim. He swore he could when he was asked. He had a difficult time in the water keeping afloat, and he drifted well up ahead of the tug.

"Luckily for him, the life-jacket had been tested. We realised that the tug must increase speed to get Kearney on the weather side of the former, before he drifted to leeward. Four men were in the water alongside of the tug trying to get aboard. I shouted to put a line around them, as the tug was going to go ahead full speed a few moments, and would drag them in the water. We gave the signal to let out on the tow-line, as the *Sonoma* shot ahead. Everything worked perfectly. Just reached Kearney as he was drifting to leeward. Another moment and he would have been across the tug's bow. It was dark when all had been rescued. The four men alongside the *Sonoma* who had been dragged ahead by us had quite a thrill. Lieutenant Clough was the worse for wear. He had to be revived after he was brought aboard.

"The tow-line that was placed on the *Huntscliffe* was a new ten-inch manila hawser. It parted the next day, and all our former work was undone. Coming to the conclusion that there was no immediate danger of the vessel sinking, we decided to place a party on board, and to hook up the *Sonoma's* wire hawser to the *Huntscliffe's* anchor chain. This hawser was 100 fathoms of steel wire rope, two and a quarter inch diameter. One of the best seamen in the tugs was Boatswain H. J. Messier of the *Genesee*. He volunteered to take a boat alongside the *Huntscliffe* and remain on board after the tow-line was secured.

"The *Genesee* lowered a boat successfully, and sent a boarding party to the *Huntscliffe*. The starboard anchor was walked back on the chain until the first shackle was on deck. The anchor and chain forward of this shackle was then stoppered off, unshackled, and the anchor end allowed to drop overboard. This left a clear end on the anchor chain to connect up the wire hawser. After connecting up the hawser the chain was veered to seventy-five fathoms. Boatswain Messier, Coxswain Warren, and Boatswain's Mate Simpson remained in the *Huntscliffe*, while the life-boat returned to the *Genesee*. One of the best displays of seamanship that was ever viewed.

"Going ahead again with the tow, everything worked beautifully, and with the *Sonoma's* towing engine operating smoothly, we were able to make good from four to six knots per hour, towards Bantry Bay. The *Genesee* towed ahead of the *Sonoma*, with a manila hawser to our bow. The *Huntscliffe* towed on our quarter, and sometimes, almost abeam, instead of astern, and it looked as if the vessel wanted to pass us.

"The sinking of the *Huntscliffe* was the greatest thrill. She sank on my watch, a little past 4 a.m., in the dark. We became cautious the evening before, when it was noticed that the south-westerly wind was dying down. Signalled to Boatswain Messier to lower one of the *Huntscliffe's* life-boats to the water's edge, stand by in this boat, and to cut the boat falls if the vessel started to sink suddenly. The securing bolts on the *Sonoma* end of the wire hawser, which were clamped to the side of the drum of the towing engine, were loosened up, and well greased, so that the bolts could be taken off quickly. Came on watch at 4 a.m., glanced astern, and could see only a small dark object where the *Huntscliffe* should be. Having become familiar with the appearance of the tow, as viewed from the bridge of the tug, perceived danger in its appearance, and immediately ran aft, flashed on the searchlight, then off. My fears were well founded. Only the upper works and masts were showing.

"The *Huntscliffe* was sinking fast. I gave orders to the watch to slip the tow-line, and as it went off the drum and overboard it was spitting fire. Meanwhile on deck things were happening fast. The *Sonoma* and *Genesee* were towing in tandem, at that time were developing their full horse-power and going full speed ahead. As the ship sank, and before the tow-line could be cast loose, the weight of the *Huntscliffe* sinking carried both vessels astern to her sinking position. The *Sonoma's* fan tail (stern) was almost to the water's edge. The bow was high out of water. As the stern was freed, by letting go of the tow-line, the tug took a beautiful nose-dive, and scooped up a huge amount of water over the bow and forecastle, which swept aft, and almost washed several of the watch overboard. Only the life-lines, which were rigged up on both sides of the tug, saved them. The *Genesee* snapped her tow-line of manila. As dawn broke, all that could be seen on the surface of the water near by were the three *Genesee* men in the life-boat, safe, and patiently waiting to be picked up. Also, a great black spot where this fine vessel went to her grave. Remember, in all these operations the two sloops were circling the horizon keeping watch for submarines. Had the *Sonoma* and *Genesee* been fortunate enough to have had about thirty more hours of favourable weather, we would have brought this ship into Bantry Bay safely."

THE COMMANDER-IN-CHIEF
Coast of Ireland.

CHAPTER XXX

VICTORY

But now a great and wonderful change had come over things.

Only a week after the *Leinster* had been torpedoed, Germany's defeat in the World War began to manifest itself. Flanders was evacuated, and this meant that four of her submarines were to be destroyed there, but the rest sent home. On October 17 a British Admiral landed at Ostende, now freed from years of German bondage. About this date German submarines were recalled from the Atlantic, on the 30th Turkey signed an Armistice, and next day the Austrian Emperor made over the Austro-Hungarian Fleet to the Jugo-Slav National Council. Ten German submarines were destroyed at Pola and Cattaro, but others got away out of the Mediterranean back to German ports. On November 11 the Armistice with Germany was signed. At 7 a.m. that day the Queenstown vessels received orders to cease hostilities.

That evening Admiral Bayly made the following signal to his officers and men :—

> The Commander-in-Chief congratulates all British and United States officers and crews under his command on the splendid victory achieved which their loyalty, ability, and ever ready energies have so greatly assisted (Stop) It will always be a source of great pride to him to have been so greatly associated with them in this Great War.

So the World War in effect had ended because the British blockade succeeded, and the German submarine blockade failed owing to the fact that it was started too late and that Anglo-American efforts had enabled the convoy system to be felt on the Western Front. Whilst it is perfectly true that had the War been protracted a little longer U-boat operations would have been confined to the North Sea, by reason of the Northern Barrage and the Dover Straits minefields; yet even if the enemy could start his campaign afresh, he would still find that the combination of fast destroyers, listening devices, and unlimited depth-charges, together with efficient convoy methods, was bound in the last resort to triumph over the submarine.

Just as we were ending, Ireland was about to begin her own fights; and even at the close of October masked Sinn Feiners were raiding houses for arms. Another war now well under way was the influenza epidemic, which brought death to many who had escaped the perils of sea. Even this, however, had its humorous aspect. One of the influenza's victims happened to be an officer who died in Haulbowline Hospital, and after dark two Irish labourers were sent to his room with a coffin. Mistaking the room's number, they entered where another officer was lying dangerously ill of pneumonia; who, seeing what the men carried, sat up in anger and cursed roundly. This sudden vivacity of a " corpse " so astounded the visitors that they dropped their burden and fled for their lives. But the story ended happily with the sick man's recovery.

It had been no small achievement to have sunk a score of enemy submarines in the Irish area, but perhaps an even greater feat was that of keeping channels moderately safe for sea traffic in spite of unchivalrous German conduct. As Sir Lewis Bayly stressed after the War, success was to be measured not only " by the number of submarines sunk (except in the case of Mystery ships and other craft whose sole duty it is to sink them), but by the number of ships, crews, and cargoes preserved from attack." And of the Americans' share in all this he wrote to the Admiralty: " It is hard to express in words the singleness of purpose which animated them; the eagerness with which they set themselves to learn all the methods which had been tried, and to improve these methods so as not to lose any chance of possible success." Shipowners and Salvage Associations wrote to thank the Commander-in-Chief for what they owed; he had " saved many thousands of tons of shipping to the nation during its period of stress and strain whilst it was endeavouring to combat an enemy who disregarded all laws of warfare and humanity." Nor did the Admiralty omit to send their appreciation.

It was not without pain that one by one British and American commanding officers came up the Hill to say good-bye after these strenuous months. Demobilisation was commenced, the huge Queenstown Fleet dispersed all over the sea, Admiral Sims went back home to take up his duties again as

SILVER ROSE BOWL PRESENTED TO ADMIRAL BAYLY
By the Queenstown Association in New York.

WHERE BRITISH AND AMERICAN NAVAL OFFICERS MET
The Royal Cork Yacht Club, Queenstown.

President of the Naval College, and by March (1919) Admiral Bayly, after more than forty years of sea service, had left the Navy to organise his Devonshire garden. But the old friendships continued, and strengthened with the passing of months. " Once a sailor, always a sailor." The sea called, the garden is not such an attraction after summer has passed and the leaves have fallen; so in the autumn of 1920 Sir Lewis Bayly, with his niece, went aboard a Blue Funnel Liner half-way round the world to Japan; which voyage was preceded by a charming invitation from the American Pacific Mail Steamship Company to travel from Yokohama across to San Francisco.

Thus the voyage became another of those unprecedented occasions. Twenty miles off the Golden Gate the steamer was met by a division of U.S. destroyers to escort the Admiral, and on arrival who should come aboard but Captain Price, late of the *Dixie*, though now head of the Naval Training Station? After passing through the Panama Canal, New York was reached, the ship being escorted by seaplanes and a dirigible, Governor's Island firing a salute. Admiral Sims and other naval officers were at the wharf to welcome.

A few days later Admiral Bayly was entertained at dinner in New York by the Queenstown Association, and presented with a silver rose-bowl in the name of his old officers. It was one of those evenings which a man never forgets. Many of the 150 members had travelled long distances—from Chicago, St. Louis, West Virginia—as a tribute of personal affection. " Tradition," said the Admiral in his speech to these officers, " is the strongest thing in the world. Sir Francis Drake is still a tradition in our Navy; his progress, seamanship and perseverance . . . let the U.S. Navy be proud of the tradition, of the days when you worked in Queenstown with an Allied country, with the greatest possible success and the admiration of everybody who watched your work."

. . . . . .

The years sped by. Some of these destroyer captains who had come over in 1917 as Lieut.-Commanders had gone from one promotion to the next, and were now Admirals a decade and a half later. Among them was J. R. Poinsett Pringle, whose untimely death in 1932 came as a great shock to his former Queenstown Chief. Therefore, in the spring of 1934

Sir Lewis Bayly once more crossed the Atlantic: this time to place at Annapolis a memorial, that all might know of the great loyalty and affection which had drawn these two sailors together. Once more a British Admiral was met by American destroyers as he entered port.

There is no courtesy such as that of the sea.

. . . . . .

Much has changed since the last warship left her Queenstown buoy, and Admiral Bayly hauled down his flag. It was not so very long afterwards that the Sinn Feiners burnt Admiralty House till it was left a mere shell. Queenstown has changed its name to Cobh. The Irish Free State has come into being. Haulbowline Dockyard is no longer a hive of naval activity: the place seems musty with memories. At the town quays of Queenstown, where the *Lusitania* survivors landed, and 7000 more stricken passengers as well as crews during the next three and a half years were destined to be brought ashore, provided with food, beds, clothing, and then sent on their way, no kindly women from the local organisations have to come out at all times of the day or night to tend the torpedoed. Ireland has had its own thrilling period, and the Great War is just one chapter farther back.

But, for all that, there are thousands of British and American seafarers, scattered over the face of land and water, for whom the mere mention of Queenstown conjures up the recollection of life's best years. To them it suggests the very opposite of strife and disunion: it perpetuates the perfect spirit of unity. The reader will remember how in an earlier chapter Admiral Bayly focussed this motive in the words " Pull together " with brass lettering. By a wonderfully felicitous spontaneity, at the close of hostilities all the American commanding officers in the port presented the Admiral with a beautiful silver halfmodel representing one of their destroyers, and named it the U.S.S. *Pulltogether*. It is cherished not less for its symbolism than as a reminder of the welcome help which came to preserve the seas' freedom in a great crisis.

The former captain of the American destroyer *Rowan* gave me the following amusing yarn for an example of " Navigation As It Should Not Be "; but there is also in this story a figurative meaning.

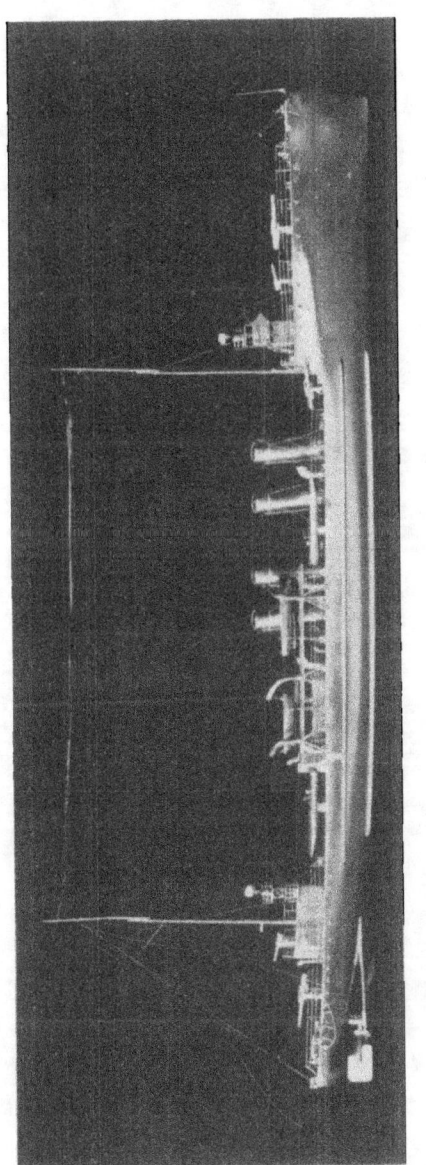
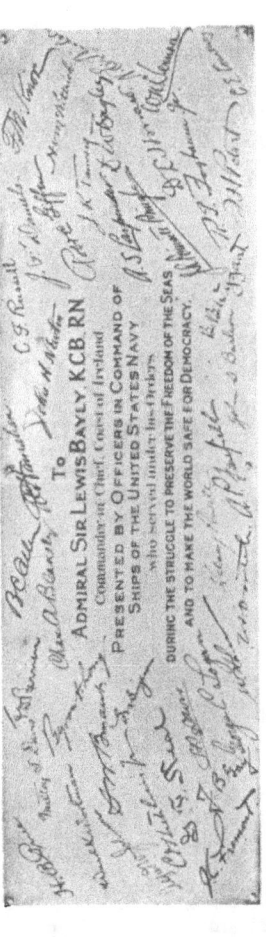

U.S.S. *PULLTOGETHER*

The silver half-model of an American destroyer, presented to Admiral Bayly by U.S. Commanding Officers, with their autographs.

"Early in December 1918, while in command of the *Rowan*, I was directed to take charge of five other destroyers, proceed from Queenstown to Portland, England, on a joy ride; after four days' stay there, to proceed to Brest and join the destroyer escort which was going out to meet President Wilson in the *George Washington*. As usual, on the day of sailing the fog was as thick as the proverbial pea soup, but by dint of some care and much luck, the detachment rendezvoused off Daunt's Rock lightship, ready for the trip.

"I set a course to pass north of the Scilly Islands between them and the mainland. In this passage there is a lightship which I hoped to pick up. The passage across was stormy, and the fog continued. It was decided that should the lightship not be sighted by 11.30 p.m., course would be changed to go round the Scilly Islands. But that hour came and no lightship in sight, so the detachment was headed due west, then due south and then east, thinking that I would now pick up the Bishop light. In a short time a light was sighted which seemed to be well down the horizon, colour white, which was the description of the Bishop light, but it was on our starboard bow instead of port. Course was altered to bring it to proper bearing. Suddenly this light seemed to pop out of the horizon somewhere over us and change colour from white to red. Almost at the same time look-outs reported breakers on the starboard bow. I knew immediately that I had made a turn out in the middle of the ocean and come back almost into the place that I was originally headed for. However, it was too late to hunt a hole, so it was ' Full left rudder,' ' Stop port engine,' a little prayer to God, with toots of the whistle and siren, for astern of me were five other destroyers making eighteen knots.

"We got out of the fix safely, but with much confusion, the boats becoming scattered, and we all lost sight of one another in the fog. Having now a good fix, I proceeded to set course around the Scilly Islands and come in past the Bishop. The next morning, in order to be sure of a land fall, I deliberately headed for the Lizard, which shortly popped out ahead of me about 200 yards. However, I was ready for this at reduced speed. The messages on file at that time prescribed a certain course from the Bill of Portland into the breakwater, at the same time notifying us of a restricted area around the lightship. Nothing was mentioned of any obstruction at either place.

"After proceeding up the Channel, the vessels still separated and lost in the fog, we took up the prescribed course from the Bill of Portland. However, the tides and the winds prevented making this course good, and the first thing I knew we were close aboard the lightship, in the so-called restricted area. Not knowing the reason for this restricted area, we sounded our way through it; much to my consternation, I afterwards found out that we had steamed our way through a mine-field. About this time I received a message from Captain Hickey, who was in command of the *Wilkes*, asking me where I was. I replied, ' I don't know, but don't come here.' Feeling that it was much too thick to find the entrance of the breakwater, I located what seemed a fine anchorage just outside of the breakwater, and headed for it.

"In a few minutes the look-out reported barrels on the starboard bow, which I thought was interesting, but did not realise the import; then in a moment barrels on the port bow. By this time I decided things were getting a little bit warm, so I let go the anchor. Imagine my embarrassment when I discovered that we were moored head and stern, ahead with an anchor, and astern with a submarine net. My propellers were beautifully fouled in the net guarding the entrance to the anchorage.

"The next morning, with my small boat, I visited the Senior Naval Officer at Portland and explained my predicament. He laughed and said, ' Well, you are the fifth one that has done it, but the other four were my own boats.' I offered the suggestion that we had no information regarding the submarine net, to which he replied, ' No, we don't tell everything we know around here.' Personally I was firmly convinced of it. In due course of time a trawler cut the net off either quarter and towed us into the harbour for the divers to unwind the net from my propellers.

"The crowning stroke was a remark made to me by a young reserve officer (who had previously been a drug-store clerk) while we were being towed in. He came on the bridge, saluted gravely, and said, ' Captain, I want to thank you for

AFTER THE WAR
All that remained of Admiralty House, Queenstown, as a result of the Sinn Fein conflagration.

the opportunity having given me the material for the first interesting letter that I have been able to write home for months.' It was too much for me; my grey hairs having increased perceptibly."

Now, the moral of this anecdote is to be cautious of your navigation; and it is not more applicable to ships of the sea than to ships of State. Queenstown during the years 1917–1918 told the world, and thereby surprised Germany, that Anglo-American courses could run parallel without anything but the happiest consequences. As the *New York Tribune* in an editorial remarked, welcoming Admiral Bayly:

> The truth is simply that the two English-speaking nations, for all their occasional surface irritations, are bound for the same port, and sailing by the same stars. Only insane folly, in addition to the evilest propaganda, can ever bring them into serious controversy.

To-day the United States Queenstown Association numbers 630 members. Between Sir Lewis Bayly and Mr. Franklin Roosevelt the friendship of Queenstown days has become stronger with the passing of time; and these considerations are not to be reckoned lightly when estimating the future of Anglo-American influence on world affairs.

APPENDIX A

SENIORITY LIST

COMMANDING OFFICERS AND THE FIRST TWENTY-EIGHT AMERICAN DESTROYERS BASED ON QUEENSTOWN, JUNE 20, 1917

Ship.	Commanding Officer.	Rank.	Seniority.
Cushing	D. C. Hanrahan	Commander	29.8.16
Wadsworth	J. K. Taussig	,,	29.8.16
Rowan	C. E. Courtney	,,	29.8.16
Conyngham	A. W. Johnson	,,	19.1.17
Porter	W. K. Wortman	Lieut.-Commander	1.7.12
Nicholson	B. A. Long	,,	7.6.13
Tucker	B. B. Wygant	,,	1.7.13
Sampson	B. C. Allen	,,	1.7.13
McDougal	A. P. Fairfield	,,	1.7.13
Cassin	W. N. Vernou	,,	11.1.14
Cummings	G. F. Neal	,,	28.4.14
Ericsson	C. T. Hutchins	,,	1.7.14
Benham	J. B. Gay	,,	1.7.14
Davis	R. F. Zogbaum	,,	1.7.14
Winslow	N. E. Nichols	,,	17.8.15
Wainwright	F. H. Poteet	,,	29.8.16
O'Brien	C. A. Blakely	,,	29.8.16
Jacob Jones	D. W. Bagley	,,	29.8.16
Jarvis	L. P. Davis	,,	29.8.16
Patterson	J. H. Newton	,,	29.8.16
Warrington	C. H. Dortch	Lieutenant	18.6.10
Drayton	D. L. Howard	,,	1.7.11
Walke	C. F. Russell	,,	1.7.13
Jenkins	W. H. Lee	,,	1.7.14
Paulding	J. S. Barleon	,,	27.6.16
Trippe	R. C. Giffen	,,	29.8.16
Sterett	G. W. Simpson	,,	29.8.16
Perkins	F. M. Knox	,,	29.8.16

APPENDIX B

Officers and Crew of German Submarine U 103

Saved.

Officers (4)

Claus Rucker.	Kapitanleutnant, Kommandant.
Bruno Krumhaar.	Kapitanleutnant, 1st officer.
Otto Grotian.	Oberleutnant, 2nd officer.
Edmund Dreyer.	Leutnant Ingenieur, Marine Ingenieur.

Crew (31)

Rausch.	Steuerman.	Arens.	Matrose
Weigelt.	Maschinist.	Kunzel.	,,
Mollmann.	Obermaat.	Lippertz.	,,
Koppeimann.	,,	Achilles	F.T. Gast.
Meier.	Bootsmaat.	Ehlers.	,,
Peters.	,,	Felsberg.	Heizer.
Schornick.	,,	Jarombeck.	,,
Tiedemann.	F.T. Maat.	Sterzenbach.	,,
Willomeit.	Obermaat.	Schuhenn.	,,
Schandert.	Masch. Maat.	Noack.	,,
Milerowitsch.	,,	Jagusch.	,,
Kunze.	,,	Schuplie.	,,
Wadewitz.	,,	Muller.	,,
Kliemeck.	Matrose.	Jensch.	,,
Frankenfeld.	,,	Stuhr.	,,
Emmich.	,,		

Missing.

Officers (1)

z. Kurt Reumann.	Leutnant, 4th officer.

Crew (8)

Schroder.	Ob. Bootsmaat.	Rudolff.	Ober Matrose.
Dorkha.	Masch. Maat.	Geb.	Heizer.
Reppert.	,,		
Mucke.	,,		
Lauxmann.	Bootsmaat.		
Kisow.	Ober. Matrose.		

INDEX

AANONSEN, Capt., *Pehr Ugland*, splendid seamanship of, 104-5
Aboukir, H.M.S., sunk by *U 9*, 25
Achilles, H.M.S., armoured cruiser, with *Dundee*, *Rena* sunk by, 24
Acker, Ernst von, internment of, 105
Active, H.M. light cruiser, 362; at Queenstown, *vice* H.M.S. *Adventure*, 285, 307; Admiral Bayly out in, to meet *Leviathan*, 314
Acworth, Lt.-Comdr. B., R.N., H.M. submarine *L 2*, experience of a depth-charge, 329-30
Admirals, British, Admiralty standard for, 200; type of, in fiction and drama, 68
Admiralty awards, *see after names of recipients*
Admiralty, new First Lord of (June 1915), matters for consideration by, 64; Naval Intelligence Department of, efficiency of, 143; appreciation by, of Admiral Bayly's search for *Genista* survivors, 195-6; desire of, to award service decorations to U.S. officers, 281; Lords of, visits of, to Queenstown, 361, 362; endorsement by, of Admiral Bayly's tribute to the share of the American vessels in the work of the Queenstown patrol, 378
Adriatic Sea, the, *U 21* ordered to, 34
Adriatic, S.S., White Star liner, escape of, 217
Adventure, H.M.S., detailed to Admiral Bayly, 67 & *n.*, 73, 103; kept ready for sea, 113; rushed to rescue of *Huronian*, 114 *sqq.*; Admiral Bayly afloat in, March 1916, 127; the *Aud* prisoners taken by, to Milford Haven, 156; sent to Kingstown, 158;

Mr. Asquith's return in, 166; Admiral Bayly's search in, for *Genista* survivors, 193, 194; Admiralty appreciation of this conduct, 195-6; submarines escorted by, to Queenstown, March 1917, 217-18; succeeded as flagship by H.M.S. *Active*, 285, 307
Aguila, S.S., sunk, 34
Air patrols round the coasts, start of, 198
Air pilots, American, training of, at Queenstown, 363
Air stations, the five in Ireland, 362
Albemarle, H.M.S., at Passage West, near Queenstown, 159
Alexandrian, S.S., escape of, from a U-boat, 192, 193, 194; torpedoed but not sunk, 202, 223; break-up of, 204
Allied shipping, U-boat danger to, 31
Amadavit, H.M. trawler, U-boat shelled by, 87; S.S. *Maxton* saved by, 87
Amazon, S.S., sunk, survivors saved, 331
America, *see also* U.S.A., influence of, on the German blockade, 93; mixed nationalities of, difficulties caused by, 45
American citizens lost in S.S. *Arabic*, probable consequences of this, 88; anger at the torpedoing of the *Sussex*, 170; intervention, effects of, 170-1
American munitions, steamers laden with, *U 78*'s attempt to blow up, 184
American Pacific Mail Steamship Company, invitation from, to Admiral Bayly to travel from Yokohama to San Francisco, 379

387

Amiral Ganteaume, French S.S., torpedoed, 26
Ammen, U.S. destroyer, 275; funnel lost by, in gale and replaced, 311
Andalusian, S.S., sunk, 31
Andromache, steam trawler, sunk, 223
Anglesey, 31, 47, 52
Anglo-American influence in world affairs, bearing on, of the Queenstown Association and of the friendship between Admiral Bayly and President Franklin Roosevelt, 383
Anglo-American operations in the West, 363
Anglo-Colombian, S.S., sunk, 97, 98
Anglo-Dutch wars, convoy system during, 199, 273
Anglo-French wars, eighteenth century, convoy system during, 273
Angroll, Lt., U.S. destroyer *Cassin*, 300
Annapolis, U.S.A., Volunteer Reserve destroyer officers trained at, 298, 299; memorial at, to Admiral J. R. Poinsett Pringle, placed by Admiral Bayly, 380
Annan, S.S., 217
Ann Ford Melville, armed trawler, U-boat fired on by, 87
Anti-Submarine Division the, inaugurated by Jellicoe, 198; co-ordination by and extension of, existing anti-submarine measures, details of, 198 & *n*.
Anti-submarine screen in the North Sea, destroyers retained for, 91
Anti-submarine warfare, craft carrying out till Dec. 1916, 198; victories in, 210 *sqq*.
Antofagasta, 104
April, 1917, the Critical Month of the Unrestricted Submarine Campaign, events of, 221 *sqq*., the peak of the U-boat onslaught, 239
Aptera, motor-boat and *Lusitania*, 40
Aquitania, S.S., Cunard liner, in collision with *Shaw*, U.S. destroyer (*q.v.*), 366 *sqq*.
Arabic, S.S., White Star liner, sunk, 88, German approval, 100; American passengers lost in, 88; indiscretion of the act, commotion due to, 88, 91, 92, 96, 103
Aral, oiler, escorted by H.M. sloop *Zinnia*, 224
Aranmore, S.S., torpedoed, 126
Archer, H.M.S., destroyer, and the October gale, 1916, 195
Ardfert, 152
Ardmore Bay, 60
Ardmore Head, U-boat attack near, 60 *sqq*.
Arethusa, oil-tanker, fuelling from, difficulties of, 337
Argyll, H.M.S., 75
Armistice, the, with Germany signed, Nov. 11, 1918, 73, 377
Asquith, Rt. Hon. H. H. (later Earl of Oxford and Asquith), visit of, to Queenstown, 166
Aster, armed steam yacht, on patrol work, 49; *Nebraskan* helped by, 51
Atalanta, S.S., set on fire by U-boat, 32, 35
Athenry, 161, 162, 163
Atlantic convoys, temptation of, to the enemy, 283-4; German ocean-keeping cruiser-submarines sent against, in 1917, 291
Atlantic liners, danger to, from Tory Island minefields, 21
Atlantic Ocean, 14, 15, 16, 258; trade routes of, 18; possible onslaught of submarines from, 19; appearance of U-boats in, 32; distance into, penetrated by U-boats, 50; torpedoing out in, 196; storms

INDEX

in, Oct. 1915, 104; *U 93*'s maiden trip in, events of, 229 *sqq.*

West, large U-boat capture in, of U.S. shipping, 354

Attentive, H.M.S., escape of, from *U 18*, 25–6

Aud, German decoy ship, course taken by, to Tralee, 148, 177, 216; the genuine Norwegian S.S. sighted by Spindler, 151; why not expected, 153; blown up, off Daunt's Rock, by Spindler, 155–6; crew and captain rescued, 156; ammunition of, raised, 157; why allowed to reach Ireland, 157, *see also* Spindler.

Audacious, H.M.S., battleship, mined, 20

August, 1917, Germany hard pressed in, 283

Ausonia, S.S., torpedoed, sufferings of the survivors, 360

Austro-Hungarian Fleet, surrender of, 1918, 377

Auten, Comdr. Harold, V.C., D.S.O., R.N.R., book by, 121 *n.*; in command Q-ship *Heather*, 272; later of *Stockforce*, fight of, with U-boat, awarded V.C. for the engagement, 365

Avonmouth, U-boat effort to close port, 64; H.M.S. *Sunflower* under repair at, 201; H.M.S. *Patia* torpedoed near, 354, 355

Awtrey, —, U.S. naval personnel, 346

Ayres, Engr. Lieut. E. A., R.N.R., death of, 295

Azores, the, 318; passage from, of U.S. s/m-chaser flotilla, 336, 337 *sqq.*; Q-ships' opportunities near, 365

BABCOCK, Comdr. J. V., U.S.N., 238, 243, 244, 250

Bagley, Lieut.-Comdr. David W., of U.S. destroyer *Jacob Jones*, rescue of, 311

Balakani, S.S., oil-tanker, barque *William T. Lewis* salved by, 94; award for this, 95; foundering of, 95

Balfour, Rt. Hon. A. J. (later Earl), First Lord of the Admiralty, 56, 57, the Queenstown command offered by, to Admiral Bayly, 66

Ballater, S.S., rescue by, of crews of *Hirose* and *Victoria*, 55

Ballycotton Bay, 40; a U-boat in, 48; German minefield off, 217

Ballyheighe Bay, Casement's landing place, 152, 154

Baltic, S.S., Walsh's trips in, 309

Baltimore, Ireland, 116, 130, 219; Fastnet area of, U-boat sighted off, 48

Baltimore, U.S.A., *Deutschland*'s departure from, 176

Bantry Bay, 49, 102, 106, 118, 269, 272, 375; *Manchester Inventor* survivors at, 204; *Queen Mary* survivors at, 225; *Stonecrop* survivors landed at, 296; air station at, 362; U.S. submarines based on and trained at, by Capt. Nasmith, 318, 319

Bardsey Island, 46; *U 21* off, 27

Barnstaple Bay, nets laid off, 46

Baron Sempill, S.S., sunk, 203

Barrels Light-ship, signal lights of, 129

Barrow-in-Furness, 27

Barrymore, Lord, courtesy shown by, to Admiral Bayly, 84

Bay of Biscay, 93, 94, 95, 96; French barque sunk in, 185; a submerged U-boat, Christmas in, 200; Campbell's crowning Q-boat achievement in, 284–5; a U-boat sunk in, 286–7

Bayano, H.M.S., sunk, 32
Bayhall, S.S., Captain of, a strange Christmas spent by, 200–1
Bayly, Admiral Sir Lewis, K.C.B., K.C.M.G., C.V.O., 192, 195, 333, 361; in command of the Royal Naval War College, 65, 251; appointment of, to the Queenstown Command, 65 *sqq.*, previous commands held by, 65 (*cf.* 49); characteristics of, 65, 68 *sqq.*, 74 & *n.*, 75 *sqq.*, 80, 81, 82, 83, 84, 102, 167, 195, 246 *sqq.*, 307; described as " the father of destroyer tactics and organisation," 65, 66, 251; studies of, in naval history, 65, and deductions therefrom, 91; circle drawn by, to indicate extent of Queenstown Command, 66; arrival of, at Queenstown, in his flag-ship H.M.S. *Adventure*, 67, 68, 103; organisation of work there, 69, 70, 73; secrecy of signals secured by, 69–70; relations of, with Bishop Browne (Bishop of Cloyne), 70–1, 166–7, 255; vessels under the command of, sloops promised in addition to, 71 *sqq.*, inadequacy of, 90; *see also* Queenstown Command; an appreciation of, by Capt. Simpson, 77; Paymaster Rear-Admiral Russell Secretary to, 79; work conducted by, 79 *sqq.*, small staff of, supplemented by his niece, 80–1; the matter of the motor car supplied to, 84; the sole hospitality accepted by, 84; three methods practicable to, for combatting U-boats, 90; views of, on decoy ships, 91, later change in, and use of them, 100, 121, 126–7, and success of, in devising them, 132 *sqq.*; *Baralong* despatched by, to intercept a U-boat, 98; vessels kept ready for emergencies, 113, 114; precautions of, as to leakage of dockyard knowledge, 133; precautions taken in anticipation of an attempt to land arms in Ireland, 143; an officer sent by, to identify Casement, 152–3, orders of, to bring *Aud* to Queenstown, 154–5; added duties and responsibilities imposed on, by the Irish Easter rebellion, further vessels and men sent to, in consequence, 158–9; visits to, of Lord Midleton, and of Mr. Asquith, 166; and a reprieve for a rebel, 166–7; praise from, for extrication of *Terpsichore*, 174; and the M.L.s, 187, 188, 189; search by, in the *Adventure* for *Genista* survivors, 193, why he went, 194–5, appreciation of his conduct by the Admiralty, 195–6; joint attack on Zeebrugge and Ostend advocated by, 197; official designation changed to Commander-in-Chief, Western Approaches, 199, 200; and the *Invercauld's* late master, 215; and Commander Nasmith, 218; and the salvage of *UC* 44, 223; a smoking conclave of, with Lieut.-Comdr. Raikes, 235; relations of, with the U.S. Naval Commanders, 239 *sqq.*, 242–3, 308 (*cf.* 74 *n.*), speed of greeting to them, effect of, American naval comment on, 246; and the film, 242–243, 250; meeting of, with Admiral Sims, parallel course of their careers, and unity of

their plans, 250-1; the two-years' strain on, 251; Admiral Sims replacing, while on holiday, 252; daily visits to, of every commanding officer, British and American, 254; and Captain Pringle, the Cork deputation received by, 256-7; and *Zylpha's* gun, 262; *Zinnia* and *Benham* congratulated by, after collision, 282; routine daily signals sent to, 290; memorandum issued by, to all his Queenstown ships, September 1917, 298; attachment felt for, by U.S. destroyer commanders, 307, 308; attitude of, to the press, an instance of, 308-9; precautions of, as to the arrival of *Leviathan*, U.S. troopship, 313; belief of, that a large vessel disguised, would have made a trap for German cruiser submarines, 317; and the Queenstown Association of British and American Naval Officers who served under him, 328; memorandum issued by, to U.S.N. officers and men on the anniversary of their arrival at Queenstown, 339; trip of, in U.S. destroyer *Trippe*, 348 *sqq.*, a U-boat depth-charged during, 353; friendship of, with President Franklin Roosevelt, 361-2, 383; sloops sent by, to the aid of S.S. *Huntscliffe*, 371; signal made by, to his officers and men on the signing of the Armistice, Nov. 11, 1918, congratulations conveyed in, 377; thanks sent to, by Shipowners and Salvage Associations, 378; tribute paid by, to the U.S. share in the work of the Queenstown patrol, endorsed by the Admiralty, 378; retirement of, 379; passage of, by Blue Funnel Liner to Japan, and thence to San Francisco, the welcome given him there, the dinner to him at New York given by the Queenstown Association and the presentation of the silver rose bowl of remembrance, speech by him on naval traditions, 379; second visit of, to U.S.A., and meeting of, on arrival by U.S. destroyers, a monument to Admiral Pringle, U.S.N. placed by, at Annapolis, 380; model of a destroyer, the *Pulltogether*, given him by all the American commanding officers at Queenstown, 380; *New York Tribune's* remarks when welcoming, on Anglo-American relations, 383;

On the Queenstown patrol as compared with the Brest patrol of the Napoleonic wars, 108; on Lieut.-Comdr. Gordon Campbell's record, 134; to Admiral Sims on the decoy ship, 135; on mistaken identifications in thick weather, 190-1; on a cargo steamer's attempt to ram a U-boat, 191; on instances of 'leading,' 194; on the arrival through mines of U.S.S. *Dixie*, 253; on the excellence of those under his command, 272; on the true measurement of success of the Queenstown patrols, 378

Bayonne, New Jersey, M.L.s constructed at, 187

Bayonne, French sailing ship, German use of the tricolour flag of, 212

Beaton, Lieut. W. D., R.N.R., Q-ship 21, 229; D.S.O. awarded to, 231
Beatty, Admiral (later Earl), flagship of, in the North Sea, 102
Bee, Lieut. W. H. A., R.N.R., of armed trawler *Lord Heneage*, the *Aud* chased by, 150–1
Begum, tramp steamer, torpedoed, 194
Belgian Prince, S.S., torpedoed by *U* 44 and survivors drowned by diving of the same, 280
Belgian refugees torpedoed, 26
Bellgrade, Norwegian barque, shelled by *U* 35, 55, 58; salvaged by Milford patrol, 58–9
Bell of Tonsberg, Norwegian barque, sunk, 144
Bempton, armed trawler, on patrol duty, 49; in rescue of *Huronian*, 114
Ben Cruachan, S.S., sunk, 28
Bengairn, barque, sunk, 144
Bengrove, S.S., sunk, 31
Berehaven, 38, 39, 51, 106, 111, 117, 130, 146, 195, 225, 227, 269, 294; small craft based on, in 1914, 71; *William T. Lewis's* crew brought into, 94, ship repaired at, 95; climate of, 101–2; Capt. H. L. P. Heard in charge at, 200; *Alexandrian*, S.S., at, 202, break-up of, 204; *Pensacola's* (collier), adventure at, 204; Mill Cove in, *Farnborough* beached at, 213; submarine flotilla at, regulations for employment of, 218; arrival at, of U.S. submarines, 318; *UB* 77 operating off, 330; U.S. s/m-chasers operated from, 336; U.S. battleships posted at, Aug., 1918, 364–5
Berehaven Auxiliary Patrol, increase of, 49
Berehaven M.L.s, the author as senior officer of, 188; amusing episodes connected with, 189–90

Bere Island, weather at, 101
Berlin Inquiry on failure of Unrestricted Submarine Campaign, 206 *sqq*.
Berlin races, 229
Berlin, S.S., ex-North German Lloyd liner, minelaying by, frustrated, 20, 21; internment of, 21
Bermuda, 183, 318, 336; Q-ship *Farnborough* at, 181
Bernays, Comdr. L. A., C.M.G., R.N., *Penshurst*, fate of, and appreciation of, 136
Bernstorff, Count, 92; and Casement, 139, 154; departure of, from America, 204, effects of, 205, 206, message from, to Berlin on "influencing Congress," 206; spying under, 206, 240; secret decisions following his departure, 237
Berrien, Comdr. F. D., U.S. destroyer *Nicholson*, 302
Berry, Ensign A. G., U.S. destroyer *Shaw*, account by, of the journey of the Fourth Troop Convoy to France, 275 *sqq*.
Berwindvale, S.S., torpedoed, 125–6, and salvaged by *Primrose*, 126
Beryl, H.M. armed yacht, a U-boat chased by, 144
Besoeki, Dutch S.S., under escort, 347
Bethmann-Hollweg, T. von, in favour of forbidding U-boat attacks on passenger steamers, 92
Big Blockade, The (Chatterton), 364 & *n*.
Bight of Heligoland, the, 17
Birkenhead shipyards, repairs at, 363
Birrell, Rt. Hon. A., Irish Secretaryship of, 168
Bishop Rock and light, Scilly Isles, 381; *U* 41 in vicinity of, 97
Blacksod Bay, mine-laying U-boat sighted W. of, a depth-charge dropped on, by *Farnborough*, 178–9

INDEX

Blackwood, Comdr. M. B. R., R.N., of Q-ship *Stonecrop*, *U* 88's attack replied to and *U* 88 sunk by, 293–4; and the boats after torpedoing of *Stonecrop*, 294–5; award to, of D.S.O., 296

Blasket or Blasquet Island, U-boat activities off, 35; oil-tanker *El Torro* aground on and later sunk, 202

Blimp, a, a U-boat spotted by, 352–3

Blockades, German and British, differences and resemblances of, 65, *see also* British, *and* German submarines.

Blommersdyk, Dutch S.S., sunk by *U* 53 off Nantucket Lightvessel, 180

Blue Funnel Liner, Admiral Bayly's voyage aboard, to Japan, 379

Bluebell, trawler, on patrol, 40; Capt. Turner rescued by, 42–3

"Bobs," police dog rescue of, from H.M.S. *Patia*, 358

Booth, Lieut. A. J., R.N.R., a U-boat bluffed by, 294; rescue of, with boat's crew by a M.L. 295; award to, of D.S.C., 296

Bordeaux, 105; convoy under escort to, 355

Borkum Roads, 34, 35, 95

Boston, U.S.A., American destroyers equipped at, and despatched from, 239, 240

Boston and Maine railway, 352

Bougainville, French sailing ship, sunk, 121

Boy-Ed, Captain, spying directed by, 240; *U* 103's sailing orders signed by, 342

Bradford, armed trawler, and *Lusitania*, 42; total loss of, 195

Braeneil, S.S., *U* 93 sunk by, 232

Brave deeds at sea, some records of, 370 *sqq.*

Bremen, ocean-going U-boat, unknown fate of, 180

Brest, sloop patrol, Napoleonic, compared with the Queenstown patrol, 108; U.S. s/m-chasers at, 336, 337; U-boat attacks off, on U.S.S. *Bridgewater*, 337; convoys for, 347, 355; U.S. destroyers based on, 348

Brewer, Skipper W. H., R.N.R., and Q-ship 21's "panic party," 230; award to, of D.S.C., 231

Bridgeport, U.S.S., U-boat attack on, 337

Bristol Channel, U-boat successes in and near, 31, 34, 53, 87, 89; 216, 354 *sqq.*; approaches to, protection of, sloops intended for, 77; German minefield in, 184, 199

British and American ships, mixed escorts of, loyal co-operation of their commanders, 282, 283

British blockade, the, effect on, of U-boat activities, 28; effect of, on relations with U.S.A., 45, 206; effect of, on Germany, 63, 274; compared with the German, 65; vessels employed in, 107–8; off North Scotland, 141; success of, contribution of, to victory, 377

British Broadcasting Corporation, 333 *n.*

British endurance and counter-measures, the failure of the Unrestricted Submarine Campaign attributed to, by German Admirals, 207

British Expeditionary Force, in transit, possible raids on, 17; 11th Cruiser Squadron as protection for, 19; *U* 9 sent to intercept, 24

British fast surface craft, effect of, on U-boats, 208

British Guiana, 128

British harbours, not one safe against torpedo attack in 1914, 71
British Home Waters, U-boat activity in, 170; rescue tugs stationed in, vessels saved by, 215–16
British Isles, sea warfare off, part of the Grand Fleet in, 56
British listening ships, 208
British merchant shipping destroyed during March and April, 1917, 216, 221, 224–5
British minefields, not referred to by Admiral Koch, 208
British signalmen, lent to U.S. destroyers, 246, 247
British submarine forces, use of, against the enemy, 217–18, *see also* Submarines.
Brock, armed trawler, and *Lusitania*, 42; U-boat sighted by, near Daunt's Rock, 48
Broke–Swift episode in Dover Straits, 241, 243, 246, 277
Brow Head, fogs off, 38; S.S. *Quantock* attacked off, 226, 227; one of *UC* 29's mines found off, 284
Browne, Most Rev. R., Bishop of Cloyne, Admiral Bayly's relations with, 70–1, 166–7, 255
Browning, Vice-Admiral M. E., in charge of the North America and West Indies Station, patrol area set by, for Q-ship *Farnborough*, 181
Bruges, German submarine base, 26
Bruhn, Lieut. Hans, prisoner from *UC* 29, 260–1
Brunsbüttel, U-boats based on, in July 1918, 361
Bryant, Lieut.-Comdr. S. W., in command of U.S. destroyer escort for *Leviathan*, 313
Buffalo, U.S.S., convoying U.S. s/m-chasers, 337
Bull Rocks and Lighthouse, 118; *Genista* sunk W. of, 193; *Ausonia* survivors with their Captain rescued near, 360

Buncrana, 233, 234; base for convoy-sloops, 258
Burdis, Capt., master of *Gafsa* (oil tanker), 219
Busch, Sub-Lieut., *U* 110, killed in conning-tower, 331
"Business as Usual," 55
Butt of Lewis, S.S. *Roanoke* torpedoed off, by Steinhauer, 232

CABOT STRAITS and Rimouski, Q-ship *Farnborough* on patrol between, 181
Cahirmore signal station and the capture of Casement, 152
Cairngowan, S.S., sunk, 145, 148; crew rescued by *Zinnia*, 146
Cairnhill, S.S., torpedoed, 224
Calais, 26, 87
Caldy Island, S.S. *Kelvinia* mined near, 184
Calf of Man, nets laid off, 47
Calf Rock, 118
California, S.S., escort of, by *Zinnia*, 201
Cambank, S.S., sunk off Point Lynas, 31
Campbell, Lieut. Gordon (later Vice-Admiral), V.C., D.S.O., R.N., book by, 121 *n.*; appointed "master" of *Lodorer*, 123; in Q-ship *Farnborough*, encounter of, with *U* 68, 126–7; honours won by, 134; and *Deutschland*, 174, 176, 177 *sqq.*; and a U-boat, 184; torpedoed by *U* 83, *U* 83 sunk by, 213; awarded the V.C. in consequence, 213; in Q-ship *Pargust*, 259, 316, torpedoed, but *UC* 29 sunk by and crew saved; *Pargust* disabled and brought in, 260–1; crowning Q-ship achievement of, 284–5; in command of Admiral Bayly's flagship *Active*, 285, 307.
Canadian, S.S., Leyland liner, 211;

INDEX

torpedoed four times, 223; crew of rescued, 224
Cannell, Lieut. H. S., R.N.R., *Brock*, U-boat sighted by, 48
Cape Clear, 15, 97, 173; U-boats off, *Lusitania* warned of, 38; steam trawler *Victoria* sunk off, 54; wrecks on, plundered, 100; heavy seas off, 188; S.S. *Nestorian* wrecked at, 202; German minefield off, 217; *St. Louis*, S.S., American armed liner off, 221
Cape Clear to Old Head of Kinsale, mines laid between by *U* 78, and swept up by paddle minesweepers, 222
Cape Cod, 240, and the *Mayflower*, 242
Cape Finisterre, 95
Cape Gris Nez, refugee ship torpedoed off, 26
Cape Henry, channel passing, events associated with, 237
Cape Horn, 105
Cape Wrath, 95
Capelle, Admiral von, on the failure of the Unrestricted Submarine Campaign, 206, 207; estimate by, of average U-boat losses upset by facts, 339
Capetown, 118
Capper, Comdr. R., D.S.C., R.N.R., *Ausonia*, sufferings of, after ship torpedoed, 360
Cargo boats rammed by each other in mistake for U-boats, 191
Carnsore Point, 40, 52
Carpendale, Commodore (later Vice-Admiral Sir Charles), Senior Naval Officer, Larne, 333 & n., 362
Carpender, Lieut. A. S., U.S.N., *Fanning*, *U* 58 wrecked by, 304
Carrigan Head, former Q-ship, Admiral Henderson's flagship, 328
Carthy Islands, 173

Casement, Sir Roger, doings of, in the Irish Rebellion, 138, 139, 142, 143; landing of, in Ireland, and fate, 152-3, 157, 158
Castlehaven, 116
Castletownbere, Bantry Bay, air station at, 362
Castletownsend, U-boats near, 36
Castro, see *Aud*.
Cattaro, U-boat base, 361; *U* 21 sent to, 34; *UB* 48 sent to, 232, 233; U-boats destroyed at, others escaping from, 377
Cawsand Bay, 108
Cayo Romano, S.S., fired on, off Fastnet, 35
Celtic, S.S., Walsh's trips in, 310
Cevic, steam trawler, a U-boat chased by, 62; Admiralty award to, 63
Chr. Knutsen, S.S., sunk by *U* 53, 180
Chancellor, S.S., sunk, 97
Chatterton, Lieut.-Comdr. E. Keble, R.N.V.R., books by, 121, 364 & n.
Cherbourg, 14
Chesapeake Bay, arrival at, of Captain John Smith and the first Virginian Settlers, 237
Chesapeake River, the, U.S. vessels in, 236
Chic, S.S., sunk, 145
Chicago City, S.S., collision of, with U.S. destroyer *Wainwright*, 282
Chinese seamen in the *Queen Mary*, admirable behaviour of, 225
Churchill, Rt. Hon. Winston, First Lord of the Admiralty, resignation of, 56
City of Exeter, S.S., Ellerman liner, attack on, by *U* 24 (Schneider), repulsed, 88
City of Glasgow, S.S., 131
City of Liverpool, S.S., army transport, saved by Milford drifters, 87
Civilians, visits of, to naval vessels forbidden, 70

Clan-na-Gael, the, 309
Clan-na-Gael of Long Island, Meyer's address to, in 1914, 140
Clan Sinclair, S.S., attacked but escaping, 225
Clifden, transatlantic wireless station, 161
Clifton, steam trawler, where patrolling, 40
Cliftonian, collier, sunk, 209
Clonakilty Bay, German mines laid off, 199; S.S. *Ghazee* beached in, after being torpedoed, 209
Clough, Lieut. H. A., U.S.N., 374
Cloyne, Bishop of, *see* Browne.
Clyde, River, paddle steamers from, sent to Tory Island, 21
Firth of, mine laying in, by *Berlin* frustrated, 21
Coal trade to France, convoy system tried out on, 199
Cobb, Lieut. Calvin H., U.S.N., affinity of, for fog, 328
Cobh, formerly Queenstown, 380
Cochrane, Comdr. W. C. O'G., *Myosotis* and *Candytuft*, escapes of, when vessels torpedoed, 292, 293
Code signalling adopted by Admiral Bayly, 170
Coke, Vice-Admiral Sir Charles H., K.C.V.O., in command at Queenstown, 18, 42; warning sent by, to *Lusitania*, 36, 38, help sent her by, 39–40; demand of, for speedier patrol craft, 47; succeeded by Admiral Bayly, 49, 69; escort of *Nebraskan* by *Scadaun* sanctioned by, 51
Cole-Hamilton, Lieut.-Comdr. J. C., R.N., *Sunflower*, on the state of H.M. sloop *Sunflower* after *Iberian* rescues, 74; *Hesperian* survivors rescued by, 96
Commander-in-Chief, Grand Fleet, retention by, of destroyers, 208
Commander-in-Chief, Western Approaches, *see* Bayly.

Cone, Captain H. I., U.S.N., twice injured by torpedoes, sufferings of, 369–70
Congress, Bernstorff's "influencing" of, 206
Coningbeg lightship, 39, 121; U-boats sighted off, 36; S.S. *Manchester Engineer* sunk off, 129; German minefield off, 217
Convoy, a huge, in Aug. 1918, not attacked, 364–5
Convoy sloops, British, based on Buncrana, 258
Convoy system, adoption of, precedents for, success of, and evolution of the Convoy Section, 198–9, 208, 273; failure of the Unrestricted Submarine Campaign largely due to, 208, 377; military reasoning on, 274; hairraising experience for ship under, 282; range of, 171
Convoys from North America, principal escort needed by and provided for, 291; stragglers from, danger to and from and difficulties of, story illustrating, 279–80
Conyngham, U.S. destroyer, 237, 273; Admiralty wish to honour, 281 *n*.; and sinking of *U* 58, 303; on convoy duty, 340; sent to Berehaven, 344; beached in fog near Kinsale but able to get back for refit, 347
Corbett, Sir Julian, *cited* on Admiral Bayly, 65
Coreopsis, H.M. drifter, surrender to, of *UB* 85, 333–4; crew taken off by, 334; crew of, reward to, 334
Cork, 14, 159; Englishman as alien in, 14; social amenities at, risks of journeys to and from, 83; frequentation of, by U.S. sailors, local jealousy aroused by, fights resulting, and the

INDEX

city put out of bounds, 256, the disappointed deputation concerning this, 256-7
Cork Harbour, anti-British sympathies at, 14, 64
Cork steamer, a, *Daffodil* damaged in collision with, 201
Cornish north coast, neutral vessels sunk off, 197
Corsewall Point, H.M.S. *Bayano* torpedoed off, 32
Cottingham, S.S., sunk, 113
Counsellor, S.S., blown up, in the Galley Head minefield, 185
Courts of Inquiry, Admiral Bayly's decision on, 248-9
Cow Rock, 118
Cowap, Comdr. C. R., R.N.R., Cunard Line, description by, of Q-ship *Zylpha*, 122-3
Craft, auxiliary, urgent necessity for, 20
Cranmore, S.S., and *Zinnia*, 224
"Cressys," the three, sinking of, effect of the news on the British public, 25
Crews of sunken ships, enemy practice of leaving destitute, 185-6
Cromorna, drifter, and *Bellgrade*, 58-9
Crompton, Oberleutnant, *U* 41, 98, rescue of, 100
Crookhaven, 195, 227
Crown of India, four-masted barque, destroyed, 55
Cruiser Squadron, 11th, as escort to B.E.F., 19
Cruiser-submarines, ocean-keeping, sent by Germany against Atlantic convoys in 1917, 291, *see also Bremen*.
Cumbrian coast, *U* 24 off, 85; entirely defenceless, 1914, 86
Cummings, S.S., U.S. destroyer *Drayton* in collision with, 281
Cunard Steamship Company, determination of, to keep the *Lusitania* running, 37
Cuxhaven, munitions from, to W. Ireland, plan for landing, 332

Cymbeline, S.S., torpedoed, 95
Cymric, S.S., White Star liner, sunk, 169

Daisy VI, H.M. armed drifter, author appointed to, 103, as temporary mail ship, 106; storm experiences of, 105, 115, 116-17, *Renfield* towed to anchorage by, 119, in Dunmanus Bay, 143; and the extrication of *Terpsichore*, 173, salvage award for, 174
Dakotan, U.S. troopship of Fourth Convoy, 275
Danish vessel, crew of *William T. Lewis* rescued by, 94
Dardanelles, the, havoc wrought in by *U* 21, 34; U-boat damage off Ireland while on passage to, 93; Nasmith's V.C. won at, 218; British submarines in, 319, lessons learned there, by Nasmith, 319
Dare, Rear-Admiral C. H., in command of the Milford base, 22, 145; small ships of, 46-7
Daunt's Rock and Light-vessel, 115, 302, 304; U-boats near, 35, 48; the *Aud* blown up off, 155-6; German minefield off, 209, 243; meeting off, with the American destroyers, 243; *U* 42 sunk on her own mines off, 291; *U* 58 sunk and captured S. of, by U.S. destroyer *Nicholson*, 302-3
Davidson, W. S., an alias for Admiral Sims, 238
Dazzle-painting of convoy sloops, German ridicule of, 258
de Chair, Admiral Sir Dudley R. S., 16, 17; Blockade Squadron of, 32, 107-8, and the sinking of *Bayano*, 32; Scandinavian vessels examined by, 139
Decoy ships, or "Mystery ships," known to the enemy as

"Trap-ships," 91 (*see also* Q-ships), success of, not mentioned by Admiral Koch, 208
Defect lists, regulations for, at Queenstown, 249
Demerara, armed S.S., saved by her gunfire, 52
Denison, Admiral John, D.S.O., Commodore at Queenstown, kindness of, to *Cullist* survivors, 290
Depth-charges (depth-bombs), U-boat crews scared by, 210; unrestricted use of, effect of on the U-boat campaign, 329; U-boats destroyed by, 212, 329, 330 *sqq.*; force of explosion of, 338, 339; German U-boat crew's interest in, 344; some U-boats' ability to submerge below range of, 345
Desire, Davis's ship, 102
Destroyers, British, needed in Dover Straits, 47; Admiral Bayly "the father" of, 65, 66, 251; temperamental nature of, 82; sent from North Sea to Queenstown and returned, 82; needed in North Sea as anti-submarine screen, 91; battleships mistaken for, 191; shortage of, keenly felt, 208; addition of, to the Queenstown Command, April 1917, 221–2; the best means of fighting U-boats, 239; successes of, German irritation over, 283
Achates, gale damage sustained by, 311
Attack, 285
Brisk, in the October gale, 195
Christopher and *Dunraven* and their rescue of Campbell, 285, 286
Cockatrice, 286
Hardy, 347
Mary Rose, at Queenstown, 222

& *n.*, survivors of Q-ship 12 picked up by, 234; U.S. destroyers met and welcomed by, 241; sunk by German cruiser, 244, 283
Moresby and *Michael*, U 110 sunk by, 331
Narwhal, at Queenstown, 222
Onslow, off Berehaven, 146
Parthian, at Queenstown, 221–2; and U.S.S. *Wadsworth*, 241
Peyton, at Queenstown, 221–2; at work, 225
Destroyers, U.S.N., longed for at Queenstown, 208, Eighth Division despatched to Queenstown, 236, 239–40, historic occasion of its arrival, welcome, and filming, 241–2, a mined area passed over by, 243–4; Commanders of, relations of, with Admiral Bayly, 74 *n.*, 239 *sqq.*, 242–3, 246, 307, 308, *see also under* Bayly, *and* Queenstown Association; instruction of, on depth charges, etc., 246; British signalmen lent to, 246, 247; further Divisions of, arriving at Queenstown, two types of, 247; used for escort duty, 273, 275, 277, 313 *sqq.*, dislike of, for this work, 277; camouflage of, 277; zigzag tactics of, 277; big turning circle of, collisions due to, 281; further arrival of, at Queenstown, 1917, 298; rolling of, 310, 311; escort of, for *Leviathan*, 313; experiences of, 314–15; hunting in the Irish Sea, 347; classification of, 349
Allen, part of escort of *Leviathan*, 313, pilot carried by, 314, escort of, for U.S.S. *George Washington*, carrying President Wilson, 381
Benham, Admiralty wish to

INDEX

honour, 281 *n.*, collision of, with *Zinnia*, 282
Burrows, a tramp rammed by, 347
Cassin, 273; excellent work of, out of Queenstown, 299, the first U.S. destroyer to be torpedoed, 299, 301, 302, perilous passage of, 310
Cummings, gale damage sustained by, 311
Cushing, 261, 273, captain of, appointed to U.S. Q-ship *Arvonian*, 316; U 104 driven down by, 334, 335
Davis, 237, 247; rescue by, and Admiral Bayly's consideration shown to, 246-7, depth-charge dropped by, on H.M. submarine L 2, 329-30, crew of U 103 rescued by, 340 *sqq.*, a further thrill experienced by, 345-6
Dixie, 311, 350, 362; dangerous entry of, into Queenstown Harbour, 253; as repair ship, 363
Downes, 313; on escort duty, 345
Drayton, collision of, with S.S. *Cummings*, 281
Duncan, bad weather experienced by, 311, and the British Admiral's "lovely" signals, 327-8, help given by, to U.S. destroyer Shaw after collision, 367
Ericsson, 273
Fanning, 273, 275, 276, 347; Admiralty wish to honour, 281 *n.*, on convoy, 302, U 58 wrecked and captured by, 303, 304, picture of sinking of, shown to Captain of U 103, 344, first American ship to capture a submarine and take prisoners, 306
Heather, a U-boat depth charged by, 347
Jacob Jones, torpedoed and sunk by U 53 off the Scillies, 310, 311, 352

Jarvis, gale losses of, 311
Jenkins, run into by H.M. sloop *Laburnum*, 261
Kimberly, aid given by to Shaw after collision, 367, 369
McCall, 347
McDougal, 237; on escort duty, 313
Nicholson, 310; Admiralty wish to honour, 281 *n.*, a U-boat chased and wrecked by, 302, 303, 305, in foul weather, 311
O'Brien, 273; Paine's trip in, 309, in foul weather, 310, on patrol, 311, rescue by, of survivors of Q-ship *Arbutus*, 312, on convoy duty, 313, 340, depth-charges dropped by, without result, 344
Parker, of Fourth Troop Convoy, 275, 276; a U-boat presumably destroyed by, 280-1, on patrol, 311, and the torpedoing of Q-ship *Arbutus*, 312
Porter, 237, 301; assistance given by to U.S. destroyer *Cassin* when torpedoed, 301, on convoy duty, 340, sent to Berehaven, 344
Rowan, an anecdote on, and its moral, 380 *sqq.*, 383
Shaw, 275, 276, 278; collision of, with S.S. *Aquitania*, fire following, ship brought to harbour, 366 *sqq.*
Sterett, on convoy duty, 347
Terry, 275, 276
Trippe, gale losses of, 311; depth-charge dropped by, on H.M. submarine L 2, 329-30; Admiral Bayly's trip in, 348 *sqq.*; on escort duty, 354
Wadsworth, 236, others of this type, 247, arrival of, at Queenstown, 241, greeted by a mine explosion, 243, Evans of the *Broke* lent to, 246, Paxton survivors rescued by,

259, Admiralty wish to decorate, 281 n., in collision with H.M. mine-sweeper *Eridge*, 282

Wainwright, 237; in collision with *Chicago City*, 282; on escort duty, 313

Warrington, standing by *Zylpha* and part of crew taken off by, 266, 267, 268

Wilkes, 382; on escort duty, 273, 313, 354, and the torpedoing of H.M. Q-ship *Arbutus*, 311

Deutsche Allgemeine Zeitung, article in by Comdr. Förstner, 74 n.

Deutsche U-Boote, Die (Gayer), cited, 92 & n.

Deutschland, first submarine to cross to America, 237, watch for on return, 174–6, evaded, 178, discomforts of, 174–6, shipping sunk by, off U.S. coasts, 339, capture by, of eleven U.S. steamers and sailing vessels, 354

Devonport, naval base, 16, 18, 75, 121, 133, 185, 311; Q-ship *Penshurst* at, 212; *Myosotis* towed to, after being torpedoed, 292

Devoy, John, on the proposed Irish rebellion (1916), 140–1; on Casement as an honest meddler, 157–8

Dictator, S.S., sunk, 96

Dierdorff, Ensign Ross A., U.S.N., gallant act of, 367

Dingle Bay, 52; *Farnborough* in action off, 134; *El Torro* oil-tanker, lost off, 202; *UC 29's* mine in, found, 284

Discovery, John Smith's vessel, 242

Donaldson, Skipper John, R.N.R., of *Setter II*, bluffed by *Aud*, 149

Donegal, 20

Doris, H.M. Cruiser, 18

Douglas, Comdr. Stopford C., R.N., of the Operations Staff, 200

Douro, S.S., sunk, 96

Dover Patrol, the, a slight jealousy felt of, at Queenstown, 250

Dover Straits, U-boat activities in, effects of, 26, 61; passage of U-boats through, 27, 303, 307; net barrage in, 27, 29, 53, 307; types of U-boat using, 34; British minefields in, 29, 208, U-boats victims of, 307; U-boats driven to alternative route, 31, 36; German destroyer raid in, 241; the *Broke–Swift* episode in, 241, 243, 246, 277; harvest in, of the drifters and trawlers, 332

Dowie, Engineer Lieutenant J. M., R.N.R., D.S.C. awarded to, 100

Downshire, S.S., sunk, 31

Drake, Sir Francis, and Drake's Pool, 16; the tradition of, in the Royal Navy, 379

Drake, H.M. Cruiser, as escort to the S.S. *Carmania*, 18

Drake, trawler, on patrol duty, 49

Drifters, based on Larne, 32; damaged in the October gale, 195; of the Queenstown fleet, 198; minesweeping by, 218; and trawlers employed by the Royal Navy, steady and splendid work done by, harvest of in Dover Straits, and success of those of the North Channel, 332–3

Dublin 13, 153; Irish request for German operations at, refused, 141; the Easter Rebellion in, 157–8, 160–1; armoured train from Queenstown to, 160; no help available from, for Galway, 163; rebels at, resentment felt by for Casement and Germany, 164; surrender and execution of, 165

Duke, 347

Dumfriesshire, barque, destroyed, 55

INDEX

Dumke, —, U.S. Naval personnel, 346
Dundee, with *Achilles*, German raider *Rena* sunk by, 24
Dunedin, S.S., escape of, from U 28, 34
Dunmanus Bay, suspect as U-boat base, 49; U-boats in, 50; October gales in, 104, 105
Dunmore Cove, H.M. paddle minesweeper beached at, 282; *UC* 44 beached at, 291
Dunsley, S.S., molested by *U* 24 near Kinsale Head, 88
Dutch steamers sunk by *U* 53 off Nantucket, 180; torpedoed by *U* 21, salved by Falmouth rescue tugs, 215

Eagle Point, S.S., torpedoed, 130
Earl of Lathom, sunk, 35
East-bound vessels, warned to keep ten miles off the Irish Coast, 185
East Coast wireless stations, U-boat positions ascertained by, 53
"Edgar" class, cruisers and the blockade, 16–7
Edith, schooner, sunk, 62
El Occidente, U.S. troopship of Fourth Convoy, 275
El Toro, oil-tanker, wreck of, off Blasquet Island, 202
El Zorro, British oil-tanker, surrender of, demanded; consequences of refusal, 113 *sqq.*
Else, German schooner, capture of; later *First Prize* and *Prize*, finally Q-ship 21, 228
Emden, U-boat base, 229, 361
Emerson, Lieut.-Comdr. A. T., of *Davis*, U.S. destroyer, on S.S. *Olympic* and *U* 103, 340 *sqq.*; on the *Davis's* encounter with H.M.S. *Resolution*, 345 *sqq.*
Empty troop transports, return of to U.S.A., in convoy and losses from German mines on U.S. coast, 354
Ems River, U-boats from, 29, 34

Endymion, H.M. cruiser, 18
England, N.E. coast of, incidents off, 63
English Channel, 17, 19; passage of U-boats through, 27; U-boat successes in, 216; U-boat attacks in, shortness of, explained, 30; Q-ship *Penshurst's* actions in, 210, 211; Q-ship opportunities in, 365
Western Atlantic, gate of, U-boat endeavour to close, 64, 87; number of vessels sunk in vicinity of, 85; only one way into, 97
English Channel ports, convoy under escort to, 355
Englishman, S.S., sunk, 127
Eridge, H.M. minesweeper in collision with U.S. destroyer *Wadsworth*, 282
Eschenberg, Engine-room Artificer Karl, of *U* 104, on *U* 104's doings before her destruction, 335
Evans, Commander E. R. G. R., R.N., of H.M.S. *Broke*, exploits of, in Dover Straits, 241, promotion after, 243; and the *Wadsworth*, a near escape of, 243, 244; lent as liaison officer to U.S. destroyer *Wadsworth*, 246; on the doings of the Queenstown patrols, 250
Eveline, S.S., escape of, 127
Express, schooner, destroyed, 55

FAIR HEAD, 332
Fair Island, 361
F A J, the call-sign of the U-boat attacked by U.S. destroyer *Parker*, 281
Falaba, S.S., first passenger-ship to be torpedoed, brutality shown to, by *U* 26, public indignation aroused by, 35; German approval of the sinking of, 100

Falmouth, 90, 100; H.M. rescue tugs from, salving by, of torpedoed Dutch steamers, 215
Falmouth Harbour, 15, 228
Fanad Head, 297
Faroe Islands, 20; watch kept off, for *Deutschland*, 177
Fastnet area, the, limit of the armed steam yacht patrol, 46; torpedoings in, 48, 50, 52, 53, 55, 73, 114, 189, 194, 202, 216, 218, 219, 224, 229; patrolling in, 189, in the October gale, 195; German minefield in, 217
Fastnet Rock lighthouse, 15, 18, 32, 35, 37, 40, 52, 93, 94, 95, 96, 97, 107, 109, 114, 125, 127, 136, 144, 145, 169, 172, 221, 226, 234, 294, 319, 360; fogs off, 38; rough seas round, 102; warnings placed seven miles south of, 185; M.L.s performances around, 188; associations of, 326
Fastnet to Tuskar, sloops stationed along, 81
Fastnet–Scillies–Tuskar triangle, U-boat successes in (1916), 127 *sqq.*
Fastnet–Ushant–Lands End–Milford–Tuskar area, U-boat concentration in, Aug. 1914, 87
Fenit Pier, Tralee Bay, proposed German landing of arms at, 141, 143; naval outlook on, object of, 148; fiasco of, 153–4
Ferndale, H.M. drifter, lost in gale, 115
Finland, American armed S.S., 221
First prize captured from Germany, see *Else*.
Fish food, endangered by lack of vessels and crews (1916), 197
Fisher, Admiral of the Fleet Lord, First Sea Lord, resignation of, 56
Fisherman-patrols, Admiralty awards to, 63
Fishermen, services of, in the War, 56

Fishguard, U 21 sighted off, 28
Fishing boats, poor wireless aboard, 56
Flanders flotilla, the, 26, 361; U-boat regulations in, 34
Flanders, U B's and U C's in, 361; German evacuation of, 377
Fleetwood, drifters based at, 46; vessel from, attacked near Porcupine Bank, 62
"Flivver" type of U.S.N. destroyers, 247
Florida Straits, Q-ship *Zylpha* sent to patrol about, 182
Flying Falcon, H.M. rescue tug, wreck of, 297
Flying Foam, H.M. rescue tug, U.S. destroyer *Cassin* in tow of, 310
Flying Fox, and *Lusitania*, 42
Flying Spray, H.M. tug, 281
Flying squadron from Queenstown, 22
Fogs, seasonal density of, off Irish coast, 38
Folkestone–Grisnez area, development of, into a veritable suicides' leap for U-boats, 307
Food supplies, threat to, by U-boat activities, 28, 239; protection of routes of, 63; of U.S. Naval forces at Queenstown, 363
Forbes, Alexander, on the visit of Franklin Roosevelt to Queenstown, 362
Formidable, H.M.S., sunk, 27, 85, 88
Förstner, Lieut.-Comdr. Freiherr von, of U 28, later of U 39, ship sunk by, 34; brutality of, to S.S. *Falaba*, 35; account by, of a sea monster, 74 *n.*; barque *William T. Lewis* shelled by, but not sunk, 94 *sqq.*; off the Irish Coast in July 1918, 361
Forth Bridge, the, reached by U 21, 24
Forth Destroyer Patrol, H.M.S. *Pathfinder*, flotilla leader, sunk by U 21, 24
Fota Island, Co. Cork, opened to Admiral Bayly, 84

INDEX

Four-point bearing, explanation of, 39 & *n.*
Fourth Troop Convoy from U.S.A. to France, under destroyer escort, narrative of the passage, 275 *sqq.*, narrow escape from minefield in Quiberon Bay, 278
Franz Josef, Emperor, surrender by, of his fleet, 377
Freesia, armed trawler, on patrol duty, 40; summoned to aid of *Lusitania*, 42
French armed trawler, *Candytuft* survivors taken off by, 293
French channel buoys said to be ruined by U.S. s/m-chasers, 339
French coasts, privateering off, object of, 91
French greetings to the Fourth Troop Convoy, 278
French tugs with s/m-chaser flotilla, 337, 338
" Friends of Irish Freedom " in New York and Stockholm, objects of, 140
" Friends of Peace " Society aims of, 140
Fulgent, S.S., destroyed off the Blaskets, 35

Gaby, Belgian trawler, U-boat reported by, off Milford, 145
Gafsa, British oil-tanker sunk, 219–20
Galley Head, 15, 116; German minefield off, 199, how discovered, 185; results of further searches, 209, 217; losses while sweeping, 218
Galveston, 182
Galway, the rebellion and its collapse, 161 *sqq.*; flight of the half-German leader, 164; other leaders placed on a sloop, 165; German designs on, 205
Galway Bay, a Spanish wreck in, 279
Galway to Sybil Point, patrols on, 169

Gansser, Lieut.-Comdr., *U* 33, sent to the Mediterranean, 93; vessels sunk by, 95
Garthwaite, Sir William, loan by, of *Prize* (Q-ship 21) to the Navy, 228
Gayer, Captain A., U-boat methods explained by, 29; book by, cited on the impracticability of the order not to sink small passenger steamers, 92 & *n.*
Geary-Hill, Comdr. S. A., H.M. sloop *Jessamine*, U 104 destroyed by, D.S.O. awarded him, 335
Geddes, Sir Eric, First Lord of the Admiralty, visit of, to Queenstown, 361–2
Genesee, U.S. tug, 318, 370, and the rescue of S.S. *Hunstcliffe*, 371, 372, 375, 376
George V., H.M., and Admiral Sims, 249; on the *Dunraven's* fight, 285
George and Mary, sailing vessel, sunk by *U* 35, 53
George Washington, American S.S., President Wilson on board, 381
Gerard, Hon. J. W., U.S. Ambassador, reminder of, to Germany, on the right of neutrals, 45
German battleships, a scare concerning, U.S. battleships sent out in consequence, 364
German cruisers, H.M.S. *Mary Rose* sunk by, 244
German efforts to hinder transport of U.S. troops across the Atlantic, 355
German Flanders flotilla based on Bruges, 26; U-boat regulations in, 34
German General Headquarters, dissension at, on U-boat sinking of passenger steamers, 92
German High Sea Fleet, 17; position of, during U-boat campaign, 56; use by, of smoke screens at Jutland, 66; Jutland

damage to, as hindering U-boat construction, 206; mutiny in, 283
German internees, bold escape of, from Vigo, 191
German landing in Ireland, preparations for, 205, and plan for landing arms, 332
German Mediterranean Submarine Flotilla, bases of, and number of, in July 1918, 361
German minefields, areas in which laid, 20, 199, 209, 216–17, 332; effect of, on movements of the Grand Fleet, 20; on U.S. coast, shipping losses due to, 354
German minelayers, *see* U-boats.
German mines, rendering of, innocuous, 200; with delay release, 217
German people, characteristics of, 93, 142; joy of, over the sinking of *Lusitania*, etc., 100, wrath of, at sinking of *U* 31; morale of, breakdown of, 334
German prisoners, escape of, as stowaways, fiasco of, 186–7
German raid on East coast of England, preparations for and against, 332
German raiders, 274; escapes of, 364 & n., *see also Greif, Moewe,* and *Rena*
German spies, U.S. naval precautions against, 240; knowledge of, of arrivals of U.S. destroyers, 252–3
German spy system, article on in the *World's Work* read with interest by prisoners from *U* 103, 344
German submarine blockade, declaration of and beginning of, 28; difficulty of providing enough U-boats, 30; successes gained, 31 *sqq.*; threat of, to merchant shipping, carried out on S.S. *Falaba*, 37; sinking of the *Lusitania (q.v.)*, and its effects on public opinion, 39 *sqq.*; inadequacy of precautions against, 40; intention of, to starve Britain, 63; success of, 63; of Western Approaches, positions plotted where, from Aug. 17, U-boats were sighted or molested steamers, 87–8; influence on, of America, 93; new U-boats for, in building and crews in training, 171, 298
German submarine campaign, new, unpreparedness for starting, 29; new policy in, results of, 31; in British Waters, temporary lull in, 92–3 & n., to what due, 96; lulls in, 96, 112, 170; in the Irish Channel, 97, 121, 125; in the Mediterranean, 100; dramatic events of, 120; climax of, 171, *see also* U-boat, U-boats.
German Submarine Flotillas, grim nickname of, 283; losses of, during the War, eleven only sunk by Q-ships, 233
German submarines, *see* U, UB, and UC boats.
German threats to passage of U.S. s/m-chasers, 336, 337
German support of the Irish rebellion, given off the East of England, 165
German-Irish organisation, means of communication of, how cut off, 205
German-Irish plotting in U.S.A., a New York agency of, 157
Germania Yard, Russian ten-knot submarine built at, in 1911, 30
Germany and Sinn Fein, 138, 140, 141, 147, 157, 165, 205, 332; shortage in, of leather and oil, reported by prisoners from *U* 58, 306; chances lost by, in 1918, 364–5
Unrestricted Submarine Cam-

INDEX

paign inaugurated by, and diplomatic relations with U.S.A. severed, 204; progress of, in 1917, February, 209, March, 216, approaching its peak, 218; April the critical month of, 221 *sqq.*; injuries done by, 213; strategy of, 216; seeming success of, 226; failure of, the two causes of, 377, German explanation of, 206 *sqq.*

Germany's High Sea Fleet (Scheer), cited, 212 & *n.*

Ghazee, S.S., torpedoed and beached, 209

Gibraltar, *U* 33 and *U* 39 at work before and after passing, 94, 95; and Malta, Q-ships on trade routes to, 180; convoys from, injured by German ocean-keeping cruiser-submarines, 291; Q-ship *Candytuft* repaired at, 292; Q-ship opportunities near in July 1918, 365

Gilmore, Captain, master of S.S. *Queen Mary*, 225

Gironde, River, U-boat off mouth of, 96

Glandore, 116

Glanville, Skipper Pascoe Philip, of *Amadavit* trawler, U-boat shelled by, and S.S. *Maxton* rescued by, 87

Glasgow, 118

Gleaves, Rear-Admiral Albert, U.S.N., orders of, to the Fourth U.S. Troop Convoy, 275; flagship of, in the Loire, 278

Glenart Castle, hospital ship, torpedoed off Lundy Island, survivors rescued, 281

Glenholm, sailing vessel, sunk, 48, 50

Glimt, Norwegian vessel, sunk, 96

Gloucester, H.M.S., 146, 159, 169; sent to watch for German attempt to land arms in Ireland, 146, 147, 148; at Galway, 162, 165, Sinn Fein prisoners taken by, to England, 162

God Speed, John Smith's vessel, 242

Golden Effort, drifter, and *Lusitania*, 42; in Kenmare River, 143

Gorman, Mary, and Casement's landing, 154

Government, change of (1915), new naval appointments by, 56–7

Graf Zeppelin, the American coast first made by, off Cape Henry, 237

Grand Fleet, the, 17; effect on its movements of minelaying, 20; subsidiary fleet for, improvising of, 20; unable to spare destroyers, 47; anomalous position of, during U-boat campaign, 56; minesweeping for, in the North Sea, 91; German attempt at indirect defeat of, 199; German mine group off E. coast of Scotland an ambush for, 332

Great Britain, optimism in, 55; period of greatest jeopardy of, 225–226, 239; increase of tonnage entering ports of, Aug. 1917, 283

Great Circle course set for *Farnborough* in hope of interception of *Deutschland*, 176, 177

Great Southern, transport, Royal Marines brought by, to Galway, 165

Great Yarmouth, bombardment of, 165

Greenore Point, loss near, of one of H.M. drifters, 195

Greif (armed merchantman), German raider, sunk, 143

Grenfell, Comdr. F. H., R.N., *Penshurst*, 136; *UB* 19 sunk by, 137; activities of, 210 *sqq.*

Greta, armed yacht, 42; despatched to help of *El Zorro*, 113, 115

Grey, Rt. Hon. Sir Edward, later Viscount Grey of Fallodon, diplomacy of, 45

Grimsby fishermen, characteristics of, 61

Gudan, Navigating Warrant Officer, *U* 41, rescue of, 100
Gulf of Mexico, Q-ship *Zylpha* sent to patrol steamer track from, 182; a false alarm in, 183
Gulf of St. Lawrence, anti-submarine tactics in, 181-2
Gulflight, first American S.S. to be torpedoed, 52 *n*.
Gun Running for Casement (Spindler), 150 & *n*.
Gunn, Norwegian barque, boarded, 144

Haldon, paddle minesweeper, 222; damaged by striking a mine, but beached, 282
Halifax, 172; Q-ship *Zylpha* at, 181
Hall, Admiral Sir Reginald, on the reason for allowing *Aud* to reach Ireland, 157
Hallwright, Lieut.-Comdr. William W., R.N. (*Laburnum*, later Q-ship 16, formerly *Heather*), 163 & *n*.; indirect firing by, in Galway, effect of, 164; death of, 163 *n*.
Hampton Roads, U.S.A., 236, naming of, 237; Taussig's start from, 233, 242
Hanan, Comdr. F. W., R.N., Senior Naval Officer, Galway, 149, and the Irish Easter rebellion, 161 *sqq*.; story told by, of a straggler from convoy, 279-280
Hancock, Lieut. L., *AL* 4, 320, 321; experience of, when she dived, 323 *sqq*.; fate of, 325
Hancock, U.S. troop-ship, of Fourth Convoy, 275
Hannah, Lieut. W. J., R.N.V.R., Q-ship 21 towed home by, 231
Hanrahan, Comdr. D. C., U.S. Q-ship *Arvonian*, previously U.S. destroyer *Cushing*, 316
Hanseatic League, merchantmen of, convoyed, 273
Hansen, Lieut.-Comdr., *U* 41, 96; vessels sunk by, 97; encounter with, and sinking of, by *Baralong* (*Wyandra*), 98 *sqq*.
Harrington Harbour, *U* 24 sighted from, 86
Hartdale, S.S., sunk, 31
Hartland Point, nets laid off, 46
Harvard Medical School, a wireless operator from, 362
Harwich, the best destroyers needed at, 47
Havre, U-boats in vicinity of, 26; attempted escape from, of German prisoners, 186-7
Hawke, H.M.S., collision of, with S.S. *Olympic*, a parallel to, 345
Heard, Captain H. L. P., R.N., in charge at Berehaven, 200
Heaton, Comdr. G. W. H., R.N., minesweeper flotilla under, 200
Heligoland, U-boat base, 17, 24, 193, 222, 223, 334; number of U-boats at, in 1918, 361
Henderson, Rear-Admiral F. H., C.M.G., and the U.S. destroyer *Duncan*, 327, "lovely" signals made by to the latter, 328
Hennig, Lieut.-Comdr., *U* 18, unsuccessful attack of, on H.M.S *Attentive*, 25-6
Henry, Prince of Wales, Cape named after, 237
Hepburn, Capt. A. J., U.S.N., in command of U.S. s/m-chasers at Queenstown, 336
Herbert, Lieut.-Comdr. G., R.N., Q-ship *Baralong*, later *Wyandra*, 98; *Nicosian* rescued by, and *U* 27 sunk, 88-9; member of the Operations Staff, 200
Herbert L. Pratt, U.S. oil-tanker, mined in Delaware Bay, 354
Hermes, H.M.S., torpedoed off Calais, 26
Heron, trawler, on patrol, 40; and the rescue of *Cassin*, 301

INDEX

Hersing, Lieut.-Comdr., *U* 21, at the Forth Bridge, 23-4; the first victory in the War achieved by, in sinking H.M.S. *Pathfinder*, 24; further exploits of, 26; passing of, through Dover Straits into the Irish Sea, 27; attack of, on airship shed, Walney Island, 27, a similar exploit by Schneider, 86; effect of his exploits on the public mind, 28; three British steamers sunk by, off the Mersey, 28; possibility of living for a fortnight in a U-boat demonstrated by, 30; results of his adventurous enterprise, 31; super-brilliance of, 32; departure of, from Irish waters for the Mediterranean, 34, 215; havoc wrought by, at the Dardanelles, 34; Dutch steamers torpedoed by, 215; on being "pestered with depth-bombs" by convoying ships, 274

Hesione, S.S., sunk, 97

Hesperian, S.S., torpedoed, survivors rescued by *Sunflower*, 96

Hewett, Lieut.-Comdr. G. O., R.N., of *Paxton*, Q-ship 25, taken prisoner, 258-9

Hick, Capt. A., S.S. *Urbino*, on her being sunk, by *U* 41, 100

Hickey, Capt. A. S., U.S. destroyer *Wilkes*, and the *Rowan*, 382

Highton, Capt. A. H., *Huronian*, on the winter storms of 1915, 117

Hirose, steam trawler, stopped and sunk by *U* 34, 54-5; crew rescued by *Ballater*, 55

H. M. Whitney, U.S.S., towing army scow with U.S. s/m-chasers, 337

Hogue, H.M.S., sunk by *U* 9, 25

Holtzendorff, Admiral von, on the object of the Unrestricted Submarine Campaign, 206-7

Holyhead, 27; U.S. s/m-chasers operated from, 336; Admiral Bayly's visit to, in a U.S. destroyer, 350 *sqq*.

Holyhead-Kingstown mail route, guarded by steam trawlers, 22; unsuccessful attack on mail boats by *U* 104, 335

Home waters, rescue tugs stationed in, vessels saved by, 215-16

Hood, Lieut. M. A. F., R.N., H.M.S. *Bluebell*, *Aud* escorted by, to Queenstown, 154-5; Spindler's mistake about, 156

Hood, Rear-Admiral the Hon. H. L. A., 25

Hughes, Capt. A., master, S.S. *Trafford*, fight of, with a U-boat but sunk, 59

Hulings, Lieut. G., U.S.N., on the underwater collision of *AL* 4 with a U-boat, 319

Hull, 95

Humby, Capt. E. G., master S.S. *Turnwell*, ship attacked but safely taken to Milford, 59, 60

Hungry Hill, Berehaven, two impressions of, 102-3

Hunting patrols of destroyers and "P"-boats, started, 198

Huntscliffe, British S.S., attempted rescue of, by U.S. tugs *Genesee* and *Sonoma*, 370 *sqq*.; sinking of, 372, 375-6

Huronian, S.S., Leyland liner, torpedoed, 114, 223, salved by H.M.S. *Adventure* and the Queenstown patrol, 114, 115, 117, 202 *n*., again at sea, 169

Hyde, Capt. G. F., later Vice-Admiral Sir George, in command of H.M.S. *Adventure*, 67 *n*., 307; on the storms of December 1915, 117

Hydrophones, in Q-ships, 197

Iberian, S.S., sunk by *U* 28, and survivors rescued by *Sunflower*, 73, 74 & *n*.

Iceland, 20; sloops at work off, 108
Igel, Wolf von, and his "advertising agency" in New York, a centre for German–Irish plotting, 157
Imperial German Government, extraordinary insults of, President Wilson on, 205, 208
Ina Williams, armed trawler, on patrol duty, 49, 135; U-boats fired on, by, 83–6
Indian Empire, trawler, where patrolling, 40, wirelessed for, to rescue of *Lusitania*, 42, 43
Influenza epidemic of 1918, 378
Ingram, O. K., lost from U.S. destroyer *Cassin*, when torpedoed, 301
Inishtooskert Island, Tralee Bay, intended rendezvous of *Aud* and a U-boat, 148–9
Inishturk Island, S.S. *Atalanta* set on fire off, 32, 35
Invercauld, barque, shelled, torpedoed and turned turtle, 211, 213 *sqq*.
Inverlyon, British barque, sunk, 145
Invincible, H.M.S., *U* 21 driven away by, 24
Ireland, remoteness of, from London, 13–14; feeling in, antagonistic to England, 14, 69, 133, 254, and hostility in, to British naval forces, 138; encirclement of, by U-boats, 35; rumours in, harm done by, 49–50, 182, 183, 252; leakage from, of naval information, 69; proposed German landing in, Berlin F.O. cable on, to Washington Embassy, 141, 205; plans for landing arms in, Irish-American, 165, and German, 332; rebellions in, 251, 309–310, Easter, 133, 147 *sqq*., Galway, 157, 161 *sqq*.; effect on, of rupture between Germany and U.S.A., 206; airstations in, 363; renewal of domestic fighting in, 378

Irish Channel, the, barque *Bellgrade* an obstruction in, till towed into St. Bride's Bay, 58; neighbourhood of, steamers sunk in, in July 1914, 73; physical conditions of, effect of, on U-boat campaign, 96; a ship in distress in, 186
Irish coasts, heavy seas off, 16; ships torpedoed off, 31; a graveyard of British shipping (August 1915), 89; seriousness of shipping situation off, appreciation of by Admiral Bayly, 90; U-boat concentration on, March 1916, 121, 126, Feb. 1917, 183; German minefields off, 199; U-boat successes off, 1917, 216
N., U-boat activity off, March 1918, 330–1
N. and E., anti-U-boat precautions on, 23
S., U-boats off each end of, 48; minefields laid off, positions chosen for, 184, 185, most destroyed, but one only found when S.S. *Ghazee* was sunk, 209
S. and S.W., patrolling of, from Queenstown, 39; atmospheric difficulties on, 38, 202
"Irish Lifeboat Service," well-merited sobriquet of the Queenstown sloops, 73
Irish naval bases, U.S. s/m-chasers operating from, 336 *sqq*.
Irish naval command, transformation made in (1915), 57; position of the "Senior officer on the Coast of Ireland," problems of, differing from those elsewhere, 64–5
Irish Republic, Declaration of, 165
Irish Sea, guarding of approaches to, 21; flying squadron in, 22; U-boats reaching, and working in, 27, 28, 29, 86, their most successful week, 225;

INDEX

alternative routes to, 31; precautions in, against U-boat warfare, 46-7; duties in, of the sloops, 77; winter gales in, 73, 104, 105, 112 *sqq.*, comparable to the gales of 1861, 106, losses during, 195; Northern and Southern entrances to, and the Western approach to the English Channel, regarded as "the decisive U-boats theatres," 207; German minefields in, 209, 210; conflict in, between *U* 84 and Q-ship *Penshurst*, 211; U-boats working in, in April 1917, 229; weather in, after September, discomfort of, 298; *U* 84 destroyed in, by *P* 62, 327

Irish Volunteers, attempted landing by, of arms foreseen and precautions taken, 143

Irish-American revolutionary Associations, 140, preparations of, for landing arms in Ireland, 165

Irishman, S.S., safely protected by *Zinnia*, 224-5

Iron Cross, exchange of, for clean shirt on board U.S. destroyer *Fanning*, 304

Isis, H.M.S., 18

Isle of Man, S.S. *Downshire* sunk off, 31; Q-ship *Cullist* torpedoed S.W. of, 287

Ivy Green, drifter, and *Bellgrade*, 58-9

JACKSON, Admiral Sir Henry, appointed First Sea Lord, 56, 57, 198

Jamaica, 183

James I, 237

James Green, trawler, *Cullist* survivors rescued by, 290

Japan, Admiral Bayly's voyage to (1920), 379

Jellicoe, Admiral Sir John (Earl Jellicoe), 136; and the Tory Island minefield, 20-1; and the increase of U-boats passing round Scotland, 34; at the Admiralty, 198, 199; the Anti-Submarine Division inaugurated by, 198; the memorial to Lieut. W. E. Sanders, R.N.R., unveiled by, in New Zealand, 233; and Admiral Sims, co-operation of, 239, convoys urged on, by Admiral Sims, 274; visit of, to Queenstown, 327

Jessop, Capt. E. P., U.S.N., U.S.S. *Bridgeport*, 337

John Hardie, S.S., sunk, 95

Johnson, Comdr. A. W., U.S.N., temporary return of, to U.S.A., 307

Johnson, Engr. Sub-Lieut. J. W., R.N.R., of *Paxton* (Q-ship 25), taken prisoner, 258

Jugo-Slav National Council, the Austro-Hungarian Fleet made over to, Oct. 30, 1918, 377

Julia, examination steamer, and *Lusitania*, 42

June 26th, 1917, memorable for the safe landing in France of the first U.S.A. troops, and the beginning of the end for Germany, 273

Juno, H.M.S., 18

Jutland, Battle of, German use at, of smoke screens, 66; lesson of, to Germany, 199; effects of, on the Unrestricted Submarine Campaign, 206

KEARNEY, —, chief gunner's mate, U.S.N., rescue of, 374

Kelvinia, S.S., mined and foundered, 184

Kenmare, River, 118, 200

Kenmare, S.S., fired at by U-boat, saved by trawler *Rodney*, 60 *sqq.*

Kerry Head, the *Aud* off, 150

Kerry Head to Mizen Head, trawlers stationed between (1916), 143
Kiel, German submarine base, 145; numbers at, in 1918, 361; submarine memorial column at, 233
Kiel Canal, the, 142 *n*.
Kilcoan, S.S., sunk, 28
Killybegs Harbour, small craft based on, 71; *Paxton* survivors landed at, 259
Kingstown, naval base at, 22; trawlers, drifters, etc., based on, in 1914, 71; *Cullist* survivors landed at, 290
Kingstown–Holyhead routes, team-trawler guard on, 22
Kinpurney, sailing ship, sunk, 203
Kirkman, Lieut.-Comdr. van L., U.S. destroyer *Shaw*, gallant act of, 367
Kish, S.S., torpedoed, 224
Kish Light-vessel, S.S. *Leinster* torpedoed off, 369
Kitchener, Lord, attitude of, to publicity and to the press, 308
Koch, Admiral von, on the cause of the failure of the Unrestricted Submarine Campaign, 207; on specific British devices which prevailed over the U-boats, 207–8; on why only one transport was sunk by submarine agency, 329
Krech, Lieut.-Comdr., *UB* 85, reason given by, for his surrender, 334
Kroll, Comdr., *U* 110, lost with his boat, 331

Laconia, S.S., Cunard liner, torpedoed, lives saved by *Laburnum*, 216
Lady Blanche, H.M. yacht, losses of, in the October gale, 195
Ladysmith, drifter, lost in gale, 115
Land's End, 17
Lansing, R., and the recall of Bernstorff, 240

Lapland, S.S., Walsh's trips in, 310
Larne, small craft based on, 22, 32, 47, 63, 71, 333
Leer, 228
Leinster, S.S., Holyhead mail-boat destroyed, 369, 377
Lerwick, 244
Leslie, Lieut.-Comdr. A. G., R.N., *Sunflower* and *Terpsichore*, 173, 174
Leviathan, S.S. (late German *Vaterland*), rendezvous disregarded by, upshot of, 313 *sqq*.
Lewis, Comdr. N. M., R.N., Q-ship 12, taken prisoner by *U* 62, later relations of, with his captor, 234
Leyland Liners, torpedoing of, 202 & *n*., 223
Libau, see *Aud*.
Light Cruiser Training Squadron at Queenstown, unsuitability of, 16–17
Lilian H., sailing-ship, sunk by U-boats, 203
Limerick, 153, 171
"Limies," German submarine crews' attitude to, 306
Linda Blanche, S.S., sunk, 28
Lion, H.M.S., Admiral Bayly's flagship, 65, 102, 114, 156, 190; mistaken for a trawler, 191
Liverpool (*see also* Mersey *and* Mersey Bar), 27, 50, 52; Atlantic liners berthing at, 14, 21; precautions at, against U-boats, 21, although supposed to be secure against these, 22; sloops intended for defence of approaches to, 77; naval base at, 22; U-boat menace to, seriousness of, 28, 87
Lizard, the, 98, 100, 381; S.S. *Olympic* attacked off, 340
Llandovery Castle, hospital ship, torpedoed by *U* 86, 361
Loch Leven, S.S., dangerous anchorage of, 106
Lody, Carl, spy, execution of, 139

Lohne, 140
Loire, River, U.S. troops disembarked in, 273, 275, 278
London and America, more mutually interested than London and Ireland, 13-14
Long Island Sound, *U* 53 off, 180
Loop Head, 150; S.S. *Tritonia* sunk near, 216
Lord Heneage, armed trawler, 216; *Aud* chased by, 150, 154
Lord Mayor of Cork, the, and the trade deputation, 256-7
L'Orient, France, 277
Lough Foyle, air station at, 362; U.S.N. quarters set up on, 363
Lough Swilly, 177, 297, an important Q-ship base, 258; approaches mined, 332
Lowca, works at, 85, fired on by *U* 24, 86, 87, enemy's knowledge of, explained, 86
Lowestoft, bombardment of, 165
Lübeck, 142 *n*., 143
Lucena, S.S., sunk, crew saved, 61, 62
Lucida, trawler, on patrol duty, 49
Luciline, oiler, torpedoed, 218
Lundy Island, 87, 113; ships torpedoed off, 34, 281; nets laid off, 46; *AL* 9 in contact with U-boat off, 319-20
Luneda, trawler, on patrol duty, 40, 49
Lusitania, S.S., Cunard liner, homeward voyage of, precautions regarding, 36, 37, 38, 39; torpedoed by *U* 20, off old Head of Kinsale, 39, 41, 48, 88, 113, 242, 349, 361; no arms or troops aboard, 37; Wireless S.O.S. from, after being torpedoed, 39; craft going to assistance of, 39-40, 42; sinking of, no second torpedo fired, 41; passengers and crew of, rescued, conditions of, 42-3, 380; official investigation of the affair, 44; not the sole aim of the U-boat's cruise evidence of, 50, repercussion of the shock on world opinion and on America, 44, 56, 88, 205; strategy employed to entrap, 87; reforms set going in consequences of the sinking, 56; other sinkings parallels to, 88, 91-2, 370; German approval of the deed, 100; its lesson not learned in Germany, 170; anniversary of, 243

MAAS LIGHTSHIP, *Aboukir*, *Cressy* and *Hogue* torpedoed near, 24-5
Macaulay, —, gunner's mate, U.S.N., 341, 346
M'Carthy, John, and Casement's landing, 152
McClaran, Lieut. J. W., U.S. destroyer *Cassin*, 300
MacGregor, Lieut. I. G., R.N.R., *Paxton*, wounded and rescued, 259
McLeod, Lieut.-Comdr. J. K., R.N., and the *Zylpha*, 123, 261; gun mounted by, amidships, 262, and the story of his adventure, 263 *sqq*. (*see also Zylpha, under* Q-ships); appointment of, to a new Q-ship, 272
Mahan, Rear-Admiral A. T., U.S.N., studies of, in naval history, 65
Maidens Lightship, surrender off, of *UB* 85, 333
Malachite, S.S., torpedoed, 26
Malin Head, S.S. *Amazon* sunk off, 331; S.S. *Englishman* sunk off, 127
Malmanger, Norwegian oil-tanker, torpedoed and sunk, 218-19
Manchester, 87; *Paxton* survivors taken to, 259
Manchester Commerce, S.S., foundering of, 20
Manchester Engineer, S.S., sunk, 129 *n*.

Manchester Inventor, S.S., sunk, crew saved, 203, 204

Manning, Capt. E., master of *William T. Lewis*, shelled but not sunk, 94 *sqq.*; on the gale of Oct. 1915, 105

Man-of-War Cove, *El Zorro* driven ashore at, 116

March 1917, intense U-boat activities during, 216 *sqq.*

Marèchal de Villars, French barque, sunk, 185

Margaretta Shoal, Galway Bay, a Spanish wreck on, 279

Marine losses unconnected with the war, in January 1917, 202

Marine Navigation Company of London, Q-ship 21 lent by, to the Navy, 228

Markievicz, Countess, arrest of, 165, 166

Martin-Leake, Commodore F., later Admiral, 362; *Pathfinder*, wounded, rescued, and later avenged, 24

Marx, Admiral J. L., Q-ship *Aubrietia*, rescue by, 196

Masurian Lakes debâcle, arms captured at, sent to Ireland, 142

Maumee, oiler, Fourth Troop Convoy "fed" by, *en voyage*, 276

Mauretania, S.S., Cunard liner, and the October gale, 195

Maximus, trawler, on patrol, 40

Maxton, S.S., saved from being sunk by armed trawler *Amadavit*, 87

May Island, *Pathfinder* sunk off, 24

Mayflower, the, the "Return of," historic episode, 47, 241-2

Mayo, Rear-Admiral H. T., U.S.N., visit of, to Queenstown, 327

Mayo coast, U-boats at work off, 52, 53, 126

Mead, Skipper W. A., R.N.R., Q-ship 21, 229; *U* 93 destroyed by, 230, D.S.C. given to for this action, 231

Mediterranean Fleet, Admiral Sir Berkeley Milne in command of, 79

Mediterranean Sea, the, steam yacht squadron despatched to, 121, disappointing as improvised warships, 121; U-boat pioneer, Hersing, in, 34, 215; U-boats detailed for, 34; sinkings by, on the way and after, 85, 93 *sqq.*, 121, 170, U-boat route to, via Scotland, 94; *Baralong* ordered to, 100; Q-boats sent to, 180; U-boats destroyed in, by M.L.s, 188; British merchant shipping destroyed in, 1917, 216

Medusa, steam yacht, in the flying squadron, 22

Megantic, S.S., White Star liner, chased by U-boat, 52

Melville, U.S. destroyer depot ship, 350, 361, 362; arrival of, 253; seamen's club run by, 255; the PULL TOGETHER board on, 254, 380; *U* 58 prisoners put aboard, 306; as repair ship, 363

Merchant service officers in charge of net barrage craft, 56

Merchant shipping, threat to, in Germany's submarine declaration, 37; storm losses of, 117

Merchant vessels disguised as men-of-war, 121; arrival of, and fitting with smoke screen apparatus, 198 (*see also* Q-ships), search by, for U-boats round Ireland, 35; U-boat sinkings of high number of, Aug. 1915, and Oct. 1916, 84; master mariners of, convoy system disliked by, 273-40

Mersey, Viscount, on Capt. Turner's justification for ignoring the wireless advice sent him, 44

Mersey River, 39; mine-laying at entrance feared, 21

Bar, 22, 52, U-boat sinkings and attacks off, 28, 31, 64;

INDEX 413

waiting at, for pilots, U.S. destroyer's difficulties because of, 315; mines near, S.S. *New York* sinking one off the Lightship, 238

Mersey Bar Examination Ship with 28 pilots aboard destroyed, 315

Mersey Bar Light-vessel, Admiral Sims' vessel mined near, 238

Messier, Boatswain H. J., of *Genesee*, tug, 375

Mexican trade routes, fear of German molestation of, Q-ship *Zylpha* sent to prevent, 182

Meyer, Kuno, disloyalty of, 138, 140

Meyer, Lieut.-Comdr., *UB* 77, S.S. *Tuscania* sunk by, 330

Middle watch, the, period when most marine accidents happen, 202

Midleton, Viscount, visit of, to Admiral Bayly, 166

Milewater, H.M. rescue tug, 297

Milford area, *U* 61 destroyed in, 331–332

Milford Haven, 186, 229; minesweepers sent from, to Tory Island, 21; naval base at, 22; net barrage at, difficulties with, 23, 87; fishing fleet of, Southern Irish Sea patrolled by, 46; U-boat working towards, 54; crews of *Hirose* and *Victoria* landed at, 55; drifters of, help given by, to transport and other vessels, 58, 87; return of *Turnwell* to, 60; small craft based on, in 1914, 71, patrols of, damaged in the Oct. gales, 195; *Ferndale* lost in entry of, 115; steam yacht patrol sent from, to Mediterranean, 121; trawlers of, minefield swept by, 184; German minefield off, 209; return to, of Q-ship 21, 231; survivors of *Arbutus* landed at, 312; Admiral Bayly's visit to, in a U.S. destroyer, 352

Milford–Scillies–Queenstown triangle, U-boat operations in, 63 *n.*, net drifters of, *UC* 65 in difficulties with, 210

Mill Cove, Berehaven, *Farnborough* beached at, 213

Miller, Rear-Admiral F. S., appointed to Northern Ireland, 258

Milne, Admiral Sir Berkeley, 79

Mimosa, S.S., sunk, 95

Minefields, British, not mentioned by Admiral Koch, 208

Mine Head, *Cassin* mined off, 300–301

Minerva, H.M.S., 18

Mine-sinking by M.L.s and sloops, 91, 217, 242

Minesweeping organisation, a special section for, evolved, 199

Mines with net barrages rarely of service, 47, *see also* mines, minefields, &c., *under* German.

Ministre Beernart, S.S., sunk, 113

Mitchell, Captain, refusal of, to surrender *El Zorro* and its consequences, 113 *sqq.*

Mizen Head, 15, 40, 48, 53, 118, 172; fogs off, 38; rough seas around, 188, 191; patrolling near, 189; the *Quantock's* crew's safe landing at, 227

Moewe, German raider, 141, 274; escape of, 364

Montanan, U.S. troop-ship of Fourth Convoy, 275; odd behaviour of, 276

Montfort, share of, in *Pomeranian* rescue, 111

Montreal, 181, 187

Mora, S.S., sunk, 96

Morgan, Junius S., account by, of the U-boat attack on H.M. Q-ship *Arbutus* and of *O'Brien's* rough passage to Queenstown, 312, 313, and on his experiences in U.S. destroyer *O'Brien* when on escort duty to *Leviathan*, 314–15

Morwenna, S.S., sunk, 52

Motor-launches (M.L.s), valuable service done by, 187 *sqq.*, praise of, by Admiral Bayly, 188, 243; at Berehaven, 188, 189–90; of the Queenstown fleet, 198; hydrophones of, 208; minesweeping and patrol work of, 217, 218; rescue by one, of Lieut. Booth, *Stonecrop*, and his boat's crew, 295; the U.S. s/m-chaser (*q.v.*), a great improvement on, 336

M.L. 181, the U.S. destroyers led by, into Queenstown Harbour, 243, 244

Motor yachts, M.L.s replacing, 187

Mull of Cantyre, 21, 332

Mull of Galloway, nets laid off, 47

Munition workers, demand for, effect of, on steamship crews, 37

Murray, Steward, 114

My Mystery Ships (Gordon Campbell), 121 *n.*

Nadine, Belgian trawler, *Van Stirum* survivors rescued by, 112–13

Nagler, —, ship's cook as oarsman, 341

Nailsea Court, sunk, 203

Nantucket Shoal Light-vessel, *U 33*'s sinkings off, 180, 181, 182; Q-ship *Zylpha* sent to cruise off, 182

Napoleonic wars, the convoy system during, 199

Nasmith, Comdr. Martin E., V.C., R.N. (now Vice-Admiral Sir Martin Dunbar-Nasmith), submarine flotilla commanded by, 218, 234; U.S. submarine patrol trained by, 318, 319

Nauen wireless station, 141, 205

Naval bases, new, 1914, 22

Naval forces at Queenstown and elsewhere in Ireland, July 1918, strength of, 362

Naval history, value of, not fully appreciated twenty years ago, 90

Naval information, leakage of, in Ireland, Admiral Bayly's precautions against, 69

Naval patrol for Irish Coast based on Queenstown, 40

Naval War Colleges in England and the U.S.A., the two first Presidents of, 65, 66, 251, 379

"Navigation as it should not be," anecdote illustrative of, 380 *sqq.*

Nebraskan, S.S., torpedoed, and enabled to escape, 50 *sqq.*, not the first U.S. ship to be torpedoed, 52 *n.*

Nelson, Admiral, and his "band of brothers," the Queenstown parallel to, 327

Nestorian, S.S., totally wrecked at Cape Clear, 202

Net barrage, cost of, 47; across St. George's Channel, 22, 23; at Milford Haven, 23, 87; in Dover Straits, time needed to organise, 27, not reliable, 29, length of, 29; *U 8* fouled by and sunk, 31, *U 32*'s encounter with, 33, when of positive value, 33, undue reliance on, 33; in the North Channel, 32, 47, efficacy of, 86; off Larne, 47; Tuskar to Smalls, weather difficulties with, 87

Net drifters, difficulties of, and tribute to the officers and men of, 23, 56, 87; increase of, 46; of the Queenstown fleet, 198

Nettleingham, Sub-Lieut. C. T., R.N.R., *Ina Williams*, U-boats fired on by, 53–4

Neuquen, S.S., sunk, 203

Neutral countries, rights of, reminder of, sent by U.S.A. to Germany, 45

Neutral vessels, U-boat sinkings of, and attacks on, 197, 219

INDEX 415

New England and Virginia, association of, with Britain in the despatch of the American destroyers, 242
New Orleans, 182
New York, 37; the American destroyers' departure from, 239
New York, S.S., mine struck by, with Admiral Sims aboard, 238; passage of, through mines, 242
New York City, S.S., sunk, 89
New York Evening Post, correspondents of, and Admiral Bayly, 308–9
New York Herald on the torpedoing of S.S. *Sussex*, 170
New York Tribune, on Anglo-American relations, 383
Newby Hall, S.S., S.O.S. from, answered by U.S. destroyer *Parker*, 280
Newcastle-on-Tyne, sloop-building at, 75
Newfoundland, 152
Newfoundland Bank, crossed by *U* 53, 180
Newport, Rhode Island, *U* 53 at, 180; U.S. submarine flotilla's passage to and from and its discomforts, 318; U.S. Naval War College at, 237
Newquay, 46
News, one way of transmitting, 273
Nicholson, Father John T., and Irish prisoners of war, 139–40
Nicosian, S.S., shelled by *U* 27, 88, 98, rescued by *Baralong*, 88–9
Niger, H.M.S., sunk, 26
Noake, Comdr. Basil S., R.N., and the *Begonia*, 132
Nodzu, armed trawler, a U-boat driven under by, 145
Noma, U.S.S., and the fight of the Q-ship *Dunraven*, 285
Non-combatants, suffering inflicted on, by the enemy, 360–1
Norbreck, trawler, sailing ship saved by gunfire of, 52
Nordyk, Swedish S.S., and *Terak*, oil-tanker, 201

Norfolk, Va., 237
North America, Q-ships sent to, 180, 181
North Channel, the, net barrage laid in, 21–2, 32, 47, 86; *UB* 77 in, 330; drifters of, *UB* 82 destroyed by, and their reward, 333
North River, Fourth Convoy's departure from, 275
North Sea, the, 17; minesweepers sent from, to Tory Island, 21; destroyers not to be spared from, 47, 91; British minefields in, 208
  U-boat activities in, 18
    (1914), 23 *sqq.*
    (1915), 63
    (1917), 216
  Prospects in, had the War continued, 377
Northern Patrol, watch kept by, for *Deutschland*, 177
Norway, 20
Norwegian grainship mined, 21
Norwegian steamer, a torpedoed, watched by an M.L., 189
November and December, 1917, bad weather during and damage to shipping, 310 *sqq.*

OCTOBER, 1916, last week of, tragedies of, due to the gale, 191 *sqq.*
Oil, use of, by *Renfield*, Norwegian barque, 118; and by U.S. tug *Sonoma*, 373
Oil-tankers, armed trawler escort of, 198
Old Head of Kinsale, 15, 35, 38, 40, 86, 87, 106, 113, 114, 116; S.S. *Lusitania* torpedoed off, 39, 41, 48, 88, 113, 242, 349; centre of U-boat efforts moved south of, 88; fog signal of, 172; German minefield off, sweeping off of, 1917, 217, 292; Q-ship 21 towed to, and from, 221

Olphert, Lieut.-Comdr. W., R.N.R., *Pioneer*, later *Scadaun*, later *Salvia*, 173, 174; help given by, to *Nebraskan*, 51-2; taken prisoner when ship sunk but information sent by, to England, 272-3

Olympic, S.S., White Star liner, attempted salvage by, of H.M.S. *Audacious*, 20; attacked by *U* 103, 340 *sqq.*, 345, 348

Oracle, H.M.S., *U* 44 sunk by, 130, 280

Orkney Islands, U-boat successes off, 216, 223

Oscar II, S.S., Casement's passage in, 139, 143

Ostende, attempted blocking of, 90, need for second attempt, 91 *n.*; wasps'-nest of, 197, freed from German bondage, 377

Ottomar, Russian barquentine, fired on by *U* 44 and finally sunk after rescue of crew, 128-9, 130, 144

Overfalls Light-vessel, Delaware Bay, *Herbert L. Pratt*, U.S. oil-tanker mined off, 354

Oversay Light, Islay, *Flying Falcon* tug wrecked off, 297

Oxlade, Commander C. H., R.D., R.N.R., lost with Q-ship *Arbutus*, 312

PADDLE MINESWEEPERS, 218; "Race-meeting" class and "Hunt" class, arrival of, at Queenstown, 222

Page, W. H., American ambassador, diplomacy of, 45

Paine, Ralph D., of the *New York Evening Post*, and Admiral Bayly, 308-9, praise of the latter by, in his book, 309 & *n.*

Panama Canal, Admiral Bayly's passage through, 379

Pascal, S.S., storm losses of, 117

Passenger ships, sinking of, public opinion on, 35, 39, 44, 45, 88, 92, 96, 103; German official view on, 92

Pathfinder, H.M.S., sunk by *U* 21, 24

Patia, H.M.S., torpedoed while under escort, story of the occurrence, 354 *sqq.*

Patzig, Lieut.-Comdr. Helmut of *U* 86, S.S. *Llandovery Castle*, hospital ship, sunk by, 361

Paulding, *Davis* and *Trippe*, U.S. destroyers, depth-charges dropped by in error over H.M. submarine *L* 2, 329-30

P-boats, object for which designed, 198 & *n.*; a U-boat scared off and sunk by, 213, 213; torpedo fired by, at *AL* 4 in mistake for a U-boat, 321-2

P 51, *U* 61 destroyed by, with depth-charges, 331-2

P 56, *U* 87 sunk by, 316

P 62, *U* 84 sunk by, 212 *n.*, 327

Pearse, D. H., untrue statement of, before execution, 165

Peat, Lieut. P. S., R.N.R., *Coreopsis*, surrender to, of *UB* 85, 333-34; award to, of D.S.O., 334

Pehr Ugland, Norwegian barque, escape of, in October storms, 104-5, 118

Pembroke, naval base, 16; *U* 58 prisoners conveyed to, 304

Pensacola, H.M. collier, adventure of, at Berehaven, 204

Pet, Irish fishing smack, *Ottomar* crew put aboard of, 130

Phelan, Captain Thomas, S.S. *Rowanmore*, taken prisoner, 193

Phipps-Hornby, Rear-Admiral R. S., commanding 12th Cruiser Squadron, 18

Phrygia, S.S., escape of, 127

Pikepool, S.S., 296

Pilot Me and *Young Fred*, H.M. drifters, *UB* 82 destroyed by, reward gained for this service, 333

INDEX

Pilots, Liverpool, carried on to New York, 14; difficulty concerning got over by Lieut.-Commander Zogbaum, 315
Pioneer, armed yacht, and the extrication of *Terpsichore*, 173, 174; award for salvage, 174
Pitt, Comdr. C. Blake, U.S. s/m-chaser, 206, account by, of the passage of the U.S. s/m-chasers from the Azores to Brest, 337 *sqq*.
Plymouth, arrival at, of U.S. s/m-chasers, 336
Poe, Lieut. B. F., U.S.N., 312
Point Lynas, Anglesey, S.S. *Cambank* sunk off, 31
Pola, U-boat base, 233, 361; U-boats destroyed at, and others escaping from, Oct. 1918, 377
Pomeranian, S.S., rescue of, difficulties of, 110–11
Ponta Delgada, Azores, 337
Porcupine Bank, *Cevic* attacked near, 62
Port Arthur, blocking-up of, failure of, 91
Portland Bill, 381; reached by U-boats, 26; course indicated near, 381-2, minefield off, and net barrage, the U.S. destroyer *Rowan* entangled therein, 382
Portsmouth, naval base, 16, 133
Powell, Comdr. H., U.S. destroyer *Parker*, U-boat attacked by, 280–1; rescue by, of *Glenart* survivors, and D.S.C. award to, 281
Price, Capt. H. B., U.S.N., U.S.S. *Melville*, later *Dixie*, 253, 362; new funnel made by, for *Ammen*, 311; Admiral Bayly met by, at San Francisco, 379
Primo, S.S., sunk, 26
Princess Victoria, S.S., sunk, 31
Pringle, Capt. J. R. P., later Admiral, *Dixie*, Chief of U.S.N. Staff, Queenstown, 253-4, 362; Admiral Bayly's opinion of, 253, 254; death of, 254, 379; daily visits to, of American captains, 254; and the Cork deputation, 256
Privateers as historical precursors of submarines, 91
Prize, three-masted schooner, later Q-ship 21, history of, 228 *sqq.*
Public opinion, effect on, of sinkings of passenger vessels, 35, 39, 44, 45, 46, 48, 92, 96, 103; German official view on, 92
PULL TOGETHER board, the, on U.S.S. *Melville*, 254, 380
Pulltogether, U.S.S., silver half-model of a destroyer, given to Admiral Bayly by all the American commanding officers at Queenstown, 380

Quantock, S.S., torpedoed, 226, wild steering of, 227, salvage of, but no prize money, 227–8
Q-boat Adventures (Auten), 121 *n*.
"Q-ships" (Decoy ships) or "Mystery ships," 90, known to the Germans as "Trap-Ships," 91 (*see also* U.S. Q-ships), Admiral Bayly's early view on, 9, change of, use by, of these vessels, and successful devising of them by him, 121, 126–7, 132 *sqq.*; description of one (*Zylpha*) sufficing for all, 121 *sqq.*; commanders of, ability of, supreme test of, 124–5; "stunts" of panic parties, and smoke screens, 124–5, 211, 293; "Flower" sloops converted into, 132; Stationed at Queenstown, Queenstown allowed to choose her own, 132-3, disguising of, at Haulbowline, 133, precautions taken as to spies, 133, limits of their cruises,

171, strain on personnel of, 134, sent to intercept *Deutschland*, 174 *sqq.*, sent into the Atlantic to intercept ocean-going cruiser submarines, 180, sent to North America, West Indies, Mediterranean and White Sea, 180, later type, laden with timber, 181; actions of, with U-boats, 197; hydrophones on, 197; P-boats fitted up as, 198 *n.*; wane of, beginning of, 228; life aboard, a gamble with death, 234; Lough Swilly an important base for 258; one lost soon after *Zylpha*, 272; one, new, commissioned with McLeod in command, 272; not so dreaded by U-boats as convoy system, 274; chances for, in the English Channel, 364; duty of, to sink U-boats, 378 Known by names,

Arbutus, adapted sloop, torpedoed and sunk, 312

Arvonian, the ideal mystery ship, 316, *see also Bendish, below*

Aubrietia, adapted sloop, 132, 327, rescue by, of crew of Q-ship *Salvia*, 196

Baralong, S.S. *Nicosian* rescued by, and *U* 27 sunk, 88–9, base of, 90, despatched to the Mediterranean, 100, success of, 91, 121, value of Q-ships demonstrated by, 91; awards to crew of, 100, *see also Wyandra, below*

Begonia (*Q* 10), adapted sloop, sunk, 132

Bendish (formerly S.S. *Arvonian* and U.S. Q-ship *Santee*), 317

Candytuft, shelled, repaired, and torpedoed, 292–3

Chagford, sunk when on first job, 130, 234, 280, 316

Cullist, a U-boat damaged by, crew rewarded, 286–7, torpedoing of, Capt. Simpson's account of, 287 *sqq.*

Dunraven, Admiral Sims's visit to, 135–6; Campbell's finest achievement effected in, 284–85; wounded of, rescued by S.S. *Noma*, 285; honours conferred after, 280

Farnborough (formerly *Lodorer*), 132; encounter of, with *U* 68 and sinking of that U-boat by, 126, awards to officer and crew after, 127, encouraging effect of this success, 127; sent to the Mediterranean, 135; on patrol, 136; and the watch for the *Deutschland*, 176 *sqq.*; coal cargo discharged at Bermuda, and timber shipped at Quebec, 181, torpedoed by *U* 78, 184; torpedoed by *U* 83 and *U* 83 sunk by, 213, saved from foundering by her timber cargo, 213

Heather (*Q* 16), 272; Hallwright killed in, 163 *n.*

Lodorer, 121; Lieut. Gordon Campbell, R.N., appointed to, 123; later called *Farnborough* (*q.v. above*), 126 *n.*

Pargust, 259, 316, torpedoed, 260, *UC* 29 sunk by, crew saved, vessel salved, prisoners disposed of, 260–1, 284

Paxton, alias Q-ship 25, sunk, prisoners taken, survivors picked up, 258–9

Penshurst, U-boats sunk by, and fought with, *U* 84 driven off by, 210, 211–12; *UB* 19 sunk by, 137, 210; *UB* 37 sunk by, 210–11; torpedoed and sunk, 212, 316

Salvia, (*Q* 15) torpedoed in the Atlantic, crew saved by *Aubrietia*, 196; other details of loss, 272

Snowdrop, 226

INDEX

Stockforce, fight of, with a U-boat, sunk, and the U-boat also sunk, 365

Stonecrop, attacked by *U* 88, the attack replied to, and *U* 88 sunk by, 293–4; sufferings of her crew in boats and rescue of those left alive, 294 *sqq.*

Suffolk Coast, the last decoy vessel, 365

Tulip (Q-ship 12), 132, sunk by *U* 62, 203; Commander of, taken to Germany, 234

Vala, sunk, 136

Viola, 224

Wyandra, formerly *Baralong* (*q.v.* above), *U* 41, sunk by, 98 *sqq.*

Zylpha, a typical vessel of this class, 121 *sqq.*, Lieut.-Comdr. J. K. McLeod appointed to, as master, 123; sent to the Mediterranean, 135; on patrol, 136; sent across the Atlantic with coal, and back with timber, 181, sent to cruise about Nantucket Shoal and to patrol the Gulf of Mexico steamer tracks, to New Orleans, Galveston and Tampico, 182; shelled off the Irish coast, 183, escape of, from a U-boat, a gun afterwards secured for, 261, a U-boat attack driven off by, 261–2; story of her torpedoing, 263 *sqq.*, helped by *Warrington* and *Daffodil*, 266 *sqq.*, gramophone records used to cheer pumping party, 266

Known by numbers,
10, *see Begonia*
12, *see Tulip*
14, attack by, on a U-boat, 203
15, *see Salvia*
16, *see Heather*
21, former *Else, First Prize, Prize*, dramatic feat of, 228 *sqq.*, H.M. submarine *D* 6 accompanying, 233, sunk by *UB* 48, 233, honours awarded to all who served on board, 231
25, *see Paxton*

Q-ships and their Story (Chatterton), 121 *n.*

Quebec, 20; *Farnborough* on patrol near, 181, and at, for timber, 181, *Zylpha* at, 181; M.L.s built at, 187

Queen Mary, S.S., torpedoed, 224

Queenstown (now Cobh), 13, 14, 15, 218, 272, 291, climate of 16; naval base, 16; before, during, and after the War, 18, 363, 380; geographical outlay of, 17; as fuelling and repairing base, 18, 362; as part of the War area, 18; U-boat warning sent from, to *Lusitania*, unacknowledged 38, all available craft sent from, to assist her when torpedoed, 39–40; Irish patrol based at, 39, 40, composition of, 71; initiation into, 77; comparison of, with the Napoleonic patrol off Brest, 108; remoteness of, from Whitehall, 64; secrecy of signals secured at, 69–70; the religious difficulty at, 70; arrival at, of the sloops, 72, *see also* Sloops; problem of recreation at, 83; antagonism at, to the King's uniform, 83; Q-ships of (*see also* Q-ships), 136, disguised at Haulbowline, 133, distant voyages of, 180, 181, 182, their home and school at, 233; actions of, with U-boats, 197; trawlers of, escort duty of, 90; minesweeper flotilla at, and its commander, 200; U-boat campaign off, lull in, 112; visits to, of Asquith and Lord Midleton, 166; anti-U-boat operations from, basic principle of, 208; the vital spot in the submarine campaign, 208, 239; *Invercauld* survivors at, 215; American destroyers despatched to, welcome of, on arrival, 240, 241 *sqq.*; why such an inspiring centre in spite of discouragement, 272; convoy system of, Admiral Zogbaum on, and on the close co-operation in this, of British and American naval forces, 282-3; more U.S. destroyers at, and Volunteer Reserve officers for destroyers, 298; Naval Training Barrack organised at, for American crews, 308; U.S. Q-ship based on, 308; soldiers at, confined to barracks in anticipation of a fresh Irish rebellion, 310; arrival at, of U.S. submarines, 318; visits to, of Admiral Mayo, U.S.N., and of Admiral Jellicoe, 327; the "band of brothers" at, 327, 383, an odd story on, 328-9; U.S. s/m-chasers based on, and co-operation of, with U.S. Air Force, 336; visit to, of Geddes and Roosevelt, 361-2; visit to, of Admiral Wemyss, 362; U.S. naval organisation at, self-sufficiency of, 362 *sqq.*; British and American tugs based at, duties of, and their execution, 370 *sqq.*; present day, 380, new name of, 380, in 1917-1918, lesson of, on Anglo-American amity, 383

Admiralty House at, 18, 114; staff and work at, 69 *sqq.*, 103, 200; signal station in, closed, 70; garden of, 83; sloop garden at, reserved for commanding officers, 83; planting in, of sloops' name-flowers, 83-4;
U.S. destroyer commanders made free of, 255; never attacked during Admiral Bayly's occupation but later burnt down by Sinn Feiners, 160, 380; "dry" under Admiral Bayly, 166; Operations Staff started at, 200, 208

Air station at, 362, U.S. air pilots training at, 363;

Base hospital at, 362

Cathedral, 70; bells of, brought over under naval care, 71

Harbour, approaches mined, 208, 209, 243, 252-3, 327; boom and net defences of, 23, 71; Drake's Pool in, 16; Roche's Point in, 16, 18, 115; Rocky Island in, 17

Haulbowline Dockyard in, 17, 65, 74, 79, 103; B.E.F. divisions despatched from, 17; dock employees at, 17, 133, 160; signal station established on, 70; communication with the shore suspended, 117; Q-ship dressing in, 132, 133; leakage of information from, 133; guarded by Royal Marines from Gallipoli, 159; *Daffodil* in dry dock at, for repairs, 201; American destroyers' excess stores landed at, 246; Y.M.C.A. at, 255; British military force removed from, 253; U.S. destroyer *Cassin* taken to, 302

Rushbrooke dry dock at, 347

Ships in, civilian visits to, prohibited, 70

Size of, 16

Spike Island in, 17

U-boat approach to, 35

U.S. destroyers in collision in, 281-2

Patrol base, 39, 40; composition of the patrols, 71; initiation into, 77, strategy of, German efforts to confuse, 218, true

INDEX

measure of their success, Admiral Bayly on, 378
Royal Yacht Club, 24 n., Clubhouse of, an informal centre for naval intelligence, 255
Sloops, rescue work done by, 73; first real test of, 106, *see also* Sloops.
Spirit of efficiency initiated at, by Admiral Bayly, 74
Submarine flotilla, moving of, to Portsmouth, 332
Triangle, U-boat effort to close up, 64
Queenstown Association, the, composition of, and a would-be member, 328–9; dinner given by, to Admiral Bayly, in New York, and presentation by, of a silver rose bowl, 379; number of members to-day (1934), 383
Queenstown Command, 67 n., 199, Admiral Sir Lewis Bayly (*q.v.*), appointed to, 66; vessels composing (Aug. 1915), 90, (autumn 1916), 197, 198, (late summer 1917), 248, (Feb. 1918), 329, (July 1918), 363; four destroyers added to, April 1917, 221–2; taken over temporarily by Admiral Sims, 252; unity of, in operations and friendship, 248–9, 327, 383, *et alibi*; orders to, to cease hostilities, Nov. 11, 1918, 377; dispersal of, 378; U.S. Commanders at, silver model of a destroyer (*Pulltogether*) presented by, to Admiral Bayly, 380
Quiberon Bay, minefield in, safely passed over by Fourth Troop Convoy, 278

RAIKES, Lieut.-Comdr. R. H. T., R.N., *E* 54, 235

Rainey, Lieut. H. F., R.N.R., from *Zylpha* to H.M.S. *Heather*, 272
Rameses, S.S., *Invercauld* survivors picked up by, 215
Rathlin Island, 21; route of shipping passing south of, 32
Lighthouse, *UB* 77 and *U* 97 operating near, 330
Reay, Lieut. Marshal, R.N.R., and the destruction of *U* 104, decoration awarded after, 335
Red tape, entanglement of, even in national crisis, 199–200
Reichart, —, U.S. naval personnel, 343
Reindeer, trawler, on patrol duty, 49
Reliance, trawler, where patrolling, 40
Rena (armed merchantman), German raider, sunk by *Achilles* and *Dundee*, 24
Renfield, Norwegian barquentine, storm experiences of, 117–19, story of, told by Captain of, 118–119
Rescue tugs, system of, established in 1917, results of their efforts, 215–16
Resolution, H.M.S., challenged by *Davis*, U.S. destroyer, 346
Restango, trawler, where patrolling, 40
Rhydwen, S.S., sunk, 225
Richardson, J. V., alias of Commander Babcock, U.S.N., 238
Riley, Ensign Edward C., U.S.N., gallant act of, 367
Roads of Adventure (Paine), superlatives in, on Admiral Bayly, 309 & *n*.
Roanoke, S.S., capture of, 232–3
Roaringwater Bay, 49; *Terpsichore* aground in, 173
Rockall, the *Aud* scrutinised off, 148
Rockall Bank, watch kept off, for *Deutschland*, 177 & *n*.
Rodney, armed trawler, Skipper Watmore, U-boat hit by, and diverted from *Kenmare*, 61-2, Admiralty award to, 63

Rohr, Lieut.-Comdr., *U* 84, and Q-ship *Penshurst*, 211–12; fate of, 212 & n.
Rome, ancient, and the convoy system, 198–9, 273
Roosevelt, Franklin (President, U.S.A.), visit of, to Queenstown in 1918, and friendship of, with Admiral Bayly, 361–2, 383
Rose, Lieut.-Comdr. Hans, *U* 53, doings of, on the U.S.A. coast, 180, 181, 182
Round Island (Scillies), signal lights of, 129
Rowanmore, S.S., torpedoed off the Fastnet, 193
Roxano, armed trawler, fight of, with U-boat, 63
Roxburgh, H.M.S., *U* 89 destroyed by, 330
Royal Forces, entry into, of steamship companies' employees, 37
Royal Irish Constabulary, the, 105, and their rifles, 163
Royal Marines at Queenstown, 159; brought to Galway, 165; departure of, 169
Royal Naval, and American Naval, staffs and ratings, unity of purpose of, 251
Royal Naval War College, Greenwich, Admiral Bayly President of, 65, 66, 251
Royal Navy, bases of, 16, 22; cruiser shortage in (1914), 19; smallness of, 20; weakness of, in defence, 32
Rucker, Kapitan-leutnant Claus, commanding *U* 103, rescue of, 342; on his mistake in attack on S.S. *Olympic*, 343, on ability to dive below depth-charges, 345
Rudd, H. W. Dwight, Volunteer Reserve U.S. destroyer officer account by, of his experience in U.S. destroyer *Cassin*, 298 *sqq*.; transferred to U.S. destroyer *Nicholson*, to which *U* 58 surrendered, 303; account by, of the sinking and surrender of *U* 58, 304 *sqq*.
Runcorn, 172, 174
Russell, Paymaster Rear-Admiral H. R., secretary to Admiral Bayly, 79, 200; in temporary charge at Queenstown, 127
Russell & Co., Messrs. (now Lithgows Ltd.), steel sailing ships built by, 118
Russian Navy, submarines for, pre-war, made in Germany, 30
Ruytingen Bank, U-boats off, 29

Sabrina, armed yacht, U-boat chased by, 87
Safeguard, H.M.S., *Ausonia* survivors rescued by, 360
Sailing ships, 14; destroyed during the War, 15, 48, 50, 53, 55, 62, 89, 96, 121, 125, 128–9, 144, 145, 185, 205, 213, 361
St. Ann's Head, a U-boat driven under near, 145
St. Bride's Bay, *Bellgrade* towed into, 58
St. George's Channel, 14; net barrage at (*q.v.*), 22; *Falaba* sunk in, 34; U-boats in, narrow escapes from, 53; number of vessels sunk in, in Aug. 1914, 85; U-boats passing through, 86; S.S. *City of Exeter* attacked in, by *U* 24, 88; U-boats sunk in, 334–5
St. Goven and Helwick Light-vessels, mines laid between by *U* 78, 184
St. Kilda, 178, 179, 361
St. Lawrence River, Q-ship *Zylpha* in, 181–2
St. Louis, S.S., first U.S. armed liner, 221, U.S. troop-ship of Fourth Convoy, 275
St. Nazaire, debarkation at, of U.S. troops, 273, 277, 278
St. Olaf, sailing vessel, sunk, 89

INDEX 423

Samuel S. *Thorp*, American schooner, rescued by *Zinnia*, 186
San Francisco, welcome at, to Admiral Bayly, 1920, 379
San Urbano, S.S., attacked by *U* 81, 234, 235
Sander, Albert, spy, organisation of, 140 & *n*.
Sanders, Lieut. W. E., V.C., D.S.O., R.N.R., Q-ship 21, brilliant action of, and its recognition, 229 *sqq*., sunk, with his crew, by *UB* 48, memorial to, in New Zealand, 233
Santiago, blocking-up of, failure of, 91
Sapphire, steam yacht, in flying squadron, 22
Sarba, trawler, on patrol, 40
Scadaun, yacht, 173, and *Lusitania*, 40, *Nebraskan* escorted by, to Liverpool, 51–2
Scandinavian vessels, evasiveness of certain, 139
Scapa Flow, command of a sloop a welcome change from, 73; *Vala* at, 136
Scheer, Admiral, the U-boat campaign called off by from May to August, 1916, 170; on the escape of *U* 84, 212 & *n*. 1; book by, 212 *n*.
Scherer, —, U.S. Naval personnel, 341, 344, 346
Schneider, Lieut.-Comdr., *U* 24, H.M.S. *Formidable* sunk by, 26–7,85; return of west about Ireland, 86, excitements of the run, 87; with Wegener and Valentiner, operations of, against the Western Approaches, 87; off the Old Head of Kinsale, 88; S.S. *Arabic* sunk by, 88; again off Irish Coast, 361
Schull, coastguard at, 173
Schwieger, Lieut.-Comdr., *U* 20, route of, to the Irish Sea, 31, 36; specialist for Irish waters, 32, work of there, 35; S.S.

Lusitania torpedoed by, 39, 41, 44, 88; sighted by yacht *Seagull*, 40; use of a second torpedo denied by, 41; still at work off Queenstown Harbour, 48
Scilly Islands, 67, 97, 347; S.S. *Andalusian* sunk off, 31; small craft based on, in 1914, 71; U-boats off, 53, 361; reversion of, to Devonport Command, 121; signal lights of, 129; Q-ships off, 136; armed trawlers as escorts up to, 198; U.S. destroyer *Jacob Jones* sunk off, 310; U.S. destroyer *Rowan* in fog near, 381
Scotland, 18, 108; increase of U-boats passing round, 34
East coast, German mine grouping on, as ambush for Grand Fleet, 332
North coast of, and the British blockade, 16; Grand Fleet off, 17; incidents off, 63–4; *U* 43 sunk off, by H.M. submarine *G* 13, 217
West coast of, incidents off, 63–4; mines off, 21
Scott, Captain R. F., R.N., and the *Terra Nova*, 250
Scottish Monarch, S.S., sunk, 62
Scouting system, improved results with, 329
Sea, the, finest school for character, stamp of, unmistakable, 68
Seagull, motor yacht, *U* 20 sighted by, 40
Seamanship, time-honoured methods of, good effect of, 118
Seamen and soldiers, books by, contrasted styles of, 68
Seaward submarine screen to port, M.L.s acting as, 221
Sea-anchor, use of, 118
Sea-luck, 203, 223
Sea-monster, a, account of, by Comdr. Förstner, 74 *n*.

Sea-raiders, German, 274; escapes of, 364 & n., *see also Greif, Moewe,* and *Rena.*
Sea Raiders, *The* (Chatterton) referred to, 364 & n.
Sea-shanties, singing of, by foreign sailors, 119
Seattle, flagship of Rear - Admiral Gleaves, U.S.N., 278
Service influences, effects of, 68
Setter II, armed trawler, and *Aud,* 149, 154
Seven Heads, German minefields off, 1917, 217
Shannon River, U-boat near mouth of, 126; *Aud* near, 148
Sheep's Head, 104
Shenandoah, dirigible, disaster, Lieut. Lewis Hancock killed, in, 325
Sherston, Comdr. G. P., R.N.,*Snowdrop,* 227; co-operation of, with Cdr. Zogbaum with a nervous convoy, 282-3
Shetland Islands, 180
Shipping routes, continual alteration of, as affecting the Unrestricted Submarine Campaign, 208
Ships destroyed by U-boats in 1916, in different months, 170, the peak of, in numbers, 171
Shore lights, not interfered with, by the enemy, 217
Siberia, American S.S., help given by, to *Begonia,* 131
Signalling mistakes, 247
Silvia, S.S., sunk, 89
Simpson, Capt. S. H., D.S.O., R.N., *Jessamine,* 75; first meeting of, with Admiral Bayly, and appreciation by, of him, 76-7; storm experience of, 107; transferred to *Cullist,* 285-6, doings of, in that ship, and account by, of her fate, 286 *sqq.*, honours conferred on and on his crew, 287
Simpson, boatswain's mate, U.S.N., 375

Sims, Admiral W. S., U.S.N., 243, 244, 308, 348, 378; amusing experience of, on *Dunraven,* 135-6; despatch of, to London in April 1917, 238, his vessel mined near Mersey Light-vessel, 238; collaboration of, with Admiral Jellicoe, 239, convoys urged by, to the latter, 274; Admiral Bayly introduced to, 239; the U.S. destroyers directed by, to Queenstown, 240, 241; on the willing co-operation of the U.S.N. officers with the Royal Navy, 249; author's meeting with, and impression of, 250; appearance and character of, 250, 251; career of, parallel of, to that of Admiral Bayly, 250-1, 378-9; temporarily replacing Admiral Bayly, 252; Admiral Bayly's letter to, on the splendid stuff in his command, 272; a visit of, to Admiral Bayly, 316; and other U.S. Naval officers, Admiral Bayly welcomed by, at San Francisco, 1920, 379
Sinn Fein activities on American soil, 205 n., 309, in Ireland, 1918, 378; intrigues of, with Germany, *see under* Germany.
Sinn Fein farmer, said to supply petrol to U-boat, at Dunmanus Bay, 49-50
Sinn Feiners, in Haulbowline dockyard, no sabotage by, 159; in Galway, arrests of, 164
Skal,—,Von, and an Irish rising (1916), 140
Skellig Rock, Q-ship *Zylpha* sunk off, 272
Skelligs, the, S.S. *Nailsea Court* torpedoed off, 203; S.S. *Canadian* torpedoed off, four times, 223

INDEX

Skokham Island, H.M. drifter *Ladysmith* lost on, 115; German minefield by, 209
Sloop and oil-tanker, collision between barely averted, 203–4
Sloop areas, letters of the alphabet assigned to, 80–1
Sloop commanders, services of, and their recognition, 70; endurance of, 73
Sloop garden, Queenstown, reserved for commanding officers, 83, planting in, of sloop's nameflowers, 83–4; U.S. destroyer commanders made free of, 255
Sloops, application of the term, 72; building of, a triumph of creation, 72; fine services rendered by, 72–3; varied utilities of, 72; behaviour of, in heavy gales, 73; nickname of, for themselves, 73; advantages of, over trawlers, 81; stationing of, along the South Irish coast, 81; maintenance of, a sea organisation for, 81–2; allowed to draw fires on arrival in port, 82; needed in North Sea, for minesweeping, 91; "Flower" class, seaworthiness of, 107–8; as comparable with Brest patrol of Napoleonic wars, 108, difficulties of, in routine work, 109–10, 111; "Flower" class, adaptation of as Q-ships (*q.v.*), 132; two torpedoed, three badly damaged, others injured through collisions at end of 1916, 201; and M.L.s keeping traffic channels clear, 1917, 221; "Flower" class compared with minesweepers, 222
Alyssum, on convoy duty, 211; taken for a destroyer by *U* 84, 212; escape of and final loss of, 218, 222

Arbutus, sunk as Q-ship, 312
Aubrietia, transformed into a Q-ship, 132
Begonia, 83; in rescue of *Huronian*, 114; damage to, and escape of, 130 *sqq.*; transformed into a Q-ship, fate of, 132
Bluebell, 151, 155, 202; *Aud* overhauled by, 154–5; souvenir in, of *Aud*, 157; S.S. *Alexandrian* towed by, to Berehaven, 202; *Tritonia* survivors saved by, 216; *Myosotis* towed by, to Devonport, 292; on convoy duty, 327
Buttercup, *Farnborough* towed by, 213; and the Captain of S.S *Invercauld*, 215
Camellia, 83; in rescue of *Huronian*, 114; rescues by, 114, 194, 311, 360; search by, for *Genista* survivors, 192; rescue by, of *Jacob Jones* survivors, 311; *Ausonia* survivors rescued by, 360
Candytuft, sunk as Q-ship, 292, 293
Crocus, *Pargust* towed in by, 260, 261
Daffodil, 83; experience of, when rescuing *Pomeranian*, 110–11; search of, for *U* 44, 130; in collision, with loss of life, 201; *Zylpha* towed nearly home by, 269, 270, 271, 272
Delphinium, 83
Genista, sunk, 192, 193, 202; rescue of survivors, 193, 194, 195
Heather, converted into Q-ship 16, 132
Iris, storm experience of, 106; attack by, on a U-boat, 203
Jessamine, 75, 76, 83, 286; faulty motor boat of, Admiral Bayly's action as to, 77–8; storm experience of, 107; and U.S. destroyer *Cassin*, 301; *U* 104 destroyed by, with depth-charges, 335;

sent to the aid of S.S. *Huntscliffe*, 371, part of crew rescued by, 372; lifeboat of, wrecked, 373

Laburnum, 83, 202; sent to Galway, effect of, her indirect shooting, 163-4; *Farnborough* towed by, 213; *Laconia* survivors rescued by, 216; in collision with U.S. destroyer *Jenkins*, 261

Lavender, 83; attempted salvage by, of S.S. *Manchester Engineer*, 129 n.; *Zent's* survivors rescued by, 144; attacked by U-boat, 218

Mignonette, sunk while minesweeping, 218, 222

Myosotis and S.S. *Alexandrian*, 202; torpedoed but missed, 203; further adventure of, 203, 292

Primrose, 83, 297; *Berwindvale* salvaged by, 126

Rosemary, 222 n.

Salvia, lost as Q-ship, 196, 272

Snowdrop, 83; help given by, to *Begonia*, 131; *Great Southern*, transport conveying Royal Marines escorted by, 165; a M.L. shelled by, 190; *Nordyk*, S.S., escorted by, 201; minesweeping by, 209; rescue of S.S. *Quantock*, 226; 227, 228; signalman's mistake concerning, 247; *Cassin*, U.S. destroyer, towed by, to Haulbowline Dockyard, 301-302, and escorted by, to Newport, Mon., 310; *U* 58 prisoners conveyed by, to Pembroke, 304

Sunflower, 83; *Iberian* survivors rescued by, 74; commendation of, by Admiral Bayly after *Iberian* rescues, order following, 74; piloted by Admiral Bayly, 74-5; *Hesperian* survivors rescued by, 96; and *Terpsichore*, 173, salvage award for, 174; damaged in collision, 201

Tamarisk, 83; turned into a Q-ship, 132; attempt of to tow U.S. destroyer *Cassin*, 301

Tulip, turned into Q-ship 12, 132

Viola, 83

Zinnia, 83, 346; gale experience of, 106-7; experience of, when rescuing *Pomeranian*, 110-11; on patrol duty, 127-8; *U* 44 sighted by, from Galley Head, 130; help given by, to *Begonia*, 131; *Cairngowan* survivors rescued by, 146; the real *Aud* seen by, 151, sent to stop her, 154; *Huronian* escorted by, 169; search of, for the *Maréchal de Villars*, 185; *Samuel S. Thorp*, American schooner salvaged by, 186; search by, for *Genista's* survivors, 192, 193; search of, for the oil-tanker *Terak*, 201; minesweeping by, 209; attempted towing by, of S.S. *Tritonia*, 216; adventures of, while on escort and towing business, 218-19; to the rescue of *Pargust*, 260, 261; activities of, on patrol, April 16, 1917, 224-5; in collision with U.S. destroyer *Benham* and rescue of ship and crew, 281-2; *Stonecrop's* crew saved by, 296; a French dory's crew rescued by, 296; on convoy duty, 302, 310, 327; Captain Capper and others of the *Ausonia* rescued by, 360; sent to the aid of S.S. *Huntscliffe*, 371, difficulties with her whaler, 372

Slow transports, armed trawler escort of, 190

Small passenger steamers, U-boat officers forbidden to sink without warning, 92

INDEX

Small ships, flotillas of, possibilities with, 336
Smalls, the (Welsh coast), nets laid off, 46, 87, 210; *Van Stirum* shelled off, 112; Q-ship *Arbutus* torpedoed near, 312
Smerwick Harbour, 216; signal station at, 150
Smiles, Lieut. N. F., R.N.R., *Stonecrop*, rafts built by, after *Stonecrop* being torpedoed, five days drifting about of, 294, 295; rescue of, by *Zinnia*, D.S.C. conferred on, 296
Smith, Captain John, arrival of, in Chesapeake Bay, 237; vessels of, 242
Smithwick, Lieut.-Comdr. A. R., R.N., H.M.S. *Roxburgh*, U 89 destroyed by, D.S.O. awarded to, for this, 330
Smoke screen, first employed by Admiral Bayly, 66; German use of, at Jutland, 66; used by Q-ships, 293, 294
Soerakarta, Dutch S.S., 135
Sommelsdyk, S.S., 140
Sonoma, U.S. tug, patrol area assigned to, 370, and the rescue of S.S. *Huntscliffe*, 370 *sqq.*
Southampton, 14, 21
South Arklow Light-vessel, 113; boarded and sunk, 217
South Point, S.S., sunk, 34
South Stack (Anglesey), nets laid off, 47
Spanish treasure ships, convoyed from the West Indies, 273
Spider, armed trawler, U-boat fired on by, 87
Spiegel von und zu Peckelsheim, Lieut.-Comdr. Freiherr, U 32, entangled in net barrage, escape of, 33, effect of this, on U-boat regulations, 34; later of U 93, fight of, with Q-ship 21, 229 *sqq.*, rescue of, 231; on his experiences in U 93, 232

Spies, precautions against, as to Q-ships, 133
Spindler, Lieut. Karl, German Naval Reserve, of S.S. *Castro*, ex-Wilson liner, later *Libau*, later *Aud*, attempt of, to effect a landing in Ireland, 142 & *n.*, 143, importance of his vessel, 147, rendezvous arranged for, 148–9; Donaldson bluffed by, 149; chased by *Lord Heneage* and *Setter II*, 150; stopped and taken to port, ship blown up by, 155–6; net result of his failure, 157, 158; some little errors of, 156–7; book by, cited, 150 & *n.*, 156, on the real *Aud*, 151
Spithead, naval review at, 18
Spring-Rice, Sir Cecil, diplomacy of, 45
Stafford, General, armoured train fitted out for, at Haulbowline Dockyard, 159–60
Start Point, Q-boat engagement off, 365
Steam drifters, as anti-submarine craft, 22
Steam trawlers, Admiralty use of, and the risks to the nation's fish food supplies, 197
Steam or motor yachts of the Queenstown fleet, 198
Steamers, cargo-carrying, use by, of smoke screens, 66; torpedoed near Coningbeg Lightship, 36
Steinhauer, Lieut.-Comdr., *UB* 48, *Roanoke* captured by, and Q-ship 21 sunk by, with all hands, 232–3; *UB* 48 eventually scuttled by, 233
Stephano, S.S., sunk by U 53 off Nantucket Light-vessel, 180
Stewart, Lieut. C., R.N.R., lost with Q-ship *Arbutus*, 312
Stockholm, 140
Storesand, Norwegian vessel, sunk, 95
Stormcock, H.M. tug, 370; and the

Lusitania rescues, 42, 43; and *Terpsichore*, 173, salvage award to, 174
Storms of Winter, 1915–16, 115 *sqq*.
Stornoway, trawlers detached from, to watch for *Deutschland*, 177
Strathcona, S.S., sunk, 223
Strathdene, S.S., sunk by *U* 53 off Nantucket Light-vessel, 180
Submarine campaign, convoy system to defeat, 274
Submarine chasers (s/m-chasers), built by U.S.A., excellence of, Atlantic passage of, and operations of, from Irish naval bases, 336 *sqq*.
Submarine warfare, scarcely begun in June, 1915, 55, *see also* U-boats, *and* Unrestricted Submarine Campaign.
Submarines
  American, *see under* U.S.A.
  British, H.M.S. *Lion* mistaken for a trawler by, 191; employment of, against U-boats, extension of, 198; Queenstown flotilla of, 234; passage of, to the Dardanelles, 318, 319
  D 3, 218
  D 6, accompanying Q-ship 21, 233
  D 7, 218
  D 8, 218
  E 32, 218
  E 54, 218; *U* 81 sunk by, 234–5
  G 13, *UC* 43 torpedoed by, 217
  H 5, 218
  L 2, depth-charged in error, 329–30
  German, *see* U-boats, all types.
  Historical precursors of, 91
Suicide Fleet, the, 283
Sunlight, barque, destroyed, 55
Susan Constant, one of John Smith's ships, 242
Susannah, schooner, destroyed, 55
Sussex, S.S., torpedoed, Americans anger at, 170
Svorono, Russian S.S., destroyed off the Blaskets, 35

Swanmere, S.S., attacked and torpedoed by *U* 43 and *U* 93, 229
Swift, H.M.S., *see Broke–Swift* episode.
Sybil Point, 52; trawler-drifter patrol from, to Carnsore Point, 198
Sydney, Cape Breton, Q-ship *Farnborough*'s departure from, with timber cargo, 182
Sydney, New South Wales, 15

TAILLA, Petty Officer Franz, *UC* 29, 261
Talbot, H.M.S., 194 & *n*.
Tampico, 182
Taussig, Captain J. K., U.S.N., on defensive measures taken by U.S.A., 236; his summons to active service, 237; and the American destroyers, equipment of, and unconvoyed passage of, across the Atlantic, 239–40; first interview of, with Admiral Bayly and prompt reply, 245; in the *Wadsworth*, *Paxton* survivors rescued by, 259; temporary return of, to U.S.A., 307
Tearaght, 151; *Tritonia* S.S., torpedoed near, 216
Tebbenjohanns, Lieut.-Comdr., *UC* 44, fate of, 223
Teiresias, S.S., *U* 21 sighted by, 36
Telconia, cable S.S. held up by weather, 109
Terpsichore, ship-rigged iron vessel, 171–2; aground in Roaringwater Bay and safely extricated, 172 *sqq*., Admiralty award for salvage of, 174
Terra Nova, Scott's ship for the Antarctic, Evans aboard, 250
Teutonian, S.S., torpedoed, 125
Teutonic, H.M. auxiliary cruiser, and S.S. *Huntscliffe*, 370–1
Thames Estuary, S.S. *Balakani* mined off, 95
Thomasina, Russian barque, destroyed, 55

Three Castles, 104
Three Rivers, Q-ship *Zylpha* loaded at, with timber, 181
Timber cargoes, not contraband, 128; flotability ensured by, 227
Tirpitz, Grand Admiral, on results of submarine warfare, 44–5; insistence of, on sinking passenger ships, 92
Tomkinsville, Fourth U.S. Convoys' departure from, 275
Torbay, 108
Torpedo attack, no British harbour safe against in August 1914, 71
Torpedo boats: No. 95, *U* 33 fired on by, 95; 050, 052, 055, race of, to aid *Lusitania*, 42; at Queenstown, fighting value of, 18; work done by, 198
"Torpedoed leave" in the Royal Navy, 358–9
Tory Island and area, 176; German minefield in, 20, 21, Norwegian grain-ship sunk by, 21; effect of, 21, 199; Q-ship *Chagford* sunk off, 130; S.S. *Belgian Prince* sunk off, 280
Towing difficulties, 216
Tozer, Capt. C. M., U.S.N., U.S.S. *Buffalo*, 337
Trade routes, transatlantic, U-boat watch on, 32, 117; natural dangers along, 118, fewness of accidents due to fog and lack of light, 201, keeping clear, 221
Trafalgar, S.S., sunk, 89
Trafford, S.S., sunk by U-boat, gallantry of her master, 59, 60
Tralee Bay, proposed German landing of arms in, 141, 205
Tramore Bay, Waterford, U-boat in, 48
Transatlantic steamers, U-boat's dead set at, in April, 1917, 221
Transports bringing U.S. troops, escorts of, 273; only one sunk by U-boats, 329

Trawler patrols, speed of, 40; increase of, 46; in the Upper Irish Sea, 46–7; concentration of, round Milford–Scillies–Queenstown triangle, 63; employment of, as escorts, 198; fitting of, with minesweeping gear, 198; limits of their powers, 224; drifters, motor-boats, armed yachts and old time torpedo-boats at various bases under Admiral Bayly's command in 1914, 71, 198; strength and weakness of, 81; Sinn Fein leaders placed aboard after arrest, 162; mistaken for U-boats, 190; damaged in the October gale, 195; minesweeping by, 209
Trayer, Lieut. James S., U.S.N., of *Sonoma* tug, and the rescue of S.S. *Huntscliffe*, 370, 371; his own account of the affair, 372 *sqq.*
Tremayne, S.S., 292; missed by a torpedo off Cape Sigli, 293
Trembeth, Sub-Lieut. G., R.N.R., Q-ship *Zylpha*, lost in another Q-ship, 272
T.N.T., a cargo of, 338
Trier, armed trawler, U-boat sunk by, 145
Tritonia, S.S., torpedoed near Tearaght, survivors saved by *Bluebell*, ship with horses aboard sunk, 216
Trondheim, *Berlin* interned at, 21
Troop transports, convoy of, 47, 199
Troy, wooden horse of, Q-ship parallel to, 91
Tugs, plucky achievements of, 370 *sqq.*
Turkey, an Armistice signed by, Oct. 30, 1918, 377
Turner, Capt., Master of the S.S. *Lusitania*, Admiralty advice to, on precautions in danger zone received by, 38; further wireless message received off

Brow Head, 38; final message not acknowledged by, 38; precautions of, in danger zone, 37, 38, 39; fate of, 44
Turnwell, S.S., shelled, bombed, and abandoned, 59; return of, to Milford, 60
Tuscania, S.S., Anchor liner, sunk by *UB* 77, 330
Tuskar Rock, 39, 51, 59, 314; *U* 84 destroyed near, 327
Tuskar to Fastnet, sloops stationed along, 81; *U* 22 attacked by trawlers off, 86
Tuskar to Smalls, net barrage of, 87, 210; *U* 84 rammed here, 327
Two Point Island, 104
Tynwald, S.S., *New York's* passengers transferred to, 238
Tyrwhitt, Admiral Sir R. Y., destroyers needed by, at Harwich, 47

UGLAND, Messrs. J. L., 104
United States of America, English relations with, closer than with Ireland, 13–14; effect on, of U-boat warfare, 23, 39, 44, 45, 92; participation of, in the War, divided opinion as to, 45–6; effect on, of the British blockade, 45, 206; and Germany, political differences between, 93, first and second Notes of protest despatched by, 46, note from, threatening rupture of diplomatic relations (April 1916), 170, relations severed by, on the inauguration of the Unrestricted Submarine Campaign (*q.v.*), 204, vast influence of these events, 205; Casement's visit to, in 1914, 139
Merchant vessels, arming of, 221
Naval organisation of, self-supporting character of, 361 *sqq.*
Share of, in the work of the Queenstown patrols, Admiral Bayly's tribute to, endorsed by the Admiralty, 378, his further tribute to, 379
Steamers and sailing vessels, eleven of them captured by *Deutschland* converted type of U-boat in the West Atlantic, 354
United States Navy
Battleships, arrival of, at Berehaven, why sent, 364–5
Destroyers, *see under* Destroyers.
Q-ships of, one based on Queenstown, 308
Arvonian, the ideal mystery ship, name changed to *Santee*, 316
Santee, formerly *Arvonian*, later H.M. Q-ship *Bendish*, torpedoed when first out, 316–17
Submarine-chasers built for, excellence of, and work of, off the Irish coast, 336
No. 206, 337, and her cook's adventure, 338–9
Submarine Flotilla, the, Queenstown Harbour approaches mined before arrival of, 327
Submarines, *AL* 1, 2, 3, 4, 9, 10, 11, Atlantic crossing of, 318
AL 2, 318; a U-boat chased by, 325–6
AL 4, 318; underwater collision of, with a U-boat, 319, other contacts of, with U-boats, 320, 321, 322; accidental dive of, 323, skidding of on the bottom and raised, 324–5
AL 9, 318; encounter with a U-boat which escaped, 319–20
AL 11, 318; torpedoed, on patrol, but not hit, 322
United States troops, arrivals of, in France, in spite of the Unrestricted Submarine Campaign, 361
U.S. Volunteer Reserve destroyer officers at Queenstown, personal records of some of them, 298 *sqq.*

INDEX

U-boats, off the Irish coast, 15, 35, 125, 221, 229; precautions against in the Irish Sea, 21; route of, to S.W. Ireland 361; havoc wrought by, during passage to the Dardanelles, Dec. 1915, 93 *n.* 1; expected confinement of, to the North Sea, 18; raids of, precautions against, 22; Admiral Bayly's three methods of combatting, 90; in Dover Straits, 25 *sqq.*; nets cut through by, 144; successes of, effect of, on the German submarine service, 25, in English waters, 28, 56, summit of, 228; use of a deck gun by, to save torpedoes, 26; temperamental qualities of, 29; final number of, 30, number of, available for the Unrestricted Campaign, 207, number of, in the English Channel, Irish Sea and Western Approaches, Feb. 1918, 329, number of, in commission in June, 1918, 361; with heavy-oil engines, object for which built, 30, 50; danger of, to Allied shipping, 31; in the Atlantic, their first appearance, 32, going out into, to avoid coastal patrols, 50, crossing of, for visits, 348, activities of, Oct. 1918, 370, 371; net-cutting apparatus fitted in, 33; increase of, round Scotland, 34; in Coningbeg Lightship area, 36; favourable position of, in British Seas, 40–1; speed of, 40; instructions to, as to attacking passenger ships after the *Lusitania* incident, 44; shelters believed to be used by, 46; oversea going, petrol not used by, 50; rumours as to, time, &c., wasted in investigating, 50; strategy of, 53; wireless signals of, picked up by English stations, 53; operations of, in the Milford–Scillies–Queenstown triangle, 63; 210-feet, concentration of, against Western Approaches, 63, 89, 96; efforts of, to close Liverpool to shipping, 64; and western patrols, separate naval warfare waged between, 64; damage by, mostly accomplished by select few, 84; failure to meet *Aud* at Tralee Bay, 148–9; occasional, sent north of Scotland to U.S.A., political tactlessness of, 174; mine-layers, 184; in the North Sea, 93 *n.* 1, 222; escape of one, from Q-ship *Farnborough*, 178–9; occasional bursts of, 197; one sighted by Q-ship 21, 231; trawlers mistaken for, 190; new types of, victims sought by, at longer distances, 197; operations, intensifying and multiplying of, German anticipations from, 199; return of, in January 1917, 202 *sqq.*; attack, description of, 214–15; operating well off land and also inshore, March 1917, 218, incidents illustrating, 218 *sqq.*; difficulties of, Aug. 1917, 283; the first conquered by U.S. naval forces, 299; long voyages of, paralleled by those of British and U.S. submarines, 318; the American submarines' contacts with, 319 *sqq.*, 325–6; efforts of, to destroy American troop convoys, 339–40; destroyed, sent home and recalled from various bases and the Atlantic, Oct. 1918, 377

Attacked, chased and sunk, 59, 60, 63, 87, 93, 96, 131, 207, 212, 234, 286–7, 327; scouting for, and the use of depth-charges as affecting, 329; weekly average destruction of, May 1918, 339

Commanders, ability and endurance of, 31, 32; as experts in certain districts, 32; callous actions of some, 185–6, 280; awe felt by, for the M.L.s, 188; camouflage of convoy sloops ridiculed by, 258; detestation by, of the convoy system, 274; desire of one, to join the Queenstown Association, 328–9

Crews, length of time able to stay at sea, 30; training of, 171, 298; growing inexperience of, and lack of morale, 332

Ocean-keeping cruiser type, 211, 291, 317; *see also Bremen, and Deutschland.*

Vessels attacked, chased and sunk by, 89, 97, 98, 113, 170–1, 192–3, 202, 203, 209–10, 212, 213, 216, 217, 223, 281, 294, 365

Warfare, Tirpitz on result of, 44–5; British shipping losses due to, 55; effect of, *see under* U.S.A.

U 8, start out of, 29; sunk after surrender of crew, 31

U 9 sent to intercept B.E.F. transports, 24; the three "Cressys" sunk by, 25

U 12, H.M.S. *Niger* sunk by, 26

U 18, unsuccessful attack of, on H.M.S. *Attentive*, 25–6

U 19, Casement's passage in, to Tralee Bay, 143, 152

U 20, sighted by *Seagull*, 40, *Lusitania* sunk by, 39, 41, 44, 88, 361

U 21, 361; at the Forth Bridge, 23–4; first U-boat victory in the War scored by, 24; sinkings by, 24, 26, 28; further records of, 26; first enemy submarine to reach the Irish coast, 27; attack by, on Walney Island, 27, 46, 86; attacked by the *Vanduara*, 28; return of, to Wilhelmshaven, 28–9, 215; despatched to the Adriatic, 34; neutral vessels attacked by, 215

U 24, H.M.S. *Formidable* sunk by, 26–7, 85; route of, to Lowca, 85, 86, 87; attacked by trawler, 86–7; off the Irish coast, Aug. 1914, 87; attack by, on S.S. *City of Exeter* repulsed, 88; S.S. *Dunsley* molested by, 88; S.S. *Arabic* torpedoed by, 88, 91, 96, 103, commotion caused by in U.S.A., 92, Count Bernstorff on punishment of the captain, 92; active off the Irish coast in July 1918, 361

U 27, late start of, for the Irish Sea, 29, new route to, found by, 31, work of there, 84–5, 87; sunk by Q-ship *Baralong* and fate of commander and crew, 89

U 28, exploits of, 34, 35; S.S. *Aguila* sunk by, 34

U 30, start of, for western cruise, 29

U 33, 93; despatched to the Mediterranean, 85; S.S. *Mimosa* and S.S. *Whitfield* sunk by, 95; fired on, by H.M. T.B. No. 95, 95

U 34, operating in Irish Seas, 53; *Hirose* attacked and sunk by, 54–5, treatment of crew by, 55; *Victoria* probably sunk by, 54; despatched to the Mediterranean, 85

U 35, British Isles encircled by, 53; *George and Mary*, sailing vessel, sunk by, 53; despatched to the Mediterranean, 85

INDEX 433

U 38, number of vessels sunk by, Aug. 1914, 85; off the Irish coast, 87; probably chased by H.M. armed yacht *Sabrina*, 87; estimated course of, 96

U 39, 93; despatched to the Mediterranean, 85; passage of, through Straits of Gibraltar, and work of, before and after this, 94, 95; *William T. Lewis*, barque, shelled by, 93 *sqq.*; active off the Irish coast, 361

U 41, particulars of, 96; vessels sunk by, 97; encounter with and sinking of, by Q-ship *Baralong*, 98 *sqq.*, 117

U 42, 291

U 44, *Ottomar* sunk by, 128 *sqq.*, 144; stated by crew to be *U* 287, 129; Q-ship sunk by, but herself damaged and later sunk by H.M.S. *Oracle*, 130 *n.*, 280; diving of, after torpedoing S.S. *Belgian Prince* and taking survivors aboard, 280

U 46, Christmas Day in, when submerged, 200–1

U 53, passage of, to U.S.A., 180, 307, 311; British and Dutch steamers sunk by, off Nantucket Light-vessel, 180, 181, 182; U.S. destroyer *Jacob Jones* sunk by, 311

U 55, safe return of, 182

U 57, *Genista* sunk by, 193

U 58, depth-charged and destroyed by U.S. destroyer *Fanning*, 302 *sqq.*; size, speed, and equipment of, and daring passage of, through Dover Straits, 303, 307

U 61, destroyed by H.M.S. *P* 51, with depth-charges, 331-2

U 62, Q-ship No. 12 sunk by, 203, 234; Comdr. Lewis captured by, 234; commander of, invited by Comdr. Lewis to come to England after the War, 234

U 67, working the Irish coast, 229

U 68, encounter of, with Q-ship *Farnborough*, and sinking of, 126–7

U 78, mines laid by, 184, 222; attack by, on S.S. *Strathcona* and steam trawler *Andromache* sunk by, on the way home, 223

U 81, sunk by H.M. submarine *E* 54, 234–5; rescue of captain of, 235

U 84, Q-ship *Penshurst's* fight with, 211–12, damage sustained by, 212; *Alyssum* taken for a destroyer by, 212; destroyed by *P* 62 near Tuskar, 212 *n.*, 327

U 86, *Llandovery Castle* sunk by, 361

U 87, in the Irish Sea, 316, Q-ship *Penshurst* damaged by; sunk by *P* 56, 316

U 88, modern type, equipment and surface speed of, 293; attacked and sunk by Q-ship *Stonecrop* off S.W. Ireland, 293–4

U 89, sunk by H.M.S. *Roxburgh*, 330

U 93, successes of, 229; fight of with Q-ship 21, 229, believed sunk by her, 230–1; amazing return of, 231–2; sunk by S.S. *Braeneil*, 232

U 97, operating off Rathlin Island Lighthouse, 330

U 103, S.S. *Olympic* attacked by, 340 *sqq.*, 345, 348; damage done to, by *Olympic*, surrender of, and rescue of survivors, 340 *sqq.*

U 104, attack on, by U.S. destroyer *Cushing*, 334; destroyed by H.M. sloop *Jessamine* with

depth-charges, 335; story of her doings, 335
U 110, S.S. *Amazon* sunk by, 331; sunk by H.M. destroyers *Moresby* and *Michael* with depth-charges, 331; survivors picked up found to be young and inexperienced, 331
U 135, 361
U 151, an ocean-keeping cruiser-submarine, advantages of, and arms carried by, 291; off the American coast, May and June 1918, 336, 337
U 156, off the American coast, May and June 1918, 336, 337
U-boat nicknamed *Penmarch Pete*, U.S.S. *Bridgeport* torpedoed by, but missed, 337
UB type, and use of Dover route, 34
19, Norwegian ship sunk by, 137; sunk by *Penshurst*, 137, 210
37, sunk by *Penshurst*, 210–11
48, *Prize* sunk by, 233
65, loss of, mystery of, 326
77 *Tuscania*, S.S. Anchor liner sunk by, 330
82, destroyed with depth-charges by H.M. drifters *Pilot Me* and *Young Fred*, 333
85, surrender of, to H.M. drifter *Coreopsis*, 333, reason given by her commander, 334, sunk by him, 334
UC type and use of Dover route, 34; in the North Sea, 63, mines laid by, *Balakani* sunk by, 95
29, Q-ship *Pargust* torpedoed by, 260; doings of, on trip from Heligoland, 260-1; sunk by *Pargust*, crew saved, 260, 284; mines laid by, found, 284
42, sunk by her own mines near Daunt's Rock Light-vessel, 291
43, torpedoed and sunk by H.M. submarine G 13, 217
44, minelayer, effect on, of depth-charges, 210; blown up by German mine off Waterford, 223; examination of, when beached, results of, 291-2
UC 65, in difficulties with Milford net-drifters, 210
Urbino, S.S., Wilson liner, sunk, crew rescued, 92, 97, 100, 112
Ushant, 97, 347; number of vessels sunk off, in Aug. 1914, 85; battle off, of Q-ship *Dunraven* with a U-boat, 284-5

VALENTIA HARBOUR, entrance mined, 184-5, 284
Valentiner, Lieut.-Comdr. Max, U 38; number of vessels sunk by, in Aug. 1914, 85; operating against the Western Approaches, 87; possibly operating off S.W. Ireland, 96
Valiant, armed steam yacht, in flying squadron, 22
Valorous, H.M. drifter, UB 85's crew rescued by, 334
Van Stirum, S.S., sunk, 112-13, survivors rescued by Belgian trawler *Nadine*, 113
Vanduara, armed steam yacht, attack by, on U 21, 28
Venus, H.M.S., 18
Vera, armed trawler, fight of, with a U-boat, 63
Verbena, trawler, on patrol, 40
Vernou, Lieut.-Comdr. W. N. (now Admiral) of *Cassin*, U.S. destroyer, on excellence of convoy work, 299; temporary return of, to U.S.A., 307
Victoria, steam trawler, sunk, 54; survivors rescued by *Ballater*, 55
Vigo, escape from, by sea, of German internees, 191
Virgen del Socorro, schooner and her crew of escaping German internees, 191

INDEX

Virginia, first settlers of, arrival of, in Chesapeake Bay, 237; Taussig's flotilla starting from, 236–7, 242

Voysey, Miss, 252, 379, hostess at Admiralty House, Queenstown, 76, tribute to, 79–80; Admiral Bayly's staff supplemented by, 80–1; and shipwrecked seamen, 246

Vulcan, H.M.S. (Capt. Nasmith), mother ship of the Berehaven submarine flotilla, 234

WADE, Chief Petty Officer, and Spindler, 156
Wade, Coxswain, 114
Wales, 22, 27
Walker, J. F., success of, in designing Q-ships, 132, 133
Walker, Skipper A., of drifter *Pilot Me*, attack of, on *UB* 82, 333
Wallflower, nickname for H.M.S. *Adventure*, 194
Walney Island, fort on, attack on, by *U* 21, 27, 46, 86
Walsh, Thomas, of the Clan-na-Gael, journeys of, to and from U.S.A., 309; arrest of, 310
Waltham, U.S. tug, mined off the U.S. coast, 354
War, the Great, 14, 15 *passim*, the end of, how brought about, 377
"War will soon End," slogan, 55
War Zone, the expansion of, through U-boat successes, 28; entry into of the Fourth U.S. Troop Convoy, 276–7
Ward, Skipper F., steam trawler *Hirose*, adventure of, with *U* 34, 54–5
Warren, Coxswain, U.S.N., 375
Warrior, H.M. tug, 370; and *Lusitania* rescues, 42; experience of, when rescuing *Pomeranian*, 110–111; help given by, to *Begonia*, 131
Warships, mistaken for destroyers, 191

"Wasser-bombs" (*see also* Depth-charges), effect of, on U-boat crews, 210; not always effectual, 211
Waterford, U-boat chased away from, by H.M. yacht *Beryl*, 144; German minefield off, *UC* 44 destroyed by, 223, 291
Watmore, Skipper, armed trawler *Rodney*, U-boat hit by and diverted from *Kenmare*, 61–62
Weeke, Messrs. B. & Sons, of Hamburg, *Terpsichore* built for, 171
Weddigen, Lieut.-Comdr., *U* 9, H.M.S. *Aboukir*, *Cressy* and *Hogue* sunk by, 24–5
Wegener, Lieut.-Comdr., *U* 27, new route taken by, to the Irish Sea, 31; *Bayano* torpedoed by, 32; pioneer and specialist in the Irish Sea, 32, 85; operations of, against the Western Approaches, 87; *Nicosian* shelled by, 88; fate of, 88–9, 91
Weisbach, Lieut.-Comdr., *U* 19, with Casement aboard, arrival of, at Irish rendezvous, 152
Wemyss, Admiral Sir Rosslyn, First Sea Lord, visit of, to Queenstown, 362
West Bay, H.M.S. *Formidable* sunk in, 26–7
West Indies, privateering in, object of, 91; Q-ships sent to, 180, 181, 183
West Point, S.S., sunk, 180
Westerbrock, 228
Western Approaches, U-boat concentration against, 63, 87, 96, 209; new methods demanded for (June 1915), 64; protection of, importance to, of Queenstown, 66; difficulties of affording, 90; U-boat activity ceasing in, May–Aug. 1916, 170; the war of, 200 *sqq*.; U-boat successes in,

1917, 216; maximum U-boat activity in, April 1917, 221
Wexford, U.S. s/m-chasers operated from, 336; air station at, 362; U.S. naval quarters at, 363
Whiddy Island, air station on, 362; U.S. naval quarters on, 363
White, Lieut.-Comdr. J., R.N., *Genista*, death of, 193, 195
White Sea, the, Q-ships sent to, 180
Whitehaven, 85
Whitfield, S.S., sunk, 95
Whytehead, Lieut.-Comdr. T. B. H., R.N.R., *Brock*, and the *Lusitania*, 42
Wilhelm II, Kaiser, 326; sinking of passenger vessels banned by, 92
Wilhelmshaven, U-boat depot, 96, 145, 303, 331; return to, of *U* 21, 28–9, 215; number of U-boats at, in July 1918, 361
William T. Lewis, barque, 165; shelled by *U* 39 but not sunk, 93 *sqq.*
Williams, Cdr. R., U.S.N., on the foul weather of Dec. 1915, 311; story told by, illustrative of Anglo-American naval brotherhood, 327–8, a later amusing experience of, 328–9
Williams, Capt. W. H., master of S.S. *Roanoke*, on the capture of the vessel, 232–3
Willie, sailing vessel, sunk by gunfire, 125
Wilmot-Smith, Lieut.-Comdr. A., R.N., *Baralong* (later *Wyandra*), 98; *U* 41 sunk by, 98, 99, 100; award to, of D.S.O., 100
Wilson, Capt. G. F. W., R.N., *Zinnia*, gale experience of, 106–7; skilful seamanship of, 111; on the real *Aud*, 151; on the capture of the German *Aud*, 154–5; on the torpedoing of the oil-tanker *Gafsa*, 219–20; on relations between crew and officers of *UC* 29, 261; on Smiles's rudimentary rafts, 296; on the pathetic sight of the *Stonecrop's* rescued men, 296
Wilson, President Woodrow, 47, diplomacy of, 45; and the American nation, influence of, on the German blockade, 93; and the entry of America into the war, 205; on the "extraordinary insults of the Imperial German government," 205, 206; destroyer escort for, 381
Wireless, on fishing boats, 48, 54
Wireless station, German, *see* Nauen.
Wireless stations, directional, East Coast, value of, 53
Wolf Rock signal lights, 129
Wood, Lieut. W. H., R.N.R., *Indian Empire*, *Lusitania* survivors rescued by, 43
Workington, 85
World-wide indignation at the sinking of passenger ships, 35, 39, 44, 45, 88, 92, 96, 103, unshared by Germany, 92
Wright, Lieut. P. T., U.S.N., *AL* 9, 319
Wyandra, *see Baralong*.

Y guns of s/m-chasers, 338
Yachts, motor, replaced by M.L.s, 187; steam, armed with guns, 22, and assigned to Milford, 46; squadron of, despatched to the Mediterranean, 121
York River, U.S.A., naval base at, 236
Young Fred, H.M. drifter, *UB* 82 destroyed by, with depth-charges, 333
Y.M.C.A. hut, Haulbowline, and Bishop Browne, 255

ZEEBRUGGE, wasps'-nest of, 197; blocking of, 90, 344 & *n*.

Zeller, Quartermaster, U.S.N., the *U* 103 prisoners tackled by, in vain, 342

Zent, S.S., torpedoed, survivors rescued by *Lavender*, 144

Zeppelin raids on East Anglia and Kent, object of, 165

Ziegler, Sub-Lieut., *U* 93 safely taken home by, 231–2

Zogbaum, Rear-Admiral R. F., U.S.N., on Admiral Bayly's opening remarks to the American captains, 246; on the Queenstown convoy system, 252–3; and the scheme for avoiding delay, etc., at the Mersey Bar, 315–16